# PAMPHLETS

ON THE

# CONSTITUTION OF THE UNITED STATES,

PUBLISHED DURING
ITS DISCUSSION BY THE PEOPLE
1787–1788.

EDITED
WITH NOTES AND A BIBLIOGRAPHY
BY
PAUL LEICESTER FORD.

THE LAWBOOK EXCHANGE, LTD.
Clark, New Jersey

ISBN-13: 9781886363953 (hardcover)
ISBN-13: 9781616190545 (paperback)

Lawbook Exchange edition 2010

*The quality of this reprint is equivalent to the quality of the original work.*

THE LAWBOOK EXCHANGE, LTD.
33 Terminal Avenue
Clark, New Jersey 07066-1321

*Please see our website for a selection of our other publications and fine facsimile reprints of classic works of legal history:*
www.lawbookexchange.com

**Library of Congress Cataloging-in-Publication Data**

Pamphlets on the Constitution of the United States, published during its discussion by the people, 1787-1788 / edited with notes and a bibliography by Paul Leicester Ford.
    p. cm.
 Originally published: Brooklyn, N.Y., 1888.
 Includes bibliographical references and index.
 ISBN 1-886363-95-1 (cloth : alk. paper)
  1. Constitutional law—United States Popular works.
2. Constitutional history—United States—Sources. 3. United States—Politics and government—1983-1789. I. Ford, Paul Leicester, 1865-1902.
KF4515.P36 1999
342.73'024—dc21                                 99-25089
                                                                           CIP

*Printed in the United States of America on acid-free paper*

# PAMPHLETS

ON THE

# Constitution of the United States,

PUBLISHED DURING
ITS DISCUSSION BY THE PEOPLE
1787–1788.

EDITED
WITH NOTES AND A BIBLIOGRAPHY
BY
PAUL LEICESTER FORD.

BROOKLYN, N. Y.:
1888.

## PREFACE.

The English speaking people have been a race of pamphleteers. Whenever a question—religious, political, military or personal—has interested the general public, it has occasioned a war of pamphlets, which, however partisan and transitory, were in a manner photographs of the public opinion, and as such have been used and valued by students and publicists.

The rarity and consequent difficulty of reaching this class of literature has been, however, a great obstacle to its use as sources of history. The name of pamphlet tells the purpose of these little publications. Written hurriedly, to effect a purpose for which there is not enough time or matter for a more elaborate volume, they are thrown by after a brief circulation and before a decade has passed, the edition has disappeared, and if any are still in existence, they are only to be found in the few public and private libraries which have taken the trouble to secure these fugitive leaflets.

The recognized value of these tractates in England has led to very extensive republications; and the *Harleian Miscellany*, the *Somers Tracts*, the issues of the Roxburghe, Bannatyne, Maitland, Chetham, Camden and Percy societies and the reprints of Halliwell, Collier, and M'Culloch, not to mention many minor collections, have placed several thousand of them within the reach of every one. But in America few attempts have been made to collect this kind of literature— Peter Force reprinted a series of pamphlets on the early settlement of the United States and a work of similar scope on Canada, containing reprints of the so called "Jesuit Relations" was printed under the patronage of the Canadian government. John Wingate Thornton and Frank Moore have collected a number of the patriotic sermons preached before and during the Revolutionary war. Franklin B. Hough republished a series of the funeral sermons and eulogies on the death of Washington, and James Spear Loring did the same for the orations delivered in Boston from 1770 to 1852. Samuel G. Drake reprinted a collection of tracts relating to King Philip's war, Joseph Sabin issued a series relating to the propagation of the gospel among the New England Indians, and William H. Whitmore edited, for the Prince Society, a number relating to the governorship of Sir Edmund Andros—but these are the only attempts worth mentioning to systematically gather these leaflets of our history, and which have singularly neglected those bearing on politics and government, in which we have so largely originated the true theories and methods.

When the student or historian comes to examine the earlier pamphlet literature of our country he encounters the greatest difficulty in their use. The lack of communication between the colonies or states, with its consequent localization of the pamphlet; the small edition caused by the high price of paper, which at that time was the costly element in the production of books; the little value attached by each generation to the pamphlets of its own time; the subsequent wars, with the destruction and high price of old paper that came with them, and the general disregard of historical material that existed for many years after the stirring times that occasioned these arguments, have all tended to make these tracts almost impossible to consult; and any one desiring to examine the original editions of the thirteen pamphlets contained in this volume would be compelled to visit the public libraries in the cities of Washington, Philadelphia, New York, Albany and Boston, while it would take a life time of patient searching and waiting to collect them from the second-hand booksellers and auction-rooms, at prices that few would care to pay.

As the rarity of these pamphlets has caused their neglect, so also has their anonymous publication. It was a time of literary masks, and we often find, like the knights of old, that when their masks were removed, they had concealed our ablest statesmen, one of whom wrote of his anonymous pamphlet, "If the reasoning in the pamphlet you allude to is just, it will have its effect on candid and discerning minds;—if weak and inconclusive, my name cannot render it otherwise," but it is certain, whatever the effect at the moment, that more attention and care would have been given these works by succeeding generations had they borne the name of one of the makers of our nation, rather than the pseudonymous mask which gave no clue to its authorship.

In America, we are too apt to forget the losing side of a question. Few to-day know of the intense struggle that took place over the ratification of our constitution, or realize that the adoption of a government which has worked so successfully, met with the strongest opposition from such men as Patrick Henry, Richard Henry Lee, George Mason, George Clinton, Samuel Chase, Elbridge Gerry, Albert Gallatin, James Monroe and others, while many equally famous were either neutral or gave it but lukewarm support. If the great fear and prediction of these men—that the general government would entirely subvert the state governments, with a consequent loss of personal freedom—has not been realized, it will nevertheless be seen in the following pages that many of their objections were embodied in the future amendments, and the disregard of others has occasioned some of our most serious national questions. If this collection presents a greater number of federal than anti-federal arguments, it is only in the proportion in which the latter was overborne by the former, both in men and writings.

Of all these partisan writings *The Federalist* has hitherto been almost the only known argument of those which for nine months kept the printers busy and the people in a turmoil, though the twenty-nine editions of that work attest the value and interest of that class of writings. That these essays equal that great series is not claimed, but I believe, nevertheless, that they, by their simpler and more popular treatment of the question, exerted quite as much influence as that "judicious and ingenious writer," who was "not well calculated for the common people," and therefore deserve in this centennial year a place on the shelf of the publicist or student, with that "political classic" of Hamilton, Madison and Jay.

PAUL LEICESTER FORD.

97 CLARK STREET,
    BROOKLYN, NEW YORK.

# CONTENTS.

|  | Page. |
|---|---|
| GERRY, ELBRIDGE. Observations on the New Constitution, and on the Federal and State Conventions. By a Columbian Patriot | 1 |
| WEBSTER, NOAH. An Examination into the leading principles of the Federal Constitution. By a Citizen of America | 25 |
| JAY, JOHN. An Address to the People of the State of New York, on the subject of the Constitution. By a Citizen of New York | 67 |
| SMITH, MELANCTHON. Address to the People of the State of New York. By a Plebeian | 89 |
| WEBSTER, PELATIAH. The Weakness of Brutus exposed: or some remarks in vindication of the Constitution. By a Citizen of Philadelphia | 117 |
| COXE, TENCH. An Examination of the Constitution of the United States of America. By an American Citizen | 134 |
| WILSON, JAMES. Speech on the Federal Constitution, delivered in Philadelphia | 155 |
| DICKINSON, JOHN. Letters of Fabius on the Federal Constitution | 163 |
| HANSON, ALEXANDER CONTEE. Remarks on the Proposed Plan of a Federal Government. By Aristides | 217 |
| RANDOLPH, EDMUND. Letter on the Federal Constitution | 259 |
| LEE, RICHARD HENRY. Observations of the System of Government proposed by the late Convention. By a Federal Farmer | 277 |
| MASON, GEORGE. Objections to the Federal Constitution | 327 |
| IREDELL, JAMES. Observations on George Mason's Objections to the Federal Constitution. By Marcus | 333 |
| RAMSAY, DAVID. An Address to the Freemen of South Carolina on the Federal Constitution. By Civis | 371 |
| Bibliography of the Constitution, 1787–1788 | 381 |
| Reference List to the history and literature of the Constitution, 1787–88. | 427 |
| Index | 443 |

Observations / On the new Constitution, and on the Federal / and State Conventions. / By a Columbian Patriot. / Sic transit gloria Americana. / [Boston: 1788.]

12 mo., pp. 19.

---

Written by Elbridge Gerry, member of the Philadelphia Convention from Massachusetts, and one of the number who refused to sign the Constitution, for reasons given in his letter to the presiding officers of the Massachusetts legislature (Elliot I, 494). Gerry made himself conspicuous in the contest in Massachusetts over the ratification, and though not elected to the State Convention, was requested by them to attend and answer questions. His life, by James T. Austin, (Boston, 1828), makes no mention of this pamphlet.

" E. G. has come out as a *Columbian Patriot*—a pitiful performance. The author sinks daily in public esteem, and his bantling goes unnoticed."—Rufus King to John Alsop, March 2d, 1788.

The first edition of this pamphlet was printed without a title page, or imprint, and an examination of the Massachusetts newspapers shows it was never for sale; making it probable that it was printed for Gerry, and not for general circulation. Greenleaf reprinted it in New York, for the [Anti] Federal Committee, who distributed sixteen hundred and thirty copies to the local county committees of that State.

" We have received yours by a Columbian Patriot—a well composed piece but in a style too sublime and florid for the common people in this part of the country."—Albany Committee to N. Y. Committee, April 12th, 1788.

P. L. F.

MANKIND may amuse themselves with theoretick systems of liberty, and trace its social and moral effects on sciences, virtue, industry and every improvement of which the human mind is capable; but we can only discern its true value by the practical and wretched effects of slavery; and thus dreadfully will they be realized, when the inhabitants of the Eastern States are dragging out a miserable existence, *only* on the gleanings of their fields; and the Southern, blessed with a softer and more fertile climate, are languishing in hopeless poverty; and when asked, what is become of the flower of their crop, and the rich produce of their farms—they may answer in the hapless stile of the Man of *La Mancha*,—" The " steward of my Lord has seized and sent it to *Madrid*."—— Or, in the more literal language of truth, The *exigencies* of government require that the collectors of the revenue should transmit it to the *Federal City*.

Animated with the firmest zeal for the interest of this country, the peace and union of the American States, and the freedom and happiness of a people who have made the most costly sacrifices in the cause of liberty,—who have braved the power of Britain, weathered the convulsions of war, and waded thro' the blood of friends and foes to establish their independence and to support the freedom of the human mind; I cannot silently [2] witness this degradation without calling on them, before they are compelled to blush at their own servitude, and to turn back their languid eyes on their lost liberties —to consider, that the character of nations generally changes at the moment of revolution.——And when patriotism is discountenanced and publick virtue becomes the ridicule of the sycophant—when every man of liberality, firmness and penetration who cannot lick the hand stretched out to oppress, is deemed an enemy to the State—then is the gulph of despotism set open, and the grades to slavery, though rapid, are scarce perceptible—then genius drags heavily its iron chain

—science is neglected, and real merit flies to the shades for security from reproach—the mind becomes enervated, and the national character sinks to a kind of apathy with only energy sufficient to curse the breast that gave it milk, and as an elegant writer observes, "To bewail every new birth as an "increase of misery, under a government where the mind is "necessarily debased, and talents are seduced to become the "panegyrists of usurpation and tyranny." He adds, "that "even sedition is not the most indubitable enemy to the pub- "lick welfare; but that its most dreadful foe is despotism "which always changes the character of nations for the worse, "and is productive of nothing but vice, that the tyrant no "longer excites to the pursuits of glory or virtue; it is not "talents, it is baseness and servility that he cherishes, and the "weight of arbitrary power destroys the spring of emulation."\* If such is the influence of government on the character and manners, and undoubtedly the observation is just, must we not subscribe to the opinion of the celebrated *Abbé Mably?* "That there are disagreeable seasons in the unhappy situation "of human affairs, when policy requires both the intention "and the power of doing mischief to be punished; and when "the senate proscribed the memory of *Cæsar* they ought to "have put *Anthony* to death, and extinguished the hopes of "*Octavius*." Self defence is a primary law of nature, which no subsequent law of society can abolish; this primæval principle, the immediate gift of the Creator, obliges every one to remonstrate against the strides of ambition, and a wanton lust of domination, and to resist the first approaches of tyranny, which at this day threaten to sweep away the rights for which the brave sons of America have fought with an heroism scarcely paralleled even in ancient republicks. [3] It may be repeated, they have purchased it with their blood, and have gloried in their independence with a dignity of spirit, which has made them the admiration of philosophy, the pride of America, and the wonder of Europe. It has been observed, with great propriety, that "the virtues and vices of a people "when a revolution happens in their government, are the "measure of the liberty or slavery they ought to expect—An

\* HELVITIUS.

"heroic love for the publick good, a profound reverence for "the laws, a contempt of riches, and a noble haughtiness of " soul, are the only foundations of a free government."* Do not their dignified principles still exist among us? Or are they extinguished in the breasts of Americans, whose fields have been so recently crimsoned to repel the potent arm of a foreign Monarch, who had planted his engines of slavery in every city, with design to erase the vestiges of freedom in this his last asylum. It is yet to be hoped, for the honour of human nature, that no combinations either foreign or domestick have thus darkned this Western hemisphere.—On these shores freedom has planted her standard, diped in the purple tide that flowed from the veins of her martyred heroes; and here every uncorrupted American yet hopes to see it supported by the vigour, the justice, the wisdom and unanimity of the people, in spite of the deep-laid plots, the secret intrigues, or the bold effrontery of those interested and avaricious adventurers for place, who intoxicated with the ideas of distinction and preferment have prostrated every worthy principle beneath the shrine of ambition. Yet these are the men who tell us republicanism is dwindled into theory—that we are incapable of enjoying our liberties—and that we must have a master.—— Let us retrospect the days of our adversity, and recollect who were then our friends; do we find them among the sticklers for aristocratick authority? No, they were generally the same men who now wish to save us from the distractions of anarchy on the one hand, and the jaws of tyranny on the other; where then were the class who now come forth importunately urging that our political salvation depends on the adoption of a system at which freedom spurns?—Were not some of them hidden in the corners of obscurity, and others wrapping themselves in the bosom of our enemies for safety? Some of them were in the arms of infancy; and others speculating for fortune, by sporting with public money; while a few, a very few of them [4] were magnanimously defending their country, and raising a character, which I pray heaven may never be sullied by aiding measures derogatory to their former exertions. But the revolutions in principle which time produces among mankind,

* ABBE MABLE.

frequently exhibits the most mortifying instances of human weakness; and this alone can account for the extraordinary appearance of a few names, once distinguished in the honourable walks of patriotism, but now found in the list of the Massachusetts assent to the ratification of a Constitution, which, by the undefined meaning of some parts, and the ambiguities of expression in others, is dangerously adapted to the purposes of an immediate *aristocratic tyranny;* that from the difficulty, if not impracticability of its operation, must soon terminate in the most *uncontrouled despotism.*

All writers on government agree, and the feelings of the human mind witness the truth of these political axioms, that man is born free and possessed of certain unalienable rights—that government is instituted for the protection, safety and happiness of the people, and not for the profit, honour, or private interest of any man, family, or class of men——That the origin of all power is in the people, and that they have an incontestible right to check the creatures of their own creation, vested with certain powers to guard the life, liberty and property of the community: And if certain selected bodies of men, deputed on these principles, determine contrary to the wishes and expectations of their constituents, the people have an undoubted right to reject their decisions, to call for a revision of their conduct, to depute others in their room, or if they think proper, to demand further time for deliberation on matters of the greatest moment: it therefore is an unwarrantable stretch of authority or influence, if any methods are taken to preclude this peaceful and reasonable mode of enquiry and decision. And it is with inexpressible anxiety, that many of the best friends of the Union of the States—to the peaceable and equal participation of the rights of nature, and to the glory and dignity of this country, behold the insiduous arts, and the strenuous efforts of the partisans of arbitrary power, by their vague definitions of the best established truths, endeavoring to envelope the mind in darkness the concomitant of slavery, and to lock the strong chains of domestic despotism on a country, which by the most glorious and successful struggles is but newly emancipated from the spectre of foreign dominion.——[5] But there are certain seasons in the course of human affairs, when Genius, Virtue, and Patriotism, seems to nod over the vices of the times, and perhaps never more remarkably, than at the present period; or we should not see such a passive disposition prevail in some, who we must candidly suppose, have liberal and enlarged sentiments; while a supple multitude are paying a blind and idolatrous homage to the opinions of those who by the most precipitate steps are treading down their dear bought privileges; and who are endeavouring by all the arts of insinuation, and influence, to betray the people of the United States, into an acceptance of a most complicated system of government; marked on the one side with the *dark, secret* and *profound intrigues*, of the statesman, long practised in the purlieus of despotism; and on the other, with the ideal projects of *young ambition*, with its wings just expanded to soar to a summit, which imagination has painted in such gawdy colours as to intoxicate the *inexperienced votary*, and to send *him* rambling from State to State, to collect materials to construct the ladder of preferment.

But as a variety of objections to the *heterogeneous phantom*, have been repeatedly laid before the public, by men of the best abilities and intentions; I will not expatiate long on a Republican *form* of government, founded on the principles of monarchy—a democratick branch with the *features* of aristocracy—and the extravagance of nobility pervading the minds of many of the candidates for office, with the poverty of peasantry hanging heavily on them, and insurmountable, from their taste for expence, unless a general provision should be made in the arrangement of the civil list, which may enable them with the champions of their cause to "*sail down the new pactolean channel.*" Some gentlemen, with laboured zeal, have spent much time in urging the necessity of government, from the embarrassments of trade—the want of respectability abroad and confidence of the public engagements at home:—These are obvious truths which no one denies; and there are few who do not unite in the general wish for the restoration of public faith, the revival of commerce, arts, agriculture, and industry, under a lenient, peaceable and energetick government: But the most sagacious advocates for the party have not by fair discusion, and rational argumentation, evinced the necessity of adopting this many headed monster; of such motley mixture, that its enemies cannot trace a feature of Democratick or Republican [6] extract; nor have its friends the courage to denominate a Monarchy, an Aristocracy, or an Oligarchy, and the favoured bantling must have passed through the short period of its existence without a name, had not Mr. *Wilson*, in the fertility of his genius, suggested the happy epithet of a *Federal Republic*.—But I leave the field of general censure on the secresy of its birth, the rapidity of its growth, and the fatal consequences of suffering it to live to the age of maturity, and will particularize some of the most weighty objections to its passing through this continent in a gigantic size.—It will be allowed by every one that the fundamental principle of a free government is the equal representation of a free people—— And I will *first* observe with a justly celebrated writer, "That " the principal aim of society is to protect individuals in the " absolute rights which were vested in them by the immediate " laws of nature, but which could not be preserved in peace, " without the mutual intercourse which is gained by the insti- " tution of friendly and social communities." And when society has thus deputed a certain number of their equals to take care of their personal rights, and the interest of the whole community, it must be considered that responsibility is the great security of integrity and honour; and that annual election is the basis of responsibility,—Man is not immediately corrupted, but power without limitation, or amenability, may endanger the brightest virtue—whereas a frequent return to the bar of their Constituents is the strongest check against the corruptions to which men are liable, either from the intrigues of others of more subtle genius, or the propensities of their own hearts,—and the gentlemen who have so warmly advocated in the late Convention of the Massachusetts, the change from annual to biennial elections; may have been in the same predicament, and perhaps with the same views that Mr. *Hutchinson* once acknowledged himself, when in a letter to *Lord Hillsborough*, he observed, " that the grand difficulty of making a "change in government against the general bent of the people "had caused him to turn his thoughts to a variety of plans, in "order to find one that might be executed in spite of opposi- "tion," and the first he proposed was that, "instead of annual, "the elections should be only once in three years:" but the Minister had not the hardiness to attempt such an innovation, even in the revision of colonial charters: nor has any one ever defended Biennial, Triennial or Septennial Elections, either in the [7] British House of Commons, or in the debates of Provincial assemblies, on general and free principles: but it is unnecessary to dwell long on this article, as the best political writers have supported the principles of annual elections with a precision, that cannot be confuted, though they may be darkned, by the sophistical arguments that have been thrown out with design, to undermine all the barriers of freedom.

2. There is no security in the profered system, either for the rights of conscience or the liberty of the Press: Despotism usually while it is gaining ground, will suffer men to think, say, or write what they please; but when once established, if it is thought necessary to subserve the purposes, of arbitrary power, the most unjust restrictions may take place in the first instance, and an *imprimator* on the Press in the next, may silence the complaints, and forbid the most decent remonstrances of an injured and oppressed people.

3. There are no well defined limits of the Judiciary Powers, they seem to be left as a boundless ocean, that has broken over the chart of the Supreme Lawgiver, "*thus far shalt thou go and no further,*" and as they cannot be comprehended by the clearest capacity, or the most sagacious mind, it would be an Herculean labour to attempt to describe the dangers with which they are replete.

4. The Executive and the Legislative are so dangerously blended as to give just cause of alarm, and everything relative thereto, is couched in such ambiguous terms—in such vague and indefinite expression, as is a sufficient ground without any objection, for the reprobation of a system, that the authors dare not hazard to a clear investigation.

5. The abolition of trial by jury in civil causes.—This mode

of trial the learned Judge Blackstone observes, "has been "coeval with the first rudiments of civil government, that "property, liberty and life, depend on maintaining in its legal "force the constitutional trial by jury." He bids his readers pauze, and with Sir Matthew Hale observes, how admirably this mode is adapted to the investigation of truth beyond any other the world can produce. 'Even the party who have been disposed to swallow, without examination, the proposals of the *secret conclave*, have started on a discovery that this essential right was curtailed; and shall a privilege, the origin of which may be traced to our Saxon ancestors—that has been a part of the law of nations, even in the fewdatory systems of France, [8] Germany and Italy—and from the earliest records has been held so sacred, both in ancient and modern Britain, that it could never be shaken by the introduction of Norman customs, or any other conquests or change of government—— shall this inestimable privilege be relinquished in America— either thro' the fear of inquisition for unaccounted thousands of public monies in the hands of some who have been officious in the fabrication of the *consolidated system*, or from the apprehension that some future delinquent possessed of more power than integrity, may be called to a trial by his peers in the hour of investigation.

6. Though it has been said by Mr. *Wilson* and many others, that a Standing-Army is necessary for the dignity and safety of America, yet freedom revolts at the idea, when the Divan, or the Despot, may draw out his dragoons to suppress the murmurs of a few, who may yet cherish those sublime principles which call forth the exertions, and lead to the best improvements of the human mind. It is hoped this country may yet be governed by milder methods than are usually displayed beneath the bannerets of military law.—Standing armies have been the nursery of vice and the bane of liberty from the Roman legions to the establishment of the artful Ximenes, and from the ruin of the Cortes of Spain, to the planting of the British cohorts in the capitals of America:—By the edicts of an authority vested in the sovereign power by the proposed constitution, the militia of the country, the bulwark of defence,

and the security of national liberty if no longer under the controul of civil authority; but at the rescript of the Monarch, or the aristocracy, they may either be employed to extort the enormous sums that will be necessary to support the civil list —to maintain the regalia of power—and the splendour of the most useless part of the community, or they may be sent into foreign countries for the fulfilment of treaties, stipulated by the President and two-thirds of the Senate.

7. Notwithstanding the delusory promise to guarantee a Republican form of government to every State in the Union —If the most discerning eye could discover any meaning at all in the engagement, there are no resources left for the support of internal government, or the liquidation of the debts of the State. Every source of revenue is in the monopoly of Congress, and if the several legislatures in their enfeebled state, should against their own feelings be necessitated to attempt a dry tax [9] for the payment of their debts, and the support of internal police, even this may be required for the purposes of the general government.

8. As the new Congress are empowered to determine their own salaries, the requisitions for this purpose may not be very moderate, and the drain for public moneys will probably rise past all calculation: and it is to be feared when America has consolidated its despotism, the world will witness the truth of the assertion—"that the pomp of an Eastern monarch may
" impose on the vulgar who may estimate the force of a nation
" by the magnificence of its palaces; but the wise man judges
" differently, it is by that very magnificence he estimates its
" weakness. He sees nothing more in the midst of this impos-
" ing pomp, where the tyrant sets enthroned, than a sumptuous
" and mournful decoration of the dead; the apparatus of a
" fastuous funeral, in the centre of which is a cold and lifeless
" lump of unanimated earth, a phantom of power ready to
" disappear before the enemy, by whom it is despised!"

9. There is no provision for a rotation, nor anything to prevent the perpetuity of office in the same hands for life; which by a little well timed bribery, will probably be done, to the exclusion of men of the best abilities from their share in

the offices of government.—By this neglect we lose the advantages of that check to the overbearing insolence of office, which by rendering him ineligible at certain periods, keeps the mind of man in equilibrio, and teaches him the feelings of the governed, and better qualifies him to govern in his turn.

10. The inhabitants of the United States, are liable to be draged from the vicinity of their own country, or state, to answer the litigious or unjust suit of an adversary, on the most distant borders of the Continent: in short the appelate jurisdiction of the Supreme Federal Court, includes an unwarrantable stretch of power over the liberty, life, and property of the subject, through the wide Continent of America.

11. One Representative to thirty thousand inhabitants is a very inadequate representation; and every man who is not lost to all sense of freedom to his country, must reprobate the idea of Congress altering by law, or on any pretence whatever, interfering with any regulations for time, places, and manner of choosing our own Representatives.

12. If the sovereignty of America is designed to be elective, the surcumscribing the votes to only ten electors in this State, [10] and the same proportion in all the others, is nearly tantamount to the exclusion of the voice of the people in the choice of their first magistrate. It is vesting the choice solely in an aristocratic junto, who may easily combine in each State to place at the head of the Union the most convenient instrument for despotic sway.

13. A Senate chosen for six years will, in most instances, be an appointment for life, as the influence of such a body over the minds of the people will be coequal to the extensive powers with which they are vested, and they will not only forget, but be forgotten by their constituents—a branch of the Supreme Legislature thus set beyond all responsibility is totally repugnant to every principle of a free government.

14. There is no provision by a bill of rights to guard against the dangerous encroachments of power in too many instances to be named: but I cannot pass over in silence the insecurity in which we are left with regard to warrants unsupported by evidence—the daring experiment of granting *writs of assistance*

in a former arbitrary administration is not yet forgotten in the Massachusetts; nor can we be so ungrateful to the memory of the patriots who counteracted their operation, as so soon after their manly exertions to save us from such a detestable instrument of arbitrary power, to subject ourselves to the insolence of any petty revenue officer to enter our houses, search, insult, and seize at pleasure. We are told by a gentleman of too much virtue and real probity to suspect he has a design to deceive—"that the whole constitution is a declaration of rights,"—but mankind must think for themselves, and to many very judicious and discerning characters, the whole constitution with very few exceptions appears a perversion of the rights of particular states, and of private citizens.——But the gentleman goes on to tell us, "that the primary object is the general gov-
"ernment, and that the rights of individuals are only incident-
"ally mentioned, and that there was a clear impropriety in
"being very particular about them." But, asking pardon for dissenting from such respectable authority, who has been led into several mistakes, more from his prediliction in favour of certain modes of government, than from a want of understanding or veracity. The rights of individuals ought to be the primary object of all government, and cannot be too securely guarded by the most explicit declarations in their favor. This has been the opinion of the Hampdens, the Pyms, and [11] many other illustrious names, that have stood forth in defence of English liberties; and even the Italian master in politicks, the subtle and renouned Machiavel acknowledges, that no republic ever yet stood on a stable foundation without satisfying the common people.

15. The difficulty, if not impracticability, of exercising the equal and equitable powers of government by a single legislature over an extent of territory that reaches from the Mississippi to the Western lakes, and from them to the Atlantic Ocean, is an insuperable objection to the adoption of the new system.—Mr. *Hutchinson*, the great champion for arbitrary power, in the multitude of his machinations to subvert the liberties in this country, was obliged to acknowledge in one of his letters, that, " from the extent of country from north to

"south, the scheme of one government was impracticable." But if the authors of the present visionary project, can by the arts of deception, precipitation and address, obtain a majority of suffrages in the conventions of the states to try the hazardous experiment, they may then make the same inglorious boast with this insidious politician, who may perhaps be their model, that "the union of the colonies was pretty well broken, "and that he hoped to never see it revewed."

16. It is an undisputed fact that not one legislature in the United States had the most distant idea when they first appointed members for a convention, entirely commercial, or when they afterwards authorized them to consider on some amendments of the Federal union, that they would without any warrant from their constituents, presume on so bold and daring a stride, as ultimately to destroy the state governments, and offer a *consolidated system*, irreversible but on conditions that the smallest degree of penetration must discover to be impracticable.

17. The first appearance of the article which declares the ratification of nine states sufficient for the establishment of the new system, wears the face of dissension, is a subversion of the union of Confederated States, and tends to the introduction of anarchy and civil convulsions, and may be a means of involving the whole country in blood.

18. The mode in which this constitution is recommended to the people to judge without either the advice of Congress, or the legislatures of the several states is very reprehensible— it is an attempt to force it upon them before it could be thoroughly understood, and may leave us in that situation, that in the first moments of slavery in the minds of the people agitated by the remembrance of their lost liberties, will be like the sea in a tempest, that sweeps down every mound of security.

But it is needless to enumerate other instances, in which the proposed constitution appears contradictory to the first principles which ought to govern mankind; and it is equally so to enquire into the motives that induced to so bold a step as the annihilation of the independence and sovereignty of the thirteen distinct states.——They are but too obvious through the whole progress of the business, from the first shutting up the doors of the federal convention and resolving that no member should correspond with gentlemen in the different states on the subject under discussion; till the trivial proposition of *recommending* a few amendments was artfully ushered into the convention of the Massachusetts. The questions that were then before that honorable assembly were profound and important, they were of such magnitude and extent, that the consequences may run parallel with the existence of the country; and to see them waved and hastily terminated by a measure too absurd to require a serious refutation, raises the honest indignation of every true lover of his country. Nor are they less grieved that the ill policy and arbitrary disposition of some of the sons of America has thus precipitated to the contemplation and discussion of questions that no one could rationally suppose would have been agitated among us, till time had blotted out the principles on which the late revolution was grounded; or till the last traits of the many political tracts, which defended the separation from Britain, and the rights of men were consigned to everlasting oblivion. After the severe conflicts this country has suffered, it is presumed that they are disposed to make every reasonable sacrifice before the altar of peace.——But when we contemplate the nature of men and consider them originally on an equal footing, subject to the same feelings, stimulated by the same passions, and recollecting the struggles they have recently made, for the security of their civil rights; it cannot be expected that the inhabitants of the Massachusetts, can be easily lulled into a fatal security, by the declamatory effusions of gentlemen, who, contrary to the experience of all ages would perswade them there is no danger to be apprehended, from vesting discretionary powers in the hands of man, which he may, or may not abuse. The very suggestion, that [13] we ought to trust to the precarious hope of amendments and redress, after we have voluntarily fixed the shackles on our own necks should have awakened to a double degree of caution.—This people have not forgotten the artful insinuations of a former

Governor, when pleading the unlimited authority of parliament before the legislature of the Massachusetts; nor that his arguments were very similar to some lately urged by gentlemen who boast of opposing his measures, "*with halters about their "necks.*"

We were then told by him, in all the soft language of insinuation, that no form of government, of human construction can be perfect—that we had nothing to fear—that we had no reason to complain—that we had only to acquiesce in their illegal claims, and to submit to the requisition of parliament, and doubtless the lenient hand of government would redress all grievances, and remove the oppressions of the people :— Yet we soon saw armies of mercenaries encamped on our plains —our commerce ruined—our harbours blockaded—and our cities burnt. It may be replied that this was in consequence of an obstinate defence of our privileges; this may be true ; and when the "*ultima ratio*" is called to aid, the weakest must fall. But let the best informed historian produce an instance when bodies of men were entrusted with power, and the proper checks relinquished, if they were ever found destitute of ingenuity sufficient to furnish pretences to abuse it. And the people at large are already sensible, that the liberties which America has claimed, which reason has justified, and which have been so gloriously defended by the swords of the brave; are not about to fall before the tyranny of foreign conquest : it is native usurpation that is shaking the foundations of peace, and spreading the sable curtain of despotism over the United States. The banners of freedom were erected in the wilds of America by our ancestors, while the wolf prowled for his prey on the one hand, and more savage man on the other; they have been since rescued from the invading hand of foreign power, by the valor and blood of their posterity; and there was reason to hope they would continue for ages to illumine a quarter of the globe, by nature kindly separated from the proud monarchies of Europe, and the infernal darkness of Asiatic slavery.——And it is to be feared we shall soon see this country rushing into the extremes of confusion and violence, in consequence of the proceeding of a set of gentlemen, who disregard-[14] ing the purposes of their appointment, have assumed powers unauthorized by any commission, have unnecessarily rejected the confederation of the United States, and annihilated the sovereignty and independence of the individual governments.—The causes which have inspired a few men to assemble for very different purposes with such a degree of temerity us to break with a single stroke the union of America, and disseminate the seeds of discord through the land may be easily investigated, when we survey the partizans of monarchy in the state conventions, urging the adoption of a mode of government that militates with the former professions and exertions of this country, and with all ideas of republicanism, and the equal rights of men.

Passion, prejudice, and error, are characteristics of human nature; and as it cannot be accounted for on any principles of philosophy, religion, or good policy; to these shades in the human character must be attributed the mad zeal of some, to precipitate to a blind adoption of the measures of the late federal convention, without giving opportunity for better information to those who are misled by influence or ignorance into erroneous opinions.——Litterary talents may be prostituted, and the powers of genius debased to subserve the purposes of ambition or avarice; but the feelings of the heart will dictate the language of truth, and the simplicity of her accents will proclaim the infamy of those, who betray the rights of the people, under the specious, and popular pretence of *justice*, *consolidation*, and *dignity*.

It is presumed the great body of the people unite in sentiment with the writer of these observations, who most devoutly prays that public credit may rear her declining head, and remunerative justice pervade the land; nor is there a doubt if a free government is continued, that time and industry will enable both the public and private debtor to liquidate their arrearages in the most equitable manner. They wish to see the Confederated States bound together by the most indissoluble union, but without renouncing their separate sovereignties and independence, and becoming tributaries to a consolidated fabrick of aristocratick tyranny.———They wish to see government established, and peaceably holding the reins with honour, energy, and dignity; but they wish for no *federal city* whose "*cloud cap't towers*" may screen the state culprit from the hand of justice; while its exclusive jurisdiction may [15] protect the riot of armies encamped within its limits.—They deprecate discord and civil convulsions, but they are not yet generally prepared with the ungrateful Israelites to ask a King, nor are their spirits sufficiently broken to yield the best of their olive grounds to his servants, and to see their sons appointed to run before his chariots—It has been observed by a zealous advocate for the new system, that most governments are the result of fraud or violence, and this with design to recommend its acceptance—but has not almost every step towards its fabrication been fraudulent in the extreme? Did not the prohibition strictly enjoined by the general Convention, that no member should make any communication to his Constituents, or to gentlemen of consideration and abilities in the other States, bear evident marks of fraudulent designs?— This circumstance is regretted in strong terms by Mr. Martin, a member from Maryland, who acknowedges "He had no "idea that all the wisdom, integrity, and virtue of the States "was contained in that Convention, and that he wished to "have corresponded with gentlemen of eminent political char- "acters abroad, and to give their sentiments due weight"— he adds, "so extremely solicitous were they, that their pro- "ceedings should not transpire, that the members were pro- "hibited from taking copies of their resolutions, or extracts "from the Journals, without express permission, by vote."— And the hurry with which it has been urged to the acceptance of the people, without giving time, by adjournments, for better information, and more unanimity has a deceptive appearance; and if finally driven to resistance, as the only alternative between that and servitude, till in the confusion of discord, the reins should be seized by the violence of some enterprizing genius, that may sweep down the last barrier of liberty, it must be added to the score of criminality with which the fraudulent usurpation at Philadelphia, may be chargeable. ——Heaven avert such a tremendous scence! and let us still hope a more happy termination of the present ferment:—may the people be calm and wait a legal redress; may the mad transport of some of our infatuated capitals subside; and every influential character through the States, make the most prudent exertions for a new general Convention, who may vest adequate powers in Congress, for all national purposes, without annihilating the individual governments, and drawing blood from every pore by taxes, impositions and illegal restrictions.—This step might [16] again re-establish the Union, restore tranquility to the ruffled mind of the inhabitants, and save America from the distresses, dreadful even in contemplation.——"The great art of governing is to lay aside all prejudices and attachments to particular opinions, classes or individual characters to consult the spirit of the people; to give way to it; and in so doing, to give it a turn capable of inspiring those sentiments, which may induce them to relish a change, which an alteration of circumstances may hereafter make necessary."——The education of the advocates for monarchy should have taught them, and their memory should have suggested that "monarchy is a species of government fit only for a people too much corrupted by luxury, avarice, and a passion for pleasure, to have any love for their country, and whose vices the fear of punishment alone is able to restrain; but by no means calculated for a nation that is poor, and at the same time tenacious of their liberty—animated with a disgust to tyranny—and inspired with the generous feeling of patriotism and liberty, and at the same time, like the ancient Spartans have been hardened by temperance and manly exertions, and equally despising the fatigues of the field, and the fear of enemies,"——and while they change their ground they should recollect, that Aristocracy is a still more formidable foe to public virtue, and the prosperity of a nation—that under such a government her patriots become mercenaries—her soldiers cowards, and the people slaves.—— Though several State Conventions have assented to, and ratified, yet the voice of the people appears at present strong against the adoption of the Constitution.——By the chicanery, intrigue, and false colouring of those who plume themselves, more on their education and abilities, than their political, patriotic, or private virtues—by the imbecility of some, and the duplicity of others, a majority of the Convention of Massachusetts have been flattered with the ideas of amendments, when it will be too late to complain——While several very worthy characters, too timid for their situation, magnified the hopeless alternative, between the dissolution of the bands of all government, and receiving the proferred system *in toto*, after long endeavouring to reconcile it to their consciences, swallowed the indegestible panacea, and in a kind of sudden desperation lent their signature to the dereliction of the honourable station they held in the Union, and have broken over the solemn compact, by which they were bound to support their own excellent constitution till the period [17] of revision. Yet Virginia, equally large and respectable, and who have done honour to themselves, by their vigorous exertions from the first dawn of independence, have not yet acted upon the question; they have wisely taken time to consider before they introduce innovations of a most dangerous nature:——her inhabitants are brave, her burgesses are free, and they have a Governor who dares to think for himself, and to speak his opinion (without first pouring libations on the altar of popularity) though it should militate with some of the most accomplished and illustrious characters.

Maryland, who has no local interest to lead her to adopt, will doubtless reject the system——I hope the same characters still live, and that the same spirit which dictated to them a wise and cautious care, against sudden revolutions in government, and made them the last State that acceded to the independence of America, will lead them to support what they so deliberately claimed.——Georgia apprehensive of a war with the Savages, has acceded in order to insure protection.—— Pennsylvania has struggled through much in the same manner, as the Massachusetts, against the manly feelings, and the masterly reasonings of a very respectable part of the Convention: They have adopted the system, and seen some of its authors burnt in effigy—their towns thrown into riot and confusion, and the minds of the people agitated by apprehension and discord.

New-Jersey and Delaware have united in the measure, from the locality of their situation, and the selfish motives which too generally govern mankind; the Federal City, and the seat of government, will naturally attract the intercourse of strangers—the youth of enterprize, and the wealth of the nation to the to the central States.

Connecticut has pushed it through with the precipitation of her neighbour, with few dissentient voices;—but more from irritation and resentment to a sister State, perhaps partiality to herself in her commercial regulations, than from a comprehensive view of the system, as a regard to the welfare of all. ——But New York has motives, that will undoubtedly lead her to rejection, without being afraid to appeal to the understanding of mankind, to justify the grounds of their refusal to adopt a Constitution, that even the framers dare not to risque to the hazard of revision, amendment, or reconsideration, least the whole superstructure should be demolished by more skilful and discreet architects.——I know not what part the Carolinas [18] will take; but I hope their determinations will comport with the dignity and freedom of this country—their decisions will have great weight in the scale.——But equally important are the small States of New Hampshire and Rhode Island:— New York, the Carolinas, Virginia, Maryland, and these two lesser States may yet support the liberties of the Continent; if they refuse a ratification, or postpone their proceedings till the spirits of the community have time to cool, there is little doubt but the wise measure of another federal convention will be adopted, when the members would have the advantage of viewing, at large, through the medium of truth, the objections that have been made from various quarters; such a measure might be attended with the most salutary effects, and prevent the dread consequences of civil feuds.——But even if some of those large states should hastily accede, yet we have frequently seen in the story of revolution, relief spring from a quarter least expected.

Though the virtues of a Cato could not save Rome, nor the abilities of a Padilla defend the citizens of Castile from falling under the yoke of Charles; yet a *Tell* once suddenly rose from a little obscure city, and boldly rescued the liberties of his country.————Every age has its Bruti and its Decci, as well as its Cæsars and Sejani:—The happiness of mankind depends much on the modes of government, and the virtues of the governors; and America may yet produce characters who have genius and capacity sufficient to form the manners and correct the morals of the people, and virtue enough to lead their country to freedom, Since their dismemberment from the British empire, America has, in many instances, resembled the conduct of a restless, vigorous, luxurious youth, prematurely emancipated from the authority of a parent, but without the experience necessary to direct him to act with dignity or discretion. Thus we have seen her break the shackles of foreign dominion, and all the blessings of peace restored on the most honourable terms: She acquired the liberty of framing her own laws, choosing her own magistrates, and adopting manners and modes of government the most favourable to the freedom and happiness of society. But how little have we availed ourselves of these superior advantages: The glorious fabric of liberty successfully reared with so much labor and assiduity totters to the foundation, and may be blown away as the bubble of fancy by the rude breath of military combinations, and politicians of yesterday.

[19] It is true this country lately armed in opposition to regal despotism—impoverished by the expences of a long war, and unable immediately to fulfil their public or private engagements that appeared in some instances, with a boldness of spirit that seemed to set at defiance all authority, government, or order, on the one hand; while on the other, there has been, not only a secret wish, but an open avowal of the necessity of drawing the reins of government much too taught, not only for a republicanism, but for a wise and limited monarchy.———— But the character of this people is not averse to a degree of subordination, the truth of this appears from the easy restoration of tranquility, after a dangerous insurrection in one of the states; this also evinces a little necessity of a complete revolution of government throughout the union. But it is a republican principle that the majority should rule; and if a spirit of

moderation should be cultivated on both sides, till the voice of the people at large could be fairly heard it should be held sacred.—And if, on such a scrutiny, the proposed constitution should appear repugnant to their character and wishes; if they, in the language of a late elegant pen, should acknowledge that "no confusion in my mind, is more terrible to them "than the stern disciplined regularity and vaunted police of "arbitrary governments, where every heart is depraved by "fear, where mankind dare not assume their natural characters, "where the free spirit must crouch to the slave in office, where "genius must repress her effusions, or like the Egyptian wor- "shippers, offer them in sacrifice to the calves in power, and "where the human mind, always in shackles, shrinks from every "generous effort." Who would then have the effrontery to say, it ought not to be thrown out with indignation, however some respectable names have appeared to support it.——But if after all, on a dispassionate and fair discussion, the people generally give their voices for a voluntary dereliction of their privileges, let every individual who chooses the active scenes of life strive to support the peace and unanimity of his country, though every other blessing may expire—And while the statesman is plodding for power, and the courtier practising the arts of dissimulation without check—while the rapacious are growing rich by oppression, and fortune throwing her gifts into the lap of fools, let the sublimer characters, the philosophic lovers of freedom who have wept over her exit, retire to the calm shades of contemplation, there they may look down with pity on the inconsistency of human nature, the revolutions of states, the rise of kingdoms, and the fall of empires.

An / Examination / into the / leading principles / of the / Federal Constitution / proposed by the late / Convention / held at Philadelphia. / With / Answers to the principal objections / that have been raised against the system. / By a Citizen of America. / —Ut patria sua felicitate cæteris præstaret, efficit. / Xenoph. Lacedæm. Resp. / Philadelphia: / Printed and sold by Prichard & Hall, in Market Street, / the second door above Lætitia Court. / M.DCC.LXXXVII.

8 vo., pp. 55.

---

Written by Noah Webster. This is reprinted from his own copy of the pamphlet, and the foot notes *in brakets* show his corrections and additions.

"This is a hasty production, written at the request of Mr. Fitzsimmons, of Philadelphia, a member of the Convention."—Indorsement by Noah Webster.

P. L. F.

TO

HIS EXCELLENCY

BENJAMIN FRANKLIN, Esq.

PRESIDENT OF THE COMMONWEALTH OF
PENNSYLVANIA,

AND

MEMBER OF THE LATE CONVENTION,
HELD AT PHILADELPHIA FOR THE PURPOSE OF
DEVISING A CONSTITUTION FOR THE
GOVERNMENT OF THE UNITED STATES,

THE FOLLOWING REMARKS UPON THE SYSTEM
RECOMMENDED BY THAT CONVENTION,

ARE MOST HUMBLY INSCRIBED

BY

HIS EXCELLENCY'S

MOST OBEDIENT

HUMBLE SERVANT,

THE AUTHOR.

PHILADELPHIA,
October 10, 1787.

OF all the memorable æras that have marked the progress of men from the savage state to the refinements of luxury, that which has combined them into society, under a wise system of government, and given form to a nation, has ever been recorded and celebrated as the most important. Legislators have ever been deemed the greatest benefactors of mankind—respected when living, and often deified after their death. Hence the fame of Fohi and Confucius—of Moses, Solon and Lycurgus—of Romulus and Numa—of Alfred, Peter the Great, and Mango Capac; whose names will be celebrated through all ages, for framing and improving constitutions of government, which introduced order into society and secured the benefits of law to millions of the human race.

This western world now beholds an æra important beyond conception, and which posterity will number with the age of Czar of Muscovy, and with the promulgation of the Jewish laws at Mount Sinai. The names of those men who have digested a system of constitutions for the American empire, will be enrolled with those of Zamolxis and Odin, and celebrated by posterity with the honors which less enlightened nations have paid to the fabled demi-gods of antiquity.

[6] But the origin of the AMERICAN REPUBLIC is distinguished by peculiar circumstances. Other nations have been driven together by fear and necessity—the governments have generally been the result of a single man's observations; or the offspring of particular interests. In the formation of our constitution, the wisdom of all ages is collected—the legislators of antiquity are consulted—as well as the opinions and interests of the millions who are concerned. In short, it is *an empire of reason*.

In the formation of such a government, it is not only the *right*, but the indispensable *duty* of every citizen to examine the principles of it, to compare them with the principles of other governments, with a constant eye to our particular situation and circumstances, and thus endeavor to foresee the future operations of our own system, and its effects upon human happiness.

Convinced of this truth, I have no apology to offer for the following remarks, but an earnest desire to be useful to my country.

In attending to the proposed Federal Constitution, the first thing that presents itself to our consideration, is the division of the legislative into two branches. This article has so many advocates in America, that it needs not any vindication.*—But it has its opposers, among whom are some respectable characters, especially in Pennsylvania; for which reason, I will state [7] some of the arguments and facts which incline me to favor the proposed division.

On the first view of men in society, we should suppose that no man would be bound by a law to which he had not given his consent. Such would be our first idea of political obligation. But experience, from time immemorial, has proved it to be impossible to unite the opinions of all the members of a community, in every case; and hence the doctrine, that the opinions of a *majority* must give law to the *whole State:* a doctrine as universally received, as any intuitive truth.

Another idea that naturally presents itself to our minds, on a slight consideration of the subject, is, that in a perfect government, all the members of a society should be present, and each give his suffrage in acts of legislation, by which he is to be bound. This is impracticable in large states; and even were it not, it is very questionable whether it would be the *best* mode of legislation. It was however practised in the free states of antiquity; and was the cause of innumerable evils. To avoid these evils, the moderns have invented the doctrine of *representation*, which seems to be the perfection of human government.

Another idea, which is very natural, is, that to complete the mode of legislation, all the representatives should be collected into *one body*, for the purpose of debating questions and enacting laws. Speculation would suggest the idea;

---

* A division of the legislature has been adopted in the new constitution of every state except Pennsylvania and Georgia.

[8] and the desire of improving upon the systems of government in the old world, would operate powerfully in its favor.

But men are ever running into extremes. The passions, after a violent constraint, are apt to run into licentiousness; and even the reason of men, who have experienced evils from the *defects* of a government, will sometimes coolly condemn the *whole system*.

Every person, moderately acquainted with human nature, knows that public bodies, as well as individuals, are liable to the influence of sudden and violent passions, under the operation of which, the voice of reason is silenced. Instances of such influence are not so frequent, as in individuals; but its effects are extensive in proportion to the numbers that compose the public body. This fact suggests the expediency of dividing the powers of legislation between the two bodies of men, whose debates shall be separate and not dependent on each other; that, if at any time, one part should appear to be under any undue influence, either from passion, obstinacy, jealousy of particular men, attachment to a popular speaker, or other extraordinary causes, there might be a power in the legislature sufficient to check every pernicious measure. Even in a small republic, composed of men, equal in property and abilities, and all meeting for the purpose of making laws, like the old Romans in the field of Mars, a division of the body into two independent branches, would be a necessary step to prevent the disorders, which arise from [9] the pride, irritability and stubborness of mankind. This will ever be the case, while men possess passions, easily inflamed, which may bias their reason and lead them to erroneous conclusions.

Another consideration has weight: A single body of men may be led astray by one person of abilities and address, who, on the first starting a proposition, may throw a plausible appearance on one side of the question, and give a lead to the whole debate. To prevent any ill consequence from such a circumstance, a separate discussion, before a different body of men, and taken up on new grounds, is a very eligible expedient.

Besides, the design of a senate is not merely to check the legislative assembly, but to collect wisdom and experience.

In most of our constitutions, and particularly in the proposed federal system, greater age and longer residence are required to qualify for the senate, than for the house of representatives. This is a wise provision. The house of representatives may be composed of new and unexperienced members—strangers to the forms of proceeding, and the science of legislation. But either positive institutions, or customs, which may supply their place, fill the senate with men venerable for age and respectability, experienced in the ways of men, and in the art of governing, and who are not liable to the bias of passions that govern the young. If the senate of Rhode Island is an exception to this observation, it is a proof that the mass of the people are corrupted, and that the senate should be elected [10] less frequently than the other house: Had the old senate in Rhode Island held their seats for three years; had they not been chosen, amidst a popular rage for paper money, the honor of that state would probably have been saved. The old senate would have stopped the measure for a year or two, till the people could have had time to deliberate upon its consequences. I consider it as a capital excellence of the proposed constitution, that the senate can be wholly renewed but once in six years.

Experience is the best instructor—it is better than a thousand theories. The history of every government on earth affords proof of the utility of different branches in a legislature. But I appeal only to our own experience in America. To what cause can we ascribe the absurd measures of Congress, in times past, and the speedy recision of whole measures, but to the want of some check? I feel the most profound deference for that honorable body, and perfect respect for their opinions; but some of their steps betray a great want of consideration—a defect, which perhaps nothing can remedy, but a division of their deliberations. I will instance only their *resolution* to build a *Federal Town*. When we were involved in a debt, of which we could hardly pay the interest, and when Congress could not command a shilling, the very proposition was extremely absurd. Congress themselves became ashamed of the resolution, and rescinded it with as much silence as possible. Many other acts of that body are equally reprehensible—but respect forbids me to mention them.

[11] Several states, since the war, have experienced the necessity of a division of the legislature. Maryland was saved from a most pernicious measure, by her senate. A rage for paper money, bordering on madness, prevailed in their house of delegates—an emission of £.500,000 was proposed; a sum equal to the circulating medium of the State. Had the sum been emitted, every shilling of specie would have been driven from circulation, and most of it from the state. Such a loss would not have been repaired in seven years—not to mention the whole catalogue of frauds which would have followed the measure. The senate, like honest, judicious men, and the protectors of the interests of the state, firmly resisted the rage, and gave the people time to cool and to think. Their resistance was effectual—the people acquiesced, and the honor and interest of the state were secured.

The house of representatives in Connecticut, soon after the war, had taken offence at a certain act of Congress. The upper house, who understood the necessity and expediency of the measure, better than the people, refused to concur in a remonstrance to Congress. Several other circumstances gave umbrage to the lower house; and to weaken or destroy the influence of the senate, the representatives, among other violent proceedings, resolved, not merely to remove the seat of government, but to make every county town in the state the seat of government, by rotation. This foolish resolution would have disgraced school-boys — the senate saved the honor of the state, by rejecting it with disdain—[12] and within two months, every representative was ashamed of the conduct of the house. All public bodies have these fits of passion, when their conduct seems to be perfectly boyish; and in these paroxisms, a check is highly necessary.

Pennsylvania exhibits many instances of this hasty conduct. At one session of the legislature, an armed force is ordered, by a precipitate resolution, to expel the settlers at Wioming from their possessions—at a succeding session, the same people are confirmed in their possessions. At one session, a charter is wrested from a corporation—at another, restored. The whole state is split into parties—everything is decided by party—any proposition from one side of the house, is sure to be damned by the other—and when one party perceives the other has the advantage, they play truant—and an officer or a mob hunt the absconding members in all the streets and alleys in town. Such farces have been repeated in Philadelphia—and *there alone*. Had the legislature been framed with some check upon rash proceedings, the honor of the state would have been saved—the party spirit would have died with the measures proposed in the legislature. But now, any measure may be carried by party in the house; it then becomes a law, and sows the seeds of dissension throughout the state.*

[13] A thousand examples similar to the foregoing may be produced, both in ancient and modern history. Many plausible things may be said in favor of pure democracy—many in favor of uniting the representatives of the people in one single house—but uniform experience proves both to be inconsistent with the peace of society, and the rights of freemen.

The state of Georgia has already discovered such inconveniences in its constitution, that a proposition has been made for altering it; and there is a prospect that a revisal will take place.

People who have heard and read of the European governments, founded on the different ranks of *monarch, nobility and people*, seem to view the *senate* in America, where there is no difference of ranks and titles, as a useless branch—or as a servile imitation of foreign constitutions of governmeut, without the same reasons. This is a capital mistake. Our senates, it

---

* I cannot help remarking the singular jealousy of the constitution of Pennsylvania, which requires that a bill shall be published for the consideration of the people, before it is enacted into a law, except in extraordinary cases. This annihilates the legislature, and reduces it to an advisory body. It almost wholly supersedes the uses of *representation*, the most excellent improvement in modern governments. Besides the absurdity of constituting a legislature, without supreme power, such a system will keep the state perpetu-

is true, are not composed of a different order of men; but the same reasons, the same necessity for distinct branches of the legislature exists in all governments. But in most of our American constitutions, we have all the advantages of checks and balance, without the danger which may arise [14] from a superior and independent order of men.

It is worth our while to institute a brief comparison between our American forms of government, and the two *best constitutions* that ever existed in Europe, the *Roman* and the *British.*

In England, the king or supreme executive officer, is hereditary. In America, the president of the United States, is elective. That this is an advantage will hardly be disputed.

In ancient Rome, the king was elective, and so were the consuls, who were the executive officers in the republic. But they were elected by the body of the people, in their public assemblies; and this circumstance paved the way for such excessive bribery and corruption as are wholly unknown in modern times. The president of the United States is also elective; but by a few men——chosen by the several legislatures——under their inspection——separated at a vast distance——and holding no office under the United States. Such a mode of election almost precludes the possibility of corruption. Besides, no state however large, has the power of chusing a president in that state; for each elector must choose at least one man, who is not an inhabitant of that State to which he belongs.

The crown of England is hereditary—the consuls of Rome were chosen annually—both these extremes are guarded against in our proposed constitution. The president is not

ally embroiled. It carries the spirit of discussion into all quarters, without the means of reconciling the opinions of men, who are not assembled to hear each others' arguments. They debate with themselves—form their own opinions, without the reasons which influence others, and without the means of information. Thus the warmth of different opinions, which, in other states, dies in the legislature, is diffused through the state of Pennsylvania, and becomes personal and permanent. The seeds of dissension are sown in the constitution, and no state, except Rhode Island, is so distracted by factions.

dis- [15] missed from his office, as soon as he is acquainted with business—he continues four years, and is re-eligible, if the people approve his conduct. Nor can he canvass for his office, by reason of the distance of the electors; and the pride and jealousy of the states will prevent his continuing too long in office.

The age requisite to qualify for this office is thirty-five years.* The age requisite for admittance to the Roman consulship was forty-three years. For this difference, good reasons may be assigned—the improvements in science, and particularly in government, render it practicable for a man to qualify himself for an important office, much earlier in life, than he could among the Romans; especially in the early part of their commonwealth, when the office was instituted. Besides it is very questionable whether any inconvenience would have attended admission to the consulship at an earlier age. [†]

The powers vested in the president resemble the powers of the supreme magistrates in Rome. They are not so extensive as those of the British king; but in one instance, the president, with concurrence of the senate, has powers exceeding those of the Roman consuls; I mean in the appointment of judges and other subordinate executive officers. The prætors or judges in Rome were chosen annually by the people. This was a defect in the Roman government. [16] One half the evils in a state arise from a lax execution of the laws; and it is impossible that an executive officer can act with vigor and impartiality, when his office depends on the popular voice. An annual popular election of executive officers is the sure source of a negligent, partial and corrupt administration. The independence of the judges in England has produced a course of the most just, impartial and energetic judicial decisions, for many centuries, that can be exhibited in any nation on earth. In this point therefore I conceive the plan proposed in America to be an improvement on the Roman constitution. In all

---

* In the decline of the republic, bribery or military force obtained this office for persons who had not attained this age—Augustus was chosen at the age of twenty; or rather obtained it with his sword.

[† "Query."]

free governments, that is, in all countries, where *laws govern*, and not *men*, the supreme magistrate should have it in his power to execute any law, however unpopular, without hazarding his person or office. The laws are the sole *guardians* of right, and when the magistrate dares not act, every person is insecure.

Let us now attend to the constitution and the powers of the senate.

The house of lords in England is wholly independent on [†] the people. The lords spiritual hold their seats by office; and the people at large have no voice in disposing of the ecclesiastical dignities. The temporal lords hold their seats by hereditary right or by grant from the king: And it is a branch of the king's prerogative to make what peers he pleases.

[17] The senate in Rome was elective; but a senator held his seat for life.*

[† of]

* I say the senate was *elective*—but this must be understood with some exceptions; or rather qualifications. The constitution of the Roman senate has been a subject of enquiry, with the first men in modern ages. Lord Chesterfield requested the opinion of the learned Vertot, upon the manner of chusing senators in Rome; and it was a subject of discussion between Lord Harvey and Dr. Middleton. The most probable account of the manner of forming the senate, and filling up vacancies, which I have collected from the best writers on this subject, is here abridged for the consideration of the reader.

Romulus chose one hundred persons, from the principal families in Rome, to form a council or senate; and reserved to himself the right of nominating their successors; that is of filling vacancies. "Mais comme Romulus avoit lui " même choisi les premiers senateurs il se reserva le droit de nommer a son " gré, leurs successeurs."—Mably, sur les Romains. Other well informed historians intimate that Romulus retained the right of nominating the president only. After the union of the Sabines with the Romans, Romulus added another hundred members to the senate, but by *consent of the people*. Tarquin, the *ancient*, added another hundred; but historians are silent as to the manner.

On the destruction of Alba by Hostilius, some of the principal Alban families were added to the senate, *by consent of the senate and people*.

After the demolition of the monarchy, Appius Claudius was admitted into the senate by *order of the people*.

Cicero testifies that, from the extinction of the monarchy, all the members of the senate were admitted by *command of the people*.

It is observable that the first creation of the senators was the act ot the monarch; and the first patrician families claimed the sole right of admission

[18] The proposed senate in America is constituted on prinples more favorable to liberty: The members are elective, and by the separate legislatures: They hold their seats for six years—they are thus rendered sufficiently dependent on their constituents; and yet are not dismissed from their office as soon as they become acquainted with the forms of proceeding.

It may be objected by the larger states, that the representation is not equal; the smallest states having the privilege of sending the same number of senators as the largest. To obviate this objection, I would suggest but two or three ideas.

1. If each state had a representation and a right in deciding questions, proportional to its property, three states would almost command the whole. Such a constitution would gradually annihilate the small states; and finally melt down the whole United States into one undivided sovereignty. The free states of Spain and the heptarchy in England, afford striking examples of this.

[19] Should it be said that such an event is desirable,·I answer; the states are all entitled to their respective sovereignties, and while they claim independence in international jurisdiction, the federal constitution ought to guarantee their sovereignty.

into the senate. "Les familles qui descendoient des deux cent senateurs que "Romulus avoit créés,—se crurent seules en droit d'entrer dans le senat."—Mably

This right however was not granted in its utmost extent ; for many of the senators in the Roman commonwealth, were taken from plebian families. For sixty years before the institution of the *censorship*, which was A. U. C. 311, we are not informed how vacancies in the senate were supplied. The most probable method was this ; to enrol, in the list of senators, the different magistrates; viz., the consuls, prætors, the two quæstors of patrician families, the five tribunes (afterwards ten) and the two ædiles of plebian families: The office of quæstor gave an immediate admission into the senate. The tribunes were admitted two years after their creation. This enrollment seems to have been a matter of course; and likewise their confirmation by the people in their comitia or assemblies.

On extraordinary occasions, when the vacancies of the senate were numerous, the consuls used to nominate some of the most respectable of the equestrian order to be chosen by the people.

On the institution of the censorship, the censors were invested with full powers to inspect the manners of the citizens,—enrol them in their proper

Another consideration has weight—There is, in all nations, a tendency toward an accumulation of power in some point. It is the business of the legislator to establish some barriers to check the tendency. In small societies, a man worth £.100,000 has but one vote, when his neighbors, who are worth but fifty pounds, have each one vote likewise. To make property the sole basis of authority, would expose many of the best citizens to violence and oppression. To make the number of inhabitants [*] in a state, the rule of apportioning power, is more equitable; and were the United States one indivisible interest, would be a perfect rule for representation. But the detached situation of the states has created some separate interests—some local institutions, which they will not resign nor throw into the hands of other states. For these peculiar interests, the states have an *equal* attachment—for the preservation and enjoyment of these, an *equal* sovereignty is necessary; and the sovereignty of each state would not be secure, had each state, in both branches of the legislature an authority in passing laws, proportioned to its inhabitants.

3. But the senate should be considered as representing the

---

ranks according to their property,—make out lists of the senators and leave out the names of such as had rendered themselves unworthy of their dignity by any scandalous vices. This power they several times exercised; but the disgraced senators had an appeal to the people.

After the senate had lost half its members in the war with Hannibal, the dictator, M. Fabius Buteo, filled up the number with the magistrates, with those who had been honored with a civic crown, or others who were respectable for age and character. One hundred and seventy new members were added at once, with *the approbation of the people*. The vacancies occasioned by Sylla's proscriptions amounted to three hundred, which were supplied by persons nominated by Sylla and *chosen by the people*.

Before the time of the Gracchi, the number of senators did not exceed three hundred. But in Sylla's time, so far as we can collect from direct testimonies, it amounted to about five hundred. The age necessary to qualify for a seat in the senate is not exactly ascertained; but several circumstances prove it to have been about thirty years.

See Vertot, Mably, and Middleton on this subject.

In the last ages of Roman splendor, the property requisite to qualify a person for a senator, was settled by Augustus at eight hundred sestertia—more than six thousand pounds sterling.

[* "Between states, and excluding negroes," added in author's copy.—P. L. F.]

confederacy in a body. It is a [20] false principle in the vulgar idea of representation, that a man delegated by a particular district in a state, is the representative of that district only; whereas in truth a member of the legislature from any town or county, is the representative of the whole state. In passing laws, he is to view the whole collective interest of the state, and act from that view; not from a partial regard to the interest of the town or county where he is chosen.

The same principle extends to the Congress of the United States. A delegate is bound to represent the true local interest of his constituents—to state in its true light to the whole body—but when each provincial interest is thus stated, every member should act for the *aggregate interest* of the whole confederacy. The design of representation is to bring the collective interest into view—a delegate is not the legislator of a single state—he is as much the legislator of the whole confederacy as of the particular state where he is chosen; and if he gives his vote for a law which he believes to be beneficial to his own state only, and pernicious to the rest, he betrays his trust and violates his oath. It is indeed difficult for a man to divest himself of local attachments and act from an impartial regard to the general good; but he who cannot for the most part do this, is not a good legislator.

These considerations suggest the propriety of continuing the senators in office, for a longer period, than the representatives. They gradually lose their partiality, generalize their views, [21] and consider themselves as acting for the whole confederacy. Hence in the senate we may expect union and firmness—here we may find the *general good* the object of legislation, and a check upon the more partial and interested acts of the other branch.

These considerations obviate the complaint, that the representation in the senate is not equal; for the senators represent the whole confederacy; and all that is wanted of the members is information of the true situation and interest of each state. As they act under the direction of the several legislatures, two men may as fully and completely represent a state, as twenty; and when the true interest of each state is known, if the senators perform the part of good legislators, and act impartially for the whole collective body of the United States, it is totally immaterial where they are chosen.*

[22] The house of representatives is the more immediate voice of the separate states—here the states are represented in proportion to their number of inhabitants—here the separate interests will operate with their full force, and the violence of parties and the jealousies produced by interfering interests, can be restrained and quieted only by a body of men, less local and dependent.

It may be objected that no separate interests should exist in a state; and a division of the legislature has a tendency to create them. But this objection is founded on mere jealousy, or a very imperfect comparison of the Roman and British governments, with the proposed federal constitution.

* It is a capital defect of most of the state-constitutions, that the senators, like the representatives, are chosen in particular districts, They are thus inspired with local views, and however wrong it may be to entertain them, yet such is the constitution of human nature, that men are almost involuntarily attached to the interest of the district which has reposed confidence in their abilities and integrity. Some partiality therefore for constituents is always expectable. To destroy it as much as possible, a political constitution should remove the grounds of local attachment. Connecticut and Maryland have wisely destroyed this attachment in their senates, by ordaining that the members shall be chosen in the *state at large*. The senators hold their seats by the suffrages of the state, *not of a district;* hence they have no particular number of men to fear or to oblige.—They represent *the state;* hence that union and firmness which the senates of those states have manifested on the most trying occasions, and by which they have prevented the most rash and iniquitous measures.

It may be objected, that when the election of senators is vested in the people, they must choose men in their own neighborhood, or else those with whom they are unacquainted. With respect to representatives, this objection does not lie; for they are chosen in small districts; and as to senators, there is, in every state, a small number of men, whose reputation for abilities, integrity and good conduct will lead the people to a very just choice. Old experienced statesmen should compose the senate; and people are generally, in this free country, acquainted with their characters. Were it possible, as it is in small states, it would be an improvement in the doctrine of representation, to give every freeman the right of voting for every member of the legislature, and the privilege of choosing the men in any part of the state. This would totally exclude bribery and undue influence; for no man can bribe a state; and it would almost annihilate partial views in legislation. But in large states it may be impracticable.

The house of peers in England is a body originally and totally independent on [*] the people—the senate in Rome was mostly composed of patrician or noble families, and after the first election of a senator, he was no longer dependent on the people—he held his seat for life. But the senate of the United States can have no separate interests from the body of the people; for they live among them—they are chosen by them—they *must* be dismissed from their place once in six years and *may* at any time be impeached for mal-practices— —their property is si- tuated among the people, and with their persons, subject to the same laws. No title can be granted, but the temporary titles of office, bestowed by the voluntary election of the people; and no pre-eminence can be acquired but by the same means.

The separation of the legislature divides the power—checks —restrains—amends the proceedings—at the same time, it creates no division of interest, that can tempt either branch to encroach upon the other, or upon the people. In turbulent times, such restraint is our greatest safety—in calm times, and in measures obviously calculated for the general good, both branches must always be unanimous.

A man must be thirty years of age before he can be admitted into the senate—which was likewise a requisite in the Roman government. What property was requisite for a senator in the early ages of Rome, I cannot inform myself; but Augustus fixed it at six hundred sestertia—between six and seven thousand pounds sterling. In the federal constitution, money is not made a requisite—the places of senators are wisely left open to all persons of suitable age and merit, and who have been citizens of the United States for nine years; a term in which foreigners may acquire the feelings and acquaint themselves with the interests, of the native Americans.

The house of representatives is formed on very equitable principles; and is calculated to guard the privileges of the people. The English house of commons is chosen by a small part of the people of England, and continues for seven years. The Romans never discovered the secret of representation—the whole body of citizens assembled for the purposes

[* of]

of legislation—a circumstance that exposed their government to frequent convulsions, and to capricious measures. The federal house of representatives is chosen by the people qualified to vote for state representatives,* and continues two years.

[25] Some may object to their continuance in power *two years*. But I cannot see any danger arising from this quarter. On the contrary, it creates less trouble for the representatives, who by such choice are taken from their professions and obliged to attend Congress, some of them at the distance of at least seven hundred miles. While men are chosen by the people, and responsible to them, there is but little danger from ambition or corruption.

If it should be said that Congress may in time become triennial, and even septennial, like the English parliaments, I answer, this is not in their power. The English parliament had power to prolong the period of their existence—but Congress will be restrained by the different legislatures, without

---

* It is said by some, that no property should be required as a qualification for an elector. I shall not enter into a discussion of the subject; but remark that in most free governments, some property has been thought requisite, to prevent corruption and secure government from the influence of an unprincipled multitude.

In ancient Rome none but the free citizens had the right of a suffrage in the *comitia* or legislative assemblies. But in Sylla's time the Italian cities demanded the rights of the Roman citizens; alledging that they furnished two-thirds of the armies, in all their wars, and yet were despised as foreigners. Vell. Paterc. lib. 2. cap. 15. This produced the *Marsic* or *social* war, which lasted two years, and caried off 300,000 men. Ibm. It was conducted and concluded by Pompey, father of Pompey the Great, with his lieutenants Sylla and Marius. But most of the cities eventually obtained *the freedom of Rome;* and were of course entitled to the rights of suffrage in the comitia. "Paulatim deinde recip-"iendo in civitatem, qui arma aut non ceperant aut deposuerant maturiùs, " vires refectæ sunt." Vell. Paterc. 2. 16.

But Rome had cause to deplore this event, for however reasonable it might appear to admit the allies to a participation of the rights of citizens, yet the concession destroyed all freedom of election. It enabled an ambitious demagogue to engage and bring into the assemblies, whole towns of people, slaves and foreigners;—and everything was decided by faction and violence. This Montesquieu numbers among the causes of the decline of the Roman greatness. De la grandeur des Romains, c. 9.

Representation would have, in some measure, prevented the consequences;

whose constitutional concurrence, no alteration can be made in the proposed system.

The fourth section, article 1, of the new constitution declares that "The times, places, and manner of holding elec-"tions for senators and representatives, shall be prescribed in "each state by the legislature thereof; *but the Congress may* "*at any time by law make or alter such regulations, except as to* "*the places of chusing senators.*" Here let us pause————What did the convention mean by giving Congress power to *make regulations*, prescribed by the legislatures? Is this expression accurate or intelligible? But the word *alter* is very intelligible, and the clause puts the election of representatives *wholly*, and [26] the senators *almost wholly*, in the power of Congress.

The views of the convention I believe to be perfectly upright—They might mean to place the election of representatives and senators beyond the reach of faction—They doubtless had good reasons, in *their* minds, for the clause—But I see no occasion for any power in Congress to interfere with the choice of their own body—They will have power to suppress insurrections, as they ought to have; but the clause in *Italics* gives *needless* and *dangerous* powers—I hope the states will reject it with decency, and adopt the whole system, without altering another syllable. [*]

The method of passing laws in Congress is much preferable to that of ancient Rome or modern Britain. Not to mention other defects in Rome, it lay in the power of a single tribune

---

but the admission of every man to a suffrage will ever open the door to corruption. In such a state as Connecticut, where there is no conflux of foreigners, no introduction of seamen, servants, &c., and scarcely an hundred persons in the state who are not natives, and very few whose education and connexions do not attach them to the government; at the same time few men have property to furnish the means of corruption, very little danger could spring from admitting every man of age and discretion to the privilege of voting for rulers. But in the large towns of America there is more danger. A master of a vessel may put votes in the hands of his crew, for the purpose of carrying an election for a party Such things have actually taken place in America. Besides, the middle states are receiving emigrations of poor people, who are not at once judges of the characters of men, and who cannot be safely trusted with the choice of legislators.

[* These two paragraphs struck out in author's copy.—P. L. F.]

to obstruct the passing of a law. As the tribunes were popular magistrates, the right was often exercised in favor of liberty; but it was also abused, and the best regulations were prevented, to gratify the spleen, the ambition, or the resentment of an individual.

The king of Great-Britain has the same power, but seldom exercises it. It is however a dangerous power—it is absurd and hazardous to lodge in *one man* the right of controlling the will of a state.

Every bill that passes a majority of both houses of Congress, must be sent to the president for [27] his approbation; but it must be returned in ten days, whether approved by him or not; and the concurrence of two thirds of both houses passes the bill into a law, notwithstanding any objections of the president. The constitution therefore gives the supreme executive a check but no negative, upon the sense of Congress.

The powers lodged in Congress are extensive; but it is presumed that they are not too extensive. The first object of the constitution is to *unite* the states into one *compact society*, for the purpose of government. If such *union* must exist, or the states be exposed to foreign invasions, internal discord, reciprocal encroachments upon each others property—to weakness and infamy, which no person will dispute; what powers must be collected and lodged in the supreme head or legislature of these states. The answer is easy: This legislature must have exclusive jurisdiction in all matters in which the states have a mutual interest. There are some regulations in which all the states are equally concerned—there are others, which in their operation, are limited to one state. The first belongs to Congress—the last to the respective legislatures. No one state has a right to supreme control, in any affair in which the other states have an interest, nor should Congress interfere in any affair which respects one state only. This is the general line of division, which the convention have endeavored to draw, between the powers of Congress and the rights of the individual states. The only question therefore is, whether the new constitution delegates to Congress any powers which [28] do not respect the general interest and welfare of the

United States. If these powers intrench upon the present sovereignty of any *state*, without having for an object the *collective interest* of the whole, the powers are too extensive. But if they do not extend to all concerns, in which the states have a mutual interest, they are too limited. If in any instance, the powers necessary for protecting the *general* interest, interfere with the constitutional rights of an *individual* state, such state has assumed powers that are inconsistent with the safety of the United States, and which ought instantly to be resigned. Considering the states as individuals, on equal terms, entering into a social compact, no state has a right to any power which may prejudice its neighbors. If therefore the federal constitution has collected into the federal legislature no more power than is necessary for the *common defence and interest*, it should be recognized by the states, however particular clauses may supersede the exercise of certain powers by the individual states.

This question is of vast magnitude. The states have very high ideas of their separate sovereignty; altho' it is certain, that while each exists in its full latitude, we can have no *Federal sovereignty*. However flattered each state may be by its independent sovereignty, we can have no union, no respectability, no national character, and what is more, no national justice, till the states resign to one *supreme head* the exclusive power of *legislating, judging and executing*, in all matters of a general nature. Every thing of [29] a private or provincial nature, must still rest on the ground of the respective state-constitutions.

After examining the limits of the proposed congressional powers, I confess I do not think them too extensive—I firmly believe that the life, liberty and property of every man, and the peace and independence of each state, will be more fully secured under such a constitution of federal government, than they will under a constitution with more limited powers; and infinitely more safe than under our boasted distinct sovereignties. It appears to me that Congress will have no more power than will be necessary for our union and general welfare; and such power they must have or we are in a wretched state. On the adoption of this constitution, I should value real estate twenty per cent. higher than I do at this moment.

I will not examine into the extent of the powers proposed to be lodged in the supreme federal head; the subject would be extensive and require more time than I could bestow upon it. But I will take up some objections, that have been made to particular points of the new constitution.

Most of the objections I have yet heard to the constitution, consist in mere insinuations unsupported by reasoning or fact. They are thrown out to instil groundless jealousies into the minds of the people, and probably with a view to prevent all government; for there are, in every society, some turbulent geniuses whose importance [30] depends solely on faction. To seek the insidious and detestable nature of these insinuations, it is necessary to mention, and to remark on a few particulars.

1. The first objection against the constitution is, that the legislature will be more expensive than our present confederation. This is so far from being true, that the money we actually lose by our present weakness, disunion and *want of government* would support the civil government of every state in the confederacy. Our public poverty does not proceed from the expensiveness of Congress, nor of the civil list; but from want of power to command our own advantages. We pay more money to foreign nations, in the course of business, and merely for *want of government*, than would, under an efficient government, pay the annual interest of our domestic debt. Every man in business knows this to be *truth;* and the objection can be designed only to delude the ignorant.

2. Another objection to the constitution, is the division of the legislature into two branches. Luckily this objection has no advocates but in Pennsylvania; and even here their number is dwindling. The factions that reign in this state, the internal discord and passions that disturb the government and the peace of the inhabitants, have detected the errors of the constitution, and will some time or other produce a reformation. The division of the legislature has been the subject of discussion in the beginning of this essay; and will be deemed,

by nineteen-twentieths of [31] the Americans, one of the principal excellencies of the constitution.

3. A third insinuation, is that the proposed federal government will annihilate the several legislatures. This is extremely disingenuous. Every person, capable of reading, must discover, that the convention have labored to draw the line between the federal and provincial powers—to define the powers of Congress, and limit them to those general concerns which *must* come under federal jurisdiction, and which *cannot* be managed in the separate legislatures—that in all internal regulations, whether of civil or criminal nature, the states retain their sovereignty, and have it guaranteed to them by this very constitution. Such a groundless insinuation, or rather mere surmise, must proceed from dark designs or extreme ignorance, and deserves the severest reprobation.

4. It is alledged that the liberty of the press is not guaranteed by the new constitution. But this objection is wholly unfounded. The liberty of the press does not come within the jurisdiction of federal government. It is firmly established in all the states either by law, or positive declarations in *bills of right;* and not being mentioned in the federal constitution, is not—and cannot be abridged by Congress. It stands on the basis of the respective state-constitutions. Should any state resign to Congress the exclusive jurisdiction of a certain district, which should include any town where presses are already established, it is in the power of the state to reserve [32] the liberty of the press, or any other fundamental privilege, and make it an immutable condition of the grant, that such rights shall never be violated. All objections therefore on this score are " *baseless visions*."

5. It is insinuated that the constitution gives Congress the power of levying internal taxes at pleasure. This insinuation seems founded on the eighth section of the first article, which declares, that " Congress shall have power to lay and collect " taxes, duties, imposts and excises, to pay the debts and pro- " vide for the common defence and general welfare of the " United States."

That Congress should have power to collect duties, imposts

and excises, in order to render them uniform throughout the United States will hardly be controverted. The whole objection is to the right of levying internal taxes.

But it will be conceded that the supreme head of the states must have power, competent to the purposes of our union, or it will be, as it now is, a *useless body*, a mere expense, without any advantage. To pay our public debt, to support foreign ministers and our own civil government, money must be raised; and if the duties and imposts are not adequate to these purposes, where shall the money be obtained? It will be answered, let Congress apportion the sum to be raised, and leave the legislatures to collect the money. Well this is all that is intended by the clause under consideration; with the addition of a fe- [33] deral power that shall be sufficient to oblige a delinquent state to comply with the requisition. [*] Such power must exist somewhere, or the debts of the United States can never be paid. For want of such power, our credit is lost and our national faith is a bye-word.

For want of such power, one state now complies fully with a requisition, another partially, and a third absolutely refuses or neglects to grant a shilling. Thus the honest and punctual are doubly loaded—and the knave triumphs in his negligence. In short, no honest man will dread a power that shall enforce an equitable system of taxation. The dis-honest are ever apprehensive of a power that shall oblige them to do what honest men are ready to do voluntarily.

Permit me to ask those who object to this power of taxation, how shall money be raised to discharge our honest debts which are universally acknowledged to be just? Have we not already experienced the inefficacy of a system without power? Has it not been proved to demonstration, that a voluntary compliance with the demands of the union can never be expected? To what expedient shall we have recourse? What is the resort of all governments in cases of delinquency? Do not the states vest in the legislature, or even in the governor and council, a power to enforce laws, even with the militia of the states? And how rarely does there exist the necessity of exerting such a power? Why should such a power be

[* Last two sentences struck out in author's copy.—P. L. F.]

more dangerous in Congress than in a legislature? Why should [34] more confidence be reposed in a member of one legislature than of another? Why should we choose the best men in the state to represent us in Congress, and the moment they are elected arm ourselves against them as against tyrants and robbers? Do we not, in this conduct, act the part of a man, who, as soon as he has married a woman of unsuspected chastity, locks her up in a dungeon? Is there any spell or charm, that instantly changes a delegate to Congress from an honest man into a knave—a tyrant? I confess freely that I am willing to trust Congress with any powers that I should dare lodge in a state-legislature. I believe life, liberty, and property is as safe in the hands of a federal legislature, organized in the manner proposed by the convention, as in the hands of any legislature, that has ever been or ever will be chosen in any particular state.

But the idea that Congress can levy taxes *at pleasure* is false, and the suggestion wholly unsupported. The preamble to the constitution is declaratory of the purposes of our union: and the assumption of any powers not necessary to *establish justice, insure domestic tranquility, provide for the common defence, promote the general welfare, and to secure the blessings of liberty to ourselves and our posterity*, will be unconstitutional, and endanger the existence of Congress. Besides, in the very clause which gives the power of levying duties and taxes, the purposes to which the money shall be appropriated are specified, viz. *to pay the debts and provide for the common de-* [35] *fence and general welfare of the United States.*\* For these purposes money must be collected, and the power of collection must be lodged, sooner or later, in a federal head; or the common defence and general welfare must be neglected.

The states in their separate capacity, cannot provide for

---

\* The clause may at first appear ambiguous. It may be uncertain whether we should read and understand it thus—"The Congress shall have power to "lay and collect taxes, duties, imposts and excises *in order to pay the debts*," &c. or whether the meaning is—"The Congress shall have power to lay and collect "taxes, duties, imposts and excises, and *shall have power to pay the debts*," &c. On considering the construction of the clause, and comparing it with the preamble, the last sense seems to be improbable and absurd. But it is not very the *common* defence; nay in case of a civil war, a state cannot secure its own existence. The only question therefore is, whether it is necessary to unite, and provide for our *common defence and general welfare.* For this question being once decided in the affirmative, leaves no room to controvert the propriety of constituting a power over the whole United States, adequate to these general purposes.

The states, by granting such power, do not throw it out of their own hands—they only throw, each its proportion, into a common stock—they merely combine the powers of the several states into one point, where they *must* be collected, before they *can* be exerted. But the powers are still in their own hands; and cannot be alienated, till they create a body independent of them- [36] selves, with a force at their command, superior to the whole yeomanry of the country.

6. It is said there is no provision made in the new constitution against a standing army in time of peace. Why do not people object that no provision is made against the introduction of a body of Turkish Janizaries; or against making the Alcoran the rule of faith and practice, instead of the Bible? The answer to such objections is simply this—*no such provision is necessary.* The people in this country cannot forget their apprehensions from a British standing army, quartered in America; and they turn their fears and jealousies against themselves. Why do not the people of most of the states apprehend danger from standing armies from their own legislatures? Pennsylvania and North Carolina, I believe, are the only states that have provided against this danger at all events. Other states have declared that " no standing armies shall be kept up without the consent of the legislature." But this leaves the power entirely in the hands of the legislature. Many of the states however have made *no provision* against this evil. What

material; for no powers are vested in Congress but what are included under the general expressions, of *providing for the common defence and general welfare of the United States.* Any powers not promotive of these purposes, will be unconstitutional;—consequently any appropriations of money to any other purpose will expose the Congress to the resentment of the states, and the members to impeachment and loss of their seats.

hazards these states suffer! Why does not a man pass a law in his family, that no armed soldier shall be quartered in his house by his consent? The reason is very plain: no man will suffer his liberty to be abridged, or endangered—his disposition and his power are uniformly opposed to any infringement of his rights. In the same manner, the principles and habits, as well as the power of the Americans are directly opposed to standing armies; and there is as little [37] necessity to guard against them by positive constitutions, as to prohibit the establishment of the Mahometan religion. But the constitution provides for our safety; and while it gives Congress power to raise armies, it declares that no appropriation of money to their support shall be for a longer term than two years.

Congress likewise are to have power to provide for organizing, arming and disciplining the militia, but have no other command of them, except when in actual service. Nor are they at liberty to call out the militia at pleasure—but only, to execute the laws of the union, suppress insurrections, and repel invasions. For these purposes, government must always be armed with a military force, if the occasion should require it; otherwise laws are nugatory, and life and property insecure.

7. Some persons have ventured to publish an intimation, that by the proposed constitution, the trial by jury is abolished in all *civil cases*. Others very modestly insinuate, that it is in *some cases* only. The fact is, that trial by jury is not affected in *any* case, by the constitution; except in cases of impeachment, which are to be tried by the senate. None but persons in office in or under Congress can be impeached; and even after a judgment upon an impeachment, the offender is liable to a prosecution, before a common jury, in a regular course of law. The insinuation therefore that trials by jury are to be abolished, is groundless, and beyond conception, wicked. It must be wicked, because the circu- [38] lation of a barefaced falsehood, respecting a privilege, dear to freemen, can proceed only from a depraved heart and the worst intentions.

8. It is also intimated as a probable event, that the federal

courts will absorb the judiciaries of the federal states. This is a mere suspicion, without the least foundation. The jurisdiction of the federal states is very accurately defined and easily understood. It extends to the cases mentioned in the constitution, and to the execution of the laws of Congress, respecting commerce, revenue, and other general concerns.

With respect to other civil and criminal actions, the powers and jurisdiction of the several judiciaries of each state, remain unimpaired. Nor is there anything novel in allowing appeals to the supreme court. Actions are mostly to be tried in the state where the crimes are committed—But appeals are allowed under our present confederation, and no person complains; nay, were there no appeal, every man would have reason to complain, especially when a final judgement, in an inferior court, should affect property to a large amount. But why is an objection raised against an appellate jurisdiction in the supreme court, respecting *fact* as well as *law?* Is it less safe to have the opinions of two juries than of one? I suspect many people will think this is no defect in the constitution. But perhaps it will destroy a material requisite of a good jury, viz. their vicinity to the cause of action. I have no doubt, that when causes were tried, in periods prior to the Christian æra, before [39] twelve men, seated upon twelve stones, arranged in a circular form, under a huge oak, there was great propriety in submitting causes to men *in the vicinity*. The difficulty of collecting evidence, in those rude times, rendered it necessary that juries should judge mostly from their own knowledge of facts or from information obtained out of court. But in these polished ages, when juries depend almost wholly on the testimony of witnesses; and when a complication of interests, introduced by commerce and other causes, renders it almost impossible to collect men, in the vicinity of the parties, who are wholly disinterested, it is no disadvantage to have a cause tried by a jury of strangers. Indeed the latter is generally the most eligible.

But the truth is, the creation of all inferior courts is in the power of Congress; and the constitution provides that Congress may make such exceptions from the right of appeals as they shall judge proper. When these courts are erected, their jurisdictions will be ascertained, and in small actions, Congress will doubtless direct that a sentence in a subordinate court shall, to a certain amount, be definite and final. All objections therefore to the judicial powers of the federal courts appear to me as trifling as any of the preceding.

9. But, say the enemies of slavery, negroes may be imported for twenty-one years. This exception is addressed to the quakers; and a very pitiful exception it is.

[40] The truth is, Congress cannot prohibit the importation of slaves during that period; but the laws against the importation into particular states, stand unrepealed. An immediate abolition of slavery would bring ruin upon the whites, and misery upon the blacks, in the southern states. The constitution has therefore wisely left each state to pursue its own measures, with respect to this article of legislation, during the period of twenty-one years.

Such are the principal objections that have yet been made by the enemies of the new constitution. They are mostly frivolous, or founded on false constructions, and a misrepresentation of the true state of facts. They are evidently designed to raise groundless jealousies in the minds of well meaning people, who have little leisure and opportunity to examine into the principles of government. But a little time and reflection will enable most people to detect such mischievous intentions; and the spirit and firmness which have distinguished the conduct of the Americans, during the conflict for independence, will eventually triumph over the enemies of union, and bury them in disgrace or oblivion.

But I cannot quit this subject without attempting to correct some of the erroneous opinions respecting *freedom* and *tyranny*, and the principles by which they are supported. Many people seem to entertain an idea, that liberty consists in *a power to act without any control.* This is more liberty than even the savages enjoy. But in civil society, political liberty consists in [41] *acting conformably to a sense of a majority of the society.* In a free government every man binds himself to obey the *public voice,* or the opinions of a majority; and the *whole society* engages to *protect each individual*. In such a government a man is *free* and safe. But reverse the case; suppose every man to act without control or fear of punishment—every man would be free, but no man would be sure of his freedom one moment. Each would have the power of taking his neighbor's life, liberty, or property; and no man would command more than his own strength to repel the invasion. The case is the same with states. If the states should not unite into one compact society, every state may trespass upon its neighbor, and the injured state has no means of redress but its own military force.

The present situation of our American states is very little better than a state of nature—Our boasted state sovereignties are so far from securing our liberty and property, that they, every moment, expose us to the loss of both. That state which commands the heaviest purse and longest sword, may at any moment, lay its weaker neighbor under tribute; and there is no superior power now existing, that can regularly oppose the invasion or redress the injury. From such liberty, O *Lord, deliver us!

But what is tyranny? Or how can a free people be deprived of their liberties? Tyranny is the exercise of some power over a man, which is not warranted by law, or necessary for the public safety. A people can never be deprived of [42] their liberties, while they retain in their own hands, a power sufficient to any other power in the state. This position leads me directly to enquire, in what consists the power of a nation or of an order of men?

In some nations, legislators have derived much of their power from the influence of religion, or from that implicit belief which an ignorant and superstitious people entertain of the gods, and their interposition in every transaction of life. The Roman senate sometimes availed themselves of this engine to carry their decrees and maintain their authority. This was particularly the case, under the aristocracy which succeeded the abolition of the monarchy. The augurs and

[* "O" changed to "good" in author's copy  P. L. F.]

priests were taken wholly from patrician families.* They constituted a distinct order of men—had power to negative any law of the people, by declaring that it was passed during the taking of the auspices.† [¶] This influence derived from the authority of opinion, was less perceptible, but as tyrannical as a military force. The same influence constitutes, at this day, a principal support of federal governments on the Eastern continent, and perhaps in South America. But in North America, by a singular concurrence of circumstances, the possibility of establishing this influence, as a pillar of government, is totally precluded.

[43] Another source of power in government is a military force. But this, to be efficient, must be superior to any force that exists among the people, or which they can command: for otherwise this force would be annihilated, on the first exercise of acts of oppression. Before a standing army can rule, the people must be disarmed; as they are in almost every kingdom in Europe. The supreme power in America cannot enforce unjust laws by the sword; because the whole body of the people are armed, and constitute a force superior to any band of regular troops that can be, on any pretence, raised in the United States. A military force, at the command of Congress, can execute no laws, but such as the people perceive to be just and constitutional; for they will possess the *power*, and jealousy will instantly inspire the *inclination*, to resist the execution of a law which appears to them unjust and oppressive. In spite of all the nominal powers, vested in Congress by the constitution, were the system once adopted in its fullest latitude, still the actual exercise of them would be frequently interrupted by popular jealousy. I am bold to say, that *ten* just and constitutional measures would be resisted, where *one* unjust or oppressive law would be enforced.

*" Quod nemo plebeius auspicia haberet, ideoque decemviros connubium diremisse, ne incerta prole auspicia turbarentur." Tit. Liv. lib. 4. cap. 6.

† Auguriis certe sacerdotisque augurum tantus honos accessit, ut nihil belli domique postea, nisi auspicato, gereretur : concilia populi, exercitus vocati, summa rerum, ubi aves non admisissent, dirimerentur. Liv. lib. 1. cap. 37.

[¶ " The " and " of " struck out—" without " substituted in author's copy— P. L. F.]

The powers vested in Congress are little more than *nominal;* nay *real* power cannot be vested in them, nor in any body, but in the *people*. The source of power is in the *people* of this country, and cannot for ages, and probably never will, be removed. [†].

In what then does *real* power consist? The answer is short and plain—in *property*. Could [44] we want any proofs of this, which are not exhibited in this country, the uniform testimony of history will furnish us with multitudes. But I will go no farther for proof, than the two governments already mentioned, the Roman and the British.

Rome exhibited a demonstrative proof of the inseparable connexion between property and dominion. The first form of its government was an elective monarchy—its second, an aristocracy; but these forms could not be permanent, because they were not supported by property. The kings at first and afterwards the patricians had nominally most of the power; but the people, possessing most of the lands, never ceased to assert their privileges, till they established a commonwealth. And the kings and senate could not have held the reigns of government in their hands so long as they did, had they not artfully contrived to manage the established religion, and play off the superstitious credulity of the people against their own power. "Thus this weak constitution of government," says the ingenious Mr. Moyle, speaking of the aristocracy of Rome,
" not founded on the true *center of dominion, land,* nor on any
" standing foundation of authority, nor rivetted in the esteem
" and affections of the people; and being attacked by strong
" passion, general interest and the joint forces of the people,
" mouldered away of course, and pined of a lingering con-
" sumption, till it was totally swallowed up by the prevailing
" faction, and the nobility were moulded into the mass of the
" people."* The people, notwithstanding [45] the nominal authority of the patricians, proceeded regularly in enlarging their own powers. They first extorted from the senate, the right of electing *tribunes,* with a negative upon the proceed-

[† Last two sentences struck out in author's copy.—P. L. F.]
* Essay on the Roman government.

ings of the senate.* They obtained the right of proposing and debating laws; which before had been vested in the senate; and finally advanced to the power of enacting laws, without the authority of the senate.† They regained the rights of election in their comitia, of which they had been deprived by Servius Tullius.‡ They procured a permanent body of laws, collected from the Grecian institutions. They destroyed the influence of augurs, or diviners, by establishing the *tributa comitia*, in which they were not allowed to consult the gods. They increased their power by large accessions of conquered lands. They procured a repeal of the law which prohibited marriages between the patricians and plebians.§ The Licinian law limited all possessions to five hundred acres of land; which, had it been fully executed, would have secured the commonwealth.‖

The Romans proceeded thus step by step to triumph over the aristocracy, and to crown their privileges, they procured the right of being elected to the highest offices of the state. By acquiring *the property* of the plebians, the nobility, several times, held most of the power of the state; but the people, by reducing the interest of money, abolishing debts, or by forcing other advantages from the patricians, generally held the power of governing in their own hands.

In America, we begin our empire with more popular privileges than the Romans ever enjoyed. We have not to struggle against a monarch or an aristocracy—power is lodged in the mass of the people.

On reviewing the English history, we observe a progress similar to that in Rome—an incessant struggle for liberty from the date of Magna Charta, in John's reign, to the revolution. The struggle has been successful, by abridging the enormous power of the nobility. But we observe that the power of the people has increased in an exact proportion to their acquisitions of property. Wherever the right of primogeniture is established, property must accumulate and remain in families. Thus the landed property in England will never be sufficiently

---

* Livy, 2. 33.   † Livy, 3. 54.   ‡ Livy, 3. 33.   § Livy, 4. 6,   ‖ Livy, 6. 35. 42.   "Ne quis plus quingenta jugera agri possideret."

distributed, to give the powers of government wholly into the hands of the people. But to assist the struggle for liberty, commerce has interposed, and in conjunction with manufacturers, thrown a vast weight of property into the democratic scale. Wherever we cast our eyes, we see this truth, that *property* is the basis of *power;* and this, being established as a cardinal point, directs us to the means of preserving our freedom. Make laws, irrevocable laws in every state, destroying and barring entailments; leave real estates to revolve from hand to hand, as time and accident may direct; and no family influence can be acquired and established for a series of genera- [47] tions—no man can obtain dominion over a large territory—the laborious and saving, who are generally the best citizens, will possess each his share of property and power, and thus the balance of wealth and power will continue where it is, in the *body of the people.*

*A general and tolerably equal distribution of landed property is the whole basis of national freedom:* The system of the great Montesquieu will ever be erroneous, till the words *property or lands in fee simple* are substituted for *virtue,* throughout his *Spirit of Laws.*

*Virtue,* patriotism, or love of country, never was and never will be, till mens' natures are changed, a fixed, permanent principle and support of government. But in an agricultural country, a general possession of land in fee simple, may be rendered perpetual, and the inequalities introduced by commerce, are too fluctuating to endanger government. An equality of property, with a necessity of alienation, constantly operating to destroy combinations of powerful families, is the very *soul of a republic*—While this continues, the people will inevitably possess both *power* and *freedom;* when this is lost, power departs, liberty expires, and a commonwealth will inevitably assume some other form.

The liberty of the press, trial by jury, the Habeas Corpus writ, even Magna Charta itself, although justly deemed the palladia of freedom, are all inferior considerations, when compared with a general distribution of real property among

[48] every class of people.* The power of entailing estates is more dangerous to liberty and republican government, than all the constitutions that can be written on paper, or even than a standing army. Let the people have property, and they *will* have power—a power that will for ever be exerted to prevent a restriction of the press, and abolition of trial by jury, or the abridgement of any other privilege. The liberties of America, therefore, and her forms of government, stand on the broadest basis. Removed from the fears of a foreign invasion and conquest, they are [49] not exposed to the convulsions that shake other governments; and the principles of freedom are so general and energetic, as to exclude the possibility of a change in our republican constitutions.

But while *property* is considered as the *basis* of the freedom of the American yeomanry, there are other auxiliary supports; among which is the *information of the people*. In no country, is education so general—in no country, have the body of the people such a knowledge of the rights of men and the

---

* Montesquieu supposed *virtue* to be the principle of a republic. He derived his notions of this form of government, from the astonishing firmness, courage and patriotism which distinguished the republics of Greece and Rome. But this *virtue* consisted in pride, contempt of strangers and a martial enthusiasm which sometimes displayed itself in defence of their country. These principles are never permanent—they decay with refinement, intercourse with other nations and increase of wealth. No wonder then that these republics declined, for they were not founded on fixed principles; and hence authors imagine that republics cannot be durable. None of the celebrated writers on government seems to have laid sufficient stress on a general possession of real property in fee-simple. Even the authors of the *Political Sketches*, in the *Museum* for the month of September, seems to have passed it over in silence; although he combats Montesquieu's system, and to prove it false, enumerates some of the principles which distinguish our governments from others, and which he supposes constitutes the support of republics.

The English writers on law and government consider Magna Charta, trial by juries, the Habeas Corpus act, and the liberty of the press, as the bulwarks of freedom. All this is well. But in no government of consequence in Europe, is freedom established on its true and immoveable foundation. The property is too much accumulated, and the accumulations too well guarded, to admit the *true principle of republics*. But few centuries have elapsed, since the body of the people were vassals. To such men, the smallest extension of popular privileges, was deemed an invaluable blessing. Hence the encomiums upon trial by juries, and the articles just mentioned. But these people have never

principles of government. This knowledge, joined with a keen sense of liberty and a watchful jealousy, will guard our constitutions, and awaken the people to an instantaneous resistance of encroachments.

But a principal bulwark of freedom is the *right of election*. An equal distribution of property is the *foundation* of a republic; but *popular elections* form the *great barrier*, which defends it from assault, and guards it from the slow and imperceptible approaches of corruption. Americans! never resign that right. It is not very material whether your representatives are elected for one year or two—but the *right* is the Magna Charta of your governments. For this reason, expunge that clause of the new constitution before mentioned, which gives Congress an influence in the election of their own body. The *time, place* and *manner* of chusing senators or representatives are of little or no consequence to Congress. The number of members and time of meeting in Congress are fixed; but the *choice* should rest with the several states. [50] I repeat it—reject the clause with decency, but with unanimity and firmness. [*]

Excepting that clause the constitution is good [†]—it guarantees the *fundamental principles* of our several constitutions—it guards our rights—and while it vests extensive powers in Congress, it vests no more than are necessary for our union. Without powers lodged somewhere in a single body, fully competent to lay and collect equal taxes and duties—to adjust

---

been able to mount to the source of *liberty, estates in fee,* or at least but partially; they are yet obliged to drink at the streams. Hence the English jealousy of certain rights, which are guaranteed by acts of parliament. But in America, and here alone, we have gone at once to the *fountain of liberty,* and raised the people to their true dignity. Let the lands be possessed by the people in fee-simple, let the fountain be kept pure, and the streams will be pure of course. Our jealousy of *trial by jury, the liberty of the press,* &c., is totally groundless. Such rights are inseparably connected with the *power* and *dignity* of the people, which rest on their *property.* They cannot be abridged. All *other* [free] nations have wrested *property* and *freedom* from *barons* and *tyrants ;* we begin our empire with full possession of property and all its attending rights.

[* Last three sentences struck out in author's copy.—P. L. F.]

[† Revise to "The constitution is generally good.—P. L. F.]

controversies between different states—to silence contending interests—to suppress insurrections—to regulate commerce—to treat with foreign nations, our confederation is a cobweb—liable to be blown asunder by every blast of faction that is raised in the remotest corner of the United States.

Every motive that can possibly influence men ever to unite under civil government, now urges the unanimous adoption of the new constitution. But in America we are urged to it by a singular necessity. By the local situation of the several states *a few* command *all* the advantages of commerce. Those states which have no advantages, made equal exertions for independence, loaded themselves with immense debts, and now are utterly [¶] unable to discharge them; while their richer neighbors are taxing them for their own benefit, merely because they *can*. I can prove to a demonstration that Connecticut, which has the heaviest internal or state debt, in proportion to its number of inhabitants, of any in the union, cannot discharge its debt, on any principles of taxation ever yet practised. Yet [51] the state pays in duties, at least 100,000 dollars annually, on goods consumed by its own people, but imported by New York. This sum, could it be saved to the state by an equal system of revenue, would enable that state to gradually sink its debt.* [†]

New Jersey and some other states are in the same situation, except that their debts are not so large, in proportion to their wealth and population.

The boundaries of the several states were not drawn with a view to independence; and while this country was subject to Great Britain, they produced no commercial or political inconveniences. But the revolution has placed things on a different footing. The advantages of some states, and the disadvantages of others are so great—and so materially affect the business and interest of each, that nothing but an equalizing

[¶ "utterly" struck out.—P. L F.]

*The state debt of Connecticut is about 3,500,000 dollars, its proportion of the federal debt about the same sum. The annual interest of the whole 420,000 dollars.

[† Last three sentences, the following paragraph and foot note struck out in author's copy.—P. L. F.]

system of revenue, that shall reduce the advantages to some equitable proportion, can prevent a civil war and save the national debt. Such a system of revenue is the *sine qua non* of public justice and tranquillity.

It is absurd for a man to oppose the adoption of the constitution, because *he* thinks some part of it defective or exceptionable. Let every man be at liberty to expunge what *he* judges to be exceptionable, and not a syllable of the constitution [52] will survive the scrutiny. A painter, after executing a masterly piece, requested every spectator to draw a pencil mark over the part that did not please him; but to his surprise, he soon found the *whole piece* defaced. Let every man examine the most perfect building by his *own* taste, and like some microscopic critics, condemn the *whole* for small deviations from the rules of architecture, and not a part of the *best* constructed fabric would escape. But let *any* man take a *comprehensive view* of the whole, and he will be pleased with the general beauty and proportions, and admire the structure. The same remarks apply to the new constitution. I have no doubt that *every* member of the late convention has exceptions to *some part* of the system proposed. Their constituents have the same, and if *every* objection must be removed, before we have a national government, the Lord have mercy on us.

Perfection is not the lot of humanity. Instead of censuring the small faults of the constitution, I am astonished that so many clashing interests have been reconciled—and so many sacrifices made to the *general interest!* The mutual concessions made by the gentlemen of the convention, reflect the highest honor on their candor and liberality; at the same time, they prove that their minds were deeply impressed with a conviction, that such mutual sacrifices are *essential to our union.* They *must* be made sooner or later by every state; or jealousies, local interests and prejudices will unsheath the sword, and some Cæsar or Cromwell will avail himself [53] of our divisions, and wade to a throne through streams of blood.

It is not our duty as freemen, to receive the opinions of any men however great and respectable, without an examination. But when we reflect that [*] some of the greatest men in America, with the venerable FRANKLIN and the illustrious WASHINGTON at their head; *some* of them the *fathers* and *saviors* of their country, men who have labored at the helm during a long and violent tempest, and guided us to the haven of peace—and *all* of them distinguished for their abilities their acquaintance with ancient and modern governments, as well as with the temper, the passions, the interests and the wishes of the Americans;—when we reflect on these circumstances, it is impossible to resist impressions of respect, and we are almost impelled to suspect our own judgements, when we call in question any part of the system, which they have recommended for adoption. Not having the same means of information, we are more liable to mistake the nature and tendency of particular articles of the constitution, or the reasons on which they were admitted. Great confidence therefore should be reposed in the abilities, the zeal and integrity of that respectable body. But after all, if the constitution should, in its future operation, be found defective or inconvenient, two-thirds of both houses of Congress or the application of two-thirds of the legislatures, may open the door for amendments. Such improvements may then be made, as experience shall dictate.

[54] Let us then consider the *New Federal Constitution*, as it really is, an *improvement* on the *best* constitutions that the world ever saw. In the house of representatives, the people of America have an equal voice and suffrage. The choice of men is placed in the freemen or electors at large; and the frequency of elections, and the responsibility of the members, will render them sufficiently dependent on their constituents. The senate will be composed of older men; and while their regular dismission from office, once in six years, will preserve their dependence on their constituents, the duration of their existence will give firmness to their decisions, and temper the factions which must necessarily prevail in the other branch. The president of the United States is elective, and what is a capital improvement on the best governments, the mode

[* "The convention was composed of." added after "that," by author.—P. L. F.]

of chusing him excludes the danger of faction and corruption. [*] As the supreme executive, he is invested with power to enforce the laws of the union and give energy to the federal government.

The constitution defines the powers of Congress; and every power not expressly delegated to that body, remains in the several state-legislatures. The sovereignty and the republican form of government of each state is guaranteed by the constitution; and the bounds of jurisdiction between the federal and respective state governments, are marked with precision. In theory, it has all the energy and freedom of the British and Roman governments, without their defects, In short, the privilges of freemen are [55] interwoven into the feelings and habits of the Americans; *liberty* stands on the immoveable basis of a general distribution of property and diffusion of knowledge; but the Americans must cease to contend, to fear, and to hate, before they can realize the benefits of independence and government, or enjoy the blessings, which heaven has lavished, in rich profusion, upon this western world.

[* "This proves how little dependence can be placed on theory Twelve years experience, or four elections demonstrates the contrary."—Note in author's copy.—P. L. F.]

An / Address / to the / People / of the / State of New-York / On the Subject of the / Constitution, / Agreed upon at Philadelphia, / The 17th of September, 1787. / New-York: / Printed by Samuel Loudon, / Printer to the State. [1788].

Sm. 4to., pp. 19.

---

By John Jay, member of the New York State Convention. The pamphlet has been partially reprinted in Elliot, I, 496.

"The good sense, forcible observations, temper and moderation with which the pamphlet is written, cannot fail, I should think, of making a serious impression upon the antifederal mind, where it is not under the influence of such local views as will yield to no argument, no proof."—George Washington.

"I likewise send you a small pamphlet written by John Jay about ten days since, and which has had a most astonishing influence in converting anti-federalism to a knowledge and belief that the new Constitution was their only political salvation."—S. B. Webb, 27 April, 1788.

"This pamphlet contains a brief recapitulation of the most striking arguments in favor of adopting the proposed Federal Constitution. Several of the observations are new, and all are penned with such moderation of temper, and sound judgment, that they cannot fail to make an impression favorable to the Constitution on minds which are open to conviction. It is wished that every friend to good order and government might 'receive this address with the same candor with which it is written,' as it is believed the author's arguments against appointing a new general Convention, for the purpose of altering and amending the constitution, are altogether unanswerable." [Noah Webster] in *American Magazine* for April, 1788.

See Jay's *Life of Jay*, I, 362; *The Federalist*, LXXXV; and the "Postcript" of *An Address to the People of the State of New York.—By a Plebian*, infra.

P. L. F.

*Friends and Fellow Citizens:*

THERE are times and seasons, when *general evils* spread general alarm and uneasiness, and yet arise from causes too complicated, and too little understood by many, to produce an unanimity of opinions respecting their remedies. Hence it is, that on such occasions, the conflict of arguments too often excites a conflict of passions, and introduces a degree of discord and animosity, which, by agitating the public mind dispose it to precipitation and extravagance. They who on the ocean have been unexpectedly enveloped with tempests, or suddenly entangled among rocks and shoals, know the value of that serene, self-possession and presence of mind, to which in such cases they owed their preservation; nor will the heroes who have given us victory and peace, hesitate to acknowledge that we are as much indebted for those blessings to the calm prevision, and cool intrepidity which planned and conducted our military measures, as to the glowing animation with which they were executed.

While reason retains her rule, while men are as ready to receive as to give advice, and as willing to be convinced themselves, as to convince others, there are few political evils from which a free and enlightened people cannot deliver themselves. It is unquestionably true, that the great body of the people love their country, and wish it prosperity; and this observation is particularly applicable to the people of a *free* country, for they have more and stronger reasons for loving it than others. It is not therefore to vicious motives that the unhappy divisions which sometimes prevail among them are to be imputed; the people at large always mean well, and although they may on certain oc- [4] casions be misled by the counsels, or injured by the efforts of the few who expect more advantage from the wreck, than from the preservation of national prosperity, yet the motives of these few, are by no means to be confounded with those of the community in general.

That such seeds of discord and danger have been disseminated and begin to take root in America, as unless eradicated will soon poison our gardens and our fields, is a truth much to be lamented; and the more so, as their growth rapidly increases, while we are wasting the season in honestly but imprudently disputing, not whether they shall be pulled up, but by whom, in what manner, and with what instruments, the work shall be done.

When the king of Great Britain, misguided by men who did not merit his confidence, asserted the unjust claim of binding us in all cases whatsoever, and prepared to obtain our submission by force, the object which engrossed our attention, however important, was nevertheless plain and simple, "What shall we do?" was the question—the people answered, let us unite our counsels and our arms. They sent Delegates to Congress, and soldiers to the field. Confiding in the probity and wisdom of Congress, they received their recommendations as if they had been laws; and that ready acquiesence in their advice enabled those patriots to save their country. Then there was little leisure or disposition for controversy respecting the expediency of measures—hostile fleets soon filled our ports, and hostile armies spread desolation on our shores. Union was then considered as the most essential of human means and we almost worshipped it with as much fervor, as pagans in distress formerly implored the protection of their tutelar deities. That union was the child of wisdom—heaven blessed it, and it wrought out our political salvation.

That glorious war was succeeded by an advantageous peace. When danger disappeared, ease, tranquility, and a sense of security loosened the bands of union; and Congress and soldiers and good faith depreciated with their apparent importance. Recommendations lost their influence, and requisitions were rendered nugatory, not by their want of propriety, but by their want of power. The spirit of private gain expelled the spirit of public good, and men became more intent on the means of enriching and aggrandizing themselves, than of enriching and aggrandizing their country. Hence the war-worn veteran, whose re- [5] ward for toils and wounds existed in written promises, found Congress without the means, and too many of the States without the disposition, to do him justice. Hard necessity compelled him, and others under similar circumstances, to sell their honest claims on the public for a little bread; and thus unmerited misfortunes and patriotic distresses became articles of speculation and commerce.

These and many other evils, too well known to require enumeration, imperceptibly stole in upon us, and acquired an unhappy influence on our public affairs. But such evils, like the worst of weeds, will naturally spring up in so rich a soil; and a good Government is as necessary to subdue the one, as an attentive gardner or husbandman is to destroy the other— Even the garden of Paradise required to be dressed, and while men continue to be constantly impelled to error and to wrong by innumerable circumstances and temptations, so long will society experience the unceasing necessity of government.

It is a pity that the expectations which actuated the authors of the existing confederation, neither have nor can be realized:—accustomed to see and admire the glorious spirit which moved all ranks of people in the most gloomy moments of the war, observing their steadfast attachment to Union, and the wisdom they so often manifested both in choosing and confiding in their rulers, those gentlemen were led to flatter themselves that the people of America only required to know what ought to be done, to do it. This amiable mistake induced them to institute a national government in such a manner, as though very fit to give advice, was yet destitute of power, and so constructed as to be very unfit to be trusted with it. They seem not to have been sensible that mere advice is a sad substitute for laws; nor to have recollected that the advice even of the allwise and best of Beings, has been always disregarded by a great majority of all the men that ever lived.

Experience is a severe preceptor, but it teaches useful truths, and however harsh, is always honest—Be calm and dispassionate, and listen to what it tells us.

Prior to the revolution we had little occasion to inquire or know much about national affairs, for although they existed and were managed, yet they were managed *for* us, but not *by* us. Intent on our domestic concerns, our internal legislative business, our agriculture, and our buying and selling, we were seldom anxious about what passed or was [6] doing in foreign Courts. As we had nothing to do with that department of policy, so the affairs of it were not detailed to us, and we took as little pains to inform ourselves, as others did to inform us of them. War, and peace, alliances, and treaties, and commerce, and navigation, were conducted and regulated without our advice or controul. While we had liberty and justice, and in security enjoyed the fruits of our "vine and fig tree," we were in general too content and too much occupied, to be at the trouble of investigating the various political combinations in this department, or to examine and perceive how exceedingly important they often were to the advancement and protection of our prosperity. This habit and turn of thinking affords one reason why so much more care was taken, and so much more wisdom displayed, in forming our State Governments, than in forming our Federal or national one.

By the Confederation as it now stands, the direction of general and national affairs is committed to a single body of men, viz. the Congress. They may make war, but are not empowered to raise men or money to carry it on. They may make peace, but without power to see the terms of it observed—They may form alliances, but without ability to comply with the stipulations on their part—They may enter into treaties of commerce, but without power to enforce them at home or abroad—They may borrow money, but without having the means of repayment—They may partly regulate commerce, but without authority to execute their ordinances—They may appoint ministers and other officers of trust, but without power to try or punish them for misdemeanors—They may resolve, but cannot execute either with dispatch or with secrecy—In short, they may consult, and deliberate, and recommend, and make requisitions, and they who please, may regard them.

From this new and wonderful system of Government, it

has come to pass, that almost every national object of every kind, is at this day unprovided for; and other nations taking the advantage of its imbecility, are daily multiplying commercial restraints upon us. Our fur trade is gone to Canada, and British garrisons keep the keys of it. Our shipyards have almost ceased to disturb the repose of the neighborhood by the noise of the axe and hammer; and while foreign flags fly triumphantly above our highest houses, the American Stars seldom do more than shed a few feeble rays about the humble masts of river sloops and coasting schooners. The greater part of our hardy seamen, are [7] plowing the ocean in foreign pay; and not a few of our ingenious shipwrights are now building vessels on alien shores. Although our increasing agriculture and industry extend and multiply our productions, yet they constantly diminish in value; and although we permit all nations to fill our country with their merchandises, yet their best markets are shut against us. Is there an English, or a French, or a Spanish island or port in the West-Indies, to which an American vessel can carry a cargo of flour for sale? Not one. The Algerines exclude us from the Mediterranean, and adjacent countries; and we are neither able to purchase, nor to command the free use of those seas. Can our little towns or larger cities consume the immense productions of our fertile country? or will they without trade be able to pay a good price for the proportion which they do consume? The last season gave a very unequivocal answer to these questions —What numbers of fine cattle have returned from this city to the country for want of buyers? What great quantities of salted and other provisions still lie useless in the stores? To how much below the former price, is our corn, and wheat and flour and lumber rapidly falling? Our debts remain undiminished, and the interest on them accumulating—our credit abroad is nearly extinguished, and at home unrestored—they who had money have sent it beyond the reach of our laws, and scarcely any man can borrow of his neighbor. Nay, does not experience also tell us, that it is as difficult to pay as to borrow? That even our houses and lands cannot command money—that law suits and usurious contracts abound—that our farms sell on executions for less than half their value, and that distress in various forms, and in various ways, is approaching fast to the doors of our best citizens.

These things have been gradually coming upon us ever since the peace—they have been perceived and proclaimed, but the universal rage and pursuit of private gain conspired with other causes, to prevent any proper efforts being made to meliorate our condition by due attention to our national affairs, until the late Convention was convened for that purpose. From the result of their deliberations, the States expected to derive much good, and should they be disappointed, it will probably be not less their misfortune than their fault. That Convention was in general composed of excellent and tried men—men who had become conspicuous for their wisdom and public services, and whose names [8] and characters will be venerated by posterity. Generous and candid minds cannot perceive without pain, the illiberal manner in which some have taken the liberty to treat them; nor forbear to impute it to impure and improper motives, zeal for public good, like zeal for religion, may sometimes carry men beyond the bounds of reason, but it is not conceivable, that on this occasion, it should find means so to inebriate any *candid* American, as to make him forget what he owed to truth and to decency, or induce him either to believe or to say, that the almost unanimous advice of the Convention, proceeded from a wicked combination and conspiracy against the liberties of their country. This is not the temper with which we should receive and consider their recommendations, nor the treatment that would be worthy either of us or them. Let us continue careful therefore that facts do not warrant historians to tell future generations, that envy, malice and uncharitableness pursued our patriotic benefactors to their graves, and that not even pre-eminence in virtue, nor lives devoted to the public, could shield them from obloquy and detraction. On the contrary, let our bosoms always retain a sufficient degree of honest indignation to disappoint and discourage those who expect our thanks or applause for calumniating our most faithful and meritorious friends.

The Convention concurred in opinion with the people, that a national government, *competent to every national object*, was indispensibly necessary; and it was as plain to them, as it now is to all America, that the present confederation does not provide for such a government. These points being agreed, they proceeded to consider how and in what manner such a government could be formed, as on the one hand, should be sufficiently energetic to raise us from our prostrate and distressed situation, and on the other be perfectly consistent with the liberties of the people of every State. Like men to whom the experience of other ages and countries had taught wisdom, they not only determined that it should be erected by, and depend on the people; but remembering the many instances in which governments vested solely in one man, or one body of men, had degenerated into tyrannies, they judged it most prudent that the three great branches of power should be committed to different hands, and therefore that the executive should be separated from the legislative, and the judicial from both. Thus far the propriety of their work is easily seen and understood, and therefore is thus far *almost* uni-[9] versally approved—for no one man or thing under the sun ever yet pleased every body.

The next question was, what particular powers should be given to these three branches? Here the different views and interests of the different states, as well as the different abstract opinions of their members on such points, interposed many difficulties. Here the business became complicated, and presented a wide field for investigation; too wide for every eye to take a quick and comprehensive view of it.

It is said that "in a multitude of counsellors there is safety," because in the first place, there is greater security for probity; and in the next, if every member cast in only his mite of information and argument, their joint stock of both will thereby become greater than the stock possessed by any one single man out of doors. Gentlemen out of doors therefore should not be hasty in condemning a system, which probably rests on more good reasons than they are aware of, especially when formed under such advantages, and recommended by so many men of distinguished worth and abilities.

The difficulties before mentioned occupied the Convention a long time and it was not without mutual concessions that they were at last surmounted. These concessions serve to explain to us the reason why some parts of the system please in some states, which displease in others; and why many of the objections which have been made to it, are so contradictory and inconsistent with one another. It does great credit to the temper and talents of the Convention, that they were able so to reconcile the different views and interests of the different States, and the clashing opinions of their members as to unite with such singular and almost perfect unanimity in any plan whatever, on a subject so intricate and perplexed. It shews that it must have been thoroughly discussed and understood; and probably if the community at large had the same lights and reasons before them, they would, if equally candid and uninfluenced, be equally unanimous.

It would be arduous, and indeed impossible, to comprise within the limits of this address, a full discussion of every part of the plan. Such a task would require a volume, and few men have leisure or inclination to read volumes on any subject. The objections made to it are almost without number, and many of them without reason—some of them are real and honest, and others merely ostensible. There are friends to [10] Union and a national Government who have serious doubts, who wish to be informed, and to be convinced; and there are others who, neither wishing for union, nor any national Government at all, will oppose and object to any plan that can be contrived.

We are told, among other strange things, that the liberty of the press is left insecure by the proposed Constitution, and yet that Constitution says neither more nor less about it, than the Constitution of the State of New York does. We are told that it deprives us of trial by jury, whereas the fact is, that it expressly secures it in certain cases, and takes it away in none —it is absurd to construe the silence of this, or of our own constitution, relative to a great number of our rights, into a total extinction of them—silence and blank paper neither grant nor take away anything. Complaints are also made that the proposed constitution is not accompanied by a bill of rights; and yet they who would make these complaints, know and are content that no bill of rights accompanied the Constitution of this State. In days and countries, where Monarchs and their subjects were frequently disputing about prerogative and privileges, the latter often found it necessary, as it were to run out the line between them, and oblige the former to admit by solemn acts, called bills of rights, that certain enumerated rights belonged to the people, and were not comprehended in the royal prerogative. But thank God we have no such disputes—we have no Monarchs to contend with, or demand admission from—the proposed Government is to be the government of the people—all its officers are to be their officers, and to exercise no rights but such as the people commit to them. The Constitution only serves to point out that part of the people's business, which they think proper by it to refer to the management of the persons therein designated—those persons are to receive that business to manage, not for themselves and as their own, but as agents and overseers for the people to whom they are constantly responsible, and by whom only they are to be appointed.

But the design of this address is not to investigate the merits of the plan, nor of the objections to it. They who seriously contemplate the present state of our affairs will be convinced that other considerations of at least equal importance demand their attention. Let it be admitted that this plan, like everything else devised by man, has its imperfections: That it does not please every body is certain and there is little [11] reason to expect one that will. It is a question of great moment to you, whether the probability of your being able seasonably to obtain a better, is such as to render it prudent and advisable to reject this, and run the risque. Candidly to consider this question is the design of this address.

As the importance of this question must be obvious to every man, whatever his private opinions respecting it may be, it becomes us all to treat it in that calm and temperate manner, which a subject so deeply interesting to the future welfare of our country and prosperity requires. Let us therefore as much as possible repress and compose that irritation in our minds, which to warm disputes about it may have excited. Let us endeavour to forget that this or that man, is on this or that side; and that we ourselves, perhaps without sufficient reflection, have classed ourselves with one or the other party. Let us remember that this is not a matter to be regarded as a matter that only touches our local parties, but as one so great, so general, and so extensive in its future consequences to America, that for our deciding upon it according to the best of our unbiassed judgment, we must be highly responsible both here and hereafter.

The question now before us now naturally leads to *three* enquiries:

1. Whether it is probable that a better plan can be obtained?

2. Whether, if attainable, it is likely to be in season?

3. What would be our situation, if after rejecting this, all our efforts to obtain a better should prove fruitless?

The men, who formed this plan are Americans, who had long deserved and enjoyed our confidence, and who are as much interested in having a good government as any of us are, or can be. They were appointed to that business at a time when the States had become very sensible of the derangement of our national affairs, and of the impossibility of retrieving them under the existing Confederation. Although well persuaded that nothing but a good national government could oppose and divert the tide of evils that was flowing in upon us, yet those gentlemen met in Convention with minds perfectly unprejudiced in favour of any particular plan. The minds of their Constituents were at that time equally unbiased, cool and dispassionate. All agreed in the necessity of doing something, but no one ventured to say decidedly what precisely ought to be done—opinions were then fluctuating and unfixed, and whatever might have been the wishes of a few individuals, yet while the Convention deliberated, the people remained in [12] silent suspence. Neither wedded to favourite systems of their own, nor influenced by popular ones abroad, the members were more desirous to receive light from, than to impress their private sentiments on, one another. These circumstances naturally opened the door to that spirit of candour, of calm enquiry, of mutual accommodation, and mutual respect, which entered into the Convention with them, and regulated their debates and proceedings.

The impossibility of agreeing upon any plan that would exactly quadrate with the local policy and objects of every State, soon became evident; and they wisely thought it better mutually to concede, and accommodate, and in that way to fashion their system as much as possible by the circumstances and wishes of different States, than by pertinaciously adhering, each to his own ideas, oblige the Convention to rise without doing anything. They were sensible that obstacles arising from local circumstances, would not cease while those circumstances continued to exist; and so far as those circumstances depended on differences of climate, productions, and commerce, that no change was to be expected. They were likewise sensible that on a subject so comprehensive, and involving such a variety of points and questions, the most able, the most candid, and the most honest men will differ in opinion. The same proposition seldom strikes many minds exactly in the same point of light; different habits of thinking, different degrees and modes of education, different prejudices and opinions early formed and long entertained, conspire with a multitude of other circumstances, to produce among men a diversity and contrariety of opinions on questions of difficulty. Liberality therefore as well as prudence, induced them to treat each other's opinions with tenderness, to argue without asperity, and to endeavor to convince the judgment without hurting the feelings of each other. Although many weeks were passed in these discussions, some points remained, on which a unison of opinions could not be effected. Here again that same happy disposition to unite and conciliate, induced them to meet each other; and enabled them, by mutual concessions, finally to complete and agree to the plan they have recommended, and that too with a degree of unanimity which, considering the variety of discordant views and ideas, they had to reconcile, is really astonishing.

They tell us very honestly that this plan is the result of accommodation—they do not hold it up as the best of all possible ones, but only as [13] the best which they could unite in, and agree to. If such men, appointed and meeting under such auspicious circumstances, and so sincerely disposed to conciliation, could go no further in their endeavors to please every State, and every body, what reason have we at present to expect any system that would give more general satisfaction?

Suppose this plan to be rejected, what measures would you propose for obtaining a better? Some will answer, let us appoint another Convention, and as everything has been said and written that can well be said and written on the subject, they will be better informed than the former one was, and consequently be better able to make and agree upon a more eligible one.

This reasoning is fair, and as far as it goes has weight; but it nevertheless takes one thing for granted, which appears very doubtful; for although the new Convention might have more information, and perhaps equal abilities, yet it does not from thence follow that they would be equally *disposed to agree.* The contrary of this position is the most probable. You must have observed that the same temper and equanimity which prevailed among the people on the former occasion, no longer exists. We have unhappily become divided into parties; and this important subject has been handled with such indiscreet and offensive acrimony, and with so many little unhandsome artifices and misrepresentations, that pernicious heats and animosities have been kindled, and spread their flames far and wide among us. When therefore it becomes a question who shall be deputed to the new Convention; we cannot flatter ourselves that the talents and integrity of the candidates will determine who shall be elected. Federal electors will vote for Fœderal deputies, and anti-Fœderal electors for anti-Fœderal ones. Nor will either party prefer the most moderate of their adherents, for as the most staunch and active partizans will be the most popular, so the men most willing and able to carry points, to oppose, and divide, and embarrass their opponents, will be chosen. A Convention formed at such a season, and of such men, would be but too exact an epitome of the great body that named them. The same party views, the same propensity to opposition, the same distrusts and jealousies, and the same unaccommodating spirit which prevail without, would be concentred and ferment with still greater violence within. Each deputy would recollect *who* sent [14] him, and *why* he was sent; and be too apt to consider himself bound in honor, to contend and act vigorously under the standard of his party, and not hazard their displeasure by prefering compromise to victory. As vice does not sow the seeds of virtue, so neither does passion cultivate the fruits of reason. Suspicions and resentments create no disposition to conciliate, nor do they infuse a desire of making partial and personal objects bend to general union and the common good. The utmost efforts of that excellent disposition were necessary to enable the late Convention to perform their task; and although contrary causes sometimes operate similar effects, yet to expect that discord and animosity should produce the fruits of confidence and agreement, is to expect "grapes from thorns, and figs from thistles."

The States of Georgia, Delaware, Jersey, and Connecticut, have adopted the present plan with unexampled unanimity; they are content with it as it is, and consequently their deputies, being apprized of the sentiments of their Constituents, will be little inclined to make alterations, and cannot be otherwise than averse to changes which they have no reason to think would be agreeable to their people—some other States, tho' less unanimous, have nevertheless adopted it by very respectable majorities; and for reasons so evidently cogent, that even the minority in one of them, have nobly pledged themselves for its promotion and support. From these circumstances, the new Convention would derive and experience difficulties unknown to the former. Nor are these the only additional difficulties they would have to encounter. Few are ignorant that there has lately sprung up a sect of politicians who teach and profess to believe that the extent of our nation is too great for the superintendance of one national Government, and on that principle argue that it ought to be divided into two or three. This doctrine, however mischievous in its tendency and consequences, has its advocates; and, should any of them be sent to the Convention, it will naturally be their policy rather to cherish than to prevent divisions; for well knowing that the institution of any national Government, would blast their favourite system, no measures that lead to it can meet with their aid or approbation.

Nor can we be certain whether or not any and what foreign influence would, on such an occasion, be indirectly exerted, nor for what purposes—delicacy forbids an ample discussion of this question. Thus much [15] may be said, without error or offence, viz. That such foreign nations as desire the prosperity of America, and would rejoice to see her become great and powerful, under the auspices of a Government wisely calculated to extend her commerce, to encourage her navigation and marine, and to direct the whole weight of her power and resources as her interest and honour may require, will doubtless be friendly to the Union of the States, and to the establishment of a Government able to perpetuate, protect and dignify it. Such other foreign nations, if any such their be, who, jealous of our growing importance, and fearful that our commerce and navigation should impair their own—who behold our rapid population with regret, and apprehend that the enterprising spirit of our people, when seconded by power and probability of success, may be directed to objects not consistent with their policy or interests, cannot fail to wish that we may continue a weak and a divided people.

These considerations merit much attention, and candid men will judge how far they render it probable that a new Convention would be able either to agree in a better plan, or with tolerable unanimity, in any plan at all. Any plan forcibly carried by a slender majority, must expect numerous opponents among the people, who, especially in their present temper, would be more inclined to reject than adopt any system so made and carried. We should in such case again see the press teeming with publications for and against it; for as the minority would take pains to justify their dissent, so would the majority be industrious to display the wisdom of their proceedings. Hence new divisions, new parties, and new distractions would ensue, and no one can foresee or conjecture when or how they would terminate.

Let those who are sanguine in their expectations of a better plan from a new Convention, also reflect on the delays and risque to which it would expose us. Let them consider whether we ought, by continuing much longer in our present humiliated condition, to give other nations further time to perfect their restrictive systems of commerce, to reconcile their own people to them, and to fence and guard and strengthen them by all those regulations and contrivances in which a jealous policy is ever fruitful. Let them consider whether we ought to give further opportunities to discord to alienate the hearts of our citizens from one another, and thereby encourage new Cromwells to bold exploits. Are we cer- [16] tain that our foreign creditors will continue patient, and ready to proportion their forbearance to our delays? Are we sure that our distresses, dissentions and weakness will neither invite hostility nor insult? If they should, how ill prepared shall we be for defence! without Union, without Government, without money, and without credit!

It seems necessary to remind you, that some time must yet elapse, before all the States will have decided on the present plan. If they reject it, some time must also pass before the measure of a new Convention, can be brought about and generally agreed to. A further space of time will then be requisite to elect their deputies, and send them on to Convention. What time they may expend when met, cannot be divined, and it is equally uncertain how much time the several States may take to deliberate and decide on any plan they may recommend—if adopted, still a further space of time will be necessary to organize and set it in motion:—In the mean time our affairs are daily going on from bad to worse, and it is not rash to say that our distresses are accumulating like compound interest.

But if for the reasons already mentioned, and others that

we cannot now perceive, the new Convention, instead of producing a better plan, should give us only a history of their disputes, or should offer us one still less pleasing than the present, where should we be then? The old Confederation has done its best, and cannot help us; and is now so relaxed and feeble, that in all probability it would not survive so violent a shock. Then "to your tents Oh Israel!" would be the word. Then every band of union would be severed. Then every State would be a little nation, jealous of its neighbors, and anxious to strengthen itself by foreign alliances, against its former friends. Then farewell to fraternal affection, unsuspecting intercourse; and mutual participation in commerce, navigation and citizenship. Then would arise mutual restrictions and fears, mutual garrisons,—and standing armies, and all those dreadful evils which for so many ages plagued England, Scotland, Wales, and Ireland, while they continued disunited, and were played off against each other.

Consider my fellow citizens what you are about, before it is too late—consider what in such an event would be your particular case. You know the geography of your State, and the consequences of your local position. Jersey and Connecticut, to whom your impost laws have been [17] unkind—Jersey and Connecticut, who have adopted the present plan, and expect much good from it—will impute its miscarriage and all the consequent evils to you. They now consider your opposition as dictated more by your fondness for your impost, than for those rights to which they have never been behind you in attachment. They cannot, they will not love you—they border upon you, and are your neighbors; but you will soon cease to regard their neighborhood as a blessing. You have but one port and outlet to your commerce, and how you are to keep that outlet free and uninterrupted, merits consideration.—What advantage Vermont in combination with others, might take of you, may easily be conjectured; nor will you be at a loss to perceive how much reason the people of Long Island, whom you cannot protect, have to deprecate being constantly exposed to the depredations of every invader.

These are short hints—they ought not to be more

developed—you can easily in your own mind dilate and trace them through all their relative circumstances and connections. —Pause then for a moment, and reflect whether the matters you are disputing about, are of sufficient moment to justify your running such extravagant risques. Reflect that the present plan comes recommended to you by men and fellow citizens who have given you the highest proofs that men can give, of their justice, their love for liberty and their country, of their prudence, of their application, and of their talents. They tell you it is the best that they could form; and that in their opinion, it is necessary to redeem you from those calamities which already begin to be heavy upon us all. You find that not only those men, but others of similar characters, and of whom you have also had very ample experience, advise you to adopt it. You find that whole States concur in the sentiment, and among them are your next neighbors; both whom have shed much blood in the cause of liberty, and have manifested as strong and constant a predilection for a free Republican Government as any State in the Union, and perhaps in the world. They perceive not those latent mischiefs in it, with which some double-sighted politicians endeavor to alarm you. You cannot but be sensible that this plan or constitution will always be in the hands and power of the people, and that [18] if on experiment. it should be found defective or incompetent, they may either remedy its defects, or substitute another in its room. The objectionable parts of it are certainly very questionable, for otherwise there would not be such a contrariety of opinions about them. Experience will better determine such questions than theoretical arguments, and so far as the danger of abuses is urged against the institution of a Government, remember that a power to do good, always involves a power to do harm. We must in the business of Government as well as in all other business, have some degree of confidence, as well as a great degree of caution. Who on a sick bed would refuse medicines from a physician, merely because it is as much in his power to administer deadly poisons, as salutary remedies.

You cannot be certain, that by rejecting the proposed plan

you would not place yourself in a very awkward situation. Suppose nine States should nevertheless adopt it, would you not in that case be obliged either to separate from the Union, or rescind your dissent? The first would not be eligible, nor could the latter be pleasant—A mere hint is sufficient on this topic—You cannot but be aware of the consequences.

Consider then, how weighty and how many considerations advise and persuade the people of America to remain in the safe and easy path of Union; to continue to move and act as they hitherto have done, as a *band of brothers;* to have confidence in themselves and in one another; and since all cannot see with the same eyes, at least to give the proposed Constitution a fair trial, and to mend it as time, occasion and experience may dictate. It would little become us to verify the predictions of those who ventured to prophecy, that *peace:* instead of blessing us with happiness and tranquility, would serve only as the signal for factions, discords and civil contentions to rage in our land, and overwhelm it with misery and distress.

Let us also be mindful that the cause of freedom greatly depends on the use we make of the singular opportunities we enjoy of governing ourselves wisely; for if the event should prove, that the people of this [19] country either cannot or will not govern themselves, who will hereafter be advocates for systems, which however charming in theory and prospect, are not reducible to practice. If the people of our nation, instead of consenting to be governed by laws of their own making, and rulers of their own choosing, should let licentiousness, disorder, and confusion reign over them, the minds of men every where, will insensibly become alienated from republican forms, and prepared to prefer and acquiesce in Governments, which, though less friendly to liberty, afford more peace and security.

*Receive this Address with the same candor with which it is written; and may the spirit of wisdom and patriotism direct and distinguish your councils and your conduct.*

*A citizen of New York.*

An / Address / to the / People / of the / State of New-York: / Showing the necessity of making / Amendments / to the / Constitution, proposed for the United States, / previous to its Adoption. / By a Plebeian. / Printed in the State of New York ; / M,DCC,LXXX,VIII.

8vo., pp. 26.

Written by Melancthon Smith of New York, a member of the Continental Congress, (1785-88), and of the New York State Convention, in which he opposed, but ultimately voted for the ratification of the new Constitution.

"This address begins with several assertions that are not fully proved. It declares that ' the advocates for the proposed constitution, having been beaten off the field of argument, on its merits, have taken new ground—admit that it is liable to well founded objections—that a number of its articles ought to be amended—that if alterations do not take place a door will be left open for an undue administration, and encroachments on the liberties of the people—and many of them go so far as to say, if it should continue for any considersble period, in its present form, it will lead to a subversion of our equal republican forms of government.'

"These assertions, it is presumed are too general to be true. *Some* friends (upon the whole) to the proposed government, may have acknowledged all this; but the *most enlightened ones* declare that, in their opinion, the constitution is as little defective as can ever be obtained—that it is *not liable to well founded objections*—that it will *preserve* our equal republican forms of government; nay, that it is their only firm support, and the guarantee of their existence—and if they consent to the additions and alterations proposed by the Massachusetts Convention, it is not so much because they think the constitution will be *better* for them; but because they think these additions will reconcile the opposition and unite all parties in a desirable harmony, without making the constitution *worse*.

"The writer, to show the happy situation of the citizens of

this State, enquires, '*Does not every man sit under his own vine and his own fig tree?*' Yes, it may be answered, and under the rich vines and fig trees of his neighbors too, '*having none to make him afraid?*' This was probably written before the late riot: And if the inhabitants of this State are not afraid of their neighbors, whose *vines and fig trees* they are enjoying, they must be very ignorant or very insensible.

"'*Does not every cne follow his own calling without impediment and receive the reward of his well earned industry? The farmer and mechanic reap the fruits of their labor. The merchant drives his commerce and none can deprive him of the gain he honestly acquires.*' Had the last assertion been mere queries, the writer might have saved his reputation. While the *war-worn veteran* is paid for his services, at a fourth or fifth of their value; while numbers of mechanics have no employment; while commerce is restricted abroad, and tender laws and depreciated paper money exist at home, the public will not be disposed to believe themselves very happy—no, not even in this State. In other States, where riots and rebellion have violated private property, disturbed government and end in bloodshed, the inhabitants will be more incredulous, and wish for the adoption of the proposed constitution."—[Noah Webster] in *American Magazine* for April, 1788.

P. L. F.

*Friends and Fellow Citizens,*

THE advocates for the proposed new constitution, having been beaten off the field of argument, on its merits, have now taken new ground. They admit it is liable to well-founded objections—that a number of its articles ought to be amended; that if alterations do not take place, a door will be left open for an undue administration, and encroachments on the liberties of the people; and many of them go so far as to say, if it should continue for any considerable period, in its present form, it will lead to a subversion of our equal republican forms of government.——But still, although they admit this, they urge that it ought to be adopted, and that we should confide in procuring the necessary alterations after we have received it. Most of the leading characters, who advocate its reception, now profess their readiness to concur with those who oppose, in bringing about the most material amendments contended for, provided they will first agree to accept the proffered system as it is. These concessions afford strong evidence, that the opposers of the constitution have reason on their side, and that they have not been influenced, in the part they have taken, by the mean and unworthy motives of selfish and private interests with which they have been illiberally charged.—As the favourers of the constitution seem, if their professions are sincere, to be in a situation similiar to that of Agrippa, when he cried out upon Paul's preaching—" almost thou persuadest me to be a christian," I cannot help indulging myself in expressing the same wish which St. Paul uttered on that occasion, " Would to God you were not only almost, but altogether such an one as I am." But alas, as we hear no more of Agrippa's christianity after this interview with Paul, so it is much to [4] be feared, that we shall hear nothing of amendments from most of the warm advocates for adopting the new government, after it gets into operation. When the government is once organized, and all the offices under it filled, the inducements which our great men will have to support it, will be much stronger than they are now to urge its reception. Many of them will then hold places of great honour and emolument, and others will then be candidates for such places. It is much harder to relinquish honours or emoluments, which we have in possession, than to abandon the pursuit of them, while the attainment is held in a state of uncertainty.—The amendments contended for as necessary to be made, are of such a nature, as will tend to limit and abridge a number of the powers of the government. And is it probable, that those who enjoy these powers will be so likely to surrender them after they have them in possession, as to consent to have them restricted in the act of granting them? Common sense says—they will not.

When we consider the nature and operation of government, the idea of receiving a form radically defective, under the notion of making the necessary amendments, is evidently absurd.

Government is a compact entered into by mankind, in a state of society, for the promotion of their happiness. In forming this compact, common sense dictates, that no articles should be admitted that tend to defeat the end of its institution. If any such are proposed, they should be rejected. When the compact is once formed and put into operation, it is too late for individuals to object. The deed is executed—the conveyance is made—and the power of reassuming the right is gone, without the consent of the parties.——Besides, when a government is once in operation, it acquires strength by habit, and stability by exercise. If it is tolerably mild in its administration, the people sit down easy under it, be its principles and forms ever so repugnant to the maxims of liberty.——It steals, by insensible degrees, one right from the people after another, until it rivets its powers so as to put it beyond the ability of the community to restrict or limit it. The history of the world furnishes many instances of a people's increasing the powers of their rulers by persuasion, but I believe it would be difficult to produce one in which the rulers have been persuaded to relinquish their powers to [5] the people. Wherever this has taken place, it has always been the effect of compulsion. These observations are so well-founded, that they are become a kind of axioms in politics; and the inference to be drawn from them is equally evident, which is this,—that, in forming a government, care should be taken not to confer powers which it will be necessary to take back; but if you err at all, let it be on the contrary side, because it is much easier, as well as safer, to enlarge the powers of your rulers, if they should prove not sufficiently extensive, than it is too abridge them if they should be too great.

It is agreed, the plan is defective—that some of the powers granted, are dangerous—others not well defined—and amendments are necessary. Why then not amend it? why not remove the cause of danger, and, if possible, even the apprehension of it? The instrument is yet in the hands of the people; it is not signed, sealed, and delivered, and they have power to give it any form they please.

But it is contended, adopt it first, and then amend it. I ask, why not amend, and then adopt it? Most certainly the latter mode of proceeding is more consistent with our ideas of prudence in the ordinary concerns of life. If men were about entering into a contract respecting their private concerns, it would be highly absurd in them to sign and seal an instrument containing stipulations which are contrary to their interests and wishes, under the expectation, that the parties, after its execution, would agree to make alterations agreeable to their desire.——They would insist upon the exceptionable clauses being altered before they would ratify the contract. And is a compact for the government of ourselves and our posterity of less moment than contracts between individuals? certainly not. But to this reasoning, which at first view would appear to admit of no reply, a variety of objections are made, and a number of reasons urged for adopting the system, and afterwards proposing amendments.—Such as have come under my observation, I shall state, and remark upon.

1. It is insisted, that the present situation of our country is such, as not to admit of a delay in forming a new govern-

ment, or of time sufficient to deliberate and agree upon the amendments which are proper, without involving ourselves in a state of anarchy and confusion.

[6] On this head, all the powers of rhetoric, and arts of description, are employed to paint the condition of this country, in the most hideous and frightful colors. We are told, that agriculture is without encouragement; trade is languishing; private faith and credit are disregarded, and public credit is prostrate; that the laws and magistrates are contemned and set at naught; that a spirit of licentiousness is rampant, and ready to break over every bound set to it by the government; that private embarrassments and distresses invade the house of every man of middling property, and insecurity threatens every man in affluent circumstances: in short, that we are in a state of the most grievous calamity at home, and that we are contemptible abroad, the scorn of foreign nations, and the ridicule of the world. From this high-wrought picture, one would suppose that we were in a condition the most deplorable of any people upon earth. But suffer me, my countrymen, to call your attention to a serious and sober estimate of the situation in which you are placed, while I trace the embarrassments under which you labor, to their true sources. What is your condition? Does not every man sit under his own vine and under his own fig-tree, having none to make him afraid? Does not every one follow his calling without impediments and receive the reward of his well-earned industry? The farmer cultivates his land, and reaps the fruit which the bounty of heaven bestows on his honest toil. The mechanic is exercised in his art, and receives the reward of his labour. The merchant drives his commerce, and none can deprive him of the gain he honestly acquires; all classes and callings of men amongst us are protected in their various pursuits, and secured by the laws in the possession and enjoyment of the property obtained in those pursuits. The laws are as well executed as they ever were, in this or any other country. Neither the hand of private violence, nor the more to be dreaded hand of legal oppression, are reached out to distress us.

It is true, many individuals labour under embarrassments, but these are to be imputed to the unavoidable circumstances of things, rather than to any defect in our governments. We have just emerged from a long and expensive war. During its existence few people were in a situation to increase their fortunes, but many to diminish them. Debts contracted before the war were left unpaid [7] while it existed, and these were left a burden too heavy to be borne at the commencement of peace. Add to these, that when the war was over, too many of us, instead of reassuming our old habits of frugality, and industry, by which alone every country must be placed in a prosperous condition, took up the profuse use of foreign commodities. The country was deluged with articles imported from abroad, and the cash of the country has been sent to pay for them, and still left us labouring under the weight of a huge debt to persons abroad. These are the true sources to which we are to trace all the private difficulties of individuals: But will a new government relieve you from these? The advocates for it have not yet told you how it will do it—And I will venture to pronounce, that there is but one way in which it can be effected, and that is by industry and economy; limit your expences within your earnings; sell more than you buy, and everything will be well on this score. Your present condition is such as is common to take place after the conclusion of a war. Those who can remember our situation after the termination of the war preceding the last, will recollect that our condition was similar to the present, but time and industry soon recovered us from it. Money was scare, the produce of the country much lower than it has been since the peace, and many individuals were extremely embarrassed with debts; and this happened although we did not experience the ravages, desolations, and loss of property, that were suffered during the late war.

With regard to our public and national concerns, what is there in our condition that threatens us with any immediate danger? We are at peace with all the world; no nation menaces us with war; nor are we called upon by any cause of sufficient importance to attack any nation. The state governments answer the purposes of preserving the peace, and providing for present exigencies. Our condition as a nation is in no respect worse than it has been for several years past. Our public debt has been lessened in various ways, and the western territory, which has been relied upon as a productive fund to discharge the national debt has at length been brought to market, and a considerable part actually applied to its reduction. I mention these things to shew, that there is nothing special, in our present situation, as it respects our national affairs, that should induce us to accept the prof- [8] fered system, without taking sufficient time to consider and amend it. I do not mean by this, to insinuate, that our government does not stand in need of a reform. It is admitted by all parties, that alterations are necessary in our federal constitution, but the circumstances of our case do by no means oblige us to precipitate this business, or require that we should adopt a system materially defective. We may safely take time to deliberate and amend, without in the meantime hazarding a condition, in any considerable degree, worse than the present.

But it is said that if we postpone the ratification of this system until the necessary amendments are first incorporated, the consequence will be a civil war among the states. On this head weak minds are alarmed with being told, that the militia of Connecticut and Massachusetts, on the one side, and of New Jersey and Pennsylvania on the other, will attack us with hostile fury; and either destroy us from the face of the earth, or at best divide us between the two states adjoining on either side. The apprehension of danger is one of the most powerful incentives to human action, and is therefore generally excited on political questions: But still, a prudent man, though he foreseeth the evil and avoideth it, yet he will not be terrified by imaginary dangers. We ought therefore to enquire what ground there is to fear such an event?— There can be no reason to apprehend, that the other states will make war with us for not receiving the constitution proposed, until it is amended, but from one of the following causes: either that they will have just cause to do it, or that they have a disposition to do it. We will examine each of these:—That they will have no just cause to quarrel with us for not acceding, is evident, because we are under no obligation to do it, arising from any existing compact or previous stipulation. The confederation is the only compact now existing between the states: By the terms of it, it cannot be changed without the consent of every one of the parties to it. Nothing therefore can be more unreasonable than for part of the states to claim of the others, as matter of right, an accession to a system to which they have material objections. No war can therefore arise from this principle, but on the contrary, it is to be presumed, it will operate strongly the opposite way.—The states will reason on the subject in the following manner: On this momentuous question, every state has an in- [9] dubitable right to judge for itself: This is secured to it by solemn compact, and if any of our sister states disagree with us upon the question, we ought to attend to their objections, and accommodate ourselves as far as possible to the amendments they propose.

As to the inclination of the states to make war with us, for declining to accede, until it is amended, this is highly improbable, not only because such a procedure would be most unjust and unreasonable in itself, but for various other reasons.

The idea of a civil war among the states is abhorrent to the principles and feelings of almost every man of every rank in the union. It is so obvious to every one of the least reflection, that in such an event we should hazard the loss of all things, without the hope of gaining anything, that the man who should entertain a thought of this kind, would be justly deemed more fit to be shut up in Bedlam, than to be reasoned with. But the idea of one or more states attacking another, for insisting upon alterations upon the system, before it is adopted, is more extravagent still; it is contradicting every principle of liberty which has been entertained by the states, violating the most solemn compact, and taking from the state the right of deliberation. Indeed to suppose, that a people, entertaining such refined ideas of the rights of human nature as to be induced to wage war with the most powerful nation on earth, upon a speculative point, and from the mere apprehension of danger only, should be so far lost to their own feelings and principles as to deny to their brethren, who were associated with them in the arduous conflict, the right of deliberation on a question of the first importance to their political happiness and safety, is equally an insult to the character of the people of America, and to common sense, and could only be suggested by a vicious heart and a corrupt mind.

The idea of being attacked by the other states, will appear visionary and chimerical, if we consider that tho' several of them have adopted the new constitution, yet the opposition to it has been numerous and formidable. The eastern states from whom we are told we have most to fear, should a civil war be blown up, would have full employ to keep in awe those who are opposed to it in their own governments. Massachusetts, after a long and dubious contest [10] in their convention, has adopted it by an inconsiderable majority, and in the very act has marked it with a stigma in its present form. No man of candour, judging from their public proceedings, will undertake to say on which side the majority of the people are. Connecticut, it is true, have acceded to it, by a large majority of their convention; but it is a fact well known, that a large proportion of the yeomanry of the country are against it:— And it is equally true, that a considerable part of those who voted for it in the convention, wish to see it altered. In both these states the body of the common people, who always do the fighting of a country, would be more likely to fight against than for it: Can it then be presumed, that a country divided among themselves, upon a question where even the advocates for it, admit the system they contend for needs amendments, would make war upon a sister state, who only insist that that should be done before they receive it, which it is granted ought to be done after, and where it is confessed no obligation lies upon them by compact to do it. Can it, I say, be imagined, that in such a case, they would make war on a sister state? The idea is preposterous and chimerical.

It is further urged we must adopt this plan because we have no chance of getting a better. This idea is inconsistent with the principles of those who advance it. They say, it must be altered, but it should be left until after it is put in operation. But if this objection is valid, the proposal of altering, after it is received, is mere delusion.

It is granted, that amendments ought to be made; that the exceptions taken to the constitution, are grounded on just principles, but it is still insisted, that alterations are not to be attempted until after it is received: But why not? Because it is said, there is no probability of agreeing in amendments previous to the adoption, but they may be easily made after it. I wish to be informed what there is in our situation or circumstances that renders it more probable that we shall agree in amendments better after, than before submitting to it? No good reason has as yet been given; it is evident none can be given: On the contrary, there are several considerations which induce a belief, that alterations may be obtained with more ease before than after its reception, and if so, every one must agree [11] it is much the safest. The importance of preserving an union, and of establishing a government equal to the purpose of maintaining that union, is a sentiment deeply impressed on the mind of every citizen of America. It is now no longer doubted, that the confederation, in its present form, is inadequate to that end: Some reform in our government must take place: In this, all parties agree: It is therefore to be presumed, that this object will be pursued with ardour and perseverance, until it is attained by all parties. But when a government is adopted that promises to effect this, we are to expect the ardour of many, yea, of most people, will be abated;— their exertions will cease or be languid, and they will sit down easy, although they may see that the constitution which provides for this, does not sufficiently guard the rights of the people, or secure them against the encroachments of their rulers. The great end they had in view, the security of the union, they will consider effected, and this will divert their attention from that which is equally interesting, safety to their liberties. Besides, the human mind cannot continue intensely engaged for any great length of time upon one object. As after a storm, a calm generally succeeds, so after the minds of a people have been ardently employed upon a subject, especially upon that of government, we commonly find that they become cool and inattentive: Add to this that those in the community who urge the adoption of this system, because they hope to be raised above the common level of their fellow citizens; because they expect to be among the number of the few who will be benefitted by it, will more easily be induced to consent to the amendments before it is received than afterwards. Before its reception they will be inclined to be pliant and condescending; if they cannot obtain all they wish, they will consent to take less. They will yield part to obtain the rest. But when the plan is once agreed to, they will be tenacious of every power, they will strenuously contend to retain all they have got; this is natural to human nature, and it is consonant to the experience of mankind. For history affords us no examples of persons once possessed of power resigning it willingly.

The reasonings made use of to persuade us, that no alterations can be agreed upon previous to the adoption of the system, are as curious as they are futile. It is alledg- [12] ed, that there was great diversity of sentiments in forming the proposed constitution; that it was the effect of mutual concessions and a spirit of accommodation, and from hence it is inferred, that farther changes cannot be hoped for. I should suppose that the contrary inference was the fair one. If the convention, who framed this plan, were possessed of such a spirit of moderation and condescension, as to be induced to yield to each other certain points, and to accommodate themselves to each other's opinions, and even prejudices, there is reason to expect, that this same spirit will continue and prevail in a future convention, and produce an union of sentiments on the points objected to. There is more reason to hope for this, because the subject has received a full discussion, and the minds of the people much better known than they were when the convention sat. Previous to the meeting of the convention, the subject of a new form of government had been little thought of, and scarcely written upon at all. It is true, it was the general opinion, that some alterations were requisite in the federal system. This subject had been contemplated by almost every thinking man in the union. It had been the subject of many well-written essays, and it was the anxious wish of every true friend to America. But it was never in the contemplation of one in a thousand of those who had reflected on the matter, to have an entire change in the nature of our federal government—to alter it from a confederation of states, to that of one entire government, which will swallow up that of the individual states. I will venture to say, that the idea of a government similar to the one proposed, never entered the minds of the legislatures who appointed the convention, and of but very few of the members who composed it, until they had assembled and heard it proposed in that body: much less had the people any conception of such a plan until after it was promulgated. While it was agitated, the debates of the convention were kept an impenetrable secret, and no opportunity was given for well informed men to offer their sentiments upon the subject. The system was therefore never publicly discussed, nor indeed could be, because it was not known to the people until after it was proposed. Since that, it has been the object of universal attention—it has been thought of by every reflecting man—been discussed in a public and private manner, in conversation and in print; [13] its defects have been pointed out, and every objection to it stated; able advocates have written in its favour, and able opponents have written against it. And what is the result? It cannot be denied but that the general opinion is, that it contains material errors, and requires important amendments. This then being the general sentiment, both of the friends and foes of the system, can it be doubted, that another convention would concur in such amendments as would quiet the fears of the opposers, and effect a great degree of union on the subject?—An event most devoutly to be wished. But it is farther said, that there can be no prospect of procuring alterations before it is acceded to, because those who oppose it do not agree among themselves with respect to the amendments that are necessary. To this I reply, that this may be urged against attempting alterations after it is received, with as much force as before; and therefore, if it concludes anything, it is that we must receive any system of government proposed to us, because those who object to it do not entirely concur in their objections. But the assertion is not true to any considerable extent. There is a remarkable uniformity in the objections made to the constitution, on the most important points. It is also worthy of notice, that very few of the matters found fault with in it, are of a local nature, or such as affect any particular state; on the contrary, they are such as concern the principles of general liberty, in which the people of New Hampshire, New York and Georgia are equally interested.

It would be easy to shew, that in the leading and most important objections that have been made to the plan, there has been and is an entire concurrence of opinion among writers, and in public bodies throughout the United States.

I have not time to fully illustrate this by a minute narration of particulars; but to prove that this is the case, I shall adduce a number of important instances.

It has been objected to that the new system, that it is calculated to, and will effect such a consolidation of the States, as to supplant and overturn the state governments. In this the minority of Pennsylvania, the opposition in Massachusetts, and all the writers of any ability or note in Philadelphia, New York, and Boston concur. It may be added, that this appears to have been the opinion of the Massachusetts convention, and gave rise to that article in [14] the amendments proposed, which confines the general government to the exercise only of powers expressly given.

It has been said that the representation in the general legislature is too small to secure liberty, or to answer the intention of representation. In this there is an union of sentiments in the opposers.

The constitution has been opposed, because it gives to the legislature an unlimited power of taxation both with respect to direct and indirect taxes, a right to lay and collect taxes, duties, imposts and excises of every kind and description, and to any amount. In this there has been as general a concurrence of opinion as in the former.

The opposers to the constitution have said that it is dangerous, because the judicial power may extend to many cases which ought to be reserved to the decision of the State courts, and because the right of trial by jury is not secured in the judicial courts of the general government, in civil cases. All the opposers are agreed in this objection.

The power of the general legislature to alter and regulate the time, place and manner of holding elections, has been stated as an argument against the adoption of the system. It has been argued that this power will place in the hands of the general government, the authority, whenever they shall be disposed, and a favorable opportunity offers, to deprive the body of the people in effect, of all share in the government. The opposers to the constitution universally agree in this objection, and of such force is it, that most of its ardent advocates admit its validity, and those who have made attempts to vindicate it, have been reduced to the necessity of using the most trifling arguments to justify it.

The mixture of legislative, judicial, and executive powers in the senate; the little degree of responsibility under which the great officers of government will be held; and the liberty granted by the system to establish and maintain a standing army without any limitation or restriction, are also objected to the constitution; and in these there is a great degree of unanimity of sentiment in the opposers.

From these remarks it appears, that the opponents to the system accord in the great and material points on which they wish amendments. For the truth of the as- [15] section, I appeal to the protest of the minority of the convention of of Pennsylvania, to all the publications against the constitution, and to the debates of the convention of Massachusetts. As a higher authority than these, I appeal to the amendments proposed by the Massachusetts; these are to be considered as the sense of that body upon the defects of the system. And it is a fact, which I will venture to assert, that a large majority of the convention were of opinion, that a number of additional alterations ought to be made. Upon reading the articles which they propose as amendments, it will appear that they object to indefinite powers in the legislature—to the power of laying direct taxes—to the authority of regulating elections—to the extent of the judicial powers, both as it respects the inferior court and the appellate jurisdiction—to the smallness of the representation, &c.—It is admitted that some writers have advanced objections that others have not noticed—that exceptions have been taken by some, that have not been insisted upon by others, and it is probable, that some of the opponents may approve what others will reject. But still these difference are on matters of small importance, and of such a nature as the persons who hold different opinions will not be tenacious of. Perfect uniformity of sentiment on so great a political subject is not to be expected. Every sensible man is impressed with this idea, and is therefore prepared to make concessions and accommodate on matters of small importance. It is sufficient that we agree in the great leading principles, which relate to the preservation of public liberty and private security. And on these I will venture to affirm we are as well agreed, as any people ever were on a question of this nature. I dare pronounce that were the principal advocates for the proposed plan to write comments upon it, they would differ more in the sense they would give the constitution, than those who oppose it do, in the amendments they would wish. I am justified in this opinion, by the sentiments advanced by the different writers in favour of the constitution.

It is farther insisted, that six states have already adopted the constitution; that probably nine will agree to it; in which case it will be put in operation. That it is unreasonable to expect that those states which have acceded [16] to it will reconsider the subject in compliance with the wishes of a minority.

To perceive the force of this objection it is proper to review the conduct and circumstances of the states which have acceded it. It cannot be controverted, that Connecticut and New Jersey were very much influenced in their determinations on the questions, by local considerations. The duty of impost laid by this state, has been a subject of complaint by those states. The new constitution transfers the power of imposing these duties from the state to the general government, and carries the proceeds to the use of the union, instead of that of those state. This is a popular matter with the people of those states, and at the same time, is not advanced by the sensible opposers to the system in this state as an objection to it. —To excite in the minds of the people of these states an attachment to the new system, the amount of the revenue arising from our impost has been magnified to a much larger sum than it produces; it has been stated to amount to from sixty to eighty thousand pounds lawful money; and a gentleman of high eminence in Connecticut has lent the authority of his name to support it. It has been said, that Connecticut pays a third of this sum annually for impost, and Jersey nearly as much. It has farther been asserted, that the avails of the impost were applied to the separate use of the state of New York. By these assertions the people have been grossly imposed upon, for neither of them are true.

The amount of the revenue from impost for two years past, has not exceeded fifty thousands pounds currency, per annum, and a drawback of duties is allowed by law, upon all goods exported to the beforementioned states, in casks or packages unbroken.

The whole of this sum, and more, has been paid into the federal treasury for the support of the government of the union. All the states therefore have actually derived equal benefit with the state of New York, from the impost. It may be said, I know, that this state has obtained credit for the amount, upon the requisitions of Congress: It is admitted, but still it is a fact, that other states, and especially those who complain, have paid no part of the monies required of them, and have scarcely made an effort to do it. The fact therefore is, that they have re- [17] ceived as much advantage from the impost of this state as we ourselves have. The proposed constitution directs to no mode, in which the deficiencies of states on former requisitions, are to be collected, but seems to hold out the idea, that we are to start out anew, and all past payments be forgotten. It is natural to expect, that selfish motives will have too powerful an influence on men's minds, and that too often, they will shut the eyes of a people to their best and true interest. The people of those states have been persuaded to believe, that this new constitution will relieve them from the burden of taxes, by providing for all the exigencies of the union, by duties which can be raised only in the neighbouring states. When they come to be convinced, that this promise is a mere delusion, as they assuredly will, by finding the continental tax-gatherer knocking at their doors, if not before, they will be among the first to urge amendments, and perhaps the most violent to obtain them. But notwithstanding the local prejudices which operate upon the people of these states, a considerable part of them wish for amendments. It is not to be doubted that a considerable majority of the people of Connecticut wish for them, and many in Jersey have the same desires, and their numbers are increasing. It cannot be disputed, that amendments would accord with the sentiments of a great majority in Massachusetts, or that they would be agreeable to the greater part of the people of Pennsylvania: There is no reason to doubt but that they would be agreeable to Delaware and Georgia—If then, the states who have already ratified the constitution, are desirous to have alterations made in it, what reason can be assigned why they should not cordially meet with overtures for that purpose from any state, and concur in appointing a convention to effect it? Mankind are easily induced to fall into measures to obtain an object agreeable to them. In this case, the states would not only be moved by this universal principle of human nature, but by the strong and powerful motive of uniting all the states under a form of government agreeable to them.

I shall now dismiss the consideration of objections made to attempting alterations previous to the adoption of the plan, but before I close, I beg your indulgence, while I make some remarks on the splendid advantages which the advocates of this system say are to be derived from it.—Hope and fear are two of the most active principles of [18] our nature: We have considered how the latter is addressed on this occasion, and with how little reason: It will appear that the promises it makes, are as little to be relied upon as its threatenings. We are amused with the fair prospects that are to open, when this government is put into operation—Agriculture is to flourish, and our fields to yield an hundred fold—Commerce is to expand her wings, and bear our productions to all the ports in the world—Money is to pour into our country through every channel—Arts and manufactures are to rear their heads, and every mecanic find full employ—Those who are in debt, are to find easy means to procure money to pay them—Public burdens and taxes are to be lightened, and yet all our public debts are soon to be discharged.—With such vain and delusive hopes are the minds of many honest and well meaning people fed, and by these means are they led inconsiderately to contend for a government, which is made to promise what it cannot perform; while their minds are diverted from contemplating its true nature, or considering whether is will not endanger their liberties, and work oppression.

Far be it from me to object to granting the general government the power of regulating trade, and of laying imposts and duties for that purpose, as well as for raising a revenue: But it is as far from me to flatter people with hopes of benefits to be derived from such a change in our government which can never be realized. Some advantages may accrue from vesting in one general government, the right to regulate commerce, but it is a vain delusion to expect anything like what is promised. The truth is, this country buys more than it sells: It imports more than it exports. There are too many merchants in proportion to the farmers and manufacturers. Until these defects are remedied, no government can relieve us. Common sense dictates, that if a man buys more than he sells, he will remain in debt; the same is true of a country.—And as long as this country imports more goods than the exports ——— the overplus must be paid for in money or not paid at all. These few remarks may convince us, that the radical remedy for the scarcity of cash is frugality and industry. Earn much and spend little, and you will be enabled to pay your debts, and have money in your pockets; and if you do not follow [19] this advice, no government that can be framed, will relieve you.

As to the idea of being relieved from taxes by this government, it is an affront to common sense, to advance it. There is no complaint made against the present confederation more justly founded than this, that it is incompetent to provide the means to discharge our national debt, and to support the national government. Its inefficacy to these purposes, which was early seen and felt, was the first thing that suggested the necessity of changing the government; other things, it is true, were afterwards found to require alterations; but this was the most important, and accordingly we find, that while in some other things the powers of this government seem to be in some measure limited, on the subject of raising money, no bounds are set to it. It is authorised to raise money to any amount, and in any way it pleases. If then, the capital embarrassment in our present government arises from the want of money, and this constitution effectually authorises the raising of it, how are the taxes to be lessened by it? Certainly money can only be raised by taxes of some kind or other; it must be got either by additional impositions on trade, by excise, or by direct taxes, or what is more probable, by all together. In either way, it amounts to the same thing, and the position is clear, that as the necessities of the nation require more money than is now raised, the taxes must be enhanced. This you ought to know, and prepare yourselves to submit to.—Besides, how is it possible that the taxes can be decreased when the expences of your government will be greatly advanced? It does not require any great skill in politics, or ability at calculation to shew, that the new government will cost more money to administer it, than the present. I shall not descend to an estimate of the cost of a federal town, the salaries of the president, vice-president, judges, and other great officers of state, nor calculate the amount of the pay the legislature will vote themselves, or the salaries that will be paid the innumerable and subordinate officers. The bare mention of these things is sufficient to convince you, that the new government will be vastly more expensive than the old: And how is the money to answer these purposes to be obtained? It is obvious, it must be taken out of the pockets of the people, by taxes, in some mode or other.

[20] Having remarked upon the arguments which have been advanced, to induce you to accede to this government, without amendments, and I trust refuted them, suffer me to close with an address dedicated by the affection of a brother, and the honest zeal of a lover of his country.

*Friends, countrymen, and fellow-citizens,*
The present is the most important crisis at which you ever have arrived. You have before you a question big with consequences, unutterably important to yourselves, to your children, to generations yet unborn, to the cause of liberty and of mankind; every motive of religion and virtue, of private happiness and public good, of honour and dignity, should urge you to consider cooly and determine wisely.

Almost all the governments that have arisen among mankind, have sprung from force and violence. The records of history inform us of none that have been the result of cool and dispassionate reason and reflection: It is reserved for this favoured country to exhibit to mankind the first example.

——————— This opportunity is now given us, and we are to exercise our rights in the choice of persons to represent us in convention, to deliberate and determine upon the constitution proposed: It will be to our everlasting disgrace to be indifferent on such a subject; for it is impossible, we can contemplate anything that relates to the affairs of this life of half the importance.

You have heard that both sides on this great question, agree, that there are in it great defects; yet the one side tell you, choose such men as will adopt it, and then amend it——— while the other say, amend previous to its adoption.——————
I have stated to you my reasons for the latter, and I think they are unanswerable.—Consider you the common people the yeomanry of the country, for to such I principally address myself, you are to be the principal losers, if the constitution should prove oppressive; When a tyranny is established, there are always masters as well as slaves; the great and well-born are generally the former, and the middling class the latter—Attempts have been made, and will be repeated, to

alarm you with the fear of consequences; but reflect there are consequences on both sides, and none can be apprehended more dreadful, than entailing on ourselves and poste-[21] rity a government which will raise a few to the height of human greatness and wealth, while it will depress the many to the extreme of poverty and wretchedness. Consequences are under the controul of that all-wise and all-powerful being, whose providence conducts the affairs of all men: Our part is to act right, and we may then have confidence that the consequences will be favourable. The path in which you should walk is plain and open before you; be united as one man, and direct your choice to such men as have been uniform in their opposition to the proposed system in its present form, or without proper alterations: In men of this description you have reason to place confidence, while on the other hand, you have just cause to distrust those who urge the adoption of a bad constitution, under the delusive expectation of making amendments after it is acceded to. Your jealousy of such characters should be the more excited, when you consider that the advocates for the constitution have shifted their ground. When men are uniform in their opinions, it affords evidence that they are sincere: When they are shifting, it gives reason to believe, they do not change from conviction. It must be recollected, that when this plan was first announced to the public, its supporters cried it up as the most perfect production of human wisdom; It was represented either as having no defects, or if it had, they were so trifling and inconsiderable, that they served only, as the shades in a fine picture, to set off the piece to the greater advantage. One gentleman in Philadelphia went so far in the ardour of his enthusiasm in its favour, as to pronounce, that the men who formed it were as really under the guidance of Divine Revelation, as was Moses, the Jewish lawgiver. Their language is now changed; the question has been discussed; the objections to the plan ably stated, and they are admitted to be unanswerable. The same men who held it almost perfect, now admit it is very imperfect; that it is necessary it should be amended. The only question between us, is simply this: Shall we accede to a bad constitution, under the uncertain prospect of getting it amended, after we have received it, or shall we amend it before we adopt it? Common sense will point out which is the most rational, which is the most secure line of conduct. May heaven inspire you with wisdom, union, moderation and firm- [22] ness, and give you hearts to make a proper estimate of your invaluable privileges, and preserve them to you, to be transmitted to your posterity unimpaired, and may they be maintained in this our country, while Sun and Moon endure.

A Plebeian.

## POSTCRIPT.

Since the foregoing pages have been put to the press, a pamphlet has appeared, entitled, "An addresss to the people of the state of New York, on the subject of the new constitution, &c." Upon a cursory examination of this performance (for I have not had time to give it more than a cursory examination) it appears to contain little more than declamation and observations that have been often repeated by the advocates of the new constitution.

An attentive reader will readily perceive, that almost everything deserving the name of an argument in this publication, has received consideration, and, I trust, a satisfactory answer in the preceding remarks, so far as they apply to prove the necessity of an immediate adoption of the plan, without amendments.

I shall therefore only beg the patience of my readers, while I make a few very brief remarks on this piece.

The author introduces his observations with a short history of the revolution, and of the establishment of the present existing federal government. He draws a frightful picture of our condition under the present confederation. The whole of what he says on that head, stripped of its artificial colouring, amounts to this, that the existing system is rather commendatory than coercive, or that Congress have not in most cases, the power of enforcing their own resolves. This he calls "a new and wonderful system." However "wonderful" it may seem, it certainly is not "new." For most of the *federal governments* that have been in the world, have been of the same nature.——The united Netherlands are governed on the same plan. There are other governments also now existing, which are in a similar condition with our's, with regard to several particulars, on account of which this author denominates it " new and wonderful."——The king of Great Britain "may make war, but has not power to raise money to carry it on." He may borrow money, but it is without the means of repayment, &c. For these he is dependent on his parliament. But it is needless to add on [24] this head, because it is admitted that the powers of the general government ought to be increased in several of the particulars this author instances. But these things are mentioned to shew, that the outcry made against the confederation, as being a system new, unheard of, and absurd, is really without foundation.

The author proceeds to depicture our present condition in the high-wrought strains common to his party.——I shall add nothing to what I have said on this subject in the former part of this pamphlet, but will only observe, that his imputing our being kept out of the possession of the western posts, and our want of peace with the Algerines, to the defects in our present government, is much easier said than proved. The British keep possession of these posts, because it subserves their interest, and probably will do so, until they perceive that we have gathered strength and resources sufficient to assert our rights with the sword. Let our government be what it will, this cannot be done without time and patience. In the present exhausted situation of the country, it would be madness in us, had we ever so perfect a government, to commence a war for the recovery of these posts.——With regard to the Algerines, there are but two ways in which their ravages can be prevented. The one is, by a successful war against them, and the other is by treaty, The powers of Congress under the confederation are completely competent either to declare war against them, or to form treaties. Money, it is true, is necessary to do both these. This only brings us to this conclusion, that the great defect in our present government, is the want of powers to provide money for the public exigencies. I am willing to grant *reasonable* powers, on this score, but not unlimited ones; commercial treaties may be made under the present powers of Congress. I am persuaded we flatter ourselves with advantages which will result from them, that will never be realized. I know of no benefits that we receive from any that have yet been formed.

This author tells us, "it is not his design to investigate merits of the plan, nor of the objections made to it." It is well he did not undertake it, for if he had, from the specimen he has given, the cause he assumes would not have probably gained much strength by it.

He however takes notice of two or three of the many objections brought against the plan.

" We are told, (says he) among other strange things, that
" the liberty of the press is left insecure by the proposed con-
" stitution, and yet that constitution says neither more nor
"less [25] about it, than the constitution of the state of New
" York does. We are told it deprives us of trial by jury,
" whereas the fact is, that it expressly secures it in certain
" cases, and takes it away in none, &c. it is absurd to construe
" the silence of this, or of our own constitution relative to a
" great number of our rights into a total extinction of them ;
" silence and a blank paper neither grant nor take away any-
" thing."

It may be a strange thing to this author to hear the people of America anxious for the preservation of their rights, but those who understand the true principles of liberty, are no strangers to their importance. The man who supposes the constitution, in any part of it, is like a blank piece of paper, has very erroneous ideas of it. He may be assured every clause has a meaning, and many of them such extensive meaning, as would take a volume to unfold. The suggestion, that the liberty of the press is secure, because it is not in express words spoken of in the constitution, and that the trial by jury is not taken away, because it is not said in so many words and letters it is so, is puerile and unworthy of a man who pretends to reason. We contend, that by the indefinite powers granted to the general government, the liberty of the press may be restricted by duties, &c. and therefore the constitution ought to have stipulated for its freedom. The trial by jury, in all civil cases is left at the discretion of the general government, except in the supreme court on the appelate jurisdiction, and in this I affirm it is taken away, not by express words, but by fair and legitimate construction and inference; for the supreme court have expressly given them an appelate jurisdiction, in every case to which their powers extend (with two or three exceptions) both as to *law and fact*. The court are the judges; every man in the country, who has served as a juror, knows, that there is a difference between the court and the jury, and that the lawyers in their pleading, make the distinction. If the court, upon appeals, are to determine both the law and the fact, there is no room for a jury, and the right of trial in this mode is taken away.

The author manifests levity in referring to the constitution of this state, to shew that it was useless to stipulate for the liberty of the press, or to insert a bill of rights in the constitution. With regard to the first, it is perhaps an imperfection in our constitution that the liberty of the press is not expressly reserved; but still there was not equal necessity of making this reservation in our State as in the general Constitution, for the common and statute law of England, and the laws of the [26] colony are established, in which this privilege is fully defined and secured. It is true, a bill of rights is not prefixed to our constitution, as it is in that of some of the states; but still this author knows, that many essential rights are reserved in the body of it; and I will promise, that every opposer of this system will be satisfied, if the stipulations that they contend for are agreed to, whether they are prefixed, affixed, or inserted in the body of the constitution, and that they will not contend which way this is done, if it be but done. I shall add but one remark, and that is upon the hackneyed argument introduced by the author, drawn from the character and ability of the framers of the new constitution.

The favourers of this system are not very prudent in bringing this forward. It provokes to an investigation of characters, which is an inviduous task. I do not wish to detract from their merits, but I will venture to affirm, that twenty assemblies of equal number might be collected, equally respectable both in point of ability, integrity, and patriotism. Some of the characters which compose it I revere; others I consider as of small consequence, and a number are suspected of being great public defaulters, and to have been guilty of notorious peculation and fraud, with regard to public property in the hour of our distress. I will not descend to personalities, nor would I have said so much on the subject, had it not been in self defence. Let the constitution stand on its own merits. If it be good, it stands not in need of great men's names to support it. If it be bad, their names ought not to sanction it.

FINIS.

The Weakness of Brutus exposed : / or, some / Remarks / in / Vindication of the Constitution / proposed by the late / Federal Convention, / against the / Objections and gloomy Fears of that Writer / Humbly offered to the Public, / By / a Citizen of Philadelphia. / Philadelphia, / Printed for, and to be had of John Sparhawk, in Market-Street, / near the Court House / M.DCC.LXXXVII.

12mo., pp. 23.

---

Written by Pelatiah Webster, a Philadelphia merchant, and author of a number of pamphlets on the finances and government of the United States, most of which he reprinted in his "Political Essays" in Philadelphia in 1791.

Brutus was the signature (of Thomas Treadwell, of Suffolk County, N. Y.?) to a series of sixteen newspaper essays in the *New York Journal*, which were extensively copied throughout the country. This is an answer to the first essay only, and was published November 4th, 1787.

P. L. F.

THE long piece signed BRUTUS, (which was first published in a New-York paper, and was afterwards copied into the Pennsylvania Packet of the 26th instant) is wrote in a very good stile; the language is easy, and the address is polite and insinuating: but the sentiments, I conceive, are not only unsound, but wild and chimerical; the dreary fears and apprehensions, altogether groundless; and the whole tendency of the piece, in this important crisis of our politics, very hurtful. I have therefore thought it my duty to make some animadversions on it; which I here offer, with all due deference, to the Author and to the Public.

His first question is, *Whether a confederated government is best for the United States?*

I answer, If Brutus, or any body else, cannot find any benefit resulting from the union of the Thirteen States; if they can do *without* as well as *with* the respectability, the protection, and the security, which the States might derive from that union, I have nothing further to say: but if that union is to be supported in any such manner as to afford [4] respectability, protection, or security to the States, I say it must be done by an adequate government, and cannot be otherwise done.

This government must have a supreme power, *superior to and able to controul* each and all of its parts. 'Tis essential to all governments, that such a power be somewhere existing in it; and if *the place* where the proposed Constitution has fixed it, does not suit Brutus and his friends, I will give him leave to stow it away in any *other place that is better:* but I will not consent to have it *annihilated;* neither will I agree to have it *cramped and pinched* for room, so as to lessen its energy; for that will *destroy* both its nature and use.

The supreme power of government ought to be *full, definite, established,* and *acknowledged.* Powers of government too limited, or uncertain and disputed, have ever proved, like

*Pandora's* box, a most fruitful source of quarrels, animosities, wars, devastation, and ruin, in all shapes and degrees, in all communities, states and kingdoms on earth.

Nothing tends more to the honour, establishment, and peace of society, than public decisions, grounded on principles of right, natural fitness and prudence; but when the powers of government are *too limited*, such decisions can't be made and enforced; so the mischief goes without a remedy: dreadful examples of which we have felt, in instances more than enough, for seven years past.

[5] Further, where the powers of government are not *definite* but *disputed*, the administration dare not make decisions on the footing of impartial justice and right; but must temporize with the parties, lest they lose friends or make enemies: and of course the *righteous* go off injured and disgusted, and the *wicked* go grumbling to; for 'tis rare that any sacrifices of a court can satisfy a prevailing party in the state.

'Tis necessary in States, as well as in private families, that controversies should have a just, *speedy*, and effectual decision, that right may be done before the contention has *time* to grow up into habits of malignity, resentment, ill nature, and ill offices. If a controversy happens between two states, must it continue undecided, and daily increase, and be more and more aggravated, by the repeated insults and injuries of the contending parties, 'till they are ripe for the decision of the sword? or must the weaker states suffer, without remedy, the groundless demands and oppressions of their stronger neighbours, because they have no avenger, or umpire of their disputes?

Or shall we institute a supreme power with full and effectual authority to controul the animosities, and decide the disputes of these strong contending bodies? In the one proposed to to us, we have perhaps every chance of a *righteous judgment*, that we have any reason [6] to hope for; but I am clearly of opinion, that even a *wrongful decision*, would, in most cases, be preferable to the continuance of such destructive controversies.

I suppose that neither Brutus nor any of his friends would

wish to see our government *embroiled abroad;* and therefore will admit it necessary to institute some federal authority, sufficient to punish *any individual or State*, who shall violate our treaties with foreign nations, insult their dignity, or abuse their citizens, and compel due reparation in all such cases.

I further apprehend, that Brutus is willing to have the *general* interest and *welfare* of the States well provided for and supported, and therefore will consent that there shall exist in the states, an authority to *do* all this *effectually;* but he seems grieved that Congress should be the *judges of this general welfare* of the states. If he will be kind enough to point out any other more suitable and proper judges, I will consent to have them admitted.

Indeed I begin to have hopes of Brutus, and think he may come right at last; for I observe (after all his fear and tremblings about the new government) the constitution he *defines and adopts*, is the very same as that which the federal convention have proposed to us, *viz.* "that the Thirteen States should continue thirteen confederated republics under the *direction and controul* of a supreme [7] federal head, for certain defined national purposes, only." Where we may observe,

1. That the new Constitution leaves all the Thirteen States, complete republics, as it found them, but all confederated under the direction and controul of a federal head, for certain defined national purposes only, *i. e.* it leaves all the dignities, authorities, and internal police of each State in free, full, and perfect condition; unless when national purposes make the controul of them by the federal head, or authority, necessary to the general benefit.

2. These powers of controul by the federal head or authority, are *defined* in the new constitution, as minutely as may be, in their principle; and any detail of them which may become necessary, is committed to the wisdom of Congress.

3. It extends the controuling power of the federal head to no one case, to which the jurisdiction or power of definitive decision of any one state, can be competent. And,

4. In every such case, the controuling power of the federal

head, is absolutely necessary to the support, dignity, and benefit of the national government, and the safety of individuals; neither of which can, by any possibility, be secured without it.

All this falls in pretty well with Brutus's sentiments; for he does not think that the new Constitution in *its present state* so very bad, [8] but fears that it will not preserve its purity of institution; but if adopted, will immediately verge to, and terminate in *a consolidation, i. e.* a destruction of the state governments. For argument, he suggests the avidity of power natural to rulers; and the eager grasp with which they hold it when obtained; and their strong propensity to abuse their power, and encroach on the liberties of the people.

He dwells on the vast powers vested in Congress by the new Constitution, *i. e.* of levying taxes, raising armies, appointing federal courts, &c.; takes it for granted, that all these powers will be abused, and carried to an oppressive excess; and then harangues on the dreadful case we shall be in, when our *wealth* is all devoured by taxes, our *liberty* destroyed by the power of the army, and our *civil rights* all sacrificed by the unbounded power of the federal courts, &c.

And when he has run himself out of breath with this dreary declamation, he comes to the conclusion he set out with, *viz.* That the Thirteen States are too big for a republican government, which requires *small territory*, and can't be supported in *more extensive nations;* that in large states liberty will soon be swallowed up, and lost in the magnitude of power requisite in the government, &c.

[9] If any conclusion at all can be drawn from this baseless assemblage of gloomy thoughts, I think it must be *against any union at all;* against *any kind of federal government.* For nothing can be plainer than this, *viz.* that *the union can't by any possibility be supported with success, without adequate and effectual powers of government?*

We must have *money* to support the union, and therefore the power of raising it must be lodged somewhere; we must have *a military force,* and of consequence the power of raising and directing it must exist; civil and criminal causes of national concern will arise, therefore there must be somewhere a power of appointing *courts* to hear and determine them.

These powers must be vested in Congress; for nobody pretends to wish to have them vested in any other body of men.

The Thirteen States have a territory very extensive, and inhabitants very numerous, and every day rapidly increasing; therefore the powers of government necessary to support their union must be great in proportion. If the ship is large the mast must be proportionately great, or it will be impossible to make her sail well. The federal powers must extend to every part of the federal territory, *i. e.* to the utmost limits of the Thirteen States, and to every part of them; and must carry with them, sufficient [10] authority to secure the execution of them; and these powers must be vested in Congress, and the execution of them must be under their direction and controul.

These powers are *vast*, I know, and the trust is of the most *weighty kind* that can be committed to human direction; and the execution and administration of it will require the greatest *wisdom, knowledge, firmness,* and *integrity* in that august body; and I hope they will have all the *abilities and virtues* necessary to that important station, and will *perform their duty well;* but if they fail, the fault is in them, not in the constitution. The best constitution possible, even a divine one, badly administered, will make a bad government.

The members of Congress will be the best we can get; they will all of them derive their appointment from the States, and if the States are not wise enough to send *good and suitable* men, great *blame*, great *sin* will lie at their door. But I suppose nobody would wish to mend this fault by taking away the election of the people, and directing the appointment of Congress to be made in any other way.

When we have got the best that can be obtained, we ought to be quiet and cease complaining. 'Tis not in the power of human wisdom to do more; 'tis the fate of human nature to *be imperfect and to err;* and [11] no doubt but Congress, with all their *dignity of station and character*, with all their *opportunities* to gain *wisdom and information*, with all their *induce-*

*ments to virtue and integrity*, will err, and abuse or misapply their powers in more or less instances. I have no expectation that they will make *a court of angels*, or be anything more than *men:* 'tis probable many of them will be *insufficient* men, and some of them may be *bad men*.

The greatest wisdom, care, and caution, has been used in the *mode* of their appointment; in the *restraints and checks* under which they must act; in the numerous *discussions and deliberations* which all their acts must pass through, before they can receive the stamp of authority; in the terrors of *punishment* if they misbehave. I say, in all *these ways* the greatest care has been used to procure and form a good Congress.

The *dignity and importance* of their station and character will afford all the inducements to virtue and effort, which can influence a mind *capable* of their force.

Their own *personal reputation*, with the eyes of all the world on them,—the *approbation of their fellow citizens*, which every man in public station naturally wishes to enjoy,—and the *dread of censure and shame*, all contribute very forceable and strong inducements to noble, upright and worthy behavior.

[12] The *particular interest* which every member of Congress has in every public order and resolution, is *another strong motive* to right action. For every act to which any member gives his sanction, if it be raising an *army*, levying a *tax*, instituting a *court*, or any other act to bind the *States*,—such act will equally bind *himself, his nearest connections, and his posterity*.

Another mighty influence to the noblest principle of action will be *the fear of God before their eyes;* for while they sit in the place of God, to give law, justice, and right to the States, they must be *monsters indeed* if they do not regard *his law*, and imitate *his character*.

If all this will not produce a Congress fit to be trusted, and worthy of the public confidence, I think we may give the matter up as impracticable. But still we must make ourselves as easy as we can, under a *mischief* which admits *no remedy*, and bear with patience an *evil* which can't be *cured:* for a government we must have; there is no safety without it; though we know it will be imperfect, we still must prefer it to anarchy or no government at all. 'Tis the height of folly and madness to reject a necessary convenience, because it is not a perfect good.

Upon this statement of facts and principles, (for the truth and reality of which, I appeal [13] to every candid man,) I beg leave to remark,

1. That the federal Convention, in the constitution proposed to us, have exerted their utmost to produce *a Congress worthy of the public confidence*, who shall have *abilities* adequate to their important duty, and shall act under every possible inducement to execute it *faithfully*.

2. That this affords every chance which the nature of the thing will admit, of a wise and upright administration.

3. Yet all this notwithstanding, 'tis very possible that Congress *may err, may abuse, or misapply* their powers, which no precaution of human wisdom can prevent.

4. 'Tis *vain*, 'tis *childish*, 'tis *contentious* to object to a constitution thus framed and guarded, on pretence that the commonwealth may suffer by a bad administration of it; or to *withhold* the *necessary powers* of government, from the supreme rulers of it, least they should *abuse* or *misapply* those powers. This is an objection which will operate with equal force against every institution that can be made in this world, whether of policy, religion, commerce, or any other human concern, which can require regulations: for 'tis not possible to form any institution however necessary, wise and good, whose uses may not be lessened or destroyed by bad management.

If Brutus, or any body else, can point out [14] any *checks*, *cautions*, or *regulations*, which have been hitherto omitted, which will make Congress more *wise*, more *capable*, more *diligent*, or more *faithful*, I am willing to attend to them. But to set Congress at the head of the government, and object to their being vested with full and sufficient power to manage all the great departments of it, appears to me *absurd*, quite *wild*, and *chimerical:* it would produce a plan which would destroy itself as it went along, would be a sort of counter position of contrary parts, and render it impossible for rulers to render those services, and secure those benefits to the States, which are the only great ends of their appointment.

The constitution under Brutus's corrections would stand thus, *viz.* Congress would have power to *raise money,* but must not direct the *quanity,* or *mode of levying* it; they might raise *armies,* but must not judge to the *number* of soldiers necessary, or direct their destination; they ought to provide for the *general welfare,* but must not be judges of what that welfare *consists in,* or in *what manner* 'tis to be provided for; they might controul the several States, for *defined national purposes,* but must not be judges of *what purposes* would come within that *definition,* &c.

Any body with half an eye, may see what sort of administration the constitution, thus corrected, would produce, *e. g.* it would [15] require much greater trouble to leave the work *undone,* than would be necessary to get it *well done,* under a constitution of sufficient powers. If any one wishes to view more minutely this blessed operation, he may see a lively sample of it, in the last seven years practice of our federal government.

5. Brutus all along sounds his objections, and fears on *extreme cases* of abuse or misapplication of supreme powers, which may *possibly* happen, under the administration of a wild, weak, or wicked Congress; but 'tis easy to observe that all institutions are liable to *extremes,* but ought not *to be judged by them;* they do not often appear, and perhaps never may; but if they should happen in the cases supposed, (which God forbid) there is a remedy pointed out, in the Constitution itself.

'Tis not supposeable that such abuses could arise to any ruinous height, before they would affect the States so much, that at least two-thirds of them would unite in pursuing a remedy in the mode prescribed by the Constitution, which will always be liable to amendment, whenever any mischiefs or abuses appear in the government, which the Constitution in its present state, can't reach and correct.

6. Brutus thinks we can never be too much afraid of the encroaching avidity of rulers; but 'tis pretty plain, that however great the natural lust of power in rulers may be, the jealousy of the people in giving it, is about [16] equal; these two opposite passions, will always operate in opposite directions to each other, and like *action* and *reaction* in natural bodies, will ever tend to a good ballance.

At any rate, the Congress can never get more power than the people will give, nor hold it any longer than they will permit; for should they assume tyrannical powers, and make incroachments on liberty without the consent of the people, they would soon attone for their temerity, with shame and disgrace, and probably with their heads.

But 'tis here to be noted, that all the danger does not arise from the extreme of power in the rulers; for when the ballance verges to the contrary extreme, and the power of the rulers becomes too much limited and cramped, all the nerves of government are weakened, and the administration must unavoidably sicken, and lose that energy which is absolutely necessary for the support of the State, and the security of the people. For 'tis a truth worthy of great attention, that laws are not made so much for the righteous as for the wicked; who never fail to shelter themselves from punishment, whenever they can, under the defects of the law, and the weakness of government.

I now come to consider the grand proposition which Brutus sets out with, concludes with, and interlards all along, and which [17] seems to be the great gift of his performance, viz. That a confederation of the Thirteen States into one great republic is not best for them: and goes on to prove by a variety of arguments, that a republican form of government is not compatible, and cannot be convenient to so extensive a territory as the said States possess. He begins by taking one assumption for granted (for I can't see that his arguments prove it at all) *viz.* That the Constitution proposed will melt down and destroy the jurisdiction of the particular States, and consolidate them all into one great republic.

I can't see the least reason for this sentiment; nor the

least tendency in the new Constitution to produce this effect. For the Constitution does not suffer the federal powers to controul in the least, or so much as to interfere in the internal policy, jurisdiction, or municipal rights of any particular State: except where great and manifest national purposes and interests make that controul necessary. It appears very evident to me, that the Constitution gives an establishment, support, and protection to the internal and separate police of each State, under the superintendency of the federal powers, which it could not possibly enjoy in an independent state. Under the confederation each State derives strength, firmness and permanency from its compact with the other States. Like a stave in a cask well bound with hoops, it [18] stands firmer, is not so easily shaken, bent, or broken, as it would be were it set up by itself alone, without any connection with its neighbours.

There can be no doubt that each State will receive from the union great support and protection against the invasions and inroads of foreign enemies, as well as against riots and insurrections of their own citizens; and of consequence, the course of their internal administration will be secured by this means against any interruption or embarrassment from either of these causes.

They will also derive their share of benefit from the respectability of the union abroad, from the treaties and alliances which may be made with foreign nations, &c.

Another benefit they will receive from the controul of the supreme power of the union is this, viz. they will be restrained from making angry, oppressive, and destructive laws, from declaring ruinous wars with their neighbours, from fomenting quarrels and controversies, &c. all which ever weaken a state, tend to its fatal disorder, and often end in its dissolution. Righteousness exalts and strengthens a nation; but sin is a reproach and weakening of any people.

They will indeed have the privilege of oppressing their own citizens by bad laws or bad administration; but the moment the mischief extends beyond their own State, and [19] begins to affect the citizens of other States strangers, or the national welfare,—the salutary controul of the supreme power will check the evil, and restore strength and security, as well as honesty and right, to the offending state.

It appears then very plain, that the natural effect and tendency of the supreme powers of the union is to give strength, establishment, and permanency to the internal police and jurisdiction of each of the particular States; not to melt down and destroy, but to support and comfirm them all.

By what sort of assurance, then, can Brutus tell us that the new Constitution, if executed, must certainly and infallibly terminate in a consolidation of the whole, into one great republic, subverting all the State authorities. His only argument is, that the federal powers may be corrupted, abused, and misapplied, 'till this effect shall be produced. 'Tis true that the constitution, like every other on earth, committed to human management, may be corrupted by a bad administration, and be made to operate to the destruction of the very capital benefits and uses, which were the great end of its institution. The same argument will prove with equal cogency, that the constitution of each particular State, may be corrupted in practice, become tyranical and inimical to liberty. In short the argument proves too much, and therefore proves nothing: [20] 'tis empty, childish, and futile, and a serious proposal of it, is, I conceive, an affront to the human understanding.

But after all, supposing this event should take place, and by some strange fatality, the several states should be melted down, and merged in the great commonwealth, in the form of counties, or districts; I don't see why a commonwealth mode of government, would not be as suitable and convenient for the great State, as any other form whatever; I cannot see any sufficient ground or reason, for the position pretty often and boldly advanced, that a republican form of government can never be suitable for any nation of extensive territory, and numerous population: for if Congress can be chosen by the several States, though under the form and name of counties, or election districts, and be in every respect, instituted as directed by the new constitution, I don't see but we shall have as suitable a national council, as wise a legislative, and as strong and safe an executive power, as can be obtained under any form of government whatever; let our territory be ever so extensive or populous.

The most despotic monarch that can exist, must have his councils, and officers of state; and I can't see any one circumstance of their being appointed under a monarchy, that can afford any chance of their being any wiser or better, than ours may be. 'Tis true indeed, [21] the despot may, if he pleases, act without any advice at all; but when he does so, I conceive it will be very rare that the nation will receive greater advantages from his unadvised edicts, than may be drawed from the deliberate acts and orders of our supreme powers. All that can be said in favour of those, is, that they will have less chance of delay, and more of secrecy, than these; but I think it probable, that the latter will be grounded on better information, and greater wisdom; will carry more weights and be better supported.

The Romans rose, from small beginnings, to a very great extent of territory, population, and wisdom; I don't think their constitution of government, was near so good as the one proposed to us, yet we find their power, strength, and establishment, were raised to their utmost height, under a republican form of government. Their State received very little acquisition of territory, strength, or wealth, after their government became imperial; but soon began to weaken and decay.

The Carthagenians acquired an amazing degree of strength, wealth, and extent of dominion, under a republican form of of government. Neither they or the Romans, owed their dissolution to any causes arising from that kind of government: 'twas the party rage, animosity, and violence of their citizens, which destroyed them both; it weakened them, 'till the [22] one fell under the power of their enemy, and was thereby reduced to ruin; the other changed their form of government, to a monarchy. which proved in the end, equally fatal to them.

The same causes, if they can't be restrained, will weaken

or destroy any nation on earth, let their form of government be what it will; witness the division and dissolution of the Roman empire; the late dismemberment of Poland; the intestine divisions, rage, and wars of Italy, of France, of Spain, and of England.

No form of government can preserve a nation which can't controul the party rage of its own citizens; when any one citizen can rise above the controul of the laws, ruin draws near. 'Tis not possible for any nation on earth, to hold their strength and establishment, when the dignity of their government is lost, and this dignity will forever depend on the wisdom and firmness of the officers of government, aided and supported by the virtue and patriotism of their citizens.

On the whole, I don't see but that any form of government may be safe and practicable, where the controuling authority of the supreme powers, is strong enough to effect the ends of its appointment, and at the same time, sufficiently checked to keep it within due bounds, and limit it to the objects of its duty; and I think it appears, that the constitution proposed to us, has all these qualities [23] in as great perfection, as any form we can devise.

But after all, the grand secret of forming a good government, is, to put good men into the administration: for wild, vicious, or idle men, will ever make a bad government, let its principles be ever so good; but grave, wise, and faithful men, acting under a good constitution, will afford the best chances of security, peace, and prosperity, to the the citizens, which can be derived from civil police, under the present disorders, and uncertainty of all earthly things.

PHILADELPHIA, Nov. 4, 1787.

FINIS.

An / Examination / of the / Constitution / for the / United States / of / America, / Submitted to the People / by the / General Convention, / At Philadelphia, the 17th Day of September, 1787, / and since adopted and ratified / by the / Conventions of Eleven States, / chosen for the purpose of considering it, being all / that have yet decided on the subject. / By an American Citizen. / To which is added, / A Speech / of the / Honorable James Wilson, Esquire, / on the same subject. / Philadelphia : / Printed by Zachariah Poulson, Junr. in Fourth- / Street, between Market and Arch-Street. / M.DCC.LXXXVIII.

8vo., pp. 33.

---

"An American Citizen" was the pseudonym of Tench Coxe, of Pennsylvania, a member of the Annapolis Convention and the Continental Congress, and author of a number of pamphlets on the finances and commerce of the United States. The four letters written over that signature were among the first to appear in favor of the Constitution, and were reprinted in many of the newspapers of the day.

I have seen three copies with "Tench Coxe, Esq.," interlined on the title page in his own handwriting below "By an American Citizen." P. L. F.

TO THE

## CANDID READER.

EVERY person, who desires to know *the true situation* of the United States of America, in regard to *the freedom and powers* of their governments, must carefully consider together the *constitution of the state* in which he lives and *the new constitution of fœderal or general government*. The *latter alone* is treated of in the following pages. The former, it is presumed, are sufficiently understood by the citizens who live under them.

# NUMBER I.

*On the Federal Government, and first on the safety of the people, from the restraints imposed on the President.*

IT is impossible for an honest and feeling mind, of any nation or country whatever, to be insensible to the present circumstances of America. Were I an East Indian, or a Turk, I should consider this singular situation of a part of my fellow creatures as the most curious and interesting. Intimately connected with the country, as a citizen of the union, I confess it entirely engrosses my mind and feelings.

To take a proper view of the ground on which we stand, it may be necessary to recollect the manner in which the United States were originally settled and [4] established. Want of charity in the religious systems of Europe, and of justice in their political governments, were the principal moving causes, which drove the emigrants of various countries to the American continent. The Congregationalists, Quakers, Presbyterians and other British dissenters, the Catholics of England and Ireland, the Hugonots of France, the German Lutherans, Calvinists and Moravians, with several other societies, established themselves in the different colonies, thereby laying the ground of that liberality in ecclesiastical affairs, which has been observable since the late revolution. Religious liberty naturally promotes corresponding dispositions in matters of government. The constitution of England as it stood on paper, was one of the freest, at that time, in the world, and the American colonies considered themselves as entitled to the fullest enjoyment of it. Thus, when the ill-judged discussions of late times in England brought into question the rights of this country, as it stood connected with the British crown, we were found more strongly impressed with their importance, and accurately acquainted with their extent, than the wisest and most learned of our brethren beyond the Atlantic.

When the greatest names in parliament insisted on the power of that body over the commerce of the colonies, and even the right to bind us in all cases whatsoever, America, seeing that it was only another form of tyranny, insisted upon the immutable truth, that taxation and representation are inseparable; and, while a desire of harmony and other considerations induced her into an acquiescence in the commercial relations of Great Britain, it was done from the declared necessity of the case, and with a cautious, full, and absolute saving of our voluntarily-suspended rights. The parliament was persevering, and America continued firm, till hostilities and open war commenced, and finally the late revolution closed the contest forever.

[5] It is evident, from this short detail, and the reflections which arise from it, that the quarrel between the United States and the parliament of Great Britain did not arise so much from objections to the form of government, though undoubtedly a better one by far is now within our reach, as from a difference concerning certain important rights, resulting from the essential principles of liberty, which their constitution actually preserved to all the subjects residing within the realm. It was not asserted by America, that the people of the island of Great Britain were slaves, but that we, though possessed absolutely of the same rights, were not admitted to enjoy an equal degree of freedom.

When the declaration of independence compleated the separation between the two countries, new governments were necessarily established. Many circumstances led to the adoption of the republican form, among which was the predilection of the people. In devising the frames of government, it may have been difficult to avoid extremes opposite to the vices of that we had just rejected; nevertheless, many of the state constitutions we have chosen are truly excellent. Our misfortunes have been, that in the first instance we adopted no national government at all; but were kept together by common danger only; and that in the confusions of a civil war, we framed a fœderal constitution, now universally admitted to be inadequate to the preservation of liberty, property, and the union. The question is not, then, how far our state constitutions are good, or otherwise—the object of our wishes is, to amend and supply the evident and allowed errors and defects of the fœderal government. Let us consider awhile, that which is now proposed to us—let us compare it with the so much boasted British form of government, and see how much more it favours the people, and how completely it secures their rights, remembering, at the same time, that we did not dissolve our connection [6] with that country so much on account of its constitution, as the perversion and mal-administration of it.

In the first place, let us look at the nature and powers of the head of that country, and those of the ostensible head of ours.

The British king is the great bishop or supreme head of an established church, with an immense patronage annexed. In this capacity he commands a number of votes in the house of lords, by creating bishops, who, besides their great incomes, have votes in that assembly, and are judges in the last resort. These prelates have also many honorable and lucrative places to bestow, and thus from their wealth, learning, dignities, powers, and patronage, give a great lustre and an enormous influence to the crown.

In America, our president will not only be without these influencing advantages, but they will be in the possession of the people at large, to strengthen their hands in the event of a contest with him. All religious funds, honors and powers, are in the gift of numberless unconnected, disunited and contending corporations, wherein the principle of perfect equality universally prevails. In short, danger from ecclesiastical tyranny, that long standing and still remaining curse of the people—that sacreligious engine of royal power in some countries—can be feared by no man in the United States. In Britain their king is for life—in America, our President will always be one of the people at the end of four years. In that country, the king is hereditary, and may be an ideot, a knave, or a tyrant by nature, or ignorant from neglect of his education, yet cannot be removed, for "he can do no wrong." This is a favorite maxim of their constitution. In America, as the President is to be one of the people at the end of his short term, so will he and his fellow citizens remember, that he was originally one of the people; and he is created by their breath. Further, he cannot be [7] an ideot, probably not a knave or tyrant, for those whom nature makes so discover it before the age of thirty-five, until which period he cannot be elected. It appears, we have not admitted that he can do no wrong, but have rather pre-supposed he may, and sometimes will do wrong, by providing for his impeachment, his trial, and his peaceable and complete removal.

In England the king has a power to create members of the upper house, who are judges in the highest court, as well as legislators. Our President not only cannot make members of the Senate, but their creation, like his own, is by the people, through their representatives: and a member of Assembly may and will be as certainly dismissed at the end of his year, for electing a weak or wicked Senator, as for any other blunder or misconduct.

The king of England has complete legislative power, while our President can only use it when the other servants of the people are divided. But in all great cases affecting the national interests or safety, his modified and restrained power must give way to the sense of two-thirds of the legislature. In fact it amounts to no more, than a serious duty imposed upon him to request both houses to re-consider any matter on which he entertains doubts or feels apprehensions; and here the people have a strong hold upon him from his sole and personal responsibility.

The President of the upper-house (or the chancellor) in in England, is appointed by their king, while our Vice-President, who is chosen by the people, through the electors and the Senate, is not at all dependant on the President, but may exercise equal powers on some occasions. In all royal governments, an helpless infant or an inexperienced youth may wear the crown. Our President must be matured by the experience of years, and being born among us, his character at thirty-five must be fully understood. Wisdom, virtue and ac-[8]tive qualities of mind and body can alone make him the first servant of a free and enlightened people.

Our President will fall very much short indeed of any prince in his annual income, which will not be hereditary, but the absolute allowance of the people, passing through the hands of their other servants from year to year, as it becomes necessary. There will be no burdens on the nation, to provide for his heir, or other branches of his family. It is probable, from the state of property in America, and other circumstances, that many citizens will exceed him in show and expense,—those dazzling trappings of kingly rank and power. He will have no authority to make a treaty, without two-thirds of the senate, nor can he appoint ambassadors or other great officers without their approbation, which will remove the idea of patronage and influence, and of personal obligation and dependence. The appointment of even the inferior officers may be taken out of his hands by an act of congress at any time; he can create no nobility or titles of honor, nor take away offices during good behaviour. His person is not so much protected as that of a member of the house of representatives; for he may be proceeded against like any other man in the ordinary course of law. He appoints no officer of the separate states. He will have no influence from placemen in the legislature, nor can he prorogue or dissolve it. He will have no power over the treasures of the state; and, lastly, as he is created through the electors, by the people at large, he must ever look up to the support of his creators. From such a servant, with powers so limited and transitory, there can be no danger, especially when we consider the solid foundations on which our national liberties are immoveably fixed, by the other provisions of this excellent constitution. Whatever of dignity or authority he possesses, is a delegated part of their majesty and their political omnipotence, transiently vested in him by the people themselves, for their own happiness.

[9] NUMBER II.
*On the safety of the people, from the restraints imposed upon the Senate.*

We have seen that the late honorable convention, in designating the nature of the chief executive office of the United States, having deprived it of all the dangerous appendages of royalty, and provided for the frequent expiration of its limited powers—As our president bears no resemblance to a king, so we shall see the senate have no similitude to nobles.

First, then, not being hereditary, their collective knowledge, wisdom, and virtue are not precarious, for by these qualities alone they are to obtain their offices; and they will have none of the peculiar follies and vices of those men, who possess power merely because their fathers held it before them, for they will be educated (under equal advantages, and with equal prospects) among and on a footing with the other sons of a free people. If we recollect the characters, who have, at various periods, filled the seats of congress, we shall find this expectation perfectly reasonable. Many young men of genius, and many characters of more matured abilities without fortunes, have been honored with that trust. Wealth has had but few representatives there, and those have been generally possessed of respectable personal qualifications. There have also been many instances of persons not eminently endowed with mental qualities, who have been sent thither from a reliance on their virtues, public and private—As the senators are still to be elected by the legislatures of the states, there can be no doubt of equal safety and propriety in their future appointment, especially as no further pecuniary qualification is required by the constitution.

[10] They can hold no other office civil or military under the United States, nor can they join in making provision for themselves, either by creating new places, or encreasing the emoluments of old ones. As their sons are not to succeed them, they will not be induced to aim at an increase or per-

petuity of their powers, at the expence of the liberties of the people, of which those sons will be a part. They possess a much smaller share of the judicial power than the upper house in Britain, for they are not, as there, the highest court in civil affairs. Impeachments alone are the cases cognizable before them, and in what other place could matters of that nature be so properly and safely determined? The judges of the fœderal courts will owe their appointments to the president and senate, therefore may not feel so perfectly free from favour, affection and influence, as the upper house who receive the power from the people, through their state representatives, and are immediately responsible to those assemblies, and finally to the nation at large—Thus we see, when a daring or dangerous offender is brought to the bar of public justice, the people, who alone can impeach him by their immediate representatives, will cause him to be tried, not by judges appointed in the heat of the occasion, but by two-thirds of a select body, chosen a long time before, for various purposes, by the collective wisdom of their State legislatures. From a pretence or affectation of extraordinary purity and excellence of character, their word of honour is the sanction under which these high courts, in other countries, have given their sentence—But with us, like the other judges of the union, like the rest of the people, of which they are never to forget they are a part, it is required that they be on oath.

No ambitious, undeserving or inexperienced youth can acquire a seat in this house by means of the most enormous wealth, or most powerful connections, till [11] thirty years have ripened his abilities, and fully discovered his merits to his country—a more rational ground of preference surely than mere property.

The senate, though more independent of the people, as to the free exercise of their judgment and abilities, than the house of representatives, by the longer term of their office, must be older and more experienced men, and are vested with less effective power; for the public treasures, the sinews of the state, cannot be called forth by their original motion. They may indeed restrain the profusion or errors of the house of representatives, but they cannot take any of the necessary measures to raise a national revenue.

The people, through the electors, prescribe them such a president as shall be best qualified to controul them.

They can only, by conviction or impeachment, remove and incapacitate a dangerous officer, but the punishment of him as a criminal remains within the province of the courts of law, to be conducted under all the ordinary forms and precautions, which exceedingly diminishes the importance of their judicial powers. They are detached, as much as possible, from local prejudices in favor of their respective states, by having a separate and independent vote, for the sensible and conscientious use of which every member will find his person, honor and character seriously bound—He cannot shelter himself, under a vote in behalf of his state, among his immediate colleagues.

As there are only two, he cannot be voluntarily or involuntarily governed by the majority of the deputation—He will be obliged, by wholesome provisions, to attend his public duty, and thus in great national questions must give a vote, of the honesty of which he will find it is necessary to convince his constituents.

The senate must always receive the exceptions of the president against any of their legislative acts, which, without [12] serious deliberation and sufficient reasons, they will seldom disregard. They will also feel a considerable check from the constitutional powers of the state legislatures, whose rights they will not be disposed to infringe, since they are the bodies to which they owe their existence, and are moreover to remain the immediate guardians of the people.

And lastly, the Senate will feel the mighty check of the House of Representatives—a body so truly popular and pure in its election, so intimately connected, by its interests and feelings, with the people at large, so guarded against corruption and influence—so much, from its nature, above all apprehensions, that it must ever be able to maintain the high ground assigned to it by the fœderal constitution.

## NUMBER III.

*On the safety of the people, from the nature of the House of Representatives.*

In pursuing the consideration of the new fœderal constitution, it remains now to examine the nature and powers of the House of Representatives—the immediate delegates of the people.

Each member of this truly popular assembly will be chosen by about six thousand electors, by the poor as well as the rich. No decayed or venal borough will have an unjust share in their determinations—no old Sarum will send thither a representative by the voice of a single elector* As we shall have no royal ministers to purchase votes, so we shall have no votes for sale; for the suffrages of six thousand enlightened and independent freemen are above all price. When the increasing population of the country shall render the body too [13] large at the rate of one member for every thirty thousand persons, they will be returned at the greater rate of one for every forty or fifty thousand, which will render the electors still more incorruptible. For this regulation is only designed to prevent a smaller number than thirty thousand from having a representative. Thus we see a provision follows, that no state shall have less than one member, for if a new and greater number than thirty thousand should hereafter be fixed on, which should exceed the whole of the inhabitants of any state, such state, without this wholesome provision, would lose its voice in the House of Representatives—a circumstance which the constitution renders impossible.

The people of England, whose House of commons is filled with military and civil officers and pensioners, say their liberties would be perfectly secured by triennial Parliaments. With us no placeman can sit among the representatives of the people, and two years are the constitutional term of their existence. Here, again, lest wealth, powerful connections, or

---

*This is the case with that British Borough.

even the unwariness of the people should place in this important trust an undeserving, unqualified or inexperienced youth, the wisdom of the Convention has proposed an absolute incapacity till the age of twenty-five. At twenty-one a young man is made the guardian of his own interest, but he cannot, for a few years more be intrusted with the affairs of the nation. He must be an inhabitant of the state that elects him, that he may be intimately acquainted with their particular circumstances—The house of Representatives is not, as the senate, to have a President chosen for them from without their body, but are to elect their speaker from their own number—They will also appoint all their other officers. In great state cases, they will be the grand inquest of the nation, for they possess the sole and uncontroulable power of impeachment. They are neither to wait the call, nor abide the prorogations and dis- [14] solutions of a perverse or ambitious Prince, for they are to meet at least once in every year, and to sit on adjournments to be agreed on between themselves and the other servants of the people. Should they differ in opinion, the President, who is a temporary fellow-servant, and not their hereditary master, has a mediatorial power to adjust it for them, but cannot prevent their constitutional meeting within the year. They can compel the attendance of their members, that their public duty may not be evaded in times of difficulty or danger—The vote of each representative can be always known, as well as the proceedings of the house, that so the people may be acquainted with the conduct of those in whom they repose so important a trust. As was observed of the Senators, they cannot make new offices for themselves, nor increase, for their own benefit, the emoluments of old ones, by which the people will be exempted from needless additions to the public expences, on such sordid and mercenary principles—They are not to be restrained from the firm and plain language, which becomes the independent representatives of freedom, for there is to be a perfect liberty of speech. Without their consent, no monies can be obtained, no armies raised, no navies provided. They, alone, can originate bills for drawing forth the revenues of the union, and they will have a negative upon every legislative act of the other house.—So far, in short, as the sphere of fœderal jurisdiction extends, they will be controulable only by the people, and, in contentions with the other branch, so far as they shall be right, they must ever finally prevail.

Such, my Countrymen, are some of the cautionary provisions of the frame of government your faithful convention have submitted to your consideration—such the foundations of peace, liberty and safety, which have been laid by their unwearied labors—They have guarded you against all servants but those "whom choice and common good ordain," against all masters, " save preserving Heaven."

[15]     NUMBER IV.

*The security for national safety and happiness, resulting from other parts of the fœderal Government.*

In considering the respective powers of the President, the Senate and the House of Representatives, under the fœderal constitution, we have seen a part of the wholesome precautions, which are contained in the new system. Let us examine what further securities for the safety and happiness of the people are contained in the general stipulations and provisions.

The United States guarantee to every state in the union a separate republican form of government. From thence it follows, that any man or body of men, however rich or powerful, who shall make an alteration in the form of government of any state, whereby the powers thereof shall be attempted to be taken out of the hands of the people at large, will stand guilty of high treason; or should a foreign power seduce or over-awe the people of any state, so as to cause them to vest in the families of any ambitious citizens or foreigners the powers of hereditary governors, whether as Kings or Nobles, that such investment of powers would be void in itself, and every person attempting to execute them would also be guilty of treason.

No religious test is ever to be required of any officer or servant of the United States. The people may employ any wise or good citizen in the execution of the various duties of the government. In Italy, Spain, and Portugal, no protestant can hold a public trust. In England every Presbyterian, and other person not of their established church, is incapable of holding an office. No such impious deprivation of the rights of men can take place under the new fœderal constitution. The con- [16] vention has the honour of proposing the first public act, by which any nation has ever divested itself of a power, every exercise of which is a trespass on the Majesty of Heaven.

No qualification in monied or landed property is required by the proposed plan; nor does it admit any preference from the preposterous distinctions of birth and rank. The office of the President, a Senator, and a Representative, and every other place of power or profit, are therefore open to the whole body of the people. Any wise, informed and upright man, be his property what it may, can exercise the trusts and powers of the state, provided he possesses the moral, religious and political virtues which are necessary to secure the confidence of his fellow citizens.

The importation of slaves from any foreign country is, by a clear implication, held up to the world as equally inconsistent with the dispositions and the duties of the people of America. A solid foundation is laid for exploding the principles of negro slavery, in which many good men of all parties in Pennsylvania, and throughout the union, have already concurred. The temporary reservation of any particular matter must ever be deemed an admission that it should be done away. This appears to have been well understood. In addition to the arguments drawn from liberty, justice and religion, opinions against this practice, founded in sound policy, have no doubt been urged. Regard was necessarily paid to the peculiar situation of our southern fellow-citizens; but they, on the other hand, have not been insensible of the delicate situation of our national character on this subject.

The people will remain, under the proposed constitution, the fountain of power and public honour. The President, the Senate, and the House of Representatives, will be the channels through which the stream [17] will flow—but it will flow from the people, and from them only. Every office, religious, civil and military will be either their immediate gift, or it will come from them through the hands of their servants. And this, as observed before, will be guaranteed to them under the state constitution which they respectively approve; for they cannot be royal forms, cannot be aristocratical, but must be republican.

The people of those states which have faithfully discharged their duty to the union will be no longer subjected alone to the weight of the public debts. Proper arrangements will call forth the just proportion of their sister states, and our national character will again be as unstained as it was once exalted. Elevation to independence, with the loss of our good name, is only to be conspicuous in disgrace. The liberties of a people involved in debt are as uncertain as the liberty of an individual in the same situation. Their virtue is more precarious. The unfortunate citizen must yield to the operation of the laws, while a bankrupt nation too easy annihilates the sacred obligations of gratitude and honour, and becomes execrable and infamous. I cannot refrain from reminding my fellow-citizens of our near approach to that deplorable situation, which must be our miserable condition, if the defects of the old confederation remain without amendment. The proposed constitution will cure the evil, and restore us to our rank among mankind.

Laws, made after the commission of the fact, have been a dreadful engine in the hands of tyrannical governors. Some of the most virtuous and shining characters in the world have been put to death, by laws formed to render them punishable, for parts of their conduct which innocence permitted, and to which patriotism impelled them. These have been called ex post facto laws, and are exploded by the new system. If a time of public contention shall hereafter arrive, [18] the firm and ardent friends to liberty may know the length to which they can push their noble opposition, on the foundation of the laws. Should their country's cause impel them further, they will be acquainted with the hazard, and using those arms which Providence has put into their hands, will make a solemn appeal to "the power above."

The destruction of the ancient republics was occasioned in every instance by their being ignorant of a great political position, which was left for America to discover and and establish. Self-evident as the truth appears, we find no friend to liberty in ancient Greece or Rome asserting, that taxation and representation were inseparable. The Roman citizens, proud of their own liberty, imposed, in the freest times of the commonwealth, the most grievous burdens on their wretched provinces. At other times we find thousands of their citizens, though residing within the walls of Rome, deprived of legislative representatives. When America asserted the novel truth, Great Britain, though boasting herself as alone free among the modern nations, denied it by her legislature, and endeavoured to refute it by her arms—the reasoning of tyrants. But the attempt was vain, for the voice of truth was heard above the thunders of the war, and reached the ears of all nations. Henceforth the people of the earth will consider this position as the only rock on which they can found the temple of liberty, that taxation and representation are inseparable. Our new constitution carries it into execution on the most enlarged and liberal scale, for a Representative will be chosen by six thousand of his fellow-citizens, a Senator by half a sovereign state, a President by a whole nation.

The old fœderal constitution contained many of the same things, which from error or disingenuousness are urged against the new ones. Neither of them have a bill of rights, nor does either notice the liberty of the press, because they are already provided for by the [19] state constitutions; and relating only to personal rights, they could not be mentioned in a contract among foreign states.

Both the old and new fœderal constitutions, and indeed the constitution of Pennsylvania, admit of courts in which no use is made of a jury. The board of property, the court of admiralty, and the high court of errors and appeals, in the state of Pennsylvania, as also the court of appeals under the old confederation, exclude juries. Trial by jury will therefore be in the express words of the Pennsylvania constitution, " as heretofore,"—almost always used, though sometimes omitted. Trials for lands lying in any state between persons residing in such state, for bonds, notes, book debts, contracts, trespasses, assumptions, and all other matters between two or more citizens of any state, will be held in the state courts by juries, as now. In these case the fœderal courts cannot interfere.* But when a dispute arises between the citizens of any state about lands lying out of the bounds thereof, or when a trial is to be had between the citizens of any state and those of another, or the government of another, the private citizen will not be obliged to go into a court constituted by the state, with which, or with the citizens of which, his dispute is. He can appeal to a disinterested fœderal court. This is surely a great advantage, and promises a fair trial, and an impartial judgment. The trial by jury is not excluded in these fœderal courts. In all criminal cases, where the property, liberty or life of the citizen is at stake, he has the benefit of a jury. If convicted on impeachment, which is never done by a jury in any country, he cannot be fined, imprisoned or punished, but only may be disqualified from doing public mischief by losing his office, [20] and his capacity to hold another. If the nature of his offence, besides its danger to his country, should be criminal in itself— should involve a charge of fraud, murder or treason—he may be tried for such crime, but cannot be convicted without a jury. In trials about property in the fœderal courts, which can only be as above stated, there is nothing in the new constitution to prevent a trial by jury. No doubt it will be the mode in every case, wherein it is practicable. This will be adjusted by law, and it could not be

*Trials between a state and its own Citizens, and between Citizens of the same state, involving questions concerning state laws that infringe this constitution, may be carried by appeal, it is presumed, into a fœderal court.

done otherwise. In short, the sphere of jurisdiction for the fœderal courts is limited, and that sphere only is subject to the regulations of our fœderal government. The known principles of justice, the attachment to trial by jury whenever it can be used, the instructions of the state legislatures, the instructions of the people at large, the operation of the fœderal regulations on the property of a president, a senator, a representative, a judge, as well as on that of a private citizen, will certainly render those regulations as favorable as possible to property; for life and liberty are put more than ever into the hands of the juries. Under the present constitution of all the states, a public officer may be condemned to imprisonment or death on impeachment, without a jury; but the new fœderal constitution protects the accused, till he shall be convicted, from the hands of power, by rendering a jury the indispensible judges of all crimes.

The influence which foreign powers may attempt to exercise in our affairs was foreseen, and a wholesome provision has been made against it; for no person holding an office under the United States is permitted to enjoy any foreign honours, powers or emoluments.

The apprehensions of the people have been excited, perhaps by persons with good intentions, about the powers of the new government to raise an army. Let us consider this point with moderation and candour. As enemies will sometimes insult us, invade our coun- [21] try and capture our property, it is clear a power in our government to oppose, restrain or destroy them, is necessary to our honor, safety and existence. The military should, however, be regarded with a watchful eye; for it is a profession that is liable to dangerous perversion. But the powers vested in the fœderal government do not go the length which has been said. A standing army is not granted or intended, for there can be no provision for its continuing three years, much less for its permanent establishment. Two years are the utmost time for which the money can be given. It will be under all the restrictions which wisdom and jealousy can suggest, and the original grant of the supplies must be made by the House of representatives, the immediate delegates of the people. The Senate and President, who also derive their power from the people, appoint the officers; and the heads of the departments, who must submit their accounts to the whole legislature, are to pay and provide them, as shall be directed by the laws that shall contain the conditions of the grant. The militia, who are in fact the effective part of the people at large, will render many troops quite unnecessary. They will form a powerful check upon the regular troops, and will generally be sufficient to over-awe them—for our detached situation will seldom give occasion to raise an army, though a few scattered companies may often be necessary. But whenever, even on the most obvious reasons, an army shall be raised, the several states will be called, by the nature of things, to attend to the condition of the militia. Republican jealousy, the guardian angel of these states, will watch the motions of our military citizens, even though they will be the soldiers of a free people. There is a wide difference however between the troops of such commonwealths as ours, founded on equal and unalterable principles, and those of a regal government, where ambition and oppression are the profession of the king. In the first case, a military officer is the occasional servant of the people, employed for their defence; in [22] the second, he is the ever ready instrument to execute the schemes of conquest or oppression, with which the mind of his royal master may be disturbed.

Observations have been made on the power given to the fœderal Government in regard to the elections of Representtives and Senators. The regulations of these elections are, by the first part of the clause, to be prescribed by the state legislatures, who are certainly the proper bodies, if they will always execute the duty. But in case the union or the public safety should be endangered by an omission of this duty, as in the case of Rhode-Island, then the legislature of the United States can name for the people a convenient time, and do other matters necessary to insure the free exercise of their right of election. The exception, in regard to the places of chusing Senators, was made from due respect to the sovereignty of the state legislatures, who are to elect the senators, and whose place of meeting ought not to be prescribed to them by any authority, except, indeed, as we always must, by the authority of the people. This power given to the fœderal legislature is no more than what is possessed by the governments of all the states. The constitution of Pennsylvania permits two-thirds of such cities and counties, as shall elect representatives, to exercise all the powers of the General Assembly, "as fully and amply as if the whole were present," should any part of the state neglect or refuse to perform their duty in this particular. In short, it is a power necessary to preserve the social compact of each state and the confederation of the United States.

Besides the securities for the liberties of the people arising out of the fœderal government, they are guarded by their state constitutions, and by the nature of things in the separate states. The Governor or President in each commonwealth, the Councils, Senates, Assemblies, Judges, Sheriffs, Grand and Pettit Juries, Officers of Militia, Clergy and Lay Officers of all churches, state and county Treasurer, Prothonotaries, Registers, [23] Presidents and other officers of Universities, Colleges and Academies, Wardens of ports and cities, Burgesses of towns, Commissioners of counties, County Lieutenants, and many other officers of power and influence, will still be chosen within each state, without any possible interference of the fœderal Government. The separate states will also choose all the members of the legislative and executive branches of the United States. The people at large in each state will choose their fœderal representative, and, unless ordered otherwise by state legislatures, may choose the electors of the President and Vice-President of the Union. And lastly, the legislature of the state will have the election of the senate, as they have heretofore had of the Members of Congress. Let us then, with a candor worthy of the subject, ask ourselves, whether it can he feared, that a majority of the Representatives, each of whom will be chosen by six thousand enlightened freemen, can betray their country?—Whether a majority of the Senate, each of whom will be chosen by the legislature of a free, sovereign and independent state, without any stipulations in favour of wealth or the contemptible distinctions of birth or rank, and who will be closely observed by the state legislatures, can destroy our liberties, controuled as they are too by the house of representatives? or whether a temporary, limited, executive officer, watched by the fœderal Representatives, by the Senate, by the state legislatures, by his personal enemies among the people of his own state, by the jealousy of the people of rival states, and by the whole of the people of the Union, can ever endanger our Freedom.*

[24] Permit me, my fellow-citizens, to close these observations by remarking, that there is no spirit of arrogance in the new fœderal constitution. It addresses you with becoming modesty, admitting that it may contain errors. Let us give it a trial; and when experience has taught its mistakes, the

---

* There is one grand operation of the new fœderal constitution, favorable to general liberty, which I do not remember to have heard from any of its friends. It is well known, that in most of the states the members of their Houses of Representatives are chosen in equal numbers from each county, and in the eastern states, in equal numbers from each town, without any regard to the number of taxable inhabitants, or the number of souls. Hence it is very frequent for a county, with ten thousaud souls, to send only the same number of members to the state house of representatives, as a county with two thousand souls, by which each person in the least populous county has five times as great a voice in electing representatives, as his fellow citizen of the most populous county. This is clearly a departure from the principles of equal liberty, and ought to be altered in the several states. I speak the more plainly because our state constitution is free from that fault in the formation of our house of Assembly. Now the new constitution expressly declares, that the fœderal Representatives shall be in the proportion of one to every thirty thousand, which accords with reason and the true principles of liberty. This house, therefore, so far as national matters go, will remedy the evil spoken of in the several states, and is one more great step towards the perfection of equal liberty and genuine republicanism in America. It must strongly recommend the fœderal constitution to the serious reflecting patriot, even though he may formerly have had doubts, and it will suggest to the several states the propriety of reconsidering that point in their respective constitutions. Pennsylvania, though right in the principles on which her legislative elections are and will be held, is less safe from the existence of this fault in the adjoining sister states of Virginia, Maryland, Jersey, Delaware and New York, and in others more remote.

people, whom it preserves absolutely all powerful, can reform and amend them. That I may be perfectly understood, I will acknowledge its acceptance by all the states, without delay, is the second wish of my heart. The first is, that our country may be virtuous and free.

An American Citizen.

# SUBSTANCE OF AN ADDRESS

TO A

## MEETING OF THE CITIZENS OF PHILADELPHIA,

DELIVERED, OCTOBER SIXTH, MDCCLXXXVII,

BY THE HONORABLE

## JAMES WILSON, Esquire,

ONE OF THE DE EGATES FROM THE STATE OF PENNSYLVANIA TO THE
LATE CONTINENTAL CONVENTION.

---

*Mr. Chairman and Fellow Citizens,*

HAVING received the honour of an appointment to represent you in the late convention, it is, perhaps, my duty to comply with the request of many gentlemen, whose characters and judgments I sincerely respect, and who have urged that this would be a proper occasion to lay before you any information, which will serve to elucidate and explain the principles and arrangements of the con- [26] stitution that has been submitted to the consideration of the United States. I confess that I am unprepared for so extensive and so important a disquisition: but the insidious attempts, which are clandestinely and industriously made to pervert and destroy the new plan, induce me the more readily to engage in its defence: and the impressions of four months constant attendance to the subject, have not been so easily effaced, as to leave me without an answer to the objections which have been raised.

It will be proper, however, before I enter into the refutation of the charges that are alleged, to mark the leading discrimination between the state constitutions, and the constitution of the United States. When the people established the powers of legislation under their separate governments, they invested their representatives with every right and authority which they did not in explicit terms reserve: and therefore upon every question, respecting the jurisdiction of the house of assembly, if the frame of government is silent, the jurisdiction is efficient and complete. But in delegating fœderal powers, another criterion was necessarily introduced: and the congressional authority is to be collected, not from tacit implication, but from the positive grant, expressed in the instrument of union. Hence, it is evident, that in the former case, everything which is not reserved, is given: but in the latter, the reverse of the proposition prevails, and every thing which is not given, is reserved. This distinction being recognized, will furnish an answer to those who think the omission of a bill of rights, a defect in the proposed constitution: for it would have been superfluous and absurd, to have stipulated with a fœderal body of our own creation, that we should enjoy those privileges, of which we are not divested either by the intention or the act that has brought that body into existence. For instance, the liberty of the [27] press, which has been a copious subject of declamation and opposition: what controul can proceed from the fœderal government, to shackle or destroy that sacred palladium of national freedom? If, indeed, a power similar to that which has been granted for the regulation of commerce, had been granted to regulate literary publications, it would have been as necessary to stipulate that the liberty of the press should be preserved inviolate, as that the impost should be general in its operation. With respect, likewise, to the particular district of ten miles, which is to be the seat of government, it will undoubtedly be proper to observe this salutary precaution, as there the legislative power will be vested in the president, senate, and house of representatives of the United States. But this could not be an object with the convention: for it must naturally depend upon a future compact; to which the citizens immediately interested, will, and ought to be parties: and there is no reason to suspect, that so popular a privilege will in that case be neglected. In truth, then, the proposed system possesses no influence whatever upon the press; and it would have been merely nugatory, to have introduced a formal declaration upon the subject; nay, that very declaration might have been construed to imply that some degree of power was given, since we undertook to define its extent.

Another objection that has been fabricated against the new constitution, is expressed in this disingenuous form—"the trial by jury is abolished in civil cases." I must be excused, my fellow citizens, if, upon this point, I take advantage of my professional experience, to detect the futility of the assertion. Let it be remembered, then, that the business of the fœderal constitution was not local, but general—not limited to the views and establishments of a single state, but co-extensive with the continent, and comprehending the [28] views and establishments of thirteen independent sovereignties. When, therefore, this subject was in discussion, we were involved in difficulties, which pressed on all sides, and no precedent could be discovered to direct our course. The cases open to a jury, differed in the different states; it was therefore impracticable, on that ground, to have made a general rule. The want of uniformity would have rendered any reference to the practice of the states idle and useless: and it could not, with any propriety, be said, that "the trial by jury shall be as heretofore:" since there has never existed any fœderal system of jurisprudence, to which the declaration could relate. Besides, it is not in all cases that the trial by jury is adopted in civil questions: for causes depending in courts of admiralty, such as relate to maritime captures, and such as are agitated in the courts of equity, do not require the intervention of that tribunal. How, then, was the line of discrimination to be drawn? The convention found the task too difficult for them: and they left the business as it stands—in the fullest confidence, that no danger could possibly ensue, since the proceedings of the supreme court are to be regulated by the congress, which is a faithful representation of the people: and the oppression of government is effectually barred, by declaring that in all criminal cases, the trial by jury shall be preserved.

This constitution, it has been further urged, is of a pernicious tendency, because it tolerates a standing army in the time of peace. This has always been a popular topic of declamation: and yet I do not know a nation in the world, which has not found it necessary and useful to maintain the appearance of strength in a season of the most profound tranquility. Nor is it a novelty with us; for under the present articles of confederation, congress certainly possesses this reprobated power: and the exercise of it is proved at this [29] moment by the cantonments along the banks of the Ohio. But what would be our national situation, where it otherwise? Every principle of policy must be subverted, and the government must declare war before they are prepared to carry it on. Whatever may be the provocation, however important the object in view, and however necessary dispatch and secrecy may be, still the declaration must precede the preparation, and the enemy will be informed of your intention, not only before you are equipped for an attack, but even before you are fortified for a defence. The consequence is too obvious to require any further delineation; and no man, who regards the dignity and safety of his country, can deny the necessity of a military force, under the controul, and with the restrictions which the new constitution provides.

Perhaps there never was a charge made with less reason, than that which predicts the institution of a baneful aristocracy in the fœderal senate. This body branches into two characters, the one legislative, and the other executive. In its legislative character, it can effect no purpose without the co-operation of the house of representatives: and in its executive character, it can accomplish no object, without the concurrence of the president. Thus fettered, I do not know any act which the senate can of itself perform: and such dependence necessarily precludes every idea of influence and superiority. But I will confess, that in the organization of this body, a compromise between contending interests is discernible: and when we reflect how various are the laws, commerce, habits, population, and extent of the confederated states, this evidence of mutual concession and accommodation ought rather to command a generous applause, than to excite jealousy and reproach. For my part, my admiration can only be equalled by my astonishment, in beholding so perfect a system formed from such heterogenous materials.

[30] The next accusation I shall consider, is that which represents the fœderal constitution as not only calculated, but designedly framed, to reduce the state governments to mere corporations, and eventually to annihilate them. Those who have employed the term corporation, upon this occasion, are not perhaps aware of its extent. In common parlance, indeed, it is generally applied to petty associations for the ease and conveniency of a few individuals; but in its enlarged sense, it will comprehend the government of Pennsylvania, the existing union of the states, and even this projected system is nothing more than a formal act of incorporation. But upon what pretence can it be alleged that it was designed to annihilate the state governments? For, I will undertake to prove that upon their existence depends the existence of the fœderal plan. For this purpose, permit me to call your attention to the manner in which the president, senate, and house of representatives, are proposed to be appointed. The president is to be chosen by electors, nominated in such manner as the legislature of each state may direct; so that if there is no legislature, there can be no senate. The house of representatives is to be composed of members chosen every second year by the people of the several states, and the electors in each state shall have the qualifications requisite to electors of the most numerous branch of the state legislature—unless, therefore, there is a state legislature, that qualification cannot be ascertained, and the popular branch of the fœderal constitution must likewise be extinct. From this view, then, it is evidently absurd to suppose, that the annihilation of the seaprate governments will result from their union; or, that, having that intention, the authors of the new system would have bound their connection with such indissoluble ties. Let me here advert to an arrangement highly advantageous; for you will perceive, with- [31] out prejudice to the powers of the legislature in the election of senators, the people at large will acquire an additional privilege in returning members to the house of representatives—whereas, by the present con-

federation, it is the legislature alone that appoints the delegates to congress.

The power of direct taxation has likewise been treated as an improper delegation to the fœderal government; but when we consider it as the duty of that body to provide for the national safety, to support the dignity of the union, and to discharge the debts contracted upon the collective faith of the states, for their common benefit, it must be acknowledged that those, upon whom such important obligations are imposed, ought, in justice and in policy, to possess every means requisite for a faithful performance of their trust. But why should we be alarmed with visionary evils? I will venture to predict, that the great revenue of the United States must, and always will, be raised by impost; for, being at once less obnoxious, and more productive, the interest of the government will be best promoted by the accommodation of the people. Still, however, the object of direct taxation should be within reach in all cases of emergency; and there is no more reason to apprehend oppression in the mode of collecting a revenue from this resource, than in the form of impost, which, by universal assent, is left to the authority of the fœderal government. In either case, the force of civil constitutions will be adequate to the purpose; and the dread of military violence, which has been assiduously disseminated, must eventually prove the mere effusion of a wild imagination, or a factious spirit. But the salutary consequences that must flow from thus enabling the government to relieve and support the credit of the union, will afford another answer to the objections upon this ground. The state of Pennsylvania, particularly, [32] which has encumbered itself with the assumption of a great proportion of the public debt, will derive considerable relief and advantage; for, as it was the imbecility of the present confederation, which gave rise to the funding law, that law must naturally expire, when a complete and energetic fœderal system shall be substituted—the state will then be discharged from an extraordinary burden, and the national creditor will find it to be to his interest to return to his original security.

After all, my fellow-citizens, it is neither extraordinary nor unexpected, that the constitution offered to your consideration, should meet with opposition. It is the nature of man to pursue his own interest, in preference to the public good; and I do not mean to make any personal reflection, when I add, that it is the interest of a very numerous, powerful, and respectable body, to counteract and destroy the excellent work produced by the late convention. All the officers of government, and all the appointments for the administration of justice and the collection of the public revenue, which are transferred from the individual to the aggregate sovereignty of the states, will necessarily turn the stream of influence and emolument into a new channel. Every person, therefore, who either enjoys, or expects to enjoy a place of profit under the present establishment, will object to the proposed innovation? not, in truth, because it is injurious to the liberties of his country, but because it effects his schemes of wealth and consequence. I will confess, indeed, that I am not a blind admirer of this plan of government, and that there are some parts of it, which, if my wish had prevailed, would certainly have been altered. But, when I reflect how widely men differ in their opinions, and that every man (and the] observation applies likewise to every state) has an equal pretension to assert his own, I am satisfied that [33] any thing nearer to perfection could not have been accomplished. If there are errors, it should be remembered, that the seeds of reformation are sown in the work itself, and the concurrence of two thirds of the congress may at any time introduce alterations and amendments. Regarding it, then, in every point of view, with a candid and disinterested mind, I am bold to assert, that it is the BEST FORM OF GOVERNMENT WHICH HAS EVER BEEN OFFERED TO THE WORLD.*

*The candid Reader will suppose Mr. WILSON here means, that it is the best form of fœderal government, which has ever been offered to the world—and it is surely true that the fœderal constitution, considered in due connexion with the state constitutions, is the best form of government that has ever been communicated to mankind.

FINIS.

The / Letters / of / Fabius, / in 1788, / on the Federal Constitution; / .... / Copy-Right Secured. / From the office of the Delaware / Gazette, Wilmington, / By W. C. Smith. / 1797. /

8vo. pp. iv., 202 (1).

---

Written by John Dickinson, the "Pennsylvania Farmer," and member of the Annapolis and Philadelphia Conventions. The Letters of Fabius were originally published in a Delaware newspaper in 1788, and were not issued in pamphlet form till 1797, when they were reprinted as above, together with a second series of letters "on the present situation of public affairs," which are omited in this reprint. They were also included in "The Political Writings of John Dickinson," printed in 1801.

P. L. F.

# THE EDITOR TO THE PUBLIC.

THE First Nine Letters in this Collection, published in the beginning of the Year 1788, were occasioned by an alarming hesitation of some States to ratify the Constitution proposed by the Federal Convention in 1787.

They appeared separately in News-papers; and have never been published together, before the present Edition.

Some Notes are added of Extracts from "*The Rights of Man*," published about three years after these Letters, containing similar sentiments, expressed with a remarkable resemblance of Language, especially on the two great subject—the *organization* of a *constitution* from original rights, and the *formation* of *government* from contributed rights, both of so much importance in laying regular *foundations* of Civil Society, and consequently in securing the advancement of *human happiness*.

## LETTER I.

THE Constitution proposed by the Federal Convention now engages the fixed attention of America.

Every person appears to be affected. Those who wish the adoption of the plan, consider its rejection as the source of endless contests, confusions, and misfortunes; and they also consider a resolution to alter, without previously adopting it, as a rejection.

Those who oppose the plan, are influenced by different views. Some of them are friends, others of them are enemies, to The United States. [2] The latter are of two classes; either men without principles or fortunes, who think they may have a chance to mend their circumstances, with impunity, under a weak government, or in public convulsions, but cannot make them worse even by the last—or men who have been always averse to the revolution; and though at first confounded by that event, yet, their hopes reviving with the declension of our affairs, have since persuaded themselves, that at length the people, tired out with their continued distresses, will return to their former connection with Great Britain. To argue with these opposers, would be vain—The other opposers of the plan deserve the highest respect.

*What concerns all, should be considered by all;* and individuals may injure a whole society, by not declaring their sentiments. It is therefore not only their right, but their duty, to declare them. Weak advocates of a good cause or artful advocates of a bad one, may endeavour to stop such communications, or to discredit them by clamour and calumny. This, however, is not the age for such tricks of controversy. Men have suffered so severely by being deceived upon subjects of the highest import, those of religion and freedom, that *truth* becomes infinitely valuable to them, not as a matter of curious speculation, but of beneficial practice—A spirit of inquiry is excited, information diffused, judgment strengthened.

Before this tribunal of *the people*, let every one freely speak, what he really thinks, [3] but with so sincere a reverence for the cause he ventures to discuss, as to use the utmost caution, lest he should lead any into errors, upon a point of such sacred concern as the public happiness.

It is not the design of this address, to describe the present derangement of our affairs, the mischiefs that must ensue from its continuance, the horrors, of a total dissolution of the union, or of the division of it into partial confederacies. Nor is it intended to describe the evils that will result from pursuing the plan of another Federal Convention; as if a better temper of conciliation, or a more satisfactory harmony of decisions, could be expected from men, after their minds are agitated with disgusts and disappointments, than before they were thus disturbed; though from an uncontradicted assertion it appears, that without such provocations, the difficulty of reconciling the interests of the several states was so near to *insuperable*, in the late convention, that after many weeks spent in the most faithful labours to promote concord, the members were upon the very point of dispersing in the utmost disorder, jealousy and resentment, and leaving the states exposed to all the tempests of passions, that have been so fatal to confederacies of republics.

All these things, with observations on particular articles of the constitution, have been laid before the public, and the writer of this address means not to repeat what has been already said. What he wishes, is to simplify [4] the subject, so as to facilitate the inquiries of his fellow citizens.

Many are the objections made to the system proposed. They should be distinguished. Some may be called local, because they spring from the supposed interests of individual states. Thus, for instance, some inhabitants of large states may desire the system to be so altered, that they may possess more authority in the decisions of the government; or some inhabitants of commercial states may desire it to be so altered, that the advantages of trade may center almost wholly among themselves; and this predilection they may think compatible with the common welfare. Their judgment being thus warp'd, at the beginning of their deliberations, objections are accumulated as very important, that, without this prepossession, would never have obtained their approbation. Certain it is, that strong understandings may be so influenced by this insulated patriotism, as to doubt—whether general benefits can be communicated by a general government.*

Probably nothing would operate so much for the correction of these errors, as the perusal of the accounts transmitted to us by the ancients, of the calamities occasioned in Greece by a conduct founded on similar mistakes. They are expressly ascribed to this cause—that each city meditated a part on its own profit and ends——insomuch that those *who seemed to contend for union*, could never relinquish their own in- [5] terests and advancement, while they deliberated for the public.

Heaven grant! that our countrymen may pause in time—duly estimate the present moment—and solemnly reflect—whether their measures may not tend to draw down the same distractions upon us, that desolated Greece.

They may now tolerably judge from the proceedings of the Federal Convention and of other conventions, what are the sentiments of America upon her present and future prospects. Let the voice of her distress be venerated—and adhering to the generous Virginian declaration, let them resolve to "*cling to Union as the political Rock of our Salvation.*"

FABIUS.

PHILADELPHIA,
*April* 10, 1788.

---

* See some late publications.

[6]         LETTER II.

But besides the objections originating from the before mentioned cause, that have been called local, there are other objections that are supposed to arise from maxims of liberty and policy.—

Hence it is inferred, that the proposed system has such inherent vices, as must necessarily produce a bad administration, and at length the oppression of a monarchy and aristocracy in the federal officers.

The writer of this address being convinced by as exact an investigation as he could make, that such mistakes may lead to the perdition of his country, esteems it his indispensable duty, strenuously to contend, that—*the power of the people* pervading the proposed system, together with the *strong confederation of the states*, forms an adequate security against every danger that has been apprehended.

If this single assertion can be supported by facts and arguments, there will be reason to hope, that anxieties will be removed from the minds of some citizens, who are truly devoted to the interests of America, and who have been thrown into perplexities, by the mazes of multiplied and intricate disquisitions.

The objectors agree, that the confederation of the states will be strong, according to the system proposed, and so strong, that many of them loudly complain of that strength. On this part of the assertion, there is no dispute: But some of the objections that have been published, [7] strike at another part of the principle assumed, and deny, that the system is sufficiently founded on the power of the people.

The course of regular inquiry demands, that these objections should be considered in the first place. If they are removed, then all the rest of the objections, concerning unnecessary taxations, standing armies, the abolishment of trial by jury, the liberty of the press, the freedom of commerce, the judicial, executive, and legislative authorities of the several states, and the rights of citizens, and the other abuses of federal government, must, of consequence, be rejected, if the principle contains the salutary, purifying, and preserving qualities attributed to it. The question then will be—not what may be done, when the government shall be turned into a tyranny; but how the government can be so turned?

Thus unembarrassed by subordinate discussions, we may come fairly to the contemplation of that superior point, and be better enabled to discover, whether our attention to it will afford any lights, whereby we may be conducted to peace, liberty, and safety.

The objections, denying that the system proposed is sufficiently founded on the power of the people, state, that the number of the federal trustees or officers, is too small, and that they are to hold their offices too long,

One would really have supposed, that smallness of number could not be termed a cause of danger, as influence must increase with enlargement. If this is a fault, it will soon be cor- [8] rected, as an addition will be often made to the number of the senators, and a much greater and more frequently, to that of the representatives; and in all probability much sooner, than we shall be able and willing to bear the expence of the addition.

As to the senate, it never can be, and it never ought to be large, if it is to possess the powers which almost all the objectors seem inclined to allot to it, as will be evident to every intelligent person, who considers those powers.

Though small, let it be remembered, that it is to be created by the sovereignties of the several states; that is, by the persons, whom the people of each state shall judge to be most worthy, and who, surely, will be religiously attentive to making a selection, in which the interest and honour of their state will be so deeply concerned. It should be remembered too, that this is the same manner, in which the members of Congress are now appointed; and that herein, the sovereignties of the states are so intimately involved, that however a renunciation of part of these powers may be desired by some of the states, it *never* will be obtained from the rest of them. Peaceable, fraternal, and benevolent as these are, they think, the concessions they have made, ought to satisfy all.

That the senate may always be kept full, without the interference of Congress, it is provided in the system, that if vacancies happen by resignation or otherwise, during the recess of the legislature of the state, the executive thereof may make temporary appointments, until the [9] next meeting of the legislature, which shall then fill up such vacancies.

As to the house of representatives, it is to consist of a number of persons, not exceeding one for every thirty thousand: But each state shall have at least one representative. The electors will reside, widely dispersed, over an extensive country. Cabal and corruption will be as impracticable, as, on such occasions, human institutions, can render them. The will of freemen, thus circumstanced, will give the fiat. The purity of election thus obtained, will amply compensate for the supposed defect of representation; and the members, thus chosen, will be most apt to harmonize in their proceedings, with the general interests, feelings, and sentiments of the people.

Allowing such an increase of population as, from experience and a variety of causes, may be expected, the representatives, in a short period, will amount to several hundreds, and most probably long before any change of manners for the worse, that might tempt or encourage our ruler to mal-administration, will take place on this continent.

That this house may always be kept full, without the interference of Congress, it is provided in the system, that when vacancies happen in any state, the executive authority thereof shall issue writs of election to fill such vacancies.

But, it seems, the number of the federal officers is not only too small: They are to hold their offices too long.

[10] This objection surely applies not to the house of representatives, who are to be chosen every two years, especially if the extent of empire, and the vast variety and importance of their deliberations, be considered. In that view, they and the senate will actually be not only legislative but also diplomatic bodies, perpetually engaged in the arduous talk of reconciling, in their determinations, the interests of several sovereign states, not to insist on the necessity of a competent knowledge of foreign affairs, relative to the states.

They who desire the representatives to be chosen every year, should exceed Newton in calculations, if they attempt to evince, that the public business would, in that case, be better transacted, than when they are chosen every two years. The idea, however, should be excused for the zeal that prompted it.

Is monarchy or aristocracy to be produced, without the consent of the people, by a house of representatives, thus constituted?

It has been unanimously agreed by the friends of liberty, that *frequent elections of the representatives of the people, are the sovereign remedy of all grievances in a free government.*— Let us pass on to the senate.

At the end of two years after the first election, one third is to be elected for six years; and at the end of four years, another third. Thus one third will constantly have but four years, and another but two years to continue in office. The whole number at first will amount to [11] twenty-six, will be regularly renovated by the biennial election of one third, and will be overlooked, and overawed by the house of representatives, nearly three times more numerous at the beginning, rapidly and vastly augmenting, and more enabled to overlook and overawe them, by holding their offices for two years, as thereby they will acquire better information, respecting national affairs. These representatives will also command the public purse, as all bills for raising revenue, must originate in their house.

As in the Roman armies, when the Principes and Hastati had failed, there were still the Triarii, who generally put things to rights, so we shall be supplied with another resource.

We are to have a president, to superintend, and if he thinks the public weal requires it, to controul any act of the representatives and senate.

This president is to be chosen, not by the people at large, because it may not be possible, that all the freemen of the empire should always have the necessary information, for directing their choice of such an officer; nor by Congress, lest it should disturb the national councils; nor *by any one standing body whatever*, for fear of undue influence.

He is to be chosen in the following manner. Each state shall appoint, as the legislature thereof may direct, a number of electors, equal to the whole number of senators and representatives, to which the state shall be entitled in Congress: but no senator or representative, or person holding an office of trust or profit under the United States, shall be appointed an elector. As these elec- [12] tors are to be appointed, as the legislature of each state may direct, the fairest, freest opening is given, for each state to chuse such electors for this purpose, as shall be most signally qualified to fulfil the trust.

To guard against undue influence these electors, thus chosen, are to meet in their respective states, and vote by ballot; and still further to guard against it, Congress may determine the time of chusing the electors, and the days on which they shall give their votes—*which day shall be the same throughout the United States.* All the votes from the several states are to be transmitted to Congress, and therein counted. The president is to hold his office for four years.

When these electors meet in their respective states, utterly vain will be the unreasonable suggestions derived for partiality. The electors may throw away their votes, mark, with public disappointment, some person improperly favored by them, or justly revering the duties of their office, dedicate their votes to the best interests of their country.

This president will be no dictator. Two thirds of the representatives and the senate may pass any law, notwithstanding his dissent; and he is removable and punishable for misbehaviour.

Can this limited, fluctuating senate, placed amidst such powers, if it should become willing, ever become able, to make America pass under its yoke? The senators will generally be inhabitants of places very distant one from another. They can scarcely be acquainted till [13] they meet. Few of them can ever act together for any length of time, unless their good conduct recommends them to a re-election; and then there will be frequent changes in a body dependant upon the acts of other bodies, the legislatures of the several states, that are altering every year. Machiavel and Cæsar Borgia together could not form a conspiracy in such a senate, destructive to any but themselves and their accomplices.

It is essential to every good government, that there should be some council, permanent enough to get a due knowledge of affairs internal and external; so constituted, that by some deaths or removals, the current of information should not be impeded or disturbed; and so regulated, as to be responsible to, and controulable by the people. Where can the authority for combining these advantages, be more safely, beneficially, or satisfactorily lodged. than in the senate, to be formed according to the plan proposed? Shall parts of the trust be committed to the president, with counsellors who shall subscribe their advices?* If assaults upon liberty are to be guarded against, and surely they ought to be with sleepless vigilance, why should we depend more on the commander in chief of the army and navy of The United States, and of the militia of the several states, and on his counsellors, whom he may secretly influence, than of the senate to be appointed by the persons exercising the sovereign authority of the several states? In truth, the [14] objections against the powers of the senate originated from a desire to have them, or at least some of them, vested in a body, in which the several states should be represented, in proportion to the number of inhabitants, as in the house of representatives. This method is *unattainable*, and the wish for it should be dismissed from every mind, that desires the existence of a confederation.

What assurance can be given, or what probability be assigned, that a board of counsellors would continue honest, longer than the senate? Or, that they would possess more useful information, respecting all the states, than the senators of all the states? It appears needless to pursue this argument any further.

How varied, balanced, concordant, and benign, is the system proposed to us? To secure the freedom, and promote the happiness of these and future states, by giving *the will of the people* a decisive influence over the whole, and over all the

* See late publications.

parts, with what a comprehensive arrangement does it embrace different modes of representation, from an election by a county to an election by an empire? What are the complicated ballot, and all the refined devices of Venice for maintaining her aristocracy, when compared with this plain-dealing work for diffusing the blessings of equal liberty and common prosperity over myriads of the human race?

All the foundations before mentioned, of the federal government, are by the proposed system to be established, in the most clear, strong, [15] positive, unequivocal expressions, of which our language is capable. Magna charta, or any other law, never contained clauses more decisive and emphatic. While the people of these states have sense, they will understand them; and while they have spirit, they will make them to be observed.

FABIUS.

[16] LETTER III.

The writer of this address hopes, that he will now be thought so disengaged from the objections against the principle assumed, that he may be excused for recurring to his assertion, that—the power of the people pervading the proposed system, together with the strong confederation of the states, will form an adequate security against every danger that has been apprehended.

It is a mournful, but may be a useful truth, that the liberty of single republics has generally been destroyed by some of the citizens, and of confederated republics, by some of the associated states.

It is more pleasing, and may be more profitable to reflect, that, their tranquility and prosperity have commonly been promoted, in proportion to the strength of their government for protecting the worthy against the licentious.

As in forming a political society, each individual contributes some of his rights, in order that he may, from *a common stock* of rights, derive greater benefits, than he could from merely *his own;* so, in forming a confederation, each political society should contribute such a share of their rights, as will, from *a common stock* of these rights, produce the largest quantity of benefits for them.

But, what is that share? and, how to be managed? Momentous questions! Here, flattery is treason; and error, destruction.

[17] Are they unanswerable? No. Our most gracious *Creator* does not condemn us to sigh for unattainable blessedness: But one thing he demands—that we should seek for happiness in his way, and not in our own.

Humility and benevolence must take place of pride and overweening selfishness. Reason, rising above these mists, will then discover to us, that we cannot be true to ourselves, without being true to others—that to love our neighbours as ourselves, is to love ourselves in the best manner—that to give, is to gain—and, that we never consult our own happiness more effectually, than when we most endeavour to correspond with *the divine designs*, by communicating happiness, as much as we can, to our fellow-creatures. *Inestimable truth!* sufficient, if they do not barely ask what it is, to melt tyrants into men, and to soothe the inflamed minds of a multitude into mildness—*Inestimable truth!* which our Maker in his providence, enables us, not only to talk and write about, but to adopt in practice of vast extent, and of instructive example.

Let us now enquire, if there be not some *principle*, simple as the laws of nature in other instances, from which, as from a *source*, the many benefits of society are deduced.

We may with reverence say, that our *Creator* designed men for society, because otherwise they cannot be happy. They cannot be happy without freedom; nor free without security; that is, without the absence of fear; nor thus secure, without society. The con- [18] clusion is strictly syllogistic—that men cannot be free without society. Of course, they cannot be equally free without society, *which freedom produces the greatest happiness.*

As these premises are invincible, we have advanced a considerable way in our enquiry upon *this deeply interesting sub-*

*ject.* If we can determine, what share of his rights, every individual must contribute to *the eommon stock* of rights in forming a society, for obtaining equal freedom, we determine at the same time, what share of their rights each political society must contribute to *the common stock* or rights in forming a confederation, which is only a larger society, for obtaining equal freedom: For, if the deposite be not proportioned to the magnitude of the association in the latter case, it will generate the same mischief among the component parts of it, from·their inequality, that would result from a defective contribution to association in the former case, among the component parts of it, from their inequality.

Each individual then must contribute such a share of his rights, as is necessary for attaining that *security* that is essential to freedom; and he is bound to make this contribution by the law of his nature, which prompts him to a participated happiness; that is, by the command of his creator; therefore, he must submit his will, *in what concerns all*, to the will of all, that is of the whole society. What does he lose by this submission; The power of doing [19] injuries to others—and the dread of suffering injuries from them. What does he gain by it? The aid of those associated with him, for his relief from the incommodities of mental or bodily weakness—the pleasure for which his heart is formed—of doing good—*protection* against injuries—a capacity of enjoying his undelegated rights to the best advantage—a repeal of his fears—and tranquility of mind—or, in other words, that perfect liberty better described in the Holy Scriptures, than any where else, in these expressions—" When every man shall sit under his vine, and under his fig-tree, and *none shall make him afraid.*"

The like submission, with a correspondent expansion and accommodation, must be made between states, for obtaining the like benefits in a confederation. *Men* are the materials of both. As the largest number is but a junction of *units*—a confederation is but an assemblage of individuals. The auspicious influence of the law of his nature, upon which the happiness of *man* depends in society, must attend him in confederation, or he becomes unhappy; for confederation should promote the happiness of individuals, or it does not *answer the intended purpose*. Herein there is a progression, not a contradiction. As *man*, he becomes a citizen ; as a citizen, he becomes a federalist. The generation of one, is not the destruction of the other. He carries into society his naked rights : These thereby improved, he carries still forward into confederation. If that sacred law before mentioned, is not here [20] observed, the confederation would not be real, but pretended. He would confide, and be deceived.*

* " The error of those who reason by precedent, drawn from antiquity, respecting the rights of man, is, that they do not go far enough into antiquity. They do not go the whole way. They stop in some of the intermediate stages of an hundred or a thousand years, and produce what was then done, as a rule for the present day. This is no authority at all. If we travel still further into antiquity, we shall find a direct contrary opinion and practice prevailing ; and if antiquity is to be authority, a thousand such authorities may be produced, successively contradicting each other : but if we proceed on, at last we shall come out right : We shall then come to the time when man came from the hand of his Maker. What was he then ? *Man*. Man was his high and only title, and a higher cannot be given him——We are now got at the origin of man, and at the origin of his rights.——Every history of the creation, and every traditionary account, whether from the lettered or unlettered world, however they may vary in their opinion or belief of certain particulars, all agree in establishing one point, the *unity* of man ; by which I mean that man is all of one degree, and consequently that all men are born equal, and with equal natural rights. By considering man in this light, it places him in a close connection with all his duties, whether to his *Creator*, or to the creation, of which he is a part ; and it is only where he forgets his *origin*, or, to use a more fashionable phrase, his birth and family, that he becomes dissolute.

" Hitherto we have spoken only (and that but in part) of the natural rights of man. We have now to consider the civil rights of man, and to shew how the one *originates* out of the other.—Man did not enter into society, to become worse than he was before, nor to have less rights than he had before, but to have those rights *better secured*. His natural rights are the foundation of all his civil rights. But in order to pursue this distinction with more precision, it will be necessary to mark the different qualities of natural and civil rights.

" A few words will explain this. Natural rights are those which appertain to man in the right of his existence—civil rights are those which appertain to man in right of his being a member of society. Every civil right has for its foundation some natural right pre-existing in the individual, but to unite his individual power is not, in all cases, sufficiently competent. Of this kind are all those which relate to *security* and *protection*.

" From this short review it will be easy to distinguish between that class of natural rights which man retains after entering into society, and those which

[21] The dilemma is inevitable. There must either be one will, or several wills. If but one will, all the people are concerned: if several wills, few comparatively are concerned. Surprizing! that this doctrine should be contended for by those, who declare, that the constitution is not founded on a bottom broad enough; and, though *the whole people* of the United States are to be *trebly* represented in it in *three different modes* of representation, and their servants will have the most advantageous situations and opportunities of acquiring all requisite information for the welfare of the [22] whole union, yet insist for a privilege of opposing, obstructing, and confounding all their measures taken with common consent for the general weal, by the delays, negligences, rivalries, or other selfish views of parts of the union.

Thus, while one state should be relied upon by the union for giving aid, upon a recommendation of Congress, to another in distress, the latter might be ruined; and the state relied upon, might suppose, it would gain by such an event.

When any persons speak of a consideration, do they, or do they not acknowledge, that the whole is interested in the safety of every part—in the agreement of parts—in the relation of parts [23] to one another—to the whole—or, to other societies? If they do—then, the authority of the whole, must be co-extensive with its interests—and if it is, the will of the whole must and ought in such cases to govern; or else the whole would have interests without an authority to manage them—a position which prejudice itself cannot digest.

If they do not acknowledge, that the whole is thus interested, the conversation should cease. Such persons mean not a confederation, but something else.

---

he throws into *common stock* as a member of society. The natural rights which he retains, are all those in which the power to execute is as perfect in the individual as the right itself.—The natural rights which are not retained, are all those in which, though the right is perfect in the individual, the power to execute them is defective: *they answer not his purpose*—those he *deposits* in the *common stock* of society, and takes the arm of society, of which he is a part, in preference and in addition to his own. Society grants him nothing. Every man is a proprietor in society, and draws on the capital as a matter of right."— "*Rights of Man*," 1791, page 30, 31.

As to the idea, that this superintending sovereign will must of consequence destroy the subordinate sovereignties of the several states, it is begging a concession of the question, by inferring, that a manifest and great usefulness must necessarily end in abuse; and not only so, but it requires an extinction of the principle of all society: for the subordinate sovereignties, or, in other words, the undelegated rights of the several states, in a confederation, stand upon the very same foundation with the undelegated rights of individuals in a society, the federal sovereign will being composed of the subordinate sovereign wills of the several confederated states. As some persons seem to think, a bill of rights is the best security of rights, the sovereignties of the several states have this best security by the proposed constitution, and more than this best security, for they are not barely declared to be rights, but are taken into it as component parts for their perpetual preservation—by themselves. In short, the government of each state is, and is to be, [24] sovereign and supreme in all matters that relate to each state only. It is to be subordinate barely in those matters that relate to the whole; and it will be their *own faults* if the several states suffer the federal sovereignty to interfere in things of their respective jurisdictions. An instance of such interference with regard to any single state, will be a dangerous precedent as to all, and therefore will be guarded against by all, as the trustees or servants of the several states will not dare, if they retain their senses, so to violate the independent sovereignty of their respective states, *that justly darling object* of American affections, to which they are responsible, besides being endeared by all the charities of life.

The common sense of mankind agrees to the devolutions of individual wills in society; and if it has not been as universally assented to in confederation, the reasons are evident, and worthy of being retained in remembrance by Americans. They were want of opportunities, or the loss of them, through defects of knowledge and virtue. The principle, however, has been sufficiently vindicated in imperfect combinations, as their prosperity has generally been commensurate to its operation.

How beautifully and forcibly does the inspired Apostle Paul, argue upon a sublimer subject, with a train of reasoning strictly applicable to the present? His words are—"If the foot shall say, because I am not the hand, I am not of the body; is it therefore not of the body? and if the ear shall say, because I am [25] not the eye, I am not of the body; is it therefore not of the body?" As plainly inferring, as could be done in that allegorical manner, the strongest censure of such partial discontents and dissentions, especially, as his meaning is enforced by his description of the benefits of union in these expressions—"But, now they are many members, yet but one body: and the eye *cannot* say to the hand, I have no need of thee."

When the commons of Rome upon a rupture with the Senate, seceded in arms at the Mons sacer, Menemius Agrippa used the like allusion to the human body, in his famous apologue of a quarrel among some of the members. The unpolished but honest-hearted Romans of that day, understood him, and were appeased.

Another comparison has been made by the learned, between a natural and a political body; and no wonder indeed, when the title of the latter was borrowed from the resemblance. It has therefore been justly observed, that if a mortification takes place in one or some of the limbs, and the rest of the body is sound, remedies may be applied, and not only the contagion prevented from spreading, but the diseased part or parts saved by the connection with the body, and restored to former usefulness. When general putrefaction prevails, death is to be expected. History sacred and profane tells us, that, *corruption of manners sinks nations into slavery.*

FABIUS.

## LETTER IV.

[26]

Another question remains. How are the contributed rights to be managed? The resolution has been in great measure anticipated, by what has been said concerning the system proposed. Some few reflections may perhaps finish it.

If it be considered separately, a *constitution* is the *organization* of the contributed rights in society. *Government* is the *exercise* of them. It is intended for the benefit of the governed; of course can have no just powers but what conduce to that end: and the awfulness of the trust is demonstrated in this—that it is founded on the nature of man, that is, on the will of his *Maker*, and is therefore sacred. It is then an offence against Heaven, to violate that trust.*

[27] If the organization of a constitution be defective, it may be amended,

A good constitution promotes, but not always produces a good administration.

---

* "We have now traced Man from a natural individual to a member of society——Civil power, properly considered as such is made up of the *aggregate* of that class of the natural rights, which become defective in the individual in point of power, and *answers not his purpose;* but when collected into a focus, becomes competent to the purpose of every one.——Let us now apply those principles to government,——

"Individuals themselves, each in his own personal and sovereign right, entered into a compact with each other, to produce a government; and this is the only mode in which governments have a right to arise, and the only principle on which they have a right to exist.

"A *constitution* is not a thing in name only, but in fact.—It has not an ideal but a real existence, and wherever it cannot be produced in a visible form, there is none. A *constitution* is a thing antecedent to a *government;* and a government is only the creature of a constitution.—A constitution of a country is not the act of its government, but of the people constituting a government. It is the body of elements to which you can refer, and quote article by article; and which contains the principles on which the government shall be established, the manner in which it shall be organized, the powers it shall have, the mode of election, the duration of parliaments, or by what other name such bodies may be called, the powers which the executive part of the government shall have; and, in fine, every thing that relates to the complete *organization* of a civil government, and the principles on which it shall act, and by which it shall be bound."—"*Rights of Man,*" page 35, 36.

The government must never be lodged in a single body. From such an one, with an unlucky composition of its parts, rash, partial, illegal, and when intoxicated with success, even cruel, insolent and contemptible edits, may at times be expected. By these, if other mischiefs do not follow, the national dignity may be impaired.

[28] Several inconveniences might attend a division of the government into two bodies, that probably would be avoided in another arrangement.

The judgment of the most enlightened among mankind, confirmed by multiplied experiments, points out the propriety of government being committed to such a number of great departments, as can be introduced without confusion, distinct in office, and yet connected in operation. It seems to be agreed, that three or four of these departments are a competent number.

[29] Such a repartition appears well calculated to express the sense of the people, and to encrease the safety and repose of the governed, which with the advancement of their happiness in other respects, are the objects of government; as thereby there will be more obstructions interposed; against errors, feuds, and frauds, in the administration, and the extraordinary interference of the people need be less frequent. Thus, wars, tumults, and uneasinesses, are avoided. The departments so constituted, may therefore be said to be balanced.

But, notwithstanding, it must be granted, that a bad admin-

---

"What is a constitution? it is the form of government, delineated by the mighty hand of the people, in which certain first principles or fundamental laws are established. The constitution is certain and fixed; it contains the permanent will of the people, and is the supreme law of the land; it is paramount to the power of the legislature, and can be revoked or altered only by the authority that made it.—What are legislatures? creatures of the constitution, they owe their existence to the constitution—they derive their powers from the constitution.—It is their commission, and therefore all their acts must be conformable to it, or else void. The *constitution* is the work or will of the *people themselves*, in their original, sovereign, and unlimited capacity. Law is the work or will of the legislature in their derivative capacity."

Judge Patterson's charge to the Jury in the Wioming case of Vanhorne's lessee against Dorrance; tried at the circuit-court for the United States, held at Philadelphia, April term, 1795.

istration may take place.—What is then to be done? The answer is instantly found—Let the Fasces be lowered before —the supreme sovereignty of the people. *It is their duty to watch, and their right to take care, that the constitution be preserved;* or in the Roman phrase on perilous occasions—*to provide, that the republic receive no damage.*

Political bodies are properly said to be balanced, with respect to this *primary origination* and *ultimate destination*, not to any intrinsic or constitutional properties.* It [30] is the *power* from which they *proceed*, and which they *serve*, that *truly and of right balances* them.†

But, as a good constitution not always produces a good administration, a defective one not always excludes it. Thus in governments very different from those of United America, general manners and customs, improvement in knowledge, and the education and disposition of princes, not unfrequently soften the features, [31] and qualify the defects. Jewels of value are substituted, in the place of the rare and genuine orient of higest price and brightest lustre: and though the sovereigns cannot even in their ministers, be brought to account by the governed, yet there are instances of their conduct indicating a veneration for the rights of the

---

* Constitutional properties are only, as has been observed at the beginning of this letter, parts in the organization of the contributed rights. As long as those parts preserve the orders assigned to them respectively by the constitution, they may so far be said to be balanced: but, when one part, without being sufficiently checked by the rest, abuses its power to the manifest danger of public happiness, or when the several parts abuse their respective powers so as to involve the commonwealth in the like peril, *the people* must restore things to that order, from which their functionaries have departed. If *the people* suffer this living principle of watchfulness and controul to be extinguished among them, they will assuredly not long afterwards experience that of their "temple," "there shall not be left one stone upon another, that shall not be thrown down."

† When the *controuling power* is in a constitution, it has the *nation* for its support, and the *natural* and the political controuling powers are together. The laws which are enacted by the governments, controul men only as individuals, but the *nation*, thro' its constitution controuls *the whole government*, and has a *natural ability* to do so. The *final controuling* power, therefore, and the *original constituting* power, *are one and the same power.*—"*Rights of Man,*" 1792, part 2d, b. 4, page 42.

people, and an internal conviction of the guilt that attends their violation. Some of them appear to be fathers of their countries. Revered princes! Friends of mankind! May peace be in their lives—and in their deaths—Hope.

By this superior will of the people, is meant a reasonable, not a distracted will. When frenzy seizes the mass, it would be equal madness to think of their happiness, that is, of their freedom. They will infallibly have a Philip or a Cæsar, to bleed them into soberness of mind. At present we are cool; and let us attend to our business.

Our goverment under the proposed confederation, will be guarded by a repetition of the strongest cautions against excesses. In the senate the sovereignties of the several states will be equally represented; in the house of representatives, the people of the whole union will be equally represented; and, in the president, and the federal independent judges, so much concerned in the execution of the laws, and in the determination of their constitutionality, the sovereignties of the several states and the people of the whole union, may be considered as conjointly represented.

[32] Where was there ever and where is there now upon the face of the earth, a government so diversified and attempered? If a work formed with so much deliberation, so respectful and affectionate an attention to the interests, feelings, and sentiments of all United America, will not satisfy, what would satisfy all United America?

It seems highly probable, that those who would reject this labour of public love, would also have rejected the Heaven-taught institution of *trial by jury*, had they been consulted upon its establishment. Would they not have cried out, that there never was framed so detestable, so paltry, and so tyrannical a device for extinguishing freedom, and throwing unbounded domination into the hands of the king and barons, under a contemptible pretence of preserving it? "What! Can freedom be preserved by imprisoning its guardians? Can freedom be preserved, by keeping twelve men closely confined without meat, drink, fire, or candle, until they unanimously agree, and this to be innumerably repeated? Can freedom be preserved, by thus delivering up a number of freemen to a monarch and an aristocracy, fortified by dependant and obedient judges and officers, to be shut up, until under duress they speak as they are ordered? Why cannot the twelve jurors separate,* after hearing the evidence, return to their respective homes, and there take time,* and think of the matter at their ease?* Is there not a variety of [33] ways, in which causes have been, and can be tried, without this *tremendous, unprecedented inquisition?* Why then is it insisted on; but because the fabricators of it know that it will, and intend that it shall reduce the people to slavery? Away with it—Freemen will never be enthralled by so insolent, so execrable, so pitiful a contrivance."

Happily for us our ancestors thought otherwise. They were not so over-nice and curious, as to refuse blessings, because, they might possibly be abused.

They perceived, that the uses included were great and manifest. Perhaps they did not foresee, that from this acorn, as it were, of their planting, would be produced a perpetual vegetation of political energies, that "would secure the just liberties of the nation for a long succession of ages,* and elevate it to the distinguished rank it has for several centuries held. As to abuses, they trusted to their own spirit for preventing or correcting them: And worthy is it of deep consideration by every friend of freedom, that abuses that seem to be but "trifles,"† may be attended by fatal consequences. What can be "trifling," that diminishes or detracts from the only defence, that ever was found against "open attacks and secret machinations?"‡ This establishment originates from a knowledge of human nature. With a superior force, wisdom, and benevolence uni- [34] ted, it rives the difficulties concerning administration of justice, that have distressed, or destroyed the rest of mankind. It reconciles contradictions—vastness of power, with safety of private station. It is ever new, and always the same.

* See late publications against the Federal Constitution.

* Blackstone, III. 279 † Idem, IV. 350. ‡ Idem, III. 381.

Trial by jury and the dependence of taxation upon representation, those corner stones of liberty, were not obtained by a bill of rights, or any other records, and have not been and cannot be preserved by them. They and all other rights must be preserved, by *soundness of sense and honesty of heart*. Compared with these, what are a bill of rights, or any characters drawn upon paper or parchment, those frail remembrances? Do we want to be reminded, that the sun enlightens, warms, invigorates, and cheers? or how horrid it would be, to have his blessed beams intercepted, by our being thrust into mines or dungeons? Liberty is the sun of society. Rights are the beams.*

[35] "It is the duty which every man owes to his country, his friends, his posterity, and himself, to maintain to the utmost of his power this valuable palladium in all its rights; to restore to its its ancient dignity, if at all impaired by the different value of property, or otherwise deviated from its first institution; to amend it, wherever it is defective;* and above all to guard with the most jealous circumspection against the new and arbitrary methods of trial, which, under a variety of plausible pretences, may in time imperceptibly undermine this best preservative of liberty."† Trial by Jury is our birth-right; and tempted to his own ruin, by some seducing spirit, must be the man, who in opposition to the genius of United America, shall dare to attempt its subversion.

In the proposed confederation, it is preserved inviolable in criminal cases, and cannot be altered in other respects, but when United America demands it.

There seems to be a disposition in men to find fault, no dif-

---

* Instead of referring to musty records and mouldy parchments to prove that the rights of the living are lost, "renounced, and abdicated for ever," by those who are now no more.——M. de la Fayette, in his address to the national assembly, applies to the living world, and says—" Call to mind the sentiments which nature has engraved in the heart of every citizen, and which take a new face when they are solemnly recognized by all. For a nation to love liberty, it is sufficient that she knows it; and to be free, it is sufficient that she wills it,"—"*Rights of Man*," page 11.

* See an enumeration of defects in trials by jury. Blackstone, III. 381.
† Idem, IV. 350.

ficult matter, rather than to act as they ought. The works of creation itself have been objected to: and one learned prince declared, that if he had been consulted, they would have been improved. With what book has so much fault been found, as with the Bible? Perhaps, principally, because it so clearly and strongly enjoins men *to do right*. How many, how plausible objections have been [36] made against it, with how much ardor, with how much pains? Yet, the book has done more good than all the books in the world; would do much more, if duly regarded; and might lead the objectors against it to happiness, if they would value it as they should.

When objections are made to a system of high import, should they not be weighed against the benefits? Are these great, positive, immediate? Is there a chance of endangering them by rejection or delay? *May they not be attained without admitting the objections at present,* supposing the objections to be well founded? If the objections are well founded, may they not be hereafter admitted, without danger, disgust, or inconvenience? Is the system so formed, that they may be thus admitted? May they not be of less efficiency, than they are thought to be by their authors? are they not designed to hinder evils, which are generally deemed to be sufficiently provided against? May not the admission of them prevent benefits, that might otherwise be obtained? In political affairs, is it not more safe and advantageous, for all to agree in measures that may not be best, than to quarrel among themselves, what are best?

When questions of this kind with regard to the plan proposed, are calmly considered, it seems reasonable to hope, that every faithful citizen of United America, will make up his mind, with much satisfaction to himself, and advantage to his country.

FABIUS.

## LETTER V.

[37] It has been considered, what are the rights to be contributed, and how they are to be managed; and it has been said, that republican tranquility and prosperity have commonly been promoted, in proportion to the strength of governnment for protecting the worthy against the licentious.

The protection herein mentioned, refers to cases between citizens and citizens, or states and states: But there is also a protection to be afforded to all the citizens, or states, against foreigners. It has been asserted, that this protection never can be afforded, but under an appropriation, collection, and application, of the general force, by the will of the whole combination. This protection is in a degree dependent on the former, as it may be weakened by internal discords and especially where the worst party prevails. Hence it is evident, that such establishments as tend most to protect the worthy against the licentious, tends most to protect all against foreigners. This position is found to be verified by indisputable facts, from which it appears, that when nations have been, as it were, condemned for their crimes, unless they first became suicides, foreigners have acted as executioners.

This is not all. As government is intended for the happiness of the people, the protection of the worthy against those of contrary characters, is calculated to promote the end of legitimate government, that is the general welfare; [38] for *the government will partake of the qualities of those whose authority is prevalent.* If it be asked, who are the worthy, we may be informed by a heathen poet—

"Vir bonus est quis?
"Qui consulta patrum, qui leges juraque servat."*

The best foundations of this protection, that can be laid by man, are a constitution and government secured, as well as can be, from the undue influence of passions either in the people or their servants. Then in a contest between citizens and citizens, or states and states, the standard of laws may be displayed, explained and strengthened by the well-remembered

* He who reverses the constitution, liberties and laws of his country.—

sentiments and examples of our fore-fathers, which will give it a sanctity far superior to that of their eagles so venerated by the former masters of the world. This circumstance will carry powerful aids to the true friends of their country, and unless counteracted by the follies of Pharsalia, or the accidents of Philippi, may secure the blessings of freedom to succeeding ages.

It has been contended that the plan proposed to us, adequately secures us against the influence of passions in the federal servants. Whether it as adequately secures us against the influence of passions in the people, or in particular states, time will determine, and *may the determination be propituous.*

[39] Let us now consider the tragical play of the passions in similar cases; or, in other words, the consequences of their irregularities. Duly governed, they produce happiness.

Here the reader, is respectfully requested, to assist the intentions of the writer, by keeping in mind, the ideas of a single republic with one democratic branch in its government, and of a confederation of republics with one or several democratic branches in the government of the confederation, or in the government of its parts, so that as he proceeds, a comparison may easily run along, between any of these and the proposed plan.

History is entertaining and instructive; but if admired chiefly for amusement, it may yield little profit. If read for improvement, it is apprehended, a slight attention only will be paid to the vast variety of particular incidents, unless they be such as may meliorate the heart. A knowledge of the distinguishing features of nations, the principles of their governments, the advantages and disadvantages of their situations, the methods employed to avail themselves of the first, and to alleviate the last, their manners, customs, and institutions, the sources of events, their progresses, and determining causes, may be eminently useful, tho' obscurity may rest upon a multitude of attending circumstances. Thus one nation may become prudent and happy, not only by the wisdom and success, but even by the errors and misfortunes of another.

[40] In Carthage and Rome, there was a very numerous

senate, strengthened by prodigious attachments, and in a great degree independent of the people. In Athens, there was a senate strongly supported by the powerful court of Arcopagus. In each of these republics, their affairs at length became convulsed, and their liberty was subverted. What cause produced these effects? Encroachments of the senate upon the authority of the people? No! but directly the reverse, according so the unanimous voice of historians; that is, encroachments of the people upon the authority of the senate. The people of these republics absolutely *laboured* for their own destruction; and never thought themselves so free, as when they were promoting their own subjugation. Though even after these encroachments had been made, and ruin was spreading around, yet the remnants of senatorial authority delayed the final catastrophe.*

[41] In more modern times, the Florentines exhibited a memorable example. They were divided into violent parties; and the prevailing one vested exorbitant powers in the house of Medici, then possessed, as it was judged, of more money than any crowned head in Europe. Though that house engaged and persevered in the attempt, yet the people were never despoiled of their liberty, until they were overwhelmed by the armies of foreign princes, to whose enterprizes their situation exposed them.

Republics of later date and various form have appeared. Their institutions consist of old errors tissued with hasty inventions, somewhat excusable, as the wills of the Romans, made with arms in their hands. Some of them were condensed†, by dangers. They are still compressed by them into

---

* The great Bacon, in enumerating the art by which Cæsar enslaved his country, says—"His first artifice was to break the strength of the *senate*, for while that remained safe, there was no opening for any person to immoderate or extraordinary power.——'*Nam initio sibi erani frangendæ senatus opes et autoritas qua salva nemini ad, immodica et extra ordinaria imperia aditus erat.*' Bossuet, bishop of Meaux, takes notice in his universal history, that the infamous Herod, to engross authority, attacked the Sanhedrim, which was in a manner the senate, where the supreme jurisdiction was exercised."

† "If we consider what the principles are that first condense man into society, and what the motive is that regulates their mutual intercourse afterwards, we shall find, by the time we arrive at what is called government, that nearly the whole of the business is performed by the natural operation of the parts upon each other."—*Rights of Man.*

a sort of union. Their well-known transactions witness, that their connection is not enough compact and arranged. They have all suffered, or are suffering through that defect. Their existence seems to depend more upon others, than upon themselves. There might be an impropriety in saying more, considering the peculiarity of their circumstances at this time.

[42] The wretched mistake of the great men who were leaders in the long parliament of England, in attempting, by not filling up vacancies, to extend their power over a brave and sensible people, accustomed to *popular representation*, and their downfal, when their victories and puissance by sea and land had thrown all Europe into astonishment and awe, shew, how difficult it is for rulers to usurp over a people who are not wanting to themselves.

Let the fortunes of confederated republics be now considered.

"The Amphictionic council," or "general court of Greece," claims the first regard. Its authority was very great: But, the parts were not sufficiently combined, to guard against the ambitious, avaricious, and selfish projects of some of them; or, if they had the power, they dared not to employ it, as the turbulent states were very sturdy, and made a sort of partial confederacies.*

[43] "The Achæan league" seems to be the next in dignity. It was at first, small, consisting of few states: afterwards, very

---

* When Xerxes invaded Greece with the largest host and the greatest fleet that ever were collected, events occurred, which being preserved in history, convey to us a very affecting and instructive information.

While the danger was at some distance, the states of Greece looked to remote friends for assistance. Disappointed in these speculations, tho' the vast armaments of their enemies were constantly rolling towards them, still there was no firmness in their union, no vigor in their resolutions.

The Persian army passed the Hellespont, and directed its march westward. It was then decided, that Thessaly was the frontier to be first attacked.

The Thessalians, than whom no people had been more forward in the common cause, hastened a remonstrance to Corinth, urging that unless they were immediately and powerfully supported, necessity would oblige them to make terms with the invaders.

This reasonable remonstrance roused the sluggish and hesitating councils extensive, constituting of many. In their diet or Congress, they enacted laws, disposed of vacant employments, declared war, made peace, entered into alliances, compelled every state of the union to [44] obey its ordinances, and managed other affairs. Not only their laws, but their magistrates, council, judges, money, weights and measures, were the same. So uniform were they, that all seemed to be but one state. Their chief officer called Strategos, was chosen in the Congress by a majority of votes. He presided in [45] the Congress, commanded the forces, and was vested with great powers, especially in time of war: but was liable to be called to an account by the Congress, and punished, if convicted of misbehaviour.

The states have been oppressed by the kings of Macedon, and insulted by tyrants. "From their incorporation," says Polybius, "may be dated the birth of that greatness, that by a constant augmentation, at length arrived to a marvellous height of prosperity. The same of their wise laws and mild government reached the Greek colonies in Italy, where the Grotoniates, the Sybarites, and the Cauloniates, agreed to adopt them, and to govern their states conformably."

Did the delegates to the Amphictionic council, or to the Congress of the Achæan league destroy the liberty of their country, by establishing a monarchy or an aristocracy among themselves? Quite the contrary. *While the several states con-*

---

of the confederacy. A body of foot was dispatched who soon occupied the valley of Tempe, the only pass from Lower Macedonia, into Thessaly.

In a few days, these troops being informed that there was another pass from Upper Macedonia, returned to the Corinthian Isthmus.

The Thessalians thus deserted made their submission.

"This retreat from Tempe appears to have been a precipate measure, rendered necessary by nothing so much as by *the want of some powers* of government extending over the several states which composed the confederacy."—Mitford's *History of Greece.*

With diminished forces, the defence of the confederates was now to be contracted. But in the conduct even of this business daily becoming more urgent, we find them laboring under the defects of their confederation.

"Destitute of any sufficient power extending over the whole, no part could confide in the protection of the whole, while the naval superiority of their enemy put it in his choice, where, when, and how to make his attacks ; and therefore *tinued faithful to the union, they prospered.* Their affairs were shattered by dissensions, emulations, and civil wars, artfully and diligently fomented by princes who thought it their interest; and in the case of the Achæan league, partly, by the folly and wickedness of Greeks not of the league, particularly the Ætolians, who repined at the glories, that constantly attended the banner of freedom, supported by virtue and conducted by prudence. Thus weakened, they all sunk together, the envied and the envying, under the domination, first of Macedon, and then of Rome.

[46] Let any man of common sense peruse the gloomy but instructive pages of their mournful story, and he will be convinced, that if any nation could successfuly have resisted those conquerors of the world, the illustrious deed had been achieved by Greece; that cradle of republics, if the several states had been cemented by some such league as the Achæan, and had honestly fulfilled its obligations.

It is not pretended, that the Achæan league was perfect, or that they were not monarchical and aristocratical factions among the people of it. Every concession of that sort, that can be asked, shall be made. It had many defects; every one of which, however, has been avoided in the plan proposed to us.

With all its defects, with all its disorders, yet such was the life and vigor communicated through the whole, by the popular representation of each part, and the close combination of

---

each republic seems to have been anxious to reserve its own strength for future contingencies.

Their generous hearts all beat at the call of freedom; but their efforts were embarrassed and enfeebled by the vices of their political constitution, to their prodigious detriment, and almost to their total destruction. For these vices, the ardor of heroism united with love of country could not compensate. These very vices therefore, may truly be said to have wasted the blood of patriots, and to have betrayed their country into the severest calamities.

If *we* shall hereafter by experience discover any vices in our constitution, let us *hasten* with prudence and a fraternal affection for each other, to correct them. We are all embarked in the same vessel, and equally concerned in repairing any defects.

all, that the true spirit of republicanism *predominated*, and thereby advanced the happiness and glory of the people to so pre-eminent a state that *our* ideas upon the pleasing theme cannot be too elevated. Here is the proof of this assertion. When the Romans had laid Carthage in ashes; had reduced the kingdom of Macedon to a province; had conquered Antiochus the great, and got the better of all their enemies in the East; these Romans, masters of so much of the then known world, determined to humble the Achæan league, because as history expressly informs us, "their great power began to raise no small jealousy at Rome."—Polybius.

[47] What a vast weight of argument do these facts and circumstances add to the maintenance of the principle contended for by the writer of this address?

FABIUS.

[48] LETTER VI.

Some of our fellow-citizens have ventured to predict the future state of United America, if the system proposed to us, shall be adopted.

Though every branch of the constitution and government is to be popular, and guarded by the strongest provisions, that until this day have occurred to mankind, yet the system will end, they say, in the oppressions of a monarchy or aristocracy by the federal servants or some of them.

Such a conclusion seems not in any manner suited to the premises. It startles, yet, not so much from its novelty, as from the respectability of the characters by which it is drawn.

We must not be too much influenced by our esteem for those characters: But, should recollect, that when the fancy is warmed, and the judgment inclined, by the proximity or pressure of particular objects, very extraordinary declarations are not unfrequently made. Such are the frailties of our nature, that genius and integrity sometimes afford no protection against them.

Probably, there never was, and never will be, such an instance of dreadful denunciation, concerning the fate of a country, as was published while the union was in agitation between England and Scotland. The English were for a joint legislature, many of the Scots for separate legislatures, and urged, that they should be in [49] a manner swallowed up and lost in the other, as then they would not possess one eleventh part in it.

Upon that occasion lord Belhaven, one of the most distinguished orators of the age, made in the Scottish parliament a famous speech, of which the following extract is part:

"My lord Chancellor,

"When I consider this affair of an union between the two nations, as it is expressed in the several articles thereof, and now the subject of our deliberation at this time, I find my mind crowded with a variety of very melancholy thoughts, and I think it my duty to disburthen myself of some of them, by laying them before and exposing them to the serious consideration of this honourable house.

"I think, *I see a free and independent kingdom* delivering up that, which all the world hath been fighting for since the days of Nimrod; yea, that, for which most of all the empires, kingdoms, states, principalities, and dukedoms of Europe, are at this very time engaged in the most bloody and cruel wars that ever were; to wit, *a power to manage their own affairs by themselves, without the assistance aud council of any other.*

"I think I see *a National Church,* founded upon a rock, secured by a claim of right, hedged and fenced about by the strictest and pointedest legal sanctions that sovereignty could contrive, voluntarily descending into a plain upon an equal level with Jews, Paptists, Soci- [50] nians, Armenians, and Anabaptists, and other Sectaries, &c.

"I think I see *the noble and honorable peerage of Scotland,* whose valiant predecessors led against their enemies upon their own proper charges and expences, now divested of their followers and vassalages, and put upon such an equal foot with their vassals, that I think, I see a petty English *exciseman* receive more homage and respect, than what was paid formerly to their quondam Mackallamors.

"I think, I see *the present peers of Scotland,* whose noble ancestors, conquered provinces, over-run countries, reduced and subjected towns and fortified places, exacted tribute through the greatest part of England, now walking in the *court of requests,* like so many English Attornies, laying aside their walking swords when in company with the English Peers, lest their self-defence should be found murder.

"I think, I see *the honorable Estate of Barons,* the bold assertors of the nations rights and liberties in the worst of times, now setting *a watch upon their lips* and *a guard upon their tongues,* lest they be found guilty of *scandalum magnatum.*

"I think I see *the royal State of Boroughs,* walking their *desolate streets,* hanging down their heads *under disappointments;* worm'd out of *all the branches of their old trade,* uncertain *what hand to turn to,* necessitated to become [51] apprentices to their unkind neighbors, and yet after all finding their *trade so fortified by companies* and secured by prescriptions, that they despair of any success therein.

"I think, I see *our learned Judges* laying aside their practiques and decisions, studying the common law of England, gravelled with certioraries, *nisi priuses*, writs of error, *ejectiones firmæ*, injunctions, demurrers, &c. and frighted with *appeals* and *avocations*, because of *the new regulations*, and *rectifications* they meet with.

"I think, I see *the valiant and gallant soldiery*, either sent to learn the plantation trade abroad, or at home petitioning for *a small subsistence*, as the reward of their honourable exploits, while their old corps are broken, the common soldiers left to beg, and the youngest English corps kept standing.

"I think, I see the *honest industrious tradesman* loaded with *new taxes and impositions*, disappointed of the equivalents, drinking water in place of ale, eating his saltless pottage, petitioning for *encouragement to his manufactories*, and answered by counter petitions.

"In short, I think I see the *laborious ploughman*, with his corn spoiling upon his hands *for want of sale*, cursing the day of his birth; dreading the expence of his burial, and uncertain whether to marry or do worse.

"I think I see the incurable difficulties of *landing men*, fettered under the golden chain of equivalents, their pretty daughters petition- [52] ing for want of husbands, and their sons for want of employments.

"I think I see *our mariners delivering up their ships* to their Dutch partners, and what through *presses and necessity* earning their bread as underlings in the English navy. But above all, my lord, I think, I see *our ancient mother Caledonia*, like Cæsar, sitting in the midst of our senate, ruefully looking round about her, covering herself with her royal garment, attending the fatal blows and breathing out her last with a
———*Et tu quoque mi fili.*

"Are not these, my lord, very afflicting thoughts? And yet they are the least part suggested to me by these dishonorable articles. Should not the considerations of these things vivify these dry bones of ours? Should not the memory of our noble predecessors' valor and constancy rouse up our drooping spirits? Are our noble predecessors' souls got so far into the English cabbage-stalks and cauliflowers, that we should shew the least inclination that way? Are our eyes so blinded? Are our ears so deafened? Are our hearts so hardened? Are our tongues so faultered? Are our hands so fettered? that in this our day, I say, my lord, that in this our day, we should not mind the things that concern the very being and well being of our ancient kingdom, before the day be hid from our eyes.

"When I consider this treaty as it hath been explained, and spoke to, before us these three weeks by past; I see the *English* constitution remaining firm, the same *two houses* of Par- [53] liament, the same *taxes*, the same *customs*, the same *excises*, the same *trading companies*, the same municipal laws and courts of judicature; *and all ours either subject to regulations or annihilations*, only we are to have *the honor* to pay *their old debts*, and to have some few persons present for witnesses, to the validity of the deed, when they are pleased to contract more."\*

Let any candid American deliberately compare that transaction with the present, and laying his hand upon his heart, solemnly answer this question to himself—Whether, he does not verily believe the eloquent Peer before mentioned, had ten-fold more cause to apprehend evils from such an unequal match between the two kingdoms, that any citizen of these states has to apprehend them from the system proposed? Indeed not only that Peer, but other persons of distinction, and large numbers of the people of Scotland were filled with the utmost aversion to the union; and if the greatest diligence and prudence had not been employed by its friends in removing misapprehensions and refuting misrepresentations, and by the then subsisting government for preserving the public peace, there would certainly have been a rebellion.

Yet, *what were the consequences* to Scotland of that *dreaded*

---

\* See objections against the Federal constitution, very similar to those made in Scotland.

union with England? The cultivation of her virtues and the correction of her errors—The emancipation of one [54] class of her citizens from the yoke of her superiors—A relief of other classes from the injuries and insults of the great—Improvements in agriculture, science, arts, trade, and manufactures—The profits of industry and ingenuity enjoyed under the protection of laws—peace and security at home, and encrease of respectability abroad. Her Church is still eminent—Her laws and courts of judicature are safe—Her boroughs grown into cities—Her mariners and soldiery possessing a larger subsistence than she could have afforded them, and her tradesmen, ploughmen, landed men, and her people of every rank, in a more flourishing condition, not only than they ever were, but in a more flourishing condition, than the clearest understanding could, at the time, have thought it possible for them to attain in so short a period, or even in many ages. England participated in the blessings. The stock of their union or ingraftment, as perhaps it may be called, being strong and capable of drawing better nutriment and in greater abundance, than they could ever have done apart,

"Ere long, to Heaven the soaring branches shoot,
"And wonder at their height, and more than native fruit."

FABIUS.

[55] LETTER VII.

Thus happily mistaken was the ingenious, learned, and patriotic lord Belhaven, in his prediction concerning the fate of his country; and thus happily mistaken, it is hoped, some of our fellow-citizens will be, in their prediction concerning the fate of their country.

Had they taken large scope, and assumed in their proposition the vicissitude of human affairs, and the passions that so often confound them, their prediction might have been a tolerably good guess. Amidst the mutabilities of terrestrial things, the liberty of United America may be destroyed. As to that point, it is our duty, humbly, constantly, fervently, to implore the protection of our most gracious maker, "who doth not afflict willingly nor grieve the children of men," and incessantly to strive, as we are commanded, to recommend ourselves to that protection, by "doing his will," diligently exercising our reason in fulfilling the purposes for which that and our existence were given to us.

How the liberty of this country is to be destroyed, is another question. Here, the gentlemen assign a cause, in no manner proportioned, as it is apprehended, to the effect.

The uniform tenor of history is against them. That holds up the *licentiousness* of the people, and *turbulent temper* of some of the states, as *the only causes* to be dreaded, not the conspiracies of federal officers. There-[56]fore, it is highly probable, that, if our liberty is ever subverted, it will be by one of the two causes first mentioned. Our tragedy will then have the same acts, with those of the nations that have gone before us; and we shall add one more example to the number already too great, of people that would not take warning, not, "know the things which belong to their peace." But, we ought not to pass such a sentence against our country, and the interests of freedom: Though, no sentence whatever can be equal to the atrocity of our guilt, if through enormity of obstinacy or baseness, we betray the cause of our posterity and of mankind, by providence committed to our parental and fraternal care.

There is reason to believe, that the calamities of nations are the punishments of their sins.

As to the first mentioned cause, it seems unnecssary to say any more upon it.

As to the second, we find, that the misbehaviour of the constituent parts acting separately, or in partial confederacies, debilitated the Greeks under The Amphictionic Council, and under The Achæan League. As to the former, it was not entirely an assembly of strictly democratical republics. Besides, it wanted a sufficiently close connection of its parts. After these observations, we may call our attention from it.

'Tis true, The Achæan League was disturbed by the misconduct of some parts, but it is as true, that it surmounted these difficulties, and wonderfully prospered, until it was dissolved in the manner that has been described.

[57] The glorious operations of its principles bear the clearest testimony to this distant age and people, that the wit of man never invented such an antidote against monarchical and aristocratical projects, as a strong combination of truly democratical republics. By strictly or truly democratical republics, the writer means republics in which all the principal officers, except the judicial, are from time to time chosen by the people.

The reason is plain. ·As liberty and equality, or as well termed by Polybius, *benignity*, were the foundations of their institutions, and the energy of the government pervaded all the parts in things relating to the whole, it counteracted for the common welfare, the designs hatched by selfishness in separate councils.

If folly or wickedness prevailed in any parts, friendly offices and salutary measures restored tranquility. Thus the public good was maintained. In its very formation, tyrannies and aristocracies submitted, by consent or compulsion. Thus, the Ceraunians, Trezenians, Epidaurians, Megalopolitans, Argives, Hermionians, and Phlyayzrians were received into the league. A happy exchange! For history informs us, that so true were they to their noble and benevolent principles, that, in their diet, " *no resolutions were taken, but what were equally advantageous to the whole confederacy, and the interest of each part so consulted, as to leave no room for complaints!"*

[58] How degrading would be the thought to a citizen of United America, that the people of these states, with institutions beyond comparison preferable to those of The Achæan league, and so vast a superiority in other respects, should not have wisdom and virtue enough, to manage their affairs, with as much prudence and affection of one for another as these ancients did.

Would this be doing justice to our country? The composition of her temper is excellent, and seems to be acknowledged equal to that of any nation in the world. Her prudence will guard its warmth against two faults, to which it may be exposed—The one, an imitation of *foreign fashions*, which from small things may lead to great. May her citizens aspire at a national dignity in every part of conduct, private as well as public. This will be influenced by the former. May *simplicity* be the characteristic feature of their manners, which, inlaid with their other virtues and their forms of government, may then indeed be compared, in the Eastern stile, to "apples of gold in pictures of silver." Thus will they long, and may they, while their rivers run, escape the contagion of luxury—that motley issue of innocence debauched by folly, and the lineal predecessor of tyranny, prolific of guilt and wretchedness. The other fault, of which, as yet, there are no symptoms among us, is the *thirst of empire*. This is a vice, that ever has been, and from the nature of things, ever must be, fatal to republican [59] forms of government. Our wants, are sources of happiness: our irregular desires, of misery. The abuse of prosperity, is rebellion against Heaven; and succeeds accordingly.

Do the propositions of gentlemen who object, offer to our view, any of *the great points* upon which, the fate, fame, or freedom of nations has turned, excepting what some of them have said about trial by jury; and which has been frequently and fully answered? Is there one of them calculated to regulate, and if needful, to *controul* those tempers and measures of constituent parts of an union, that have been so baneful to the weal of every confederacy that has existed? Do not some of them tend to enervate the authority evidently designed thus to regulate and controul? Do not others of them discover a bias in their advocates to particular connections, that if indulged to them, would enable persons of less understanding and virtue, to repeat the disorders, that have so often violated public peace and honor? Taking them altogether, would they afford as strong a security to our liberty, as the frequent election of the federal officers by the people, and the repartition of power among those officers, according to the proposed system?

It may be answered, that, they would be an additional security. In reply, let the writer be permitted at present to refer to what has been said.

The principal argument of gentlemen who object, involves a direct proof of the point contended for by the writer of this address, and as [60] far as it may be supposed to be founded, a plain confirmation of Historic evidence.

They generally agree, that the great danger of a monarchy or aristocracy among us, will arise from the federal senate.

The members of this senate, are to be chosen by men exercising the sovereignty of their respective states. These men therefore must be monarchically or aristocratically disposed, before they will chuse federal senators thus disposed; and what merits particular attention, is, that these men must have obtained an overbearing influence in their respective states, before they could with such disposition arrive at the exercise of the sovereignty in them: or else, the like disposition must be prevalent among the people of such states.

Taking the case either way, is not this a disorder in parts of the union, and ought it not to be rectified by the rest? Is it reasonable to expect, that the disease will seize all at the same time? If it is not, ought not the sound to possess a right and power, by which they may prevent the infection from spreading? And will not *the extent* of our territory, and the *number* of states within it, vastly increase the difficulty of any political disorder diffusing its contagion, and the probability of its being repressed?

From the annals of mankind, these conclusions are deducible—that confederated states may act prudently and honestly, and apart foolishly and knavishly; but, that it is a defiance [61] of all probability, to suppose, that states conjointly shall act with folly and wickedness, and yet separately with wisdom and virtue.

FABIUS.

[62] LETTER VIII.

The proposed confederation offers to us a system of diversified representation in the legislative, executive, and judicial departments, as essentially necessary to the good government of an extensive republican empire. Every argument to recommend it, receives new force, by contemplating events, that must take place. The number of states in America will increase. If not united to the present, the consequences are evident. If united, it must be by a plan that will communicate equal liberty and assure just protection to them. These ends can never be attained, but by a close combination of the several states.

It has been asserted, that a very extensive territory cannot be ruled by a government of republican form. What is meant by this proposition? Is it intended to abolish all ideas of connection, and to precipitate us into the miseries of division, either as single states, or partial confederacies? To stupify us into despondence, that destruction may certainly seize us? The fancy of poets never feigned so dire a Metamorphosis, as is now held up to us. The Ægis of their Minerva was only said to turn men into stones. This spell is to turn "a band of brethren," into a monster, preying on itself, and preyed upon by all its enemies.

If hope is not to be abandoned, common sense teaches us to attempt the best means of preservation. This is all that men can do, and [63] this they ought to do. Will it be said, that any kind of disunion, or a connection tending to it, is preferable to a firm union? Or, is there any charm in that despotism, which is said, to be alone competent to the rule of such an empire? There is no evidence of fact, nor any deduction of reason, that justifies the assertion. It is true, that extensive territory has in general been arbitrarily governed; and it is as true, that a number of republics, in such territory, loosely connected, must inevitably rot into despotism.

It is said—Such territory has never been governed by a confederacy of republics. Granted. But, where was there ever a confederacy of republics, in such territory, united, as these states are to be by the proposed constitution? Where was there ever a confederacy, in which, the sovereignty of each state was equally represented in one legislative body, the people of each state equally represented in another, and the sovereignties and people of all the states conjointly represented, possessed such a qualified and temperating authority in making laws? Or, in which the appointment to federal offices was vested in a chief magistrate chosen as our president is to be? Or, in which, the acts of the executive department were regulated, as they are to be with us? Or, in which, the federal judges were to hold their offices independently and during good behaviour? Or, in which, the authority over the militia and troops was so distributed and controuled, as it is to be with us? Or, in which, the people were so drawn together by religion, blood, language, manners and [64] customs, undisturbed by former feuds or prejudices? Or, in which, the affairs relating to the whole union, were to be managed by an assembly of several representative bodies, invested with different powers that became efficient only in concert, without their being embarrassed by attention to other business? Or, in which, a provision was made for the federal revenue, without recurring to coercion against states, the miserable expedient, of every other confederacy that has existed, an expedient always attended with odium, and often with a delay productive of irreparable damage? Where was there ever a confederacy, that thus adhered to the first principle in civil society; obliging by its direct authority every individual, to contribute, when the public good necessarily required it, a just proportion of aid to the support of the commonwealth protecting him—without disturbing him in the discharge of the duties owing by him to the state of which he is an inhabitant; and at the same time, so amply, so anxiously provided, for bringing the interests, and even the wishes of every sovereignty and of every person of the union, under all their various modifications and impressions, into their full operation and efficacy in the national councils? The instance never existed. The conclusion ought not to be made. It is without premises. So far is the assertion from being true, that "a very extensive territory cannot be ruled by a government of a republican form," that such a territory cannot be well-ruled by a government of any other form.

[65] The assertion has probably been suggested by reflections on the democracies of antiquity, without making a proper distinction between them and the democracy of The United States.

In the democracies of antiquity, the people assembled together and governed personally. This mode was incompatible with greatness of number and dispersion of habitation.

In the democracy of The United States, the people act by their representatives. This improvement collects the will of millions upon points concerning their welfare, with more advantage, than the will of hundreds could be collected under the ancient form.

There is another improvement equally deserving regard, and that is, the varied representation of sovereignties and people in the constitution now proposed.

It has been said, that this representation was a mere compromise.

It was not a mere compromise. *The equal representation of each state in one branch of the legislature,* was an original substantive proposition, made in convention, very soon after the draft offered by Virginia, to which last mentioned state United America is much indebted not only in other respects, but for her merit in the origination and prosecution of this momentous business.

The proposition was expressly made upon this principle, that a territory of such extent as that of United America, could not be safely and advantageously governed, but by a combination of republics, each retaining all the rights of supreme [66] sovereignty, excepting such as ought to be contributed to the union; that for the securer preservation of these sovereignties, they ought to be represented in a body by themselves, and with equal suffrage; and that they would be annihilated, if both branches of the legislature were to be formed of representatives of the people, in proportion to the number of inhabitants in each state.*

The principle appears to be well founded in reason, Why cannot a very extensive territory be ruled by a government of republican form? They answered, because its power must languish through distance of parts. Granted, if it be not a " body by joints and bands having nourishment ministered and knit together." If it be such a body, the objection is removed. Instead of such a perfect body, framed upon the principle that commands men to associate, and societies to confederate; that, which by communicating and extending happiness, corresponds with the gracious intentions of our maker towards us his creatures? what is proposed? Truly, that the natural legs and arms of this body should be cut off, because they are too weak, and their places supplied by strongest limbs of wood and metal.

[67] Monarchs, it is said, are enabled to rule extensive territories, because they send viceroys to govern certain districts; and thus the reigning authority is transmitted over the whole empire. Be it so: But what are the consequences? Tyranny, while the viceroys continue in submission to their masters, and the distraction of civil war besides, when they revolt, to which they are frequently tempted by the very circumstances of their situation, as the history of such governments indisputably proves.

* Justice Blackstone argues in like manner, after admitting the "expediency" of titles of nobility. " It is also expedient that their owners should form an independent and separate branch of the legislature "—otherwise "their privileges would soon be borne down and overwhelmed."—Comment. 2. 157.

America is, and will be, divided into several sovereign states, each possessing every power proper for governing within its own limits for its own purposes, and also for acting as a member of the union.

They will be civil and military stations, conveniently planted throughout the empire, with lively and regular communications. A stroke, a touch upon any part, will be immediately felt by the whole. Rome famed for imperial arts, had a glimpse of this great truth; and endeavoured, as well as her hard-hearted policy would permit, to realize it in her *colonies*. They were miniatures of the capital: But wanted the vital principal of sovereignty, and were too small. They were melted down into, or overwhelmed by the nations around them. Were they now existing, they might be called curious automatons—something like to our living originals. These, will bear a remarkable resemblance to the mild features of patriarchal government, in which each son ruled his own household, and in other matters the whole family was directed by the common ancestor.

[68] Will a people thus happily situated, ever desire to exchange their condition, for subjection to an absolute ruler; or can they ever look but with veneration, or act but with deference to that union, that alone can, under providence, preserve them from such subjugation?

Can any government be devised, that will be more suited to citizens, who wish for equal freedom and common prosperity; better calculated for preventing corruption of manners; for advancing the improvements that endear or adorn life; or that can be more conformed to the understanding, to the best affections, to the very nature of *man*? What harvests of happiness may grow from the seeds of liberty that are now sowing? The cultivation will indeed demand continual attention, unceasing diligence, and frequent conflict with difficulties: but, to object against the benefits offered to us by our Creator, by excepting to the terms annexed, is a crime to be equalled only by its folly.

Delightful are the prospects that will open to the view of United America—her sons well prepared to defend their own happiness, and ready to relieve the misery of others—her fleets formidable, but only to the unjust—her revenue sufficient, yet unoppressive—her commerce affluent, but not debasing—peace and plenty within her borders—and the glory that arises from a proper use of power, encircling them.

Whatever regions may be destined for servitude, let us hope, that some portions of this land may be blessed with liberty; let us be con- [69] vinced, that *nothing short of such an union* as has been proposed, can preserve the blessing; and therefore let us be resolved to adopt it.

As to alterations, a little *experience* will cast more light upon the subject, than a multitude of debates. Whatever qualities are possessed by those who object, they will have the candor to confess, that they will be encountered by opponents, not in any respect inferior, and yet differing from them in judgment, upon every point they have mentioned.

Such untired industry to serve their country, did the delegates to the federal convention exert, that they not only laboured to form the best plan they could, but, *provided for making at any time amendments on the authority of the people*, without shaking the stability of the government. For this end, the Congress, whenever two-thirds of both houses shall deem it necessary, shall propose amendments to the constitution, or, on the application of the legislatures of two-thirds of the several states, *shall* call a convention for proposing amendments, which, in either case, shall be valid to all intents and purposes, as part of the constitution, when ratified by the legislatures of three-fourths of the several states, or by conventions in three-fourths thereof, as one or the other mode of ratification may be proposed by Congress.

Thus, by a gradual progress, we may from time to time *introduce every improvement in our constitution*, that shall be [70] suitable to our situation. For this purpose, it may perhaps be advisable, for every state, as it sees occasion, to form with the utmost deliberation, drafts of alterations respectively required by them, and to enjoin their representatives, to employ every proper method to obtain a ratification.

In this way of proceeding, the undoubted sense of every

state, collected in the coolest manner, not the sense of individuals, will be laid before the whole union in congress, and that body will be enabled with the clearest light that can be afforded by every part of it, and with the least occasion of irritation, to compare and weigh the sentiments of all United America; forthwith to adopt such alterations as are recommended by general unanimity; by degrees to devise modes of conciliation upon contradictory propositions; and to give the revered advice of our common country, upon those, if any such there should be, that in her judgment are inadmissible, because they are incompatible with the happiness of these states.

It cannot be with reason apprehended, that Congress will refuse to act upon any articles calculated to promote the *common* welfare, though they may be unwilling to act upon such as are designed to advance *partial* interests: but, whatever their sentiments may be, they *must* call a convention for proposing amendents, on applications of two-thirds of the legislatures of the several states.

May those good citizens, who have sometimes turned their thoughts towards a second [71] convention, be pleased to consider, that there are men who speak as they do, yet do not mean as they do. These borrow the sanction of their respected names, to conceal desperate designs. May they also consider, whether persisting in the suggested plan, in preference to the constitutional provision, may not kindle flames of jealousy and discord, which all their abilities and virtues can never extinguish.

FABIUS.

[72]     LETTER IX.

When the sentiments of some objectors, concerning the British constitution, are considered, it is surprising, that they should apprehend so much danger to United America, as, they say, will attend the ratification of the plan proposed to us, by the late federal convention.

These gentlemen will acknowledge, that Britain has sustained many internal convulsions, and many foreign wars, with a gradual advancement in freedom, power, and prosperity. They will acknowledge, that no nation has existed that ever so perfectly united those distant extremes, private security of life, liberty, and property, with exertion of public force—so advantageously combined the various powers of militia, troops, and fleets—or so happily blended together arms, arts, science, commerce, and agriculture. From what spring has flowed this stream of happiness? The gentlemen will acknowledge, that these advantages are derived from a single democratical branch in her legislature. They will also acknowledge, that in this branch, called the house of commons, only one hundred and thirty-one are members for counties: that nearly one half of the whole house is chosen by about five thousand seven hundred persons, mostly of no property; that fifty-six members are elected by about three hundred and seventy [73] persons, and the rest in an enormous disproportion* to the numbers of inhabitants who ought to vote.†

Thus are all the millions of people in that kingdom, said to be represented in the house of commons.

Let the gentlemen be so good, on a subject so familiar to them, as to make a comparison between the British constitution, and that proposed to us. Questions like these will then

* No member of parliament ought to be elected by fewer than the majority of 800, upon the most moderate calculation, according to Doctor Price.

† By the constitution proposed to us, a majority of the house of representatives, and of the senate, makes a quorum to do business: but, if the writer is not mistaken, about a fourteenth part of the members of the house of commons, makes a quorum for that purpose.

probably present themselves: Is there more danger to our liberty, from such a president as we are to have, than to that of Britons from an hereditary monarch with a vast revenue—absolute in the erection and disposal of offices, and in the exercise of the whole executive power—in the command of the militia, fleets, and armies, and the direction of their operations—in the establishments of fairs and markets, the regulation of weights and measures, and coining of money—who can call parliaments with a breath, and dissolve them with a nod—who can, at his will, make war, peace, and treaties irrevocably binding the nation—and who can [74] grant pardons and titles of nobility, as it pleases him? Is there more danger to us, from twenty-six senators, or double the number, than to Britons, from an hereditary aristocratic body, consisting of many hundreds, possessed of enormous wealth in lands and money—strengthened by a host of dependants—and who, availing themselves of defects in the constitution, send many of these into the house of commons—who hold a third part of the legislative power in their own hands—and who form the highest court of judicature in the nation? Is there more danger to us, from a house of representatives, to be chosen by all the freemen of the union, every two years, than to Britons, from such a sort of representation as they have in the house of commons, the members of which, too, are chosen but every seven years? Is there more danger to us, from the intended federal officers, than to Britons, from such a monarch, aristocracy, and house of commons together? *What bodies* are there in Britain, vested with such capacities for enquiring into, checking, and regulating the conduct of national affairs, *as our sovereign states?* What proportion does the number of *free holders* in Britain bear to the number of people? And what is the proportion in United America?

If any person, after considering such questions, shall say, there will be more danger to our freedom under the proposed plan, than to that of Britons under their constitution, he must mean, that Americans are, or will be, beyond all comparison, inferior to Britons in under- [75] standing and virtue; otherwise, with a constitution and government, every branch of which is so extremely popular, they certainly might guard their rights, at least at well, as Britons can guard theirs, under such political institutions as they have; unless the person has some inclination to an opinion, that monarchy and aristocracy are favourable to the preservation of their rights. If he has, he cannot too soon recover himself. If ever monarchy or aristocracy appears in this country, in must be in the hideous form of despotism.

What an infatuated, depraved people must Americans become, if, with such unequalled advantages, committed to their trust in a manner almost miraculous, they lose their liberty? Through a single organ of representation, in the legislature only, of the kingdom just mentioned, though that organ is diseased, such portions of popular sense and integrity have been conveyed into the national councils, as have purified other parts, and preserved the whole in its present state of healthfulness. To their own vigour and attention, therefore, is that people, under providence, indebted for the blessings they enjoy. They have held, and now hold *the true balance* in their government. While they retain their enlightened spirit, they will continue to hold it; and *if they regard what they owe to others*, as well as what they owe to themselves, they will, most probably, continue to be happy.\*

[76] They know, that there are powers that cannot be expressly limited, without injury to themselves; and their mag-

---

\* If to the union of England and Scotland, a just connection with Ireland be added, ecclesiastical establishments duly amended; additions to the peerage regulated, and representation of the commons properly improved, it is to be expected, that the tranquility, strength, reputation, and prosperity of the empire will be greatly promoted, the monarchy will probably change into a republic, if representation in the house of commons is not encreased by additions from the counties and great trading cities and towns, without this precaution, an increase of the peerage seems likely to accelerate an alteration. These two measures should have, it is apprehended, in such a government and in such a progress of human affairs, a well-tempered co-operation. The power of the crown might thereby become more dignified, moderated, and secured.

The discussion of this subject would embrace a very great number of considerations; but the conclusion seems to approach as near to demonstration, as an investigation of this kind can do.

nanimity scorns any fear of such powers. This magnanimity taught Charles the first, that he was but a royal servant; and this magnanimity caused James the second's army, raised, paid, and kept up by himself, to confound him with huzzas for liberty.

They ask not for compacts, of which the national welfare, and, in some cases, its existence, may demand violations. They despise such dangerous provisions against danger.

They know, that all powers whatever, even those that, according to the forms of the con- [77] stitution, are irresistible and absolute, of which there are many, ought to be exercised for the public good; and that when they are used to the public detriment, they are unconstitutionally exerted.

This plain text, commented upon by their experienced intelligence, has led them safe through hazards of every kind: and they now are, what we see them. Upon the review, one is almost tempted to believe, that their insular situation, soil, climate, and some other circumstances, have compounded a peculiarity of temperature, uncommonly favourable to the union of reason and passion.

Certainly, 'tis very memorable, with what life, impartiality, and prudence, they have interposed on great occasions; have by their patriotism communicated temporary soundness to their disordered representation; and have bid public confusions to cease. Two instances out of many may suffice. The excellent William the third was distressed by a house of commons. He dissolved the parliament, and appealed to the people. They relieved him. His successor, the present king, in the like distress, made the same appeal; and received equal relief.

Thus they have acted: but Americans, who have the same blood in their veins, have, it seems, very different heads and hearts. We shall be enslaved by a president, senators, and representatives, chosen by ourselves, and continually rotating within the period of time assigned for the continuance in office of members in the house of commons? 'Tis strange: but, we are told, 'tis true. It may be so. As we [78] have our all at stake, let us enquire, in what way this event is to be brought about. Is it to be before or after a general corruption of manners? If after, it is not worth attention. The loss of happiness then follows of course. If before, how is it to be accomplished? Will a virtuous and sensible people choose villains or fools for their officers? Or, if they should choose men of wisdom and integrity, will these lose both or either, by taking their seats? If they should, will not their places be quickly supplied by another choice? Is the like derangement again, and again, and again, to be expected? Can any man believe, that such astonishing phænomena are to be looked for? Was there ever an instance, where rulers, thus selected by the people from their own body, have, in the manner apprehended, outraged their own tender connexions, and the interests, feelings, and sentiments of their affectionate and confiding countrymen? Is such a conduct more likely to prevail in this age of mankind, than in the darker periods that have preceded? Are men more disposed now than formerly, to prefer uncertainties to certainties, things perilous and infamous to those that are safe and honorable? Can all the mysteries of such iniquity, be so wonderfully managed by treacherous rulers, that none of their enlightened constituents, nor any of their honest associates, acting with them in public bodies, shall ever be able to discover the conspiracy, till at last it shall burst with destruction to the whole federal constitution? Is it not ten thousand times less probable, that such [79] transactions will happen, than it is, that we shall be exposed to innumerable calamities, by rejecting the plan proposed, or even by delaying to accept it?

Let us consider our affairs in another light. Our difference of government, participation in commerce, improvement in policy, and magnitude of power, can be no favourite objects of attention to the Monarchies and Sovereignties of Europe. Our loss will be their gain—our fall, their rise—our shame, their triumph. Divided, they may distract, dictate, and destroy. United, their efforts will be waves dashing themselves into foam against a rock. May our national character be—an animated moderation, that seeks only its own, and will not be satisfied with less.

To his beloved fellow-citizens of United America, the writer dedicates this imperfect testimony of his affection, with fervent prayers, for a perpetuity of freedom, virtue, piety, and felicity, to them and their posterity.

FABIUS.

Remarks / on the / Proposed Plan / of a / Federal Government, / Addressed to the Citizens of the / United States of America, / And Particularly to the People of Maryland, / By Aristides. / " As a confederated government is composed of petty re- / " publics, it enjoys the internal happiness of each; and with / " regard to its external situation, by means of the associa- / " tion, it possesses all the advantages of extensive monarchies." / Mont. Sp. of Laws, B. 9, Ch. 1. / Annapolis ; / Printed by Frederick Green, Printer to the State.

8vo., pp. 42.

---

Written by Alexander Contee Hanson, a member of the Maryland State Convention, and Chancellor of Maryland from 1789 till his death in 1806. Both Drake and Lanman have confused Hanson and his son in their sketches of him, and the best account is given in Hanson's *Old Kent*.

"These remarks are not all original, but they are very judicious, calculated to remove objections to the proposed plan of government." [Noah Webster.] in *American Magazine*.

P. L. F.

To GEORGE WASHINGTON, Esquire.

Not as a Tribute to the Worth, which no Acknowledgement, or Distinctions, can reward; but to do himself an Honour, which, by labouring in the same Common Cause, he flatters himself, in some Degree, he hath deserved; the Author begs Leave to inscribe the following imperfect Essay.

IT is my intention, with all possible plainness, to examine the proposed plan of a Federal Government. Its enemies and its advocates have laid particular stress on the names, wherewith it is subscribed. As one side would obtain your implicit assent, by a reference to characters, and as the other would defeat measures by exciting your jealousy of men, permit me, in the first place, to make some general observations on the persons who composed the late memorable convention.

In general, they had been distinguished by their talents and services. They were not principally the men to whom the idea of the convention first suggested itself, and it is notorious that, in general, they accepted their appointments with reluctance. It would seem, however, according to some vague insinuations, that, no sooner did they find themselves convened, than their natures changed; and fatally have they combined for the destruction of your liberties. Now this altogether shocks my faith. I should sooner imagine that the sacredness of the trust, the unparalleled grandeur of the occasion, and the fellowhip of the great and good, might have elevated the soul of the most abandoned wretch, had it been possible for such to obtain a seat in that illustrious assemblage.

If those, who would inspire suspicion and distrust, can suggest any precise idea, it must be this, that the members of the convention will be elected into the first federal congress, and there combining again will compose a body capable of bearing down all opposition to their own aggrandisement.

By their scheme, however, thus deeply concerted, the house of representatives is to be chosen by the people once in [6] two years; and if they have acted so as to warrant any reasonable apprehension of their designs, it will be easy at any time, to prevent their election. The truth is, that very few of them either wish to be elected, or would consent to serve, either in that house, or in the senate. I have exercised my imagination to devise in what manner they or any other men, supposing them to bear full sway in both houses, could erect this imaginary fabric of power. I request any person to point out any law, or system of laws, that could be possibly contrived for that purpose, obtain the final assent of each branch, and be carried into effect, contrary to the interests and wishes of a free, intelligent, prying people, accustomed to the most unbounded freedom of inquiry. To begin by an attempt to restrain the press, instead of promoting their designs, would be the most effectual thing to prevent them.

I am apprized of the *almost* universal disposition for the increase and abuse of authority. But if we are to withhold power because there is a possibility of its perversion, we must abolish government, and submit to those evils, which it was intended to prevent. The perfection of political science consists chiefly in *providing mutual checks amongst the several departments of power, preserving at the same time, the dependance of the greatest on the people.* I speak with reference to a single government. The necessity of another species of government, for the mutual defence and protection of these American states, no man of sense and honesty, that I know of, has ever yet denied.

The convention had the above principle constantly in their view. They have contrived, that it shall be extremely difficult, if not altogether impracticable, for any person to exceed or abuse his lawful authority. There is nothing in their plan like the cloathing of individuals with power, for their own gratification. Every delegation, and every advantage that may be derived to individuals, has a strict reference to the general good.

To examine their constitution, by article and section, would be a painful and needless undertaking. I shall endeavor to answer such objections, as I have already heard, to anticipate others; to point out some advantages not general- [7] ly known; and to correct certain errors, with respect to construction. When the convention was appointed, I much feared that the numerous seeds, and principles of discord amongst the states, would, for ever, prevent them from agreeing to any efficient system whatever. I apprehended, in particular, that the dispute about representation would be the rock, on which the vessel containing all our hopes would be dashed. When, therefore, I discerned that equitable compromise between the larger and lesser states, my anxiety was instantly removed, and my soul enlightened by a sudden ray.

How then was I, some months after, disgusted at the repetition, of the arguments respecting the inequality of representatives in the first branch. We were told, that the minority in convention reasoned on first principles, that, as all men, in a state of nature, are equal with respect to rights, so also are equal all separate and distinct states;—that, when individuals form a free government, they must all have equal suffrage, either in framing laws by themselves, or in choosing representatives, although one man be ten times stronger, richer, or wiser than another; so also, when several states unite, for common convenience, they must meet on terms of perfect equality, although one be ten times more wealthy, expensive and populous than another;—that, under our present compact, the states are equal, and that no injury has resulted from the equality.

To these arguments, we may imagine, was opposed something like the following: "You talk of first principles, and, at the same time, would let 180,000 free inhabitants of Maryland have no more to do in the choice of representatives than only 30,000 inhabitants of Delaware. Do you propose, that these 30,000 shall bear an equal part of burthens and impositions? As to no injury having resulted from the equality, as you call it, under the articles of confederation, we think the reverse; and that this pretended * equality was a poison, which pervaded all our affairs." [8]

The anticipation of arguments like these had raised those apprehensions of an irreconcilable difference. It were needless

---

* Against what is called equality in representation, the great Montesquieu seems to have declared by the strongest implication. In his Spirit of Laws, b. ch. 2, he says, that the confederate republic of Lycia contained twenty-three associated towns: that, in the common council, the larger towns had three votes, the middling towns two, and the lesser only one; that they contributed to the common expence according to the proportion of suffrages; and, that were he to give the model of an excellent confederate republic, it should be that of Lycia. Could the immortal spirit of Montesquieu revisit the earth, and

to repeat more. Had an angel been the umpire, he could propose no expedient more equitable and more politic, not only as a compromise, but to establish such a decided difference between the two branches of congress, as will make them, indeed, two distinct bodies, operating by way of mutual balance and check.

By this expedient, is safety secured to the lesser states, as completely as if the senate were the only legislative body. It is possible (*if such a thing can be devised*) that, from the inequality in the first branch, propositions will be made to give the larger states some advantage over the lesser; but the equality in the senate will, for ever, preclude its adoption. It is well worthy of remark, that not more than three of the thirteen are, at present, deemed larger states, in the peculiar sense of the word. There is no reason for supposing, in the federal, like a state, legislature, the senate will be intimidated or overawed, by the more numerous branch. A demagogue may declaim, rave, menace and foam, with as little impression as the roaring billows produce upon the solid [9] beach. Were it not for this equality in one, and inequality in the other, a jealousy might be entertained of too perfect a coincidence of sentiment.

The convention has been censured for an excess of its authority. But with no other power was it invested, than is possessed by every free citizen of the states. Its office was to advise, and no further has it proceeded. Had it been even invested with full powers to amend the present compact, their proposed plan would not have exceeded their trust. Amendment, in parliamentary language, means either addition, or diminution, or striking out the whole, and substituting something in its room. The convention were not limited. The states did not tell them, this article must stand, this must be

behold the model now offered to America, how quickly would his favorite republic sink in his estimation. In a new quarter of the globe scarcely heard of by the greater part of Europeans in his day, and since the commencement of the present century, he would see men who have attained a perfection in the science most conducive to human happiness, in that study which was the principal occupation of his life, in which his predecessors had acquired only a few glimmering lights, and of which it was reserved for him to develope most of the true first principles.

struck out, and this may be altered. The avowed object of a convention was to consult on the additional power necessary to be vested in congress. But the members of this convention perceiving, from the experience of these states, from the history of ancient and modern states, and, I may add, from the principles of human nature, that the same body of men ought not to make and execute laws; and that one body alone ought not to do the first, have separated the executive, so far as was proper, from the legislative; and this last they have divided into two branches, composed of different materials, distinct from, and totally independent of, each other.

The house of representatives* is to be the immediate choice of the people, and one man is to represent 30,000 souls. In an affair of so much importance, and in districts containing so many suffrages, it is not to be supposed, that a worthless character will succeed by those arts, which have, sometimes, prevailed in county elections. It is to be expected, that, in general, the people will choose men of talents and character. Were they even so inclined, they can choose none but of ripe age, who have been, at least, seven [10] years citizens of the United States, and, at the time of election, residents of the respective state. Whatever laws shall be proposed, or assented to by these men, are to bind themselves, their children, and their connections. If a single man, or a party, shall propose a measure, calculated to promote private interest, at the expense of public good, is it conceivable, that the whole house will be brought into the measure? Suppose it should. The measure cannot be adopted into a law, without the concurrence of another house, consisting of men still more select, possessing superior qualifications of residence and age, and equally bound by the laws. After gaining the assent of the senate, the bill must be submitted to the objections of the president. He is not in any manner dependent on the legislature, which can, in no manner, punish him, except for some crime known to the

* Whether the state of Maryland shall be divided into six districts, for each to choose one man, or the people at large give their suffrage for the whole six, is hereafter to be settled by the assembly. The latter mode, on a variety of occasions, would be preferable.

laws. He is elected by persons chosen for that special purpose. He receives a compensation, which cannot be diminished or increased, during his continuance in office. . The term of his commission is limited to four years, unless he shall have acted so as to merit the people's favour. From the mode of his election, it is impossible he can intrigue to advantage; and, from the nature of other things, he will never succeed by bribery and corruption. Like any other individual, he is liable to punishment. Finally, at the expiration of his office, he returns into the mass of the people.

In spite of all these circumstances, an idea is gone forth amongst the enemies of the plan, and they labour to impress it on your minds, that whatever power may be exercised by these delegates of the people, will be used contrary to the interests of their constituents. This is a supposition, so repulsive to my mind, that I wonder any man of the least generosity, or reflection, can possibly adopt it. The assembly of Maryland, with respect to internal regulations, is almost omnipotent. And yet, is there a man who supposes the assembly would, intentionally, pass laws injurious to the people? Why then should we distrust the federal assembly, chosen for a short term, bound by the same ties, and selected on account of their talents and patriotism?

But, say the objectors, although we might probably confide with safety in congress, it is not consistent with pru- [11] dence, without a manifest necessity, to empower any men to do us an injury.

Whenever the proposed plan delegates authority, which you imagine might safely be denied, be assured, that a little reflection will suggest abundant reason for granting it. At the same time you may be convinced, that, as some powers were not intended to be exercised, so they never will be exercised, without absolute necessity.

I have been amused by the writings of an avowed friend to the plan. "Let no man," says he, "think of proposing amendments. Should each person object, and should his objections prevail, not a title of the system will be left. You are to accept the whole, or reject the whole." After speaking in this very sensible way, he advises the states to reject, with unanimity and firmness, the following provision.

"Art. I, sect. 4. The times, places, and manner of holding "elections for senators and representatives, shall be prescribed "in each state, by the legislature thereof; *but the congress may,* "*at any time, by law, make or alter such regulations, except as* "*to the places of choosing senators.*"

Can this writer imagine, that congress will presume to use this power, without the occurrence of some one or more of the cases, the contemplation whereof induced the convention to create it. These are the cases of invasion by a foreign power; of neglect, or obstinate refusal, in a state legislature; of the prevalance of a party, prescribing so as to suit a sinister purpose, or injure the general government. Others might perhaps occur in the convention. But these may suffice to evince the propriety of such a power in the federal head. It was never meant, that congress should at any time interfere, unless on the failure of a state legislature, or to alter such regulations as may be obviously improper. The exercise of this power must at all times be so very invidious, that congress, will not venture upon it without some very cogent and substantial reason. Let congress, even officiously, exert every power given by this clause, the representatives must still be chosen by the people, and the senate by the state legislatures. The provision cannot by any possibility admit of a different construction. [12]

Should the bare appointment to congress have the magic to pervert the tempers and principles of men, I perceive not the temptation for abusing this, or any other of their powers. There are bad men to be found at times, in every numerous assembly. But, under all circumstances, I predict, that, in congress, their party will be small. Should there be thither sent the most prostituted character, that ever acted, like a pest, to his own state; should he possess talents superior to the rest, I should have little dread of his influence, unless I could suppose, that a majority of like characters may be chosen. Even then, I repeat it—they will be under no temptation sufficient to influence a sensible mind; and no man of ripe age was ever yet wicked for the sake of wickedness alone.

You have heard, that, by the privilege of nominating persons to office, the president will find the congress obsequious enough to pass any laws, he shall think fit to propose. It is incumbent on the authors of this suggestion to show some interest in the president, inducing him to propose prejudicial measures. I have remarked, that under the constitution, his salary can be neither augumented nor curtailed, during his commission; and, to change the constitution, is not in the power of congress. Should he, however, devise, and endeavour to procure, some dangerous act of the body, can we conceive, that this lure will be powerful enough to corrupt a majority in each house. No member can be appointed to an office, created, or of which the profits shall be increased, during the time for which he was elected. And the expectation of such, as may fall vacant, within four years, will hardly corrupt even the smallest number, that can, in any possible case, be a majority, in the two houses. To make the members of each house ineligible to any other office whatever, would be even impolitic, on account of its precluding these states from the services perhaps of its best men. And it would be unjust to deny men the possibility of benefits, which might be attained by others less deserving.

In ascertaining and defining this obvious principle, the convention evidently pursued this obvious principle, that all [13] things, which concern the union in general, should be regulated by the federal head; and that each state legislature should regulate those things, which concern only its own internal government, together with the separate interests of its citizens. The enemies of the proposed constitution have deemed it material to shew, that such a one never existed before. It does not indeed agree with definitions in books, taken from the Amphyctyonic council, the United Netherlands, or the Helvetic body. They would therefore infer, that it is wrong. This mode of reasoning deserves not a serious refutation. The convention examined those several constitutions, if such a thing they can be called. It found them either woefully defective, as to their own particular object, or inapplicable to ours. Peradventure, our own articles of confederation, in theory, appear more perfect than any of them. These articles were made according to rule; the legislative and executive authorities being vested in one assembly. The extreme caution of its framers to secure the independence of the several states, on account of its principle, was much to be commended. But experience having fully demonstrated this constitution to be inadequate to the purposes for which it was framed, and a general conviction of its defects having occasioned the convention, it is astonishing, that attempts are now made to prefer still a theory, not founded on the nature of things, but derived merely from a few deplorable examples. If two branches in a state legislature be proper, why, in the name of common sense, are they not so in a confederate legislature?—Many instances of hasty unadvised proceedings of congress, as a legislature, have by other writers been adduced; and so long as mankind shall remain under the influence of passion or interest, there will be such proceedings in every numerous assembly of men,

It is universally, by good writers, agreed, that where any one political body possesses *full* powers, legislative and executive, whether it be a single man, or a select few, or a numerous assembly, it matters not;—the government must, in a short time, become despotic. That in a free government, therefore, the legislative and executive ought to be ever distinct and separate, is a position in the Maryland de- [14] claration of rights. This hackneyed principle, has been urged, with great confidence, against constituting the senate a council to the president. It has been urged too, even by the men who would have the whole power of the federal government centred in a single assembly. I mean the men who insist that the convention ought to have done no more than advise in what manner the powers of the present congress should be increased. Let us understand the principle in its proper extent. It does not follow, that a body, whose assent is required, in making laws, but who cannot, by themselves, do any legislative act, may not be a fit council to the supreme executive magistrate, deriving his authority, like them, from the people, in no manner dependent on them, or the immediate of the people, for any private advantage, and possessed of no share in legislation, except that of offering his advice.

The objection to this part of the constitution, I confess, at first, appeared formidable. The reasons which I now conjecture to have influenced the convention, did not then occur. But I have long adhered to a maxim, which I warmly recommend to others—never to condemn, absolutely, even within myself, any one kind, until I can hit upon some other kind which I *conceive* better. As no human institution can possess absolute perfection, it is an easy matter to espy some fault or defect in almost everything, which the wit of man can contrive, or at least, to reason plausibly against it. But this faculty of finding faults is by no means sufficient to constitute the politician or statesman. I deliberated what kind of council might be preferable, under all circumstances, to the senate. The plainest thing in nature! Exclaims he, who solves all difficulties at once. Why not appoint a body to act as council and nothing else?

One reason, and that not very unpopular, is the great additional expence. However, this reason I deem the lightest of all; and the general proposition involves a great variety of other considerations.

It is essential to a council, that the members be free, as possible, from all bias, or improper influence. This separate and distinct council must be elected by the people, or [15] by special electors; by the legislature, or by one of its branches; or by some department; or by the president.

That the people should either make laws to bind themselves, or elect persons, without whose consent, no laws shall be made, is essential to their freeedom. But universal experience forbids, that they should immediately choose persons for the execution of the laws. Shall the legislature then, or the senate, or the house of representatives, have this appointment? A council thus chosen would be dependent on its electors; and it would be the same thing in many respects, as if the legislature should execute its own laws. Can you believe, that a council, chosen annually, or once in two or three years, would dare to pursue, in all cases, the dictates of its own judgment, contrary to the known will of those, who will soon have an opportunity of removing them? Would they not be emulous to please leading men; and there not be opened, at every period of election, a fine field for intrigue and cabal? There would be one way only of rendering a council, thus chosen, independent of their electors; and that is, the choosing them for life, with salaries, not to be augmented or diminished.

Against choosing an executive for life the reasons are weighty indeed. Should they then hold their commissions during good behaviour, there must be some tribunal to determine on that good behaviour; and what body it can be, except the congress, would be difficult to decide. Besides good behaviour in a member of council is not determinable, like that of a judge, which has relation to the laws, and things universally known. In the office of the former, there is much left to discretion, that I cannot conceive with what propriety he can hold it on the condition of good behaviour. There can be no sure criterion, and the decision must therefore unavoidably depend on the discretion or mere opinion of his judges, founded on no established principles whatever.

A council, chosen by the president himself, would probably consist of creatures devoted to his will. I can discern no reason, wherefore any officer of the government [16] should make the appointment, There remains then only the people's choosing electors, and placing the council of the president on the same footing with himself. Here occurs the objection of expence; and here again would arise the controversy respecting equality of representation.

The senate, will, in all human likelihood, consist of the most important characters, men of enlightened minds, mature in judgment, independent in their circumstances, and not deriving their principal subsistence from their pay, as probably would the members of a board, distinct and separate from all other public employments.

I am not, therefore, barely reconciled to the article in question. It commands my warmest admiration, and entire applause.

Is there any power improperly trusted to that select assembly, in which all the states have equal interest, and to which they will assuredly make a determined point of sending their best men? It is this equality, almost as much as any other circumstance, which recommends it as an executive council. The senate are to try impeachments. By their advice only, may the president make treaties, appoint ambassadors, ministers, counsels, judges of the supreme court, and officers, not otherwise provided for in the constitution. Let us reflect, whether these things could be better done, by any other body, and whether it be proper for any one man (suppose even the saviour of his country to be immortal) to have the appointment of all those important officers. It has always appeared to me, that neither one man, nor many men, should possess this transcendant authority, in a republic. A single man, in high power, if he always means right, can with difficulty discern the true characters of men. Continual efforts are made to impose on his judgment. But, indeed, a single man *generally* confers by favour. In a large assembly there is perhaps equal partiality; and elections are conducted by intrigue and cabal. A select assembly is open to direct application; and although each may be supposed to entertain his partialities, he cannot recommend his favourites, without pointing out their essential qualifications and becoming, in some measure, responsible for their conduct. It is here, that characters are most fairly [17] investigated, and appointments are most deliberately made. I appeal to universal experience, whether these remarks be not founded on fact, and whether the most judicious appointments have not been made by small select assemblies. I confess, that the number of the senators for this purpose only is excessive. But I can confidently rely on the extraordinary selection to compensate for the excess.

The power of the president is alarming peculiarly to that class, who cannot bear to view others in possession of that fancied blessing, to which, alas! they must themselves aspire in vain. They tell you, this supreme magistrate, although he be called the modest name of president, and elected for only four years, will, in every essential, be an emperor, king, or stadtholder at least; and that his dignity in a few years, will become hereditary. Let us examine the foundation of this alarming prediction.

Before this appointment can be *entailed*, and before even the term can be enlarged, the constitution must be changed, by consent of the people. By what method, then, shall the president effect this alteration? Every citizen in the union will be a censor on his conduct. Not even his person is particularly protected; and the means of oppression are little in his power. Let the jealousy of the people once take the alarm, and, at the expiration of his term, he is dismissed, as inevitably as light succeeds to darkness. The election of a president is not carried on in a single assembly, where the several arts of corruption may be essayed. He is elected by persons chosen on the same day, in thirteen different assemblies, in thirteen different states. An elective monarchy has long been severely reprobated. But had the countries, where it prevailed, enjoyed regulations like these, they would perhaps, at this time, be preferred to the rules of hereditary succession, which have so often placed fools and tyrants on the throne.

It seems, however, that the president may possibly be continued for life. He may so, provided he deserve it. If [18] not, he retires to obscurity, without even the consolation of having produced any of the convulsions, attendant usually on grand revolutions. Should he be wicked or frantic enough to make the attempt, he atones for it, with the certain loss of wealth, liberty or life.

I return to the powers of congress. They are almost universally admitted to be proper for a federal head, except only the *sweeping clause*, and the power of raising fleets and armies, without any stint or limitation, in time of peace. The clause runs thus:—

ART. I, sec. 8, par. the last. "To make all laws, which shall be necessary and be proper for carrying into execution the foregoing powers, and all other powers vested by this constitution, in the government of the United States, or in any department or officer thereof."

It is apprehended, that this *sweeping clause* will afford pretext, for freeing congress from all constitutional restraints.

I will not here again insist on the pledge we enjoy, in the common interest, and sure attachment of the representatives and senate; setting aside the little probability of a majority in each branch lying under the same temptation. Consider the import of the words.

I take the construction of these words to be precisely the same, as if the clause had preceded further and said, "No act " of congress shall be valid, unless it have relation to the fore- "going powers, and be necessary and proper for carrying them "into execution." But say the objectors, "The congress, being "itself to judge of the necessity and propriety, may pass any "act, which it may deem *expedient*, for any other purpose." This objection applies with equal force to each particular power, defined by the constitution; and, if there were a bill of rights, congress might be said to be the judge of that also. They may reflect however, that every judge in the union, whether of federal or state appointment, (and some persons would say every jury) will have a right to reject any act, handed to him as a law, which he may conceive repugnant to the constitution.

It may nevertheless strike you at first view, that a provision, so obviously apt to excite distrust, might have well [19] been omitted. So indeed it might, were there a possibility of providing every thing, necessary and proper, for carrying into effect the various powers, intended to be conferred. Without this general clause, it were easy to suppose cases, wherein a particular clause might be incompetent to its own purpose.

For want of some plain and obvious distinctions, there has been vented so much senseless clamour against standing armies, that they are become a political bugbear. A limited monarch, with the means of maintaining, at all times, an army devoted to his will, might soon trample on the natural and civil rights of his subjects. Could the present congress find means of augmenting the force, which it now maintains, which of you, on that account, would experience the slightest anxiety? Which of all the European powers is destitute of an army? Which of them if they were free, could be secure of remaining so without a standing force? I might go further, and demand, whether any of them have lost their liberties, by means of a *standing* army? The troops, continually kept up in Great Britain, are formidable to its neighbors, and yet no rational Englishman apprehends the destruction of his rights. It is true, that he knows, these troops cannot be maintained, without the consent of his representatives, annually obtained. But the necessity of an army he readily conceives; and the number he leaves to the discretion of parliament. Ought then an American to have greater fears of a president, than an Englishman has of his king? Or may he not trust his representatives and the senate, with as much confidence, as the Englishman reposes in the commons and lords?

Let the federal head be constituted as it may, there can be no perfect security, without both a land force, and naval armament. It is impossible to say how much will, at all times of peace, be sufficient. We have the same security against the abuse of this, as of any other authority. The expenses of an army might indeed raise fears of a different kind,—that we shall not be able to maintain force enough for the most proper occasion.

Suppose a limitation in time of peace. What then is to be done on the prospect of a war? Should you make the [20] distinction between profound peace and a *threatened* war, who is there, but congress, to determine on the exigency? If you make no distinction, then it will be expedient to declare war, at the instant in which the danger shall be conceived, in order that it may be lawful to prepare for only a just defence. In fine, I consider this grand objection, as a mere pretext for terrifying you, like children, with spectres and hobgoblins. It may be material here to remark, that although a well regulated militia has ever been considered as the true defence of a free republic, there are always honest purposes, which are not to be answered by a militia. If they were, the burthen of the militia would be so great, that a free people would, by no means, be willing to sustain it. If indeed it be possible in the nature of things, that congress shall, at any future period, alarm us by an improper augmentation of troops, could we not, in that case, depend on the militia, which is ourselves. In such a case it would be ridiculous to urge that the federal government, is invested with a power over the whole militia of the union. Even when congress shall exercise this power, on the most proper occasions, it is provided in the constitution, that each state shall officer and train its own militia.

The objections against the judiciary are probably more sincere. The article has been generally misconceived, or misrepresented; and after bestowing much attention, I am not certain that I fully comprehend it. I am, however, at length satisfied, that no rational construction can be given to this part of the proposed plan, either to warrant a rejection of the whole, or to place matters on a worse footing, than they are at present.

The judiciary power is to be vested in one supreme court, fixed at the seat of government, with the ease and convenience of the people, the congress may hereafter appoint inferior courts in each of the states. The jurisdiction of this supreme court is to be partly original, and partly appellate. With respect to the extent of either, there can be no possible doubt, as there is neither ambiguity nor uncertainty in the relative expressions. [21].

The original jurisdiction of the supreme court extends:—

1. To all cases, in which may be concerned an ambassador, any public minister, or a consul.

2. To all cases whatever, in which a state may be a party. —This second division may be branched into 1. Cases between the United States, and one or more of the individual states. 3. Cases between two or more states. 3. Cases between a state and its own citizens. 4. Cases between a state, and the citizens of another state. 5. Cases between a state, and a foreign state. 6. Cases between a state, and the citizens, or subjects of a foreign state.

The appellate jurisdiction of the supreme court extends:—

1. To all cases whatever between parties of every kind, in law and equity, arising under this constitution, and the laws of congress, passed agreeably thereto, and to treaties already, or hereafter to be, made.

2. To all cases of admiralty or maritime jurisdiction.

3. To all cases, in which the United States shall be a party.

4. To all cases between citizens of different states.

5. To all cases between citizens of the same state, claiming lands under the grants of different states.

6. To all cases between citizens of a state, and foreign states, or their citizens or subjects.

One doubt arising on the judiciary article is, whether in these cases of appellate jurisdiction, the appeal lies both from the state courts, and the inferior federal courts, or only from the former, or only from the latter.

Another doubt is, whether the inferior courts are to be branches of the supreme court, constituted for convenience, and having equal jurisdiction, both original and appellate, with the supreme court, or whether the inferior courts are to be confined to an *original* jurisdiction in those cases, wherein the supreme court has *appellate* jurisdiction.

I shall not presume to decide absolutely on the genuine construction of an article, which is said to have caused much private debate and perplexity. I am however fully persuaded, that, as the article speaks of an original and appellate jurisdiction, of a supreme court, and inferior courts; and, as there is no intimation of appeals from the several [22] state tribunals, the inferior federal courts are intended to have original jurisdiction in all cases, wherein the supreme court has appellate jurisdiction; and the appeal lies only from them. I can, almost, with confidence, maintain, that, as there is no express clause, or necessary implication, to oust the jurisdiction of state courts, an action, after the adoption of the plan, may be instituted in any court, having, at this time, a jurisdiction. And if an action be brought in a state court, I do not, at present, perceive, that it can, in any manner, be transferred to the supreme or inferior federal court.

According then to the best of my judgment the affair stands thus. The supreme federal court will have an exclusive original jurisdiction in all cases relative to the rights of ambassadors, other ministers, and consuls; because, as I humbly conceive, the several state governments have at this time nothing to do with these cases. With respect to the cases, in which a state may be party, the supreme federal court, and the several state courts, will have, I conceive, concurrent original jurisdiction, *provided a state may, at this time, institute an action in its own name, in the courts of another state.* The inferior federal courts, and the state courts, will, I conceive, have concurrent original jurisdiction in all the enumerated cases wherein an appeal lies to the supreme court, *except only the cases created by or under the proposed constitution, in which, as they do not now exist, the inferior federal courts will have exclusive jurisdiction.* From the state inferior courts, I further apprehend, that an appeal will lie, in all cases, to their own high courts of appeal, as heretofore.

A choice of jurisdictions has been ever esteemed a valuable right, even where there are both of the same kind. The purpose of extending so far the jurisdiction of the federal judiciary, is to give every assurance to the general government, of a faithful execution of its laws, and to give citizens, states, and foreigners, an assurance of the impartial administration of justice. Without the salutary institution, the federal government might frequently be obstructed, and its servants want protection. It is calculated not as an engine of oppression, but to secure the blessings of peace and good [23] order. The provisions respecting different states, their citizens, and foreigners, if not absolutely necessary, are much to be applauded. The human mind is so framed, that the slightest circumstance may prevent the most upright and well known tribunal from giving complete satisfaction; and there may happen a variety of cases, where the distrust and suspicion may not be altogether destitute of a just foundation.

On these principles, an appeal as to fact is no less proper, than the appeal from judges of law. A jury, whose legal qualifications are only property and ripe age, may more probably incur the imputation of weakness, partiality, or undue influence. But in regard to appeals, it is very material to remark, that congress is to make such regulations and exceptions, as upon mature deliberation, it shall think proper. And indeed, before such regulations and exceptions shall be made, the manner of appeal will not be ascertained. Is it then to be presumed, that, in making regulations and exceptions, this appellate jurisdiction shall be calculated as an engine of oppression, or to serve only the purpose of vexation and delay.

As the rod of Aaron once swallowed up the rods of the Egyptian *magi*, so also is it feared, that these federal courts, will, at length, swallow up the state tribunals. A miracle, in one case, is as necessary, as in the other.

But let not the officers of state courts be overmuch alarmed! The causes, which, by possibility, may be* instituted in the federal courts bear no comparison to the rest. [24] In the course of ten years, not one action, that I know of, in Maryland, has concerned either another state, or an ambassador, consul, or other minister. It is hoped, that actions by foreigners, will, in a few years, become much rarer than at any time heretofore, and these may still be determined in the state courts. [25]

A gentleman, as it is conjectured, in the law department of a neighboring state, has been pleased to infer, that fictions, similar to those in the king's bench and exchequer of England, will be contrived, to draw causes into the federal courts. He seems not aware, that, even in England, the established fictions of law are not of modern date. They were ingenious devices, to remedy defects in the common law, *without the aid*

---

\* The importance of having the western territory determined a common stock, needs only to be mentioned, to excite attention.

As the articles of confederation contain no provision, for adjusting the dispute between the United States, and particular states, Maryland, for a long time, refused her ratification. An adequate provision is made by the proposed plan. That the United States will assuredly institute actions against two of the states, setting up claims equally wild and extensive, may appear from the following statement.

New Hampshire, Rhode Island, New Jersey, Delaware and Maryland, have been always interested in making good the common claim; as they never laid any particular claim to the territory in question.

Massachusetts, if the province of Maine be separate, is likewise become interested in the common claim.

Connecticut, and New York, have both made cessions, which congress has accepted. These two are therefore become interested.

Pennsylvania, although very extensive, has her limits ascertained. She likewise is interested.

*of parliament.* The fundamental principle however, with respect to their adoption, was, that they *consist with equity, and be requisite for the advancement of justice.* Now every man, who would establish over his cause a jurisdiction in a federal court, must shew, that such cause comes under the description of the constitution. If he do not, there will be wanting that equity, which is the support of legal fiction. But can any man seriously imagine, that fiction will be permitted, to give the judges a power of legislation, denied to congress itself? Wherefore should the judges, holding their commissions during good behaviour, be guilty of such gross falsehood, perjury, and breach of trust? Would there not be a general revolt against such barefaced impudent innovations. Away then with your trumpery of fictions! Accuse not the illustrious members of the convention of having in their contemplation such sophistry, pettifogging and chicane! But another fear is, that whatever actions may be instituted in the federal courts will there seek an admission, on account of a more speedy decision. That man alone, "on whose brow shame is ashamed to sit," will avow his opposition to a more speedy administration of justice.

The institution of the trial by jury has been sanctified by the experience of ages. It has been recognised by the consti-

---

Virginia, having made a cession to congress, has since relinquished a part of the reserved lands, or at least offered independence, to Kentucky.

North Carolina, having once made a cession, thought proper, in the omnipotence of her destined sovereignty, to repeal the act. Will not the cession be determined valid, and the repeal void?

South Carolina also, it is said, has ceded part of that territory, which lately she disputed with Georgia. In this case the United States have their claim fortified.

But Georgia, the weakest of all, lays claim to an immense tract of country. In this territory there are warlike and independent tribes of the aborigines, now carrying terror and desolation towards the heart of the country occupied by the whites. It is expected, that this circumstance, with a consciousness of the weak foundation of her claims, will dispose Georgia to give up without a suit, and consent to be circumscribed within narrower limits, so soon as a proper tribunal shall have power to enter upon a rational investigation.

N. B.—For the above statement I am principally indebted to a member of the late continental convention, and who for a considerable time, was a member of congress, a gentleman of established honour and accuracy.

tution of every state in the union. It is deemed the birthright of Americans; and it is imagined, that liberty cannot subsist without it. The proposed plan expressly adopts it, for the decision of all criminal accusations, except impeachment; and is silent with respect to the determination of facts in civil causes.

The inference, hence drawn by many, is not warranted by the premises. By recognising the jury trial in criminal cases, the constitution effectually provides, that it shall pre-[26] vail, so long as the constitution itself shall remain unimpaired and unchanged. But, from the great variety of civil cases, arising under this plan of government, it would be unwise and impolitic to say aught about it, in regard to these. Is there not a great variety of cases, in which this trial is taken away in each of the states? Are there not many more cases, where it is denied in England? For the convention to ascertain in what cases it shall prevail, and in what others it may be expedient to prefer other modes was impracticable. On this subject a future congress is to decide; and I see no foundation under Heaven for the opinion that congress will despise the known prejudices and inclination of their countrymen. A very ingenious writer of Philadelphia has mentioned the objections without deigning to refute that, which he conceives to have originated in "sheer malice."

I proceed to attack the whole body of anti-federalists in their strong hold. The proposed constitution contains no *bill of rights*.

Consider again the nature and intent of a federal republic. It consists of an assemblage of distinct states, each completely organized for the protection of its own citizens, and the whole consolidated, by express compact, under one head, for the general welfare and common defence.

Should the compact authorize the sovereign, or head to do all things it may think necessary and proper, then there is no limitation to its authority; and the liberty of each citizen in the union has no other security, than the sound policy, good faith, virtue, and perhaps proper interests, of the head.

When the compact confers the aforesaid general power,

making nevertheless some special reservations and exceptions, then is the citizen protected further, so far as these reservations and exceptions shall extend.

But, when the compact ascertains and defines the power delegated to the federal head, then cannot this government, without manifest usurpation, exert any power not expressly, or by *necessary* implication, conferred by the compact.

This doctrine is so obvious and plain, that I am amazed any good man should deplore the omission of a bill of rights.

[27] When we were told, that the celebrated Mr. Wilson had advanced this doctrine in effect, it was said, Mr. Wilson would not dare to speak thus to a CONSTITUTIONALIST. With talents inferior to that gentleman's, I will maintain the doctrine against any CONSTITUTIONALIST who will condescend to enter the lists, and behave like a gentleman.

It is, however, the idea of another most respectable character, that, as a bill of rights could do no harm, and might quiet the minds of many good people, the convention would have done well to indulge them. With all due deference, I apprehend, that a bill of rights might not be this innocent quieting instrument. Had the convention entered on the work, they must have comprehended within it everything, which the citizens of the United States claim as a natural or a civil right. An omission of a single article would have caused more discontent, than is either felt or pretended, on the present occasion. A multitude of articles might be the source of infinite controversy, by clashing with the powers intended to be given. To be full and certain, a bill of rights might have cost the convention more time, than was expended on their other work. The very appearance of it might raise more clamour than its omission,—I mean from those who study pretexts for condemning the whole fabric of the constitution. —"What! (might they say) did these exalted spirits imagine, " that the natural rights of mankind depend on their gracious " concession. If indeed they possessed that tyrannic sway, " which, the kings of England had once usurped, we might hum- " bly thank them for their *magna charta*, defective as it is. As " that is not the case, we will not suffer it to be understood,

" that their *new-fangled* federal head shall domineer with the
"powers not excepted by their precious bill of rights. What!
" if the owner of 1,000 acres of land thinks proper to fell one
" half, is it necessary to take a release from the vendee of the
" other half? Just as necessary is it for the people to have a
" grant of their natural rights from a government which derives
" everything it has, from the grant of the people." [28]

The restraints laid on the state legislatures will tend to secure domestic tranquility, more than all the bills, or declarations, of rights, which human policy could devise. It is very justly asserted, that the plan contains an avowal of many rights. It provides that no man, shall suffer by expost facto laws or bills of attainder. It declares, that gold and silver only shall be a tender for specie debts; and that no law shall impair the obligation of a contract.

I have here perhaps touched a string, which secretly draws together many of the foes to the plan. Too long have we sustained evils, resulting from injudicious emissions of paper, and from the operation of tender laws. To bills of credit as they are now falsely called, may we impute the entire loss of confidence between men. Hence it is, that specie has, in a great degree, ceased its proper office, and been confined to speculations, baneful to the public, and enriching a few enterprising sharp-sighted men, at the expence not only of the ignorant, slothful, and needy, but of their country's best benefactors. Hence chiefly are the bankruptcies throughout America, and the disreputable ruinous state of our commerce. Hence is it principally, that America hath lost its credit abroad, and American faith become a proverb. The convention plainly saw, that nothing short of a renunciation of the right to emit bills of credit could produce that grand consummation of policy, the RESTORATION OF PUBLIC AND PRIVATE FAITH.

Were it possible for the nations abroad to suppose Great Britain would emit bills on the terms whereon they have issued in America, how soon would the wide arch of that mighty empire tumble into ruins? In no other country in the universe has prevailed the idea of supplying, by *promissory notes*, the want of coin, for commerce and taxes. In America, indeed, they have heretofore served many valuable purposes. It is this consideration, which has so powerfully attached to them many well meaning honest citizens; and they talk of gratitude to paper money, as if it were a sensible benefactor, entitled to the highest rank and distinction; and as if, to abandon it, would be a deadly sin. But when everything demonstrates the season to be past; when the credit of America, in all places, depends on the security she shall give to [29] contracts, it would be madness in the states to be tenacious of their right. So long as Europe shall believe we regard not justice, gratitude and honour, so long will America labour under the disadvantages of an individual, who attempts to make good his way through the world with a blasted reputation. To the man, who shall say, "it is of no consequence to "consult national honour," I only answer thus,—"If thy soul "be so narrow and depraved, as to believe this, it were a need- "less attempt to cure thee of thy error."

On this subject there is no necessity for enlarging, to the people of my native state; their conduct on a recent occasion having acquired them great and deserved applause. Is it necessary to enlarge on the propriety of giving more efficient powers to a federal head? At this moment, congress is little more than a name, without power to effect a single thing, which is the object of a confederate republic. Reflect on the recent period, when, in a sister state, a numerous body of her frantic citizens appeared armed for the destruction of a government, framed by the people. When that unhappy state was devoted to the miseries of a civil war, did congress even dare to interpose? Conscious of its inability to protect, it could only await the result, in silence and in terror. It indeed ventured to *make application* to the states for a small body of troops, under the poor pretext of another, and a necessary, destination. But, notwithstanding the universal contagion of the alarm, did the states, on *that* occasion, comply with the *requisition?* Suppose even an invasion by a foreign power,— in what manner could congress provide for its own defence? In the contemptible light in which America has lately stood, is it reasonable to expect she will be suffered to remain long in peace? The distance between the two continents is the only circumstance on which we can rely. All Europe is now in suspence; and the result of your deliberations will instruct her in the part she shall act.

With amazement, her nations contemplate a scene, of which the world is too young to furnish a parallel. We assembled our sages, patriots, and statesmen, to consult what mode of government is capable of producing the greatest sum [30] of general good, with the least mixture of general, and partial evil. Not that each individual in this august assembly was expected to offer a system; but that the product of their joint wisdom should be referred to the several states, to be adopted, or rejected, as the great body of the people shall determine on a free and full deliberation.

As the occasion was unparalleled so also is the plan, which, after many months of painful investigation, is submitted, with an unanimity, also unparalleled.

If there be any man, who approves the great outlines of the plan, and, at the same time, would reject it, because he views some of the minute parts as imperfect, he should reflect, that, if the states think as he does, an alteration may be hereafter effected, at leisure. When the convention determined, that the whole should be received, or the whole fail, they did not on an arrogant conceit of their own infallibility, but on the soundest principles of policy and common sense. Were each state legislature, or convention, to take it up, article by article, and section by section, with the liberty of adopting some, and rejecting the rest, in all probability, so small a part would be approved by nine states, on the narrow view which each has of the subject, and attached as each is to its own supposed interest, that, in its mutilated condition, it would be worse than the present confederation. For thirteen different assemblies, in that way, to approve so much of any plan whatever, as might merit the name of system, the convention well knew to be impossible. Were there any one body of men, invested with full power, in behalf of the whole United States, to consider, and amend the plan, then would it be proper to debate it by sections, in the same manner as it was originally debated.

With a view to defeat totally the plan, another general convention is proposed; not with the power of giving a finishing hand to a constitution; but *again* to consider objections, to strike out, to add, and *again* to make their report to the several states.

In this way, there can never be an end. We must at last return to this,—that whatever is agreed on, by the assembly appointed to propose, must be either adopted in the whole, or in the whole rejected. [31]

The idea of a new convention is started by some men, with the vain expectation of having amendments made to suit a particular state, or to advance their own selfish views. Were this fatal idea adopted, I should bid a last adieu to that elevated hope, which now inspires me, of living under the happiest form of government which the sun ever beheld. Recollect again and again, that almost every state in the union made a determined point of delegating its first characters to this grand convention. Reflect upon the time spent in the arduous work, and the sacrifices which those distinguished persons made to their country. Should the same men be deputed again, would they not, think you, with the same unanimity, subscribe and recommend the same plan? So far as I have been informed, those members, who, in the progression of the plan, had opposed certain parts, and yet afterwards subscribed cheerfully to the whole, have, with the candour which becomes them, acknowledged their errors in debate. Even an illustrious character, who was of the minority, consisting only of three, I have been told, has since regretted his refusal.

Suppose then a second convention, with a different choice of delegates. These too would either speedily subscribe, or they might propose some other system, to be debated, paragraph by paragraph, in thirteen different assemblies; and then there would be the same probability of a mutilated plan; or they would propose something, to be adopted or rejected in the whole; and there would be the same necessity of another convention. Besides, as the second convention, if it consist of different men, must *inevitably* be inferior to the first, there is little probability that their work will be superior. Never again, in an assembly constituted as that was, will there be found the same liberality of sentiment, "the same spirit of amity, and the same mutual deference and concession."

If it be contended, that the second, being possessed of the various objections from the several states, must be better able to determine, I would ask, what conduct this second convention should adopt? Are they to take the proposed plan, and strike out every thing objected to by nine states? Or may they likewise adopt and recommend the entire plan? In short, to [32] appoint a second convention, merely to consult and propose, would be the most absurd expedient, that ever, in a matter of this amazing magnitude, was proposed. Does any man then entertain the thought of another kind of convention, invested with full powers to consult, amend, adopt, and confirm? A scheme like this was never yet, I trust, in agitation. But, if it were, I would propose this single question. Whether is it better to amend, before it be tried, that plan, which may be termed the result of the wisdom of America, or leave it to be amended, at leisure, as mature experience shall direct?

Although a very great variety of ostensible objections have been publicly offered, the real and sincere objections are hardly ever disclosed in private. There is a class, opposed to the union of *thirteen different states*, and the reason they assign, is the vast extent of our territory. Let us consider well their objection,

To consolidate the whole thirteen states into a single organization, was out of the convention's contemplation,—for two unanswerable reasons. In the first place, they were satisfied, that not one of the states would renounce its sovereignty. In the next place, they considered, that, in a single government, with a great extent of territory, the advantages are most unequally diffused. As the extreme parts are scarcely sensible of its protection, so are they scarcely under its domination. It is generally agreed, that a great extended nation can long continue under no *single* form of government, except a despotism into which, either a republic, or a limited monarchy, will be certain to degenerate. And hence, if I understand the man who styles himself a *Centinel*, he insinuates, that, if these states will persist in remaining under one head, they must soon fall under the dominion of a despot. But, my fellow-citizens, in a confederate republic, consisting of distinct states, completely organized within themselves, and each of no greater extent than is proper for a republican form, almost all the blessings of government are equally diffused. Its protection extends to the remotest corner, and there every man is under restraint of laws. [33]

A true federal republic is always capable of accession by the peaceable and friendly admission of new single states. *Its true size is neither greater nor less than that, which may comprehend all the states, which, by their contiguity, may become enemies, unless united under one common head, capable of reconciling all their differences.* Such a government as this, excels any single government, extending over the same territory, as a band of brothers is superior to a band of slaves, or as thirteen common men, for the purposes of agriculture, would be superior to a giant, enjoying strength of body equal to them all.

The idea of a balance has long influenced the politics of Europe. But how much superior to this almost impracticable balance would be a general league, constituting a kind of federal republic, consisting of all the independent powers of Europe, for preventing the impositions and encroachments of one upon another! A true and perfect confederate government, however, in her situation, is not to be attained; although the great soul of HENRY THE FOURTH is said to have conceived the idea.

Shall America then form one grand federal republic? Or shall she, after experiencing the benefits of even an imperfect union, and when a union the most perfect is requisite for her permanent safety;—shall she, in this situation, divide into thirteen contemptible single governments, exposed to every insult and wrong from abroad, and watching each other's motions, with all the captiousness of jealous rivals? Or shall she divide into two or more federal republics, actuated by the same malignant dispositions? In either of these cases, after struggling through infinite toils, difficulty, and danger, should the thirteen single states be, at last, delivered from foreign foes, they will fall upon each other; and no man can predict, what forms of government, or division of territory, shall finally obtain———. Two or three federal republics might possibly retain their independence. But they would be in the same situation, with respect to each other, as France, England, and Spain, scarcely ever free from war; practicing the arts of dissimulation and intrigue; in vain striving to impose, by endless negotiation; and, after all, relying only on the immense naval and land forces, which they continually maintain. [34]

Let us then, my countrymen, embrace those blessings which Providence is ready to shower on us. Open and extend your views! Let the prospect comprehend the present and future generations, yourselves, your children, your relatives, your fellow-citizens, dwellers on the same continent, and inhabitants of the whole terraqueous globe.

With the prospect of my country's future glory, presented to my glowing imagination, it is difficult to resist the strong impulse of enthusiasm. But it is neither *my* talent, nor desire, to mislead. I wish only to impress the genuine advantages of the proposed plan; and, if possible, to rouse every man from that supineness, into which he is lulled by the present deceitful calm. To acquit themselves, like men, when visible danger assails; and, when it is repelled, to sink like savages, into indolence, is said to be characteristic of Americans. I am not, however, one of those, who imagine a necessity for embracing almost any scheme, which the convention might have devised, for giving to the union more efficient powers. Had the plan, they have proposed, contained the seeds of much, though distant, evil, perhaps a *faithful patriot* might address you thus:

"Let us not, my friends, in a fit of unmanly apprehension,
"betray that immense charge, with which Americans, at this
"day are entrusted! Let us confide in *the wisdom of our great*
"*men*, with the assistance of Heaven, to establish yet our
"safety and happiness! Let us, in the meantime, sustain all
"our evils, with resignation and firmness. Let us hope, that

"no foreign power, or lawless internal combinations, shall do
"us a mighty injury! Let us be frugal, economical, industri-
"ous! Let us suspend the cruel collection of debts! Let
"commerce continue to droop! Let us awhile submit even to
"infamy; and turn a callous ear to the indignant reproaches
"of our late faithful and affectionate servants, friends and
"benefactors."

To this purpose might a man plausibly declaim; provided the proposed plan contained many and great faults; provided it were not calculated to promote the general good, without violating the *just rights* of a single individual; and provided it were not the best, which, under all circumstances, could be reasonably expected. It was the parting declaration of [35] the American NESTOR, to his exalted fellow-labourers, that "he would subscribe, because he thought it good, and because "he did not know, but it was the best that could be contrived." My own declaration, which would be the same, were I now standing on the verge of eternity, is, that if the whole matter were left to my discretion, I would not change a single part. On reflection, I was pleased with the conduct of the Virginia and Maryland assemblies, in appointing distant days for the meeting of their state conventions. Not that I greatly admired the supposed motive; but because I sincerely wished every man might have time to comprehend and weigh the plan, before the ultimate decision of these two states should be pronounced. The longer it is contemplated, after it is understood, the greater, I am persuaded, will be the approbation of those, who wish the public good, and to whose private views and expectations, nothing, which tends to promote that good, can be greatly detrimental.

But alas! My fellow citizens, on the adoption of this fatal plan, and when every part of the great complicated machine shall be put in motion, the lustre of our state assemblies will be diminished by the superior splendour of the federal head. This single consideration, although many hesitate to avow it, will cause more opposition, than all the rest united. Weigh well the objection. If ever it be material to inquire, by whom reasons are adduced, it is on this peculiar occasion.

From the objection itself, may perhaps be discerned the danger we are opposed to, from the secret views and selfish considerations of the objector.

What at this moment to the nations abroad is the state of Maryland? The poor member of a defenceless system of petty republics. In what light is she viewed by her sister states? Whatever rank she now possesses, will remain after the great alteration of the system. They will all rise or fall in the proportion which now exists. What then are the powers an individual state will lose? She will no longer be able to deny congress that, which congress, at this moment, has a right to demand. She will have no power to enter into a treaty, alliance, or confederation. She shall, in time of war, grant no letters of marque and reprisal. She shall [36] coin no money, emit no bills of credit, nor make any thing but gold and silver a tender in payment of debts. She shall pass no bill of attainder, or ex post facto law, or law impairing the obligation of a contract. She shall grant no title of nobility. She shall not, *without consent of congress*, lay any duty on imports or exports, except what may be necessary for executing her inspection laws. She shall not, *without consent of congress*, lay any duty on tonnage, keep troops or\* ships of war, in time of peace; enter into any agreement, or compact, with another state, or with a foreign power; or engage in war, unless actually invaded, or in such imminent danger, as will not admit of delay.

Of the several powers, from which an individual state is thus restrained, some are improper to be used at all; others belong not even now to the individual states; and the rest are strictly proper for only the federal head. The aversion from ceding them to congress, is just as reasonable as in a state of nature would be the reluctance of an individual to relinquish any of his natural rights, upon entering into a state of society. The principle, on which, at length, he surrenders, is the necessity of every one's making a cession of some rights, to enable the

---

\* The advantage derived from this to the southern states, is easily perceived. Have not serious apprehensions been entertained on account of the vast superiority of the eastern states by sea?

sovereign to protect the rest. Each state is fully sensible, that she cannot protect herself; and yet she would enjoy the advantages of an union, without making the necessary contributions. To discern how preposterous is the idea, requires not more than a moment's reflection.

For the honour of my countrymen, I hope this extreme reluctance to surrender power is confined to those, whose ambition, or private interest, would have all things subservient to the omnipotence of assembly. In the few years that the state constitutions have endured, has not every one seen pregnant proofs of the vain love of domination? Has he not also seen decisive marks of overbearing secret influence? Where are the instances of exalted patriotism? But I forbear. [37] Far from me is the wish to cast wantonly one stinging or disagreeable reflection. The subject naturally required the general remark, and I hope, this short hint may be excused.

Is there a possible advantage to be derived to the public, from a single state's exercising powers proper only for the federal head; suppose even each state should use them properly and alike; which, in the nature of things, is not to be expected? If there be men, who delight in parliamentary warfare; who choose a fair wide field for displaying their talents; who wish to see every servant of the public prostrate before them; whose ears soothed by humble supplication; they may still enjoy rich sources of gratification. Are not the regulations of property, the regulations of the penal law, the protection of the weak, the promotion of useful arts, the whole internal government of their respective republics; are not these the main objects of every wise and honest legislature? Are not these things still in their power; and, whilst free from invasion or injuries abroad, are not these almost the only things, in which sovereignty is exercised?

That the state legislatures will soon "drop out of sight," is an idea most extravagant and absurd; because, in addition to the importance of their duties, the very existence of the congress depends upon them. That they will, at least, dwindle into something like city corporations, is an apprehension, founded on no better principle. May the Ruler of the universe inspire them with wisdom to discharge those numerous and extensive duties, which they will find remaining. To do this, as they ought, will be far preferable to the\* breaking all useful national measures, and marring the concerns of a continent. To do this, as they ought, will afford more true pleasure to a good mind, than the carrying, by consummate eloquence and address, the most interesting federal measure, which cannot be contrived by an enlightened honest politician, in a state assembly, possessing all its darling sovereignties!

You have been assured, that, soon as this fatal plan shall [38] succeed, an host of rapacious collectors will *invade* the land; that they will wrest from you the hard product of your industry, turn out your children from their dwellings, perhaps commit your bodies to a jail; and your own immediate representatives will have no power to relieve you. This is the mere phrenzy of declamation, the ridiculous conjuration of spectres and hobgobblins!

To the five per cent. impost most of the states have more than once given their assent. This is the only tax which congress wishes immediately to impose. Of the imposition of assessment, capitation, or direct taxes of any kind, the congress entertains no idea at present; and although it be proper for the federal head to possess this power in reserve, nothing but some unforeseen disaster will ever drive them to such ineligible expedients. Setting aside the immediate advantages of revived credit and trade, and the increased value of your property and labour, you will be delivered, in a great measure, from that load of direct taxation, which has been so unequally borne, and produced so little substantial good.

Permit me to demand, what mighty benefit has resulted from the exercise of those sovereign rights, that, in general, you should be loth to resign them? Has not a perpetual clamour been kept up (it matters not whether justly or otherwise) concerning the enormous impositions on the people? And what are the advantages derived to the people of the respective states, to the union, or to meritorious individuals?

---

\* Is it possible to reflect, without indignation, on the fate of the five per cent. impost scheme?

Has not the far greater part of a state's internal expences been owing to the extreme length of sessions? Have not these sessions been consumed in disgusting altercation, and in passing laws, serving to little better purpose, than to swell the statute book, encourage a negligence of duty, and obstruct the administration of justice?

To trace each real and ostensible objection up to its proper course, would be a task equally invidious, irksome and unnecessary. The characters of the principal advocates and opponents are well known. To him who declines not a public avowal of his sentiments, some credit is due, for his candour; and he is entitled to your patient attention. But, he that prefers a secret corner, for dealing forth his ob- [39] jections, and expositions, should be heard with caution and distrust. It is in a land of slavery alone, where truth shuns the open day.— Each side has imputed to the other illiberal and selfish motives. Consider then the particular interests of each; and bear this in your minds, that an interest may be either honourable and praiseworthy, or directly the reverse.

You have been told that the proposed plan was calculated peculiarly for the rich. In all governments, not merely despotic, the wealthy must, in most things, find an advantage, from the possession of that, which is too much the end and aim of mankind. In the proposed plan, there is nothing like a discrimination in their favour. How this amazing objection is to be supported, I am at a loss to conjecture. Is it a just cause of reproach, that the constitution effectually secures property? Or would the objectors introduce a general scramble? In eligibility to office, in suffrage, and in every other civil right, men are all on terms of perfect equality. And yet, notwithstanding this just equality, each man is to pay taxes in proportion to his ability, or his expences.

A still more surpassing objection remains to be considered. "This new constitution, so much bepraised, and admired, will "commence in a moderate aristocracy. To a corrupt and op- "pressive one the transition is easy, and inevitable, unless "some Cæsar, or a Cromwell, in their stead, shall make a seiz- "ure of their liberties. As to the house of representatives, "they will either be insignificant spectators of the contest "between the president and the senate, or their weight will be "thrown in to one of the scales."

No man, indeed, has exactly used these words; but they contain the sum and scope of several recent publications.

In the course of my remarks, I have already said enough to expose the futility of certain objections, which are ushered to the world, under the auspices of a pair of honourable names. Notwithstanding the care and pomposity, with which they are circulated, it is not worth while to draw invidious comparison. One gentleman, whose name is thus *freely* used, I think, calls the house of representatives a mere [40] shred, or rag of representation. Does he consider the distinction between the objects of a confederate republic, and of a single government? It is a poor return for that singular respect which the convention paid to the majesty of the people, in contriving, that congress shall not only be a representation of states, as heretofore, but also an immediate representation of the people. Were 5, 10, or even 20,000, the ratio proposed, then peradventure the honourable objector might clamour about the expence of a mobbish legislature.

The fact is, that the new government, constructed on the broad basis of equality, mutual benefits, and national good, is not calculated to secure a single state all her natural advantages at the expence of the natural and acquired advantages of her respectable brethren of New England.

His real objection against constituting the senate an executive council arises, I conceive, from the equality of representation. As to the trite maxim, that the legislative and executive ought ever to be distinct and separate, I would, in addition to my foregoing observations on this head, refer him to Montesquieu's chapter on the English government. I could wish, the writings of that great man, and of Judge Blackstone, so often either copied, or cited for conclusive authority, were better understood. Should a second, or a third convention, be obtained, the aforesaid honourable gentlemen can never be *fully* indulged in their main object of a proportionate representation.

The examples of a genuine aristocracy are rare. They were founded in times of profound ignorance, and when the mass of property was in the hands of a few, whilst the rest pined in want and wretchedness. One European aristocratic government, if such it can be called, has grown out of the original defective form, the offspring of necessity, and commenced amidst the horrors of a civil war. Although the people of that country fought, and intended, to be free, their compact of government never was complete; they did not attend to the principle of rotation, and checks; and a genuine representation did never there prevail.

An aristocracy can perhaps subsist with only a moderate extent of territory and population, But it is a farce to talk of an aristocracy; when there are two branches, so dif-[41] ferently formed ; when the members of each are chosen for a reasonable term ; and when their reappointment depends on the good opinion of their countrymen. It is not in nature, that a man with the least portion of *common* sense can believe the people of America will consent to such a deplorable change in their constitution, as shall confine all power to a few noble families, or that, without their consent, the change will be effected, by internal policy, or force.

Whilst mankind shall believe freedom to be better than slavery; whilst our lands shall be generally distributed, and not held by a few insolent barons, on the debasing terms of vassalage; whilst we shall teach our children to read and write; whilst the liberty of the press, that grand palladium, which tyrants are compelled to respect, shall remain; whilst a spark of public love shall animate even a small part of the people; whilst even self-love shall be the general ruling principle; so long will it be impossible for an aristocracy to arise from the proposed plan.—Should Heaven, in its wrath, inflict blindness on the people of America; should they reject this fair offer of permanent safety and happiness; to predict what species of government shall at last spring from disorder, is beyond the short reach of political foresight.

Believe me, my fellow citizens, that no overweening self conceit, no vain ambition, no restless meddling spirit, has produced this address. Long had I waited to see this vast question treated, as it deserves; and the publication disseminated in my native state. Many judicious observations had appeared in newspapers and handbills. But no publication, that I have seen, has gone fully into the merits, considered the objections, and explained that, which is doubtful and obscure. On this account I, at length, made the attempt. That my performance is equal to my wishes, I can by no means believe. I have, however, a consolation in reflecting, that it will be difficult for any man to demonstrate, that, in this business, I have a particular interest. In many of my remarks, I have been anticipated by writings, which I have seen; and I have collected ma- [42] terials, wherever I could find them. Could I be convinced, that I have said nothing, which had not before been said or thought by thousands, the reflection would yield far less mortification than pleasure.

ARISTIDES.

Annapolis, January 1st, 1788.

Letter on the Federal Constitution, October 16, 1787, By Edmund Randolph [Richmond: Printed by Augustin Davis, 1787.]

16 mo. pp. 16.

---

Edmund Randolph was a member of the Annapolis, Philadelphia, and Virginia Conventions, in all of which he took a prominent though equivocal position. His letter on the Constitution was widely circulated in the newspapers, and was printed in pamphlet form as above, a copy of which is in the Library of Congress, but cannot be found, so I am compelled to give the title from Sabin's *Dictionary of Books relating to America.*

"I do not know what impression the letter may make in Virginia. It is generally understood here that the arguments contained in it in favor of the Constitution are much stronger than the objections which prevent his assent. His arguments are forcible in all places, and with all persons. His objections are connected with his particular way of thinking on the subject, in which many of the adversaries to the Constitution do not concur." *Madison to Washington,* Jan. 25, 1788.

P. L. F.

RICHMOND, Oct. 10, 1787.

THE HONORABLE THE SPEAKER OF THE HOUSE OF DELEGATES:

*Sir,—*

The constitution which I enclosed to the general assembly in a late official letter, appears without my signature. This circumstance, although trivial in its own nature, has been rendered rather important to myself at least by being misunderstood by some, and misrepresented by others.—As I disdain to conceal the reasons for withholding my subscription, I have always been, still am, and ever shall be, ready to proclaim them to the world. To the legislature, therefore, by whom I was deputed to the federal convention, I beg leave now to address them; affecting no indifference to public opinion, but resolved not to court it by an unmanly sacrifice of my own judgment.

As this explanation will involve a summary, but general review of our federal situation, you will pardon me, I trust, although I should transgress the usual bounds of a letter.

Before my departure for the convention, I believed, that the confederation was not so eminently defective, as it had been supposed. But after I had entered into a free communication with those who were best informed of the condition and interest of each State; after I had compared the intelligence derived from them with the properties which ought to characterize the government of our union, I became persuaded, that the confederation was destitute of every energy, which a constitution of the United States ought to possess.

For the objects proposed by its institution were, that it should be a shield against foreign hostility, and a firm resort against domestic commotion; that it should cherish trade, and promote the prosperity of the States under its care.

But these are not among the attributes of our present

union. Severe experience under the pressure of war—a ruinous weakness manifested since the return of peace; and the contemplation of those dangers, which darken the future prospect, have condemned the hope of grandeur and of safety under the auspices of the confederation.

In the exigencies of war, indeed, the history of its effects is but short; the final ratification having been delayed until the year 1781. But however short, this period is distinguished by melancholy testimonies of its inability to maintain in harmony, the social intercourse of the States, to defend congress against encroachments on their rights, and to obtain by requisitions, supplies to the federal treasury, or recruits to the federal armies. I shall not attempt an enumeration of the particular instances; but leave to your own remembrance and the records of congress the support of the assertions.

In the season of peace too, not many years have elapsed; and yet each of them has produced fatal examples of delinquency, and sometimes of pointed opposition to federal duties. To the various remonstrances of congress, I appeal, for a gloomy, but unexaggerated narrative of the injuries which our faith, honor and happiness, have sustained by the failure of the States.

But these evils are past; and some may be led by an honest zeal to conclude that they cannot be repeated. Yes, sir, they will be repeated as long as the confederation exists, and will bring with them other mischiefs springing from the same source, which cannot yet be foreseen in their full array of terror.

If we examine the constitution and laws of the several States, it is immediately discovered that the law of nations is unprovided with sanctions in many cases, which deeply affect public dignity and public justice. The letter however of the confederation does not permit congress to remedy these defects, and such an authority, although evidently deducible from its spirit, cannot without violation of the second article, be assumed. Is it not a political phenomenon, that the head of the confederacy should be doomed to be plunged into war, from its wretched impotency to check offences against this law; and sentenced to witness in unavailing anguish the infraction of their engagements to foreign sovereigns?

And yet this is not the only grevious point of weakness. After a war shall be inevitable, the requisitions of congress for quotas of men or money, will again prove unproductive and fallacious. Two causes will always conspire to this baneful consequence.

1. No government can be stable, which hangs on human inclination alone, unbiassed by the coercion; and 2, from the very connection between States bound to proportionate contributions, jealousies and suspicions naturally arise, which at least chill the ardor, if they do not excite the murmurs of the whole. I do not forget indeed, that by one sudden impulse our part of the American continent has been thrown into a military posture, and that in the earlier annals of the war, our armies marched to the field on the mere recommendations of congress. But ought we to argue from a contest, thus signalized by the magnitude of its stake, that as often as a flame shall be hereafter kindled, the same enthusiasm will fill our legions, or renew them, as they may be filled by losses?

If not, where shall we find protection? Impressions, like those, which prevent a compliance with requisitions of regular forces, will deprive the American republic of the services of militia. But let us suppose that they are attainable, and acknowledge as I always shall, that they are the natural support of a free government. When it is remembered, that in their absence agriculture must languish; that they are not habituated to military exposures and the rigour of military discipline, and that the necessity of holding in readiness successive detachments, carries the expense far beyond that of enlistments—This resource ought to be adopted with caution.

As strongly too, am I persuaded, that the requisitions for money will not be more cordially received. For besides the distrust, which would prevail with respect to them also; besides the opinion, entertained by each state of its own liberality and unsatisfied demands against the United States, there is another consideration not less worth of attention—the first rule for determining each quota of the value of all lands granted or surveyed, and of the buildings and improvements thereon. It is no longer doubted that an equitable, uniform mode of estimating that value is impracticable; and therefore twelve States have substituted the number of inhabitants under certain limitations, as the standard according to which money is to be furnished. But under the subsisting articles of the union, the assent of the thirteenth State is necessary, and has not yet been given. This does of itself lessen the hope of procuring a revenue for federal uses; and the miscarriage of the impost almost rivets our despondency.

Amidst these disappointments, it would afford some consolation, if when rebellion shall threaten any State, an ultimate asylum could be found under the wing of congress. But it is at least equivocal whether they can intrude forces into a State, rent asunder by civil discord, even with the purest solicitude for our federal welfare, and on the most urgent entreaties of the State itself. Nay the very allowance of this power would be pageantry alone, from the want of money and men.

To these defect of congressional power, the history of man has subjoined others not less alarming. I earnestly pray that the recollection of common sufferings, which terminated in common glory, may check the sallies of violence, and perpetuate mutual friendship between the States. But I cannot presume, that we are superior to those unsocial passions, which under like circumstances have infested more ancient nations. I cannot presume, that through all time, in the daily mixture of American citizens with each other, in the conflicts for commercial advantages, in the discontents which the neighborhood of territory has been seen to engender in other quarters of the globe, and in the efforts of faction and intrigue—thirteen distinct communities under no effective superintending control, (as the United States confessedly now are, notwithstanding the bold terms of the confederation) will avoid a hatred to each other deep and deadly.

In the prosecution of this enquiry, we shall find the general prosperity to decline under a system thus unnerved. No sooner is the merchant prepared for foreign ports, with the treasures which this new world kindly offers to his acceptance, than it is announced to him, that they are shut against American shipping, or opened under oppressive regulations. He urges congress to a counter-policy, and is answered only by a condolence on the general misfortune. He is immediately struck with the conviction, that until exclusion shall be opposed to exclusion, and restriction to restriction, the American flag will be disgraced. For who can conceive, that thirteen legislatures, viewing commerce under different regulations, and fancying themselves discharged from every obligation to concede the smallest of their commercial advantages for the benefit of the whole, will be wrought into a concert of action and defiance of every prejudice? Nor is this all: Let the great improvements be recounted, which have enriched and illustrated Europe: Let it be noted, how few those are, which will be absolutely denied to the United States, comprehending within their boundaries, the choicest blessings of climate, soil and navigable waters; then let the most sanguine patriot banish, if he can, the mortifying belief that all these must sleep, until they shall be roused by the vigor of a national government.

I have not exemplified the preceding remarks by minute details; because they are evidently fortified by truth, and the consciousness of the United States of America. I shall, therefore, no longer deplore the unfitness of the confederation to secure our peace; but proceed with a truly unaffected distrust of my own opinions to examine what order of powers the government of the United States ought to enjoy? How they ought to be defended against encroachments? Whether they can be interwoven in the confederation, without an alteration of its very essence, or must be lodged in new hands? Showing, at the same time, the convulsions which seem to await us, from a dissolution of the union or partial confederacies.

To mark the kind and degree of authority which ought to be confided to the government of the United States, is no more than to reverse the description which I have already given, of the defects of the confederation.

From thence it will follow, that the operations of peace and war will be clogged without regular advances of money, and that these will be slow indeed, if dependent on supplication alone. For what better name do requisitions deserve, which may be evaded or opposed without the fear of coercion? But although coercion is an indispensable ingredient, it ought not to be directed against a State, as a State; it being impossible to attempt it except by blockading the trade of the delinquent, or carrying war into its bowels. Even if these violent schemes were eligible, in other respects, both of them might, perhaps, be defeated by the scantiness of the public chest; would be tardy in their complete effect, as the expense of the land and naval equipments must be first reimbursed; and might drive the proscibed State into the desperate resolve of inviting foreign alliances. Against each of them lie separate unconquerable objections. A blockade is not equally applicable to all the States, they being differently circumstanced in commerce and in ports; nay an excommunication from the privilege of the union would be vain, because every regulation or prohibition may be easily eluded under the rights of American citizenship, or of foreign nations. But how shall we speak of the intrusion of troops? Shall we arm citizens against citizens, and habituate them to shed kindred blood? Shall we risk the inflicting of wounds which will generate a rancour never to be subdued? Would there be no room to fear, that an army accustomed to fight for the establishment of authority, would salute an emperor of their own? Let us not bring these things into jeopardy. Let us rather substitute the same process by which individuals are compelled to contribute to the government of their own States. Instead of making requisitions to the legislatures, it would appear more proper that taxes should be imposed by the federal head, under due modifications and guards; that the collectors should demand from the citizens their respective quotas, and be supported as in the collection of ordinary taxes.

It follows, too, that, as the general government will be responsible to foreign nations, it ought to be able to annul any offensive measure, or enforce any public right. Perhaps among the topics on which they may be aggrieved or complain, the commercial intercourse, and the manner in which contracts are discharged, may constitute the principal articles of clamor.

It follows, too, that the general government ought to be the supreme arbiter for adjusting every contention among the States In all their connections, therefore, with each other, and particularly in commerce, which will probably create the greatest discord, it ought to hold the reins.

It follows, too, that the general government ought to protect each State against domestic as well as external violence.

And lastly, it follows, that through the general government alone, can we ever assume the rank to which we are entitled by our resources and situation.

Should the people of America surrender these powers, they can be paramount to the constitutions and ordinary acts of legislation, only by being delegated by them. I do not pretend to affirm, but I venture to believe, that if the confederation had been solemnly questioned in opposition to our constitution, or even to one of our laws, posterior to it, it must have given away. For never did it obtain a higher ratification, than a resolution of assembly in the daily form.

This will be one security against encroachment, But another not less effectual is, to exclude the individual States from any agency in the national government, as far as it may be safe, and their interposition may not be absolutely necessary.

But now, sir, permit me to declare, that in my humble judgment, the powers by which alone the blessings of a general government can be accomplished, cannot be interwoven in the confederation, without a change in its very essence, or, in other words, that the confederation must be thrown aside. This is almost demonstrable from the inefficacy of requisitions, and from the necessity of converting them into acts of authority. My suffrage, as a citizen, is also for additional powers. But to whom shall we commit those acts of authority, these additional powers? To congress? When I formerly lamented the defects in the jurisdiction of congress, I had no view to indicate any other opinion, than that the federal head ought not to be so circumscribed. For free as I am at all times to profess my reverence for that body, and the individuals who compose it, I am yet equally free to make known my aversion to repose such a trust in a tribunal so constituted. My objections are not the visions of theory, but the results of my own observations in America, and of the experience of others abroad. 1. The legislative and executive are concentred in the same persons. This, where real power exists, must eventuate in tyranny. 2. The representation of the States bears no proportion to their importance. This is an unreasonable subjection of the will of the majority to that of the minority. 2. The mode of election and the liability of being recalled, may too often render the delegates rather partizans of their own States than representatives of the union. 4. Cabal and intrigue must consequently gain an ascendancy in a course of years. 5. A single house of legislation will sometimes be precipitate, perhaps passionate. 6. As long as seven States are required for the smallest, and nine for the greatest votes, may not foreign influence at some future day insinuate itself, so as to interrupt every active exertion? 7. To crown the whole, it is scarce within the verge of possibility, that so numerous an assembly should acquire that secrecy, dispatch, and vigour, which are the test of excellence in the executive department.

My inference from these facts and principles, is, that the new powers must be deposited in a new body, growing out of a consolidation of the union, as far as the circumstances of the State will allow. Perhaps, however, some may meditate its dissolution, and others partial confederacies.

The first is an idea awful indeed, and irreconcilable with a very early, and hitherto uniform conviction, that without union, we must be undone. For, before the voice of war was heard, the pulse of the then colonies was tried, and found to beat in unison. The unremitted labor of our enemies was to divide, and the policy of every congress to bind us together. But in no example was this truth more clearly displayed, than in the prudence with which independence was unfolded to the sight, and in the forbearance to declare it, until America almost unanimously called for it. After we had thus launched into troubles, never before explored, and the hour of heavy distress, the remembrance of our social strength not only forbade despair, but drew from congress the most illustrious repetition of their settled purpose to depise all terms, short of independence.

Behold, then, how successful and glorious we have been, while we acted in fraternal concord. But let us discard the illusion, that by this success, and this glory, the crest of danger has irrecoverably fallen. Our governments are yet too youthful to have acquired stability from habit. Our very quiet depends upon the duration of the union. Among the upright and intelligent, few can read without emotion the future fate of the States, if severed from each other. Then shall we learn the full weight of foreign intrigue. Then shall we hear of partitions of our country. If a prince, inflamed by the lust of conquest, should use one State as the instrument of enslaving others—if every State is to be wearied by perpetual alarms, and compelled to maintain large military establishments—if all questions are to be decided by an appeal to arms, where a difference of opinion cannot be removed by negociation—in a word, if all the direful misfortunes which haunt the peace of rival nations, are to triumph over the land, for what have we to contend? why have we exhausted our wealth? why have we basely betrayed the heroic martyrs of the federal cause.

But dreadful as the total dissolution of the union is to my mind, I entertain no less horror at the thought of partial confederacies. I have not the least ground for supposing that an overture of this kind would be listened to by a single State, and the presumption is, that the politics of the greater part of the States, flow from the warmest attachment to an union of the whole. If, however, a lesser confederacy could be obtained by Virginia, let me conjure my countrymen well to weigh the probable consequences, before they attempt to form it.

On such an event, the strength of the union would be divided in two, or perhaps three parts. Has it so increased since the war as to be divisible—and yet remain sufficient for our happiness?

The utmost limit of any partial confederacy, which Virginia could expect to form, would comprehend the three southern States, and her nearest northern neighbour. But they, like ourselves, are diminished in their real force, by the mixture of of an unhappy species of population.

Again, may I ask, whether the opulence of the United States has been augmented since the war? This is answered in the negative, by a load of debt, and the declension of trade.

At all times must a southern confederacy support ships of war, and soldiery? As soon would a navy move from the forest, and a army from the earth, as such a confederacy, indebted, impoverished in its commerce, and destitute of men, could, for some years at least, provide an ample defence for itself.

Let it not be forgotten, that nations which can enforce their rights, have large claims against the United States, and that the creditor may insist on payment from any of them. Which of them would probably be the victim? The most productive and the most exposed When vexed by reprisals of war, the southern States will sue for alliance on this continent or beyond sea. If for the former, the necessity of an union of the whole is decided; if for the latter, America will, I fear, re-act the scenes of confusion and bloodshed, exhibited among most of those nations, which have, too late, repented the folly of relying on auxiliaries.

Two or more confederacies cannot but be competitors for power. The ancient friendship between the citizens of America, being thus cut off, bitterness and hostility will succeed in its place; in order to prepare against surrounding danger, we shall be compelled to vest some where or other, power approaching near to military government.

The annals of the world have abounded so much with instances of a divided people being a prey to foreign influence, that I shall not restrain my apprehensions of it, should our union be torn asunder. The opportunity of insinuating it, will be multiplied in proportion to the parts into which we may be broken.

In short, sir, I am fatigued with summoning up to my imagination the miseries which will harass the United States, if torn from each other, and which will not end until they are superseded by fresh mischiefs under the yoke of a tyrant.

I come, therefore, to the last, and perhaps only refuge in our difficulties, a consolidation of the union, as far as circumstances will permit. To fulfil this desirable object, the constitution was framed by the federal convention. A quorum of eleven States, and the only member from a twelfth have subscribed it; Mr. Mason, of Virginia, Mr. Gerry, of Massachusetts, and myself having refused to subscribe.

Why I refused, will, I hope, be solved to the satisfaction of those who know me, by saying, that a sense of duty commanded me thus to act. It commanded me, sir, for believe me, that no event of my life ever occupied more of my reflection. To subscribe, seemed to offer no inconsiderable gratification, since it would have presented me to the world as a fellow laborer with the learned and zealous statesmen of America.

But it was far more interesting to my feelings, that I was about to differ from three of my colleagues, one of whom is, to the honor of the country which he has saved, embosomed in their affections, and can receive no praise from the highest lustre of language; the other two of whom have been long enrolled among the wisest and best lovers of the commonwealth; and the unshaken and intimate friendship of all of whom I have ever prized, and still do prize, as among the happiest of all acquisitions.—I was no stranger to the reigning partiality for the members who composed the convention, and had not the smallest doubt, that from this cause, and from the ardor of a reform of government, the first applauses at least would be loud and profuse. I suspected, too, that there was something in the human breast which for a time would be apt to construe a temperateness in politics, into an enmity to the union. Nay, I plainly foresaw, that in the dissensions of parties, a middle line would probaby be interpreted into a want of enterprise and decision.—But these considerations, how seducing soever, were feeble opponents to the suggestions of my conscience. I was sent to exercise my judgment, and to exercise it was my fixed determination; being instructed by even an imperfect acquaintance with mankind, that self approbation is the only true reward which a political career can bestow, and that popularity would have been but another name for perfidy, if to secure it, I had given up the freedom of thinking for myself.

It would have been a peculiar pleasure to me to have ascertained before I left Virginia, the temper and genius of my fellow citizens, considered relatively to a government, so substantially differing from the confederation as that which is now submitted. But this was, for many obvious reasons, impossible; and I was thereby deprived of what I thought the necessary guides.

I saw, however, that the confederation was tottering from its own weakness, and that the sitting of a convention was a signal of its total insufficiency. I was therefore ready to assent to a scheme of government, which was proposed, and which went beyond the limits of the confederation, believing, that without being too extensive it would have preserved our tranquility, until that temper and that genius should be collected.

But when the plan which is now before the general assembly, was on its passage through the convention, I moved, that the State conventions should be at liberty to amend, and that a second general convention should be holden, to discuss the amendments, which should be suggested by them. This motion was in some measure justified by the manner in which the confederation was forwarded originally, by congress to the State legislatures, in many of which amendments were proposed, and those amendments were afterwards examined in congress. Such a motion was doubly expedient here, as the delegation of so much power was sought for. But it was negatived. I then expressed my unwillingness to sign. My reasons were the following:

1. It is said in the resolutions which accompany the constitution, that it is to be submitted to a convention of delegates chosen is each State by the people thereof, for their assent and ratification. The meaning of these terms is allowed universally to be, that the convention must either adopt the constitution in the whole, or reject it in the whole, and is pos-

itively forbidden to amend. If therefore, I had signed, I should have felt myself bound to be silent as to amendments, and to endeavor to support the constitution without the correction of a letter. With this consequence before my eyes, and with a determination to attempt an amendment, I was taught by a regard for consistency not to sign.

2. My opinion always was, and still is, that every citizen of America, let the crisis be what it may, ought to have a full opportunity to propose, through his representatives, any amendment which in his apprehension, tends to the public welfare. By signing, I should have contradicted this sentiment.

3. A constitution ought to have the hearts of the people on its side. But if at a future day it should be burdensome after having been adopted in the whole, and they should insinuate that it was in some measure forced upon them, by being confined to the single alternative of taking or rejecting it altogether, under my impressions, and with my opinions, I should not be able to justify myself had I signed.

4. I was always satisfied, as I have now experienced, that this great subject would be placed in new lights and attitudes by the criticism of the world, and that no man can assure himself how a constitution will work for a course of years, until at least he shall have heard the observations of the people at large. I also fear more from inaccuracies in a constitution, than from gross errors in any other composition; because our dearest interests are to be regulated by it; and power, if loosely given, especially where it will be interpreted with great latitude, may bring sorrow in its execution. Had I signed with these ideas, I should have virtually shut my ears against the information which I ardently desired.

5. I was afraid that if the constitution was to be submitted to the people, to be wholly adopted or wholly rejected by them, they would not only reject it, but bid a lasting farewell to the union. This formidable event I wished to avert, by keeping myself free to propose amendments, and thus, if possible, to remove the obstacles to an effectual government. But it will be asked, whether all these arguments, were not be well weighed in convention. They were, sir, with great candor.

Nay, when I called to mind the respectability of those, with whom I was associated, I almost lost confidence in these principles. On other occasions, I should cheerfully have yielded to a majority; on this the fate of thousands yet unborn, enjoined me not to yield until I was convinced.

Again, may I be asked, why the mode pointed out in the constitution for its amendment, may not be a sufficient security against its imperfections, without now arresting it in its progress? My answers are—1. That it is better to amend, while we have the constitution in our power, while the passions of designing men are not yet enlisted, and while a bare majority of the States may amend than to wait for the uncertain assent of three fourths of the States. 2. That a bad feature in government, becomes more and more fixed every day. 3. That frequent changes of a constitution, even if practicable, ought not to be wished, but avoided as much as possible. And 4. That in the present case, it may be questionable, whether, after the particular advantages of its operation shall be discerned, three fourths of the States can be induced to amend.

I confess, that it is no easy task, to devise a scheme which shall be suitable to the views of all. Many expedients have occurred to me, but none of them appear less exceptionable than this; that if our convention should choose to amend, another federal convention be recommended: that in that federal convention the amendments proposed by this or any other State be discussed; and if incorporated in the constitution or rejected, or if a proper number of the other States should be unwilling to accede to a second convention, the constitution be again laid before the same State conventions, which shall again assemble on the summons of the executives, and it shall be either wholly adopted, or wholly rejected, without a further power of amendment. I count such a delay as nothing in comparison with so grand an object; especially too as the privilege of amending must terminate after the use of it once.

I should now conclude this letter, which is already too long, were it not incumbent on me, from having contended for amendments, to set forth the particulars, which I conceive to require correction. I undertake this with reluctance: because it is remote from my intentions to catch the prejudices or prepossessions of any man But as I mean only to manifest that I have not been actuated by caprice, and now to explain every objection at full length would be an immense labour, I shall content myself with enumerating certain heads, in which the constitution is most repugnant to my wishes.

The two first points are the equality of suffrage in the senate, and the submission of commerce to a mere majority in the legislature, with no other check than the revision of the president. I conjecture that neither of these things can be corrected; and particularly the former, without which we must have risen perhaps in disorder.

But I am sanguine in hoping that in every other justly obnoxious clause, Virginia will be seconded by a majority of the States. I hope that she will be seconded. 1. In causing all ambiguities of expression to be precisely explained. 2. In rendering the president ineligible after a given number of years. 3. In taking from him the power of nominating to the judiciary offices, or of filling up vacancies which may there happen during the recess of the senate, by granting commissions which shall expire at the end of their next sessions. 4. In taking from him the power of pardoning for treason at least before conviction. 5. In drawing a line between the powers of congress and individual States; and in defining the former, so as to leave no clashing of jurisdictions nor dangerous disputes; and to prevent the one from being swallowed up by the other, under cover of general words, and implication. 6. In abridging the power of the senate to make treaties supreme laws of the land. 7. In incapacitating the congress to determine their own salaries. And 8. In limiting and defining the judicial power.

The proper remedy must be consigned to the wisdom of the convention; and the final step which Virginia shall pursue, if her overtures shall be discarded, must also rest with them.

You will excuse me, sir, for having been thus tedious. My feelings and duty demanded this exposition; for through no other channel could I rescue my omission to sign from misrepresentation, and no more effectual way could I exhibit to the general assembly an unreserved history of my conduct.

I have the honor, sir, to be with great respect, your most obedient servant,

EDMUND RANDOLPH.

Observation / leading to a fair examination / of the / system of government, / proposed by the late / Convention; / and to several essential and neces- / sary alterations in it. / In a number of / Letters / from the / Federal Farmer to the Republican. [New York:] Printed [by Thomas Greenleaf] in the year M,DCC,LXXXVII.

8vo. pp. 40.

---

Written by Richard Henry Lee, who was appointed a member of the Philadelphia Convention, but declined to serve. He was one of the foremost in opposition to the Constitution, both in the Continental Congress and before the people, and was the subject of numerous attacks in the press.

The "Letters of the Federal Farmer" was one of the most popular of arguments against the new government, "four editions (and several thousands) of the pamphlet...being in a few months printed and sold in the several states," which induced Lee to write "an additional number of Letters," but it is largely repetitions of the first, and I have therefore omitted its republication. A short review will be found in the American Magazine for May, 1788, and an elaborate reply by Timothy Pickering in Pickering's Life of Pickering, II, 352.

P. L. F.

## LETTER I.

OCTOBER 8th, 1787.

DEAR SIR,

MY letters to you last winter, on the subject of a well balanced national government for the United States, were the result of a free enquiry; when I passed from that subject to enquiries relative to our commerce, revenues, past administration, &c. I anticipated the anxieties I feel, on carefully examining the plan of government proposed by the convention. It appears to be a plan retaining some federal features; but to be the first important step, and to aim strongly at one consolidated government of the United States. It leaves the powers of government, and the representation of the people, so unnaturally divided between the general and state governments, that the operations of our system must be very uncertain. My uniform federal attachments, and the interest I have in the protection of property, and a steady execution of the laws, will convince you, that, if I am under any bias at all, it is in favor of any general system which shall promise those advantages. The instability of our laws increases my wishes for firm and steady government; but then, I can consent to no government, which, in my opinion, is not calculated equally to preserve the rights of all orders of men in the community. My object has been to join with those who have endeavoured to supply the defects in the forms of our governments by a steady and proper administration of them. Though I have long apprehended that fraudalent debtors, and embarrassed men, on the one hand, and men, on the other, unfriendly to republican equality, would produce an uneasiness among the people, and prepare the way, not for cool and deliberate reforms in the governments, but for changes calculated to promote the interests of particular orders of men. Acquit me, sir, of any agency in the formation of the new system; I shall be satisfied with seeing, if it shall be adopted with a prudent administration. Indeed I am so much convinced of the truth of Pope's maxim, that "That which is best [4] administered is best," that I am much inclined to subscribe to it from experience. I am not disposed to unreasonably contend about forms. I know our situation is critical, and it behoves us to make the best of it. A federal government of some sort is necessary. We have suffered the present to languish; and whether the confederation was capable or not originally of answering any valuable purposes, it is now but of little importance. I will pass by the men, and states, who have been particularly instrumental in preparing the way for a change, and perhaps, for governments not very favourable to the people at large. A constitution is now presented which we may reject, or which we may accept with or without amendments, and to which point we ought to direct our exertions is the question. To determine this question with propriety; we must attentively examine the system itself, and the probable consequences of either step. This I shall endeavour to do, so far as I am able, with candor and fairness; and leave you to decide upon the propriety of my opinions, the weight of my reasons, and how far my conclusions are well drawn. Whatever may be the conduct of others, on the present occasion, 1 do not mean hastily and positively to decide on the merits of the constitution proposed. I shall be open to conviction and always disposed to adopt that which, all things considered, shall appear to me to be most for the happiness of the community. It must be granted, that if men hastily and blindly adopt a system of government, they will as hastily and as blindly be led to alter or abolish it; and changes must ensue, one after another, till the peaceable and better part of the community will grow weary with changes, tumults and disorders, and be disposed to accept any government however despotic, that shall promise stability and firmness.

The first principal question that occurs, is, Whether, considering our situation, we ought to precipitate the adoption of the proposed constitution? If we remain cool and temperate, we are in no immediate danger of any commotions; we are in a state of perfect peace, and in no danger of invasions; the state governments are in the full exercise of their powers; and our governments answer all present exigencies, except the regulation of trade, securing credit, in some cases, and providing for the interest, in some instances, of the public debts; and whether we adopt a change three or nine months hence, can make but little odds with the private circumstances of individuals; their happiness and prosperity, after all, depend principally upon their own exertions. We are hardly recovered from a long and distressing war: The farmers, fishmen, &c. have not fully repaired the waste made by it. Industry [5] and frugality are again assuming their proper station. Private debts are lessened, and public debts incurred by the war have been, by various ways, diminished; and the public lands have now become a productive source for diminishing them much more. I know uneasy men, who with very much to precipitate, do not admit all these facts; but they are facts well known to all men who are thoroughly informed in the affairs of this country. It must, however, be admitted, that our federal system is defective, and that some of the state governments are not well administered; but, then, we impute to the defects in our governments many evils and embarrassments which are most clearly the result of the late war. We must allow men to conduct on the present occasion, as on all similar one's. They will urge a thousand pretences to answer their purposes on both sides. When we want a man to change his condition, we describe it as wretched, miserable, and despised; and draw a pleasing picture of that which we would have him assume. And when we wish the contrary, we reverse our descriptions. Whenever a clamor is raised, and idle men get to work, it is highly necessary to examine facts carefully, and without unreasonably suspecting men of falshood, to examine, and enquire attentively, under what impressions they act. It is too often the case in political concerns that men state facts not as they are, but as they wish them to be; and almost every man, by calling to mind past scenes, will find this to be true.

Nothing but the passions of ambitious, impatient, or disorderly men, I conceive, will plunge us into commotions, if time should be taken fully to examine and consider the system proposed. Men who feel easy in their circumstances, and such as are not sanguine in their expectations relative to the consequences of the proposed change, will remain quiet under the existing governments. Many commercial and monied men, who are uneasy, not without just cause, ought to be respected; and by no means, unreasonably disappointed in their expectations and hopes; but as to those who expect employments under the new constitution; as to those weak and ardent men who always expect to be gainers by revolutions, and whose lot it generally is to get out of one difficulty into another, they are very little to be regarded; and as to those who designedly avail themselves of this weakness and ardor, they are to be despised. It is natural for men, who wish to hasten the adoption of a measure, to tell us, now is the crisis—now is the critical moment which must be seized or all will be lost; and to shut the door against free enquiry, whenever conscious the thing presented has defects in it, which time and investigation will probably discover. This has been the custom of tyrants, [6] and their dependants in all ages. If it is true, what has been so often said, that the people of this country cannot change their condition for the worse, I presume it still behoves them to endeavour deliberately to change it for the better. The fickle and ardent, in any community are the proper tools for establishing despotic government. But it is deliberate and thinking men, who must establish and secure governments on free principles. Before they decide on the plan proposed, they will enquire whether it will probably be a blessing or a curse to this people.

The present moment discovers a new face in our affairs. Our object has been all along, to reform our federal system, and to strengthen our governments—to establish peace, order and justice in the community—but a new object now presents. The plan of government now proposed is evidently calculated totally to change, in time, our condition as a people. Instead of being thirteen republics, under a federal head, it is clearly designed to make us one consolidated government. Of this, I think, I shall fully convince you, in my following letters on this subject. This consolidation of the states has been the object of several men in this country for some time past. Whether such a change can ever be effected, in any manner; whether it can be effected without convulsions and civil wars; whether such a change will not totally destroy the liberties of this country—time only can determine.

To have a just idea of the government before us, and to shew that a consolidated one is the object in view, it is necessary not only to examine the plan, but also its history, and the politics of its particular friends.

The confederation was formed when great confidence was placed in the voluntary exertions of individuals, and of the respective states; and the framers of it, to guard against usurpation, so limited, and checked the powers, that, in many respects, they are inadequate to the exigencies of the union. We find, therefore, members of congress urging alterations in the federal system almost as soon as it was adopted. It was early proposed to vest congress with powers to levy an impost, to regulate trade, &c. but such was known to be the caution of the states in parting with power, that the vestment even of these, was proposed to be under several checks and limitations. During the war, the general confusion, and the introduction of paper money, infused in the minds of people vague ideas respecting government and credit. We expected too much from the return of peace, and of course we have been disappointed. Our governments have been new and unsettled; and several legislatures, by making tender, suspension, and paper money laws, [7] have given just cause of uneasiness to creditors. By these and other causes, several orders of men in the community have been prepared, by degrees, for a change of government; and this very abuse of power in the legislatures, which in some cases has been charged upon the democratic part of the community, has furnished aristocratical men with those very weapons, and those very means, with which, in great measure, they are rapidly effecting their favourite object. And should an oppressive government be the consequence of the proposed change, prosperity may reproach not only a few overbearing, unprincipled men, but those parties in the states which have misused their powers.

The conduct of several legislatures, touching paper money, and tender laws, has prepared many honest men for changes in government, which otherwise they would not have thought of —when by the evils, on the one hand, and by the secret instigations of artful men, on the other, the minds of men were become sufficiently uneasy, a bold step was taken, which is usually followed by a revolution, or a civil war. A general convention for mere commercial purposes was moved for—the authors of this measure saw that the people's attention was turned solely to the amendment of the federal system; and that, had the idea of a total change been started, probably no state would have appointed members to the convention. The idea of destroying ultimately, the state government, and forming one consolidated system, could not have been admitted ——a convention, therefore, merely for vesting in congress power to regulate trade was proposed. This was pleasing to the commercial towns; and the landed people had little or no concern about it. September, 1786, a few men from the middle states met at Annapolis, and hastily proposed a convention to be held in May, 1787, for the purpose, generally, of amending the confederation——this was done before the delegates of Massachusetts, and of the other states arrived——still not a word was said about destroying the old constitution, and making a new one—The states still unsuspecting, and not aware that they were passing the Rubicon, appointed members to the new convention, for the sole and express purpose of revising and amending the confederation——and, probably, not one man in ten thousand in the United States, till within these ten or twelve days, had an idea that the old ship was to be destroyed, and he put to the alternative of embarking in the new ship presented, or of being left in danger of sinking—The States, I believe, universally supposed the convention would report alterations in the confederation, which would pass an examination in congress, and after being agreed to there, would be confirmed by all the legislatures, [8] or be rejected. Virginia made a very respectable appointment, and placed at the head of it the first man in America. In this appointment there was a mixture of political characters; but Pennsylvania appointed principally those men who are esteemed aristocratical. Here the favourite moment for changing the government was evidently discerned by a few men, who seized it with address. Ten other states appointed, and tho' they chose men principally connected with commerce and the judicial department yet they appointed many good republican characters—had they all attended we should now see, I am persuaded, a better system presented. The non-attendance of eight or nine men, who were appointed members of the convention, I shall ever consider as a very unfortunate event to the United States.——Had they attended, I am pretty clear that the result of the convention would not have had that strong tendency to aristocracy now discernable in every part of the plan. There would not have been so great an accumulation of powers, especially as to the internal police of this country in a few hands as the constitution reported proposes to vest in them—the young visionary men, and the consolidating aristocracy, would have been more restrained than they have been. Eleven states met in the convention, and after four months close attention presented the new constitution, to be adopted or rejected by the people. The uneasy and fickle part of the community may be prepared to receive any form of government; but I presume the enlightened and substantial part will give any constitution presented for their adoption a candid and thorough examination; and silence those designing or empty men, who weakly and rashly attempt to precipitate the adoption of a system of so much importance—We shall view the convention with proper respect——and, at the same time, that we reflect there were men of abilities and integrity in it, we must recollect how disproportionately the democratic and aristocratic parts of the community were represented——Perhaps the judicious friends and opposers of the new constitution will agree, that it is best to let it rely solely on its own merits, or be condemned for its own defects.

In the first place, I shall premise, that the plan proposed is a plan of accommodation—and that it is in this way only, and by giving up a part of our opinions, that we can ever expect to obtain a government founded in freedom and compact. This circumstance candid men will always keep in view, in the discussion of this subject.

The plan proposed appears to be partly federal, but principally however, calculated ultimately to make the states one consolidated government.

The first interesting question, therefore suggested, is, how [9] far the states can be consolidated into one entire government on free principles. In considering this question extensive objects are to be taken into view, and important changes in the forms of government to be carefully attended to in all their consequences. The happiness of the people at large must be the great object with every honest statesman, and he will direct every movement to this point. If we are so situated as a people, as not to be able to enjoy equal happiness and advantages under one government, the consolidation of the states cannot be admitted.

There are three different forms of free government under which the United States may exist as one nation; and now is, perhaps, the time to determine to which we will direct our views. 1. Distinct republics connected under a federal head. In this case the respective state governments must be the principal guardians of the peoples rights, and exclusively regulate their internal police; in them must rest the balance of government. The congress of the states, or federal head, must consist of delegates amenable to, and removable by the respective states: This congress must have general directing powers; powers to require men and monies of the states; to make treaties; peace and war; to direct the operations of armies, &c. Under this federal modification of government, the powers of congress would be rather advisory or recommendatory than coercive. 2. We may do away the federal state governments, and form or consolidate all the states into one entire government, with one executive, one judiciary, and one legislature, consisting of senators and representatives collected from all parts of the union: In this case there would be a compleat consolidation of the states. 3. We may consoldate the states as to certain national objects, and leave them severally distinct independent republics, as to internal police generally. Let the general government consist of an executive, a judiciary, and balanced legislature, and its powers extend exclusively to all foreign concerns, causes arising on the seas to commerce, imports, armies, navies, Indian affairs, peace and war, and to a few internal concerns of the community; to the coin, post-offices, weights and measures, a general plan for the militia, to naturalization, *and, perhaps to bankruptcies,* leaving the internal police of the community, in other respects, exclusively to the state governments; as the administration of justice in all causes arising internally, the laying and collecting of internal taxes, and the forming of the militia according to a general plan prescribed. In this case there would be a compleat consolidation, *quoad* certain objects only.

Touching the first, or federal plan, I do not think much can be said in its favor: The sovereignty of the nation, without [10] coercive and efficient powers to collect the strength of it, cannot always be depended on to answer the purposes of government; and in a congress of representatives of foreign states, there must necessarily be an unreasonable mixture of powers in the same hands.

As to the second, or compleat consolidating plan, it deserves to be carefully considered at this time by every American: If it be impracticable, it is a fatal error to model our governments, directing our views ultimately to it.

The third plan, or partial consolidation, is, in my opinion, the only one that can secure the freedom and happiness of this people. I once had some general ideas that the second plan was practicable, but from long attention, and the proceedings of the convention, I am fully satisfied, that this third plan is the only one we can with safety and propriety proceed upon. Making this the standard to point out, with candor and fairness, the parts of the new constitution which appear to be improper, is my object. The convention appears to have proposed the partial consolidation evidently with a view to collect all powers ultimately, in the United States into one entire government; and from its views in this respect, and from the tenacity of the small states to have an equal vote in the senate, probably originated the greatest defects in the proposed plan.

Independent of the opinions of many great authors, that a free elective government cannot be extended over large territories, a few reflections must evince, that one government and general legislation alone never can extend equal benefits to all parts of the United States: Different laws, customs, and opinions exist in the different states, which by a uniform system of laws would be unreasonably invaded. The United States contain about a million of square miles, and in half a century will, probably, contain ten millions of people; and from the center to the extremes is about 800 miles.

Before we do away the state governments or adopt measures that will tend to abolish them, and to consolidate the states into one entire government several principles should be considered and facts ascertained :——These, and my examination into the essential parts of the proposed plan, I shall pursue in my next.

Your's, &c.

THE FEDERAL FARMER.

[11]      LETTER II.

OCTOBER 9, 1787.

DEAR SIR,

The essential parts of a free and good government are a full and equal representation of the people in the legislature, and the jury trial of the vicinage in the administration of justice—a full and equal representation, is that which possesses the same interests, feelings, opinions, and views the people themselves would were they all assembled—a fair representation, therefore, should be so regulated, that every order of men in the community, according to the common course of elections, can have a share in it—in order to allow professional men, merchants, traders, farmers, mechanics, &c. to bring a just proportion of their best informed men respectively into the legislature, the representation must be considerably numerous—We have about 200 state senators in the United States. and a less number than that of federal representatives cannot, clearly, be a full representation of this people, in the affairs of internal taxation and police, were there but one legislature for the whole union. The representation cannot be equal, or the situation of the people proper for one government only—if the extreme parts of the society cannot be represented as fully as the central—It is apparently impracticable that this should be the case in this extensive country——it would be impossible to collect a representation of the parts of the country five, six, and seven hundred miles from the seat of government.

Under one general government alone, there could be but one judiciary, one supreme and a proper number of inferior courts. I think it would be totally impracticable in this case to preserve a due administration of justice, and the real benefits of the jury trial of the vicinage——there are now supreme courts in each state in the union, and a great number of county and other courts subordinate to each supreme court——most of these supreme and inferior courts are itinerant, and hold their sessions in different parts every year of their respective states, counties and districts—with all these moving courts, our citizens, from the vast extent of the country, must travel very considerable distances from home to find the place where justice is administered. I am not for bringing justice so near to individuals as to afford them any temptation to engage in law suits; though I think it one of the greatest benefits in a good government, that each citizen should find a court of justice within a reasonable distance, perhaps, within a day's travel of his [12] home; so that, without great inconveniences and enormous expense, he may have the advantages of his witnesses and jury—it would be impracticable to derive these advantages from one judiciary——the one supreme court at most could only set in the centre of the union, and move once a year into the centre of the eastern and southern extremes of it—and, in this case, each citizen, on an average, would travel 150 or 200 miles to find this court——that, however, inferior courts might be properly placed in the different counties, and districts of the union, the appellate jurisdiction would be intolerable and expensive.

If it were possible to consolidate the states, and preserve the features of a free government, still it is evident that the middle states, the parts of the union, about the seat of government, would enjoy great advantages, while the remote states would experience the many inconveniences of remote provinces. Wealth, offices, and the benefits of government would collect in the centre: and the extreme states; and their principal towns, become much less important.

There are other considerations which tend to prove that the idea of one consolidated whole, on free principles, is ill-founded——the laws of a free government rest on the confidence of the people, and operate gently—and never can extend the influence very far——if they are executed on free principles, about the centre, where the benefits of the government induce the people to support it voluntarily; yet they must be executed on the principles of fear and force in the extremes——This has been the case with every extensive republic of which we have any accurate account.

There are certain unalienable and fundamental rights, which in forming the social compact, ought to be explicitly ascertained and fixed—a free and enlightened people, in forming this compact, will not resign all their rights to those who govern, and they will fix limits to their legislators and rulers, which will soon be plainly seen by those who are governed, as well as by those who govern: and the latter will know they cannot be passed unperceived by the former, and without giving a general alarm——These rights should be made the basis of every constitution; and if a people be so situated, or have such different opinions that they cannot agree in ascertaining and fixing them, it is a very strong argument against their attempting to form one entire society, to live under one system of laws only.——I confess, I never thought the people of these states differed essentially in these respects; they having derived all these rights from one common source, the British systems; and having in the formation of their state constitutions, discovered that their ideas [13] relative to these rights are very similar. However, it is now said that the states differ so essentially in these respects, and even in the important article of the trial by jury, that when assembled in convention, they can agree to no words by which to establish that trial, or by which to ascertain and establish many other of these rights, as fundamental articles in the social compact. If so, we proceed to consolidate the states on no solid basis whatever.

But I do not pay much regard to the reasons given for not bottoming the new constitution on a better bill of rights. I still believe a complete federal bill of rights to be very practicable. Nevertheless I acknowledge the proceedings of the convention furnish my mind with many new and strong reasons, against a complete consolidation of the states. They tend to convince me, that it cannot be carried with propriety very far—that the convention have gone much farther in one respect than they found it practicable to go in another; that is, they propose to lodge in the general government very extensive powers—*powers* nearly, if not altogether, complete and unlimited, over the purse and the sword. But, in its organization, they furnish the strongest proof that the proper limbs, or parts of a government, to support and execute those powers on proper principles (or in which they can be safely lodged) cannot be formed. These powers must be lodged somewhere in every society; but then they should be lodged where the strength and guardians of the people are collected. They can be wielded, or safely used, in a free country only by an able executive and judiciary, a respectable senate, and a secure, full, and equal representation of the people. I think the principles I have premised or brought into view, are well founded—I think they will not be denied by any fair reasoner. It is in connection with these, and other solid principles, we are to examine the constitution. It is not a few democratic phrases, or a few well formed features, that will prove its merits; or a few small omissions that will produce its rejection among men of sense; they will enquire what are the essential powers in a community, and what are nominal ones; where and how the essential powers shall be lodged to secure government, and to secure true liberty.

In examining the proposed constitution carefully, we must clearly perceive an unnatural separation of these powers from the substantial representation of the people. The state government will exist, with all their governors, senators, representatives, officers and expences; in these will be nineteen twentieths of the representatives of the people; they will have a near connection, and their members an immediate intercourse with the people; and the probability is, that the state governments will possess the [14] confidence of the people, and be considered generally as their immediate guardians.

The general government will consist of a new species of executive, a small senate, and a very small house of representatives. As many citizens will be more than three hundred miles from the seat of this government as will be nearer to it, its judges and officers cannot be very numerous, without making our governments very expensive. Thus will stand the state and the general governments, should the constitution be adopted without any alterations in their organization; but as to powers, the general government will possess all essential ones, at least on paper, and those of the states a mere shadow of power. And therefore, unless the people shall make some great exertions to restore to the state governments their powers in matters of internal police; as the powers to lay and collect, exclusively, internal taxes, to govern the militia, and to hold the decisions of their own judicial courts upon their own laws final, the balance cannot possibly continue long; but the state governments must be annihilated, or continue to exist for no purpose.

It is however to be observed, that many of the essential powers given the national government are not exclusively given; and the general government may have prudence enough to forbear the exercise of those which may still be exercised by the respective states. But this cannot justify the impropriety of giving powers, the exercise of which prudent men will not attempt, and imprudent men will, or probably can, exercise only in a manner destructive of free government. The general government, organized as it is, may be adequate to many valuable objects, and be able to carry its laws into execution on proper principles in several cases; but I think its warmest friends will not contend, that it can carry all the powers proposed to be lodged in it into effect, without calling to its aid a military force, which must very soon destroy all elective governments in the country, produce anarchy, or establish despotism. Though we cannot have now a complete idea of what will be the operations of the proposed system, we may, allowing things to have their common course, have a very tolerable one. The powers lodged in the general government, if exercised by it, must intimately effect the internal police of the states, as well as external concerns; and there is no reason to expect the numerous state governments, and their connections, will be very friendly to the execution of federal laws in those internal affairs, which hitherto have been under their own immediate management. There is more reason to believe, that the general government, far removed from the people, and none of its members elected oftener than once in two years, will be forgot [15] or neglected, and its laws in many cases disregarded, unless a multitude of officers and military force be continually kept in view, and employed to enforce the execution of the laws, and to make the government feared and respected. No position can be truer than this. That in this country either neglected laws, or a military execution of them, must lead to a revolution, and to the destruction of freedom. Neglected laws must first lead to anarchy and confusion; and a military execution of laws is only a shorter way to the same point—despotic government.

Your's, &c.

THE FEDERAL FARMER.

## LETTER III.

OCTOBER 10th, 1787.

DEAR SIR,

The great object of a free people must be so to form their government and laws, and so to administer them, as to create a confidence in, and respect for the laws; and thereby induce the sensible and virtuous part of the community to declare in favor of the laws, and to support them without an expensive military force. I wish, though I confess I have not much hope, that this may be the case with the laws of congress under the new constitution. I am fully convinced that we must organize the national government on different principals, and make the parts of it more efficient, and secure in it more effectually the different interests in the community; or else leave in the state governments some powers proposed to be lodged in it—at least till such an organization shall be found to be practicable. Not sanguine in my expectations of a good federal administration, and satisfied, as I am, of the impracticability of consolidating the states, and at the same time of preserving the rights of the people at large, I believe we ought still to leave some of those powers in the state governments, in which the people, in fact, will still be represented—to define some other powers proposed to be vested in the general government, more carefully, and to establish a few principles to secure a proper exercise of the powers given it. It is not my object to multiply objections, or to contend about inconsiderable powers or amendments. I wish the system adopted with a few alterations; but those, in my mind, are essential ones; if adopted without, [16] every good citizen will acquiesce, though I shall consider the duration of our governments, and the liberties of this people, very much dependant on the administration of the general government. A wise and honest administration, may make the people happy under any government; but necessity only can justify even our leaving open avenues to the abuse of power, by wicked, unthinking, or ambitious men, I will examine, first, the organization of the proposed government, in order to judge; 2d, with propriety, what powers are improperly, at least prematurely lodged in it. I shall examine, 3d, the undefined powers; and 4th, those powers, the exercise of which is not secured on safe and proper ground.

First. As to the organization——the house of representatives, the democrative branch, as it is called, is to consist of 65 members: that is, about one representative for fifty thousand inhabitants, to be chosen biennially——the federal legislature may increase this number to one for each thirty thousand inhabitants, abating fractional numbers in each state.——Thirty-three representatives will make a quorum for doing business, and a majority of those present determine the sense of the house.——I have no idea that the interests, feelings, and opinions of three or four millions of people, especially touching internal taxation, can be collected in such a house.——In the nature of things, nine times in ten, men of the elevated classes in the community only can be chosen——Connecticut, for instance, will have five representatives——not one man in a hundred of those who form the democrative branch in the state legislature, will, on a fair computation, be one of the five.—The people of this country, in one sense, may all be democratic; but if we make the proper distinction between the few men of wealth and abilities, and consider them, as we ought, as the natural aristocracy of the country, and the great body of the people, the middle and lower classes, as the democracy, this federal representative branch will have but very little democracy in it, even this small representation is not secured on proper principles.——The branches of the legislature are essential parts of the fundamental compact, and ought to be so fixed by the people, that the legislature cannot alter itself by modifying the elections of its own members. This, by a part of Art. 1, Sect. 4, the general legislature may do, it may evidently so regulate elections as to secure the choice of any particular description of men.——It may make the whole state one district—make the capital, or any places in the state, the place or places of election—it may declare that the five men (or whatever the number may be the state may chuse) who shall have the most votes shall be considered as chosen.

——In this [17] case it is easy to perceive how the people who live scattered in the inland towns will bestow their votes on different men—and how a few men in a city, in any order or profession, may unite and place any five men they please highest among those that may be voted for——and all this may be done constitutionally, and by those silent operations, which are not immediately perceived by the people in general.

——I know it is urged, that the general legislature will be disposed to regulate elections on fair and just principles :——This may be true—good men will generally govern well with almost any constitution: but why in laying the foundation of the social system, need we unnecessarily leave a door open to improper regulations?—This is a very general and unguarded clause, and many evils may flow from that part which authorises the congress to regulate elections.——Were it omitted, the regulations of elections would be solely in the respective states, where the people are substantially represented; and where the elections ought to be regulated, otherwise to secure a representation from all parts of the community, in making the constitutions, we ought to provide for dividing each state into a proper number of districts, and for confining the electors in each district to the choice of some men, who shall have a permanent interest and residence in it; and also for this essential object, that the representative elected shall have a majority of the votes of those electors who shall attend and give their votes.

In considering the practicability of having a full and equal representation of the people from all parts of the union, not only distances and different opinions, customs and views, common in extensive tracts of country, are to be taken into view, but many differences peculiar to Eastern, Middle, and Southern States. These differences are not so perceivable among the members of congress, and men of general information in the states, as among the men who would properly form the democratic branch. The Eastern states are very democratic, and composed chiefly of moderate freeholders; they have but few rich men and no slaves; the Southern states are composed chiefly of rich planters and slaves; they have but few moderate freeholders, and the prevailing influence, in them is generally a dissipated aristocracy: The Middle states partake partly of the Eastern and partly of the Southern character.

Perhaps, nothing could be more disjointed, unweildly and incompetent to doing business with harmony and dispatch, than a federal house of representatives properly numerous for the great objects of taxation, &c. collected from the federal states; whether such men would ever act in concert; whether they would not worry along a few years, and then be the means of [18] separating the parts of the union, is very problematical?——View this system in whatever form we can, propriety brings us still to this point, a federal government possessed of general and complete powers, as to those national objects which cannot well come under the cognizance of the internal laws of the respective states, and this federal government, accordingly, consisting of branches not very numerous.

The house of representatives is on the plan of consolidation, but the senate is entirely on the federal plan; and Delaware will have as much constitutional influence in the senate, as the largest state in the union: and in this senate are lodged legislative, executive and judicial powers: Ten states in this union urge that they are small states, nine of which were present in the convention.—They were interested in collecting large powers into the hands of the senate, in which each state still will have its equal share of power. I suppose it was impracticable for the three large states, as they were called, to get the senate formed on any other principles: But this only proves, that we cannot form one general government on equal and just principles—and proves, that we ought not to lodge in it such extensive powers before we are convinced of the practicability of organizing it on just and equal principles. The senate will consist of two members from each state, chosen by the state legislatures, every sixth year. The clause referred to, respecting the elections of representatives, empowers the general legislature to regulate the elections of senators also, "except as to the places of chusing senators."—There is, therefore, but little more security in the elections than in those of representatives: Fourteen senators make a quorum for business, and a majority of the senators present give the vote of the senate, except in giving judgment upon an impeachment, or in making treaties, or in expelling a member, when two-thirds of the senators present must agree—The members of the legislature are not excluded from being elected to any military offices, or any civil offices, except those created, or the emoluments of which shall be increased by themselves: two-thirds of the members present, of either house, may expel a member at pleasure. The senate is an independant branch of the legislature, a court for trying impeachments, and also a part of the executive, having a negative in the making of all treaties, and in appointing almost all officers.

The vice president is not a very important, if not an unnecessary part of the system—he may be a part of the senate at one period, and act as the supreme executive magistrate at another——The election of this officer, as well as of the president of the United States seems to be properly secured; but [19] when we examine the powers of the president, and the forms of the executive, we shall perceive that the general government, in this part, will have a strong tendency to aristocracy, or the government of the few. The executive is, in fact, the president and senate in all transactions of any importance; the president is connected with, or tied to the senate; he may always act with the senate, but never can effectually counteract its views: The president can appoint no officer, civil or military, who shall not be agreeable to the senate; and the presumption is, that the will of so important a body will not be very easily controuled, and that it will exercise its powers with great address.

In the judicial department, powers ever kept distinct in well balanced governments, are no less improperly blended in the hands of the same men—in the judges of the supreme court is lodged the law, the equity and the fact. It is not necessary to pursue the minute organical parts of the general government proposed.—There were various interests in the convention, to be reconciled, especially of large and small states; of carrying and non-carrying states; and of states more and states less democratic—vast labour and attention were by the convention bestowed on the organization of the parts of the constitution offered; still it is acknowledged there are many things radically wrong in the essential parts of this constitution —but it is said that these are the result of our situation: On a full examination of the subject, I believe it; but what do the laborious inquiries and determination of the convention prove? If they prove any thing, they prove that we cannot consolidate the states on proper principles: The organization of the government presented proves, that we cannot form a general government in which all power can be safely lodged; and a little attention to the parts of the one proposed will make it appear very evident, that all the powers proposed to be lodged in it, will not be then well deposited, either for the purposes of government, or the preservation of liberty. I will suppose no abuse of power in those cases, in which the abuse of it is not well guarded against—I will suppose the words authorizing the general government to regulate the elections of its own members struck out of the plan, or free district elections, in each state, amply secured.—That the small representation provided for shall be as fair and equal as it is capable of being made—I will suppose the judicial department regulated on pure principles, by future laws, as far as it can be by the constitution, and consist with the situation of the country—still there will be an unreasonable accumulation of powers in the general government if all be granted, enumerated in the plan proposed. The plan does not present a well balanced government: The senatorial [20] branch of the legislative and the executive are substantially united, and the president, or the state executive magistrate, may aid the senatorial interest when weakest, but never can effectually support the democratic, however it may be opposed;—the excellency, in my mind, of a well-balanced government is that it consists of distinct branches, each sufficiently strong and independant to keep its own station, and to aid either of the other branches which may occasionally want aid.

The convention found that any but a small house of representatives would be expensive, and that it would be impracticable to assemble a large number of representatives. Not only the determination of the convention in this case, but the situation of the states, proves the impracticability of collecting, in any one point, a proper representation.

The formation of the senate, and the smallness of the house, being, therefore, the result of our situation, and the actual state of things, the evils which may attend the exercise of many powers in this national government may be considered as without a remedy.

All officers are impeachable before the senate only—before the men by whom they are appointed, or who are consenting to the appointment of these officers. No judgment of conviction, on an impeachment, can be given unless two thirds of the senators agree. Under these circumstances the right of impeachment, in the house, can be of but little importance; the house cannot expect often to convict the offender; and, therefore, probably, will but seldom or never exercise the right. In addition to the insecurity and inconveniences attending this organization beforementioned, it may be observed, that it is extremely difficult to secure the people against the fatal effects of corruption and influence. The power of making any law will be in the president, eight senators, and seventeen representatives, relative to the important objects enumerated in the constitution. Where there is a small representation a sufficient number to carry any measure, may, with ease, be influenced by bribes, offices and civilities; they easily form private juntoes, and out-door meetings, agree on measures, and carry them by silent votes.

Impressed, as I am, with a sense of the difficulties there are in the way of forming the parts of a federal government on proper principles, and seeing a government so unsubstantially organized, after so arduous an attempt has been made, I am led to believe, that powers ought to be given to it with great care and caution.

In the second place it is necessary, therefore, to examine the extent, and the probable operations of some of those ex- [21] tensive powers proposed to be vested in this government. These powers, legislative, executive, and judicial, respect internal as well as external objects. Those respecting external objects, as all foreign concerns, commerce, imposts, all causes arising on the seas, peace and war, and Indian affairs, can be lodged no where else, with any propriety, but in this government. Many powers that respect internal objects ought clearly to be lodged in it; as those to regulate trade between the states, weights and measures, the coin or current monies, post-offices, naturalization, &c. These powers may be exercised without essentially effecting the internal police of the respective states: But powers to lay and collect internal taxes, to form the militia, to make bankrupt laws, and to decide on appeals, questions arising on the internal laws of the respective states, are of a very serious nature, and carry with them almost all other powers. These taken in connection with the others, and powers to raise armies and build navies, proposed to be lodged in this government, appear to me to comprehend all the essential powers in this community, and those which will be left to the states will be of no great importance.

A power to lay and collect taxes at discretion, is, in itself, of very great importance. By means of taxes, the government may command the whole or any part of the subject's property. Taxes may be of various kinds; but there is a strong distinction between external and internal taxes. External taxes are import duties, which are laid on imported goods; they may usually be collected in a few seaport towns, and of a few individuals, though ultimately paid by the consumer; a few officers can collect them, and they can be carried no higher than trade will bear, or smuggling permit—that in the very nature of commerce, bounds are set to them. But internal taxes, as poll and land taxes, excises, duties on all written instruments, &c. may fix themselves on every person and species of property in the community; they may be carried to any lengths, and in proportion as they are extended, numerous officers must be employed to assess them, and to enforce the collection of them. In the United Netherlands the general government has compleat powers, as to external taxation; but as to internal taxes, it makes requisitions on the provinces. Internal taxation in this country is more important, as the country is so very extensive. As many assessors and collectors of federal taxes will be above three hundred miles from the seat of the federal government as will be less. Besides, to lay and collect taxes, in this extensive country, must require a great number of congressional ordinances, immediately operating upon the body of the people; these must continually interfere with the state laws, [22] and thereby produce disorder and general dissatisfaction, till the one system of laws or the other, operating on the same subjects, shall be abolished. These ordinances alone, to say nothing of those respecting the milita, coin, commerce, federal judiciary, &c. &c. will probably soon defeat the operations of the state laws and governments.

Should the general government think it politic, as some administration (if not all) probably will, to look for a support in a system of influence, the government will take every occasion to multiply laws, and officers to execute them, considering these as so many necessary props for its own support. Should this system of policy be adopted, taxes more productive than the impost duties will, probably, be wanted to support the government, and to discharge foreign demands, without leaving any thing for the domestic creditors. The internal sources of taxation then must be called into operation, and internal tax laws and federal assessors and collectors spread over this immense country. All these circumstances considered, is it wise, prudent, or safe, to vest the powers of laying and collecting internal taxes in the general government, while imperfectly organized and inadequate; and to trust to amending it hereafter, and making it adequate to this purpose? It is not only unsafe but absurd to lodge power in a government before it is fitted to receive it? It is confessed that this power and representation ought to go together. Why give the power first? Why give the power to the few, who, when possessed of it, may have address enough to prevent the increase of representation? Why not keep the power, and, when necessary, amend the constitution, and add to its other parts this power, and a proper increase of representation at the same time? Then men who may want the power will be under strong inducements to let in the people, by their representatives, into the government, to hold their due proportion of this power. If a proper representation be impracticable, then we shall see this power resting in the states, where it at present ought to be, and not inconsiderately given up.

When I recollect how lately congress, conventions, legislatures, and people contended in the cause of liberty, and carefully weighed the importance of taxation, I can scarcely believe we are serious in proposing to vest the powers of laying and collecting internal taxes in a government so imperfectly organized for such purposes. Should the United States be taxed by a house of representatives of two hundred members, which would be about fifteen members for Connecticut, twenty-five for Massachusetts, &c. still the middle and lower classes of people could have no great share, in fact, in taxation. I am aware it is said, that the representation proposed by the new [23] constitution is sufficiently numerous; it may be for many purposes; but to suppose that this branch is sufficiently numerous to guard the rights of the people in the administration of the government, in which the purse and sword is placed, seems to argue that we have forgot what the true meaning of representation is. I am sensible also, that it is said that congress will not attempt to lay and collect internal taxes; that it is necessary for them to have the power, though it cannot probably be exercised.———I admit that it is not probable that any prudent congress will attempt to lay and collect internal taxes, especially direct taxes: but this only proves, that the power would be improperly lodged in congress, and that it might be abused by imprudent and designing men.

I have heard several gentlemen, to get rid of objections to this part of the constitution, attempt to construe the powers relative to direct taxes, as those who object to it would have them; as to these, it is said, that congress will only have power to make requisitions, leaving it to the states to lay aud collect them. I see but very little colour for this construction, and the attempt only proves that this part of the plan cannot be defended. By this plan there can be no doubt, but that the powers of congress will be complete as to all kinds of taxes whatever—Further, as to internal taxes, the state governments will have concurrent powers with the general government, and both may tax the same objects in the same year; and the objection that the general government may suspend a state tax, as a necessary measure for the promoting the collection of a federal tax, is not without foundation.—— As the states owe large debts, and have large demands upon them individually, there clearly will be a propriety in leaving in their possession exclusively, some of the internal sources of taxation, at least until the federal representation shall be properly encreased : The power in the general government to lay and collect internal taxes, will render its powers respecting armies, navies and the militia, the more exceptionable. By the constitution it is proposed that congress shall have power " to raise and support armies, but no appropriation of money to that use shall be for a longer term than two years; to provide and maintain a navy; to provide for calling forth the militia to execute the laws of the union; suppress insurrections, and repel invasions : to provide for organizing, arming, and disciplining the militia;" reserving to the states the right to appoint the officers, and to train the militia according to the discipline prescribed by congress ; congress will have unlimited power to raise armies, and to engage officers and men for any number of years; but a legislative act applying money for their support can have operation for no longer term than two years, and if a subsequent congress do [24] not within the two years renew the appropriation, or further appropriate monies for the use of the army, the army will be left to take care of itself. When an army shall once be raised for a number of years, it is not probable that it will find much difficulty in getting congress to pass laws for applying monies to its support. I see so many men in America fond of a standing army, and especially among those who probably will have a large share in administering the federal system; it is very evident to me, that we shall have a large standing army as soon as the monies to support them can be possibly found. An army is not a very agreeable place of employment for the young gentlemen of many families. A power to raise armies must be lodged some where; still this will not justify the lodging this power in a bare majority of so few men without any checks; or in the government in which the great body of the people, in the nature of things, will be only nominally represented. In the state governments the great body of the people, the yeomanry, &c. of the country, are represented: It is true they will chuse the members of congress, and may now and then chuse a man of their own way of thinking; but it is not impossible for forty, or thirty thousand people in this country, one time in ten to find a man who can possess similar feelings, views, and interests with themselves: Powers to lay and collect taxes and to raise armies are of the greatest moment; for carrying them into effect, laws need not be frequently made, and the yeomanry, &c. of the country ought substantially to have a check upon the passing of these laws; this check ought to be placed in the legislatures, or at least, in the few men the common people of the country, will, probably, have in congress, in the true sense of the word, "from among themselves." It is true, the yeomanry of the country possess the lands, the weight of property, possess arms, and are too strong a body of men to be openly offended — and, therefore, it is urged, they will take care of themselves, that men who shall govern will not dare pay any disrespect to their opinions. It is easily perceived, that if they have not their proper negative upon passing laws in congress, or on the passage of laws relative to taxes and armies, they may in twenty or thirty years be by means imperceptible to them, totally deprived of that boasted weight and strength: This may be done in a great measure by congress, if disposed to do it, by modelling the militia, Should one fifth or one eighth part of the men capable of bearing arms, be made a select militia, as has been proposed, and those the young and ardent part of the community, possessed of but little or no property, and all the others put upon a plan that will render them of no importance, the former will answer all the purposes of an [25] army, while the latter will be defenceless. The state must train the militia in such form and according to such systems and rules as congress shall prescribe: and the only actual influence the respective states will have respecting the militia will be in appointing the officers. I see no provision made for calling out the *posse comitatus* for executing the laws of the union, but provision is made for congress to call forth the militia for the execution of them—and the militia in general, or any select part of it, may be called out under military officers, instead of the sheriff to enforce an execution of federal laws, in the first instance, and thereby introduce an entire military execution of the laws. I know that powers to raise taxes, to regulate the military strength of the community on some uniform plan, to provide for its defence and internal order, and for duly executing the laws, must be lodged somewhere; but still we ought not so to lodge them, as evidently to give one order of men in the community, undue advantages over others; or commit the many to the mercy, prudence, and moderation of the few. And so far as it may be necessary to lodge any of the peculiar powers in the general government, a more safe exercise of them ought to be secured, by requiring the consent of two-thirds or three-fourths of congress thereto— until the federal representation can be increased, so that the democratic members in congress may stand some tolerable chance of a reasonable negative, in behalf of the numerous, important, and democratic part of the community.

I am not sufficiently acquainted with the laws and internal police of all the states to discern fully, how general bankrupt laws, made by the union, would effect them, or promote the public good. I believe the property of debtors, in the several states, is held responsible for their debts in modes and forms very different. If uniform bankrupt laws can be made without producing real and substantial inconveniences, I wish them to be made by congress.

There are some powers proposed to be lodged in the general government in the judicial department, I think very unnecessarily, I mean powers respecting questions arising upon the internal laws of the respective states. It is proper the federal judiciary should have powers co-extensive with the federal legislature—that is, the power of deciding finally on the laws of the union. By Art. 3, Sec. 2. the powers of the federal judiciary are extended (among other things) to all cases between a state and citizens of another state—between citizens of different states—between a state or the citizens thereof, and foreign states, citizens or subjects. Actions in all these cases, except against a state government, are now brought and finally [26] determined in the law courts of the states respectively and as there are no words to exclude these courts of their jurisdiction in these cases, they will have concurrent jurisdiction with the inferior federal courts in them; and, therefore, if the new constitution be adopted without any amendment in this respect, all those numerous actions, now brought in the state courts between our citizens and foreigners, between citizens of different states, by state governments against foreigners, and by state governments against citizens of other states, may also be brought in the federal courts; and an appeal will lay in them from the state courts or federal inferior courts to the supreme judicial court of the union. In almost all these cases, either party may have the trial by jury in the state courts; except paper money and tender laws, which are wisely guarded against in the proposed constitution; justice may be obtained in these courts on reasonable terms; they must be more competent to proper decisions on the laws of their respective states, than the federal states can possibly be. I do not, in any point of view, see the need of opening a new jurisdiction in these causes—of opening a new scene of expensive law suits, of suffering foreigners, and citizens of different states, to drag each other many hundred miles into the federal courts. It is true, those courts may be so organized by a wise and prudent legislature, as to make the obtaining of justice in them tolerably easy; they may in general be organized on the common law principles of the country: But this benefit is by no means secured by the constitution. The trial by jury is secured only in those few criminal cases, to which the federal laws will extend—as crimes committed on the seas, against the laws of nations, treason and counterfeiting the federal securities and coin: But even in these cases, the jury trial of the vicinage is not secured—particularly in the large states, a citizen may be tried for a crime committed in the state, and yet tried in some states 500 miles from the place where it was committed; but the jury trial is not secured at all in civil causes. Though the convention have not established this trial, it is to be hoped that congress, in putting the new system into execution, will do it by a legislative act, in all cases in which it can be done with propriety. Whether the jury trial is not excluded the supreme judicial court is an important question. By Art. 3, Sec. 2, all cases affecting ambassadors, other public ministers, and consuls, and in those cases in which a state shall be party, the supreme court shall have jurisdiction. In all the other cases beforementioned, the supreme court shall have appellate jurisdiction, both as to *law and fact*, with such exception, and under such regulations as the congress shall make. By court is understood a court consisting of judges; and the [27] idea of a jury is excluded. This court, or the judges, are to have jurisdiction on appeals, in all the cases enumerated, as to law and fact; the judges are to decide the law and try the fact, and the trial of the fact being assigned to the judges by the constitution, a jury for trying the fact is excluded; however, under the exceptions and powers to make regulations, congress may, perhaps, introduce the jury, to try the fact in most necessary cases.

There can be but one supreme court in which the final jurisdiction will centre in all federal causes—except in cases where appeals by law shall not be allowed: The judicial powers of the federal courts extend in law and equity to certain cases: and, therefore, the powers to determine on the law, in equity, and as to the fact, all will concentrate in the supreme court:— These powers, which by this constitution are blended in the same hands, the same judges, are in Great-Britain deposited in different hands—to wit, the decision of the law in the law judges, the decision in equity in the chancellor, and the trial of the fact in the jury. It is a very dangerous thing to vest in the same judge power to decide on the law, and also general powers in equity; for if the law restrain him, he is only to step into his shoes of equity, and give what judgment his reason or opinion may dictate; we have no precedents in this country, as yet, to regulate the divisions in equity as in Great Britain; equity, therefore, in the supreme court for many years will be mere discretion. I confess in the constitution of this supreme court, as left by the constitution, I do not see a spark of freedom or a shadow of our own or the British common law.

This court is to have appellate jurisdiction in all the other cases before mentioned: Many sensible men suppose that cases before mentioned respect, as well the criminal cases as the civil ones mentioned antecedently in the constitution, if so an appeal is allowed in criminal cases—contrary to the usual sense of law. How far it may be proper to admit a foreigner or the citizen of another state to bring actions against state governments, which have failed in performing so many, promises made during the war is doubtful: How far it may be proper so to humble a state, as to oblige it to answer to an individual in a court of law, is worthy of consideration; the states are now subject to no such actions; and this new jurisdiction will subject the states, and many defendants to actions, and processes, which were not in the contemplation of the parties, when the contract was made; all engagements existing between citizens of different states, citizens and foreigners, states and foreigners; and states and citizens of other states were made the parties contemplating the remedies then existing on the laws of the states——[28] and the new remedy proposed to be given in the federal courts, can be founded on no principle whatever.

Your's, &c,

THE FEDERAL FARMER.

## LETTER IV.

OCTOBER 12th, 1787.

DEAR SIR,

It will not be possible to establish in the federal courts the jury trial of the vicinage so well as in the state courts.

Third, there appears to me to be not only a premature deposit of some important powers in the general government—but many of those deposited there are undefined, and may be used to good or bad purposes as honest or designing men shall prevail. By Art. 1, Sec. 2, representatives and direct taxes shall be apportioned among the several states, &c.——same art. sect. 8, the congress shall have powers to lay and collect taxes, duties, &c. for the common defence and general welfare, but all duties, imposts and excises, shall be uniform throughout the United States: By the first recited clause, direct taxes shall be apportioned on the states. This seems to favour the idea suggested by some sensible men and writers that congress, as to direct taxes, will only have power to make requisitions; but the latter clause, power to lay and collect taxes, &c. seems clearly to favour the contrary opinion, and, in my mind, the true one, the congress shall have power to tax immediately individuals, without the intervention of the state legislatures, in fact the first clause appears to me only to provide that each state shall pay a certain portion of the tax, and the latter to provide that congress shall have power to lay and collect taxes, that is to assess upon, and to collect of the individuals in the state, the states quota; but these still I consider as undefined powers, because judicious men understand them differently.

It is doubtful whether the vice-president is to have any qualifications; none are mentioned; but he may serve as president, and it may be inferred, he ought to be qualified therefore as the president; but the qualifications of the president are required only of the person to be elected president. By art. 2, sect. 2, "But the congress may by law vest the appointment of such inferior officers as they think proper in the president alone, in the courts of law, or in the heads of the departments:" Who are inferior officers? May not a congress disposed to vest the appointment of all officers in the president, [29] under this clause, vest the appointment of almost every officer in the president alone, and destroy the check mentioned in the first part of the clause, and lodged in the senate. It is true, this check is badly lodged, but then some check upon the first magistrate in appointing officers, ought it appears by the opinion of the convention, and by the general opinion, to be established in the constitution. By art. 3, sect. 2, the supreme court shall have appellate jurisdiction as to law and facts with such exceptions, &c. to what extent is it intended the exceptions shall be carried——Congress may carry them so far as to annihilate substantially the appellate jurisdiction, and the clause be rendered of very little importance.

4th. There are certain rights which we have always held sacred in the United States, and recognized in all our constitutions, and which, by the adoption of the new constitution in its present form, will be left unsecured. By article 6, the proposed constitution, and the laws of the United States, which shall be made in pursuance thereof; and all treaties made, or which shall be made under the authority of the United States, shall be the supreme law of the land; and the judges in every state shall be bound thereby; anything in the constitution or laws of any state to the contrary notwithstanding.

It is to be observed that when the people shall adopt the proposed constitution it will be their last and supreme act; it will be adopted not by the people of New Hampshire, Massachusetts, &c., but by the people of the United States; and wherever this constitution, or any part of it, shall be incompatible with the ancient customs, rights, the laws or the constitutions heretofore established in the United States, it will entirely abolish them and do them away: And not only this, but the laws of the United States which shall be; made in pursuance of the federal constitution will be also supreme laws, and wherever they shall be incompatible with those customs, rights, laws or constitutions heretofore established, they will also entirely abolish them and do them away.

By the article before recited, treaties also made under the authority of the United States, shall be the supreme law: It is not said that these treaties shall be made in pursuance of the constitution—nor are there any constitutional bounds set to those who shall make them: The president and two-thirds of the senate will be empowered to make treaties indefinitely, and when these treaties shall be made, they will also abolish all laws and state constitutions incompatible with them. This power in the president and senate is absolute, and the judges will be bound to allow full force to whatever rule, article or thing the president and senate shall establish by treaty, whether it be [30] practicable to set any bounds to those who make treaties, I am not able to say; if not, it proves that this power ought to be more safely lodged.

The federal constitution, the laws of congress made in pursuance of the constitution, and all treaties must have full force and effect in all parts of the United States; and all other laws, rights and constitutions which stand in their way must yield: It is proper the national laws should be supreme, and superior to state or district laws; but then the national laws ought to yield to unalienable or fundamental rights——and national laws, made by a few men, should extend only to a few national objects. This will not be the case with the laws of congress: To have any proper idea of their extent, we must carefully examine the legislative, executive and judicial powers proposed to be lodged in the general government, and consider them in connection with a general clause in art. 1, sect. 8, in these words (after enumerating a number of powers) " To make all laws which shall be necessary and proper for carrying into execution the foregoing powers, and all other powers vested by this constitution in the government of the United States, or in any department or officer thereof."——The powers of this government as has been observed, extend to internal as well as external objects, and to those objects to which all others are subordinate; it is almost impossible to have a just conception of their powers, or of the extent and number of the laws which may be deemed necessary and proper to carry them into effect, till we shall come to exercise those powers and make the laws. In making laws to carry those powers into effect, it is to be expected, that a wise and prudent congress will pay respect to the opinions of a free people, and bottom their laws on those principles which have been considered as essential and fundamental in the British, and in our government: But a congress of a different character will not be bound by the constitution to pay respect to those principles.

It is said that when people make a constitution, and delegate powers, that all powers are not delegated by them to those who govern, is reserved in the people; and that the people, in the present case, have reserved in themselves, and in their state governments, every right and power not expressly given by the federal constitution to those who shall administer the national government. It is said, on the other hand, that the people, when they make a constitution, yield all power not expressly reserved to themselves. The truth is, in either case, it is mere matter of opinion, and men usually take either side of the argument, as will best answer their purposes: But the general [31] presumption being, that men who govern, will in doubtful cases, construe laws and constitutions most favourably for increasing their own powers; all wise and prudent people, in forming constitutions, have drawn the line, and carefully described the powers parted with and the powers reserved. By the state constitutions, certain rights have been reserved in the people; or rather, they have been recognized and established in such a manner, that state legislatures are bound to respect them, and to make no laws infringing upon them. The state legislatures are obliged to take notice of the bills of rights of their respective states. The bills of rights, and the state constitutions, are fundamental compacts only between those who govern, and the people of the same state.

In the year 1788 the people of the United States made a federal constitution, which is a fundamental compact between them and their federal rulers; these rulers, in the nature of things, cannot be bound to take notice of any other compact. It would be absurd for them, in making laws, to look over thirteen, fifteen, or twenty state constitutions, to see what rights are established as fundamental, and must not be infringed upon, in making laws in the society. It is true, they would be bound to do it if the people, in their federal compact, should refer to the state constitutions, recognize all parts not inconsistent with the federal constitution, and direct their federal rulers to take notice of them accordingly; but this is not the case, as the plan stands proposed at present; and it is absurd, to suppose so unnatural an idea is intended or implied. I think my opinion is not only founded in reason, but I think it is supported by the report of the convention itself. If there are a number of rights established by the state constitutions, and which will remain sacred, and the general government is bound to take notice of them—it must take notice of one as well as another; and if unnecessary to recognize or establish one by the federal constitution, it would be unnecessary to recognize or establish another by it. If the federal constitution is to be construed so far in connection with the state constitution, as to leave the trial by jury in civil causes, for instance, secured; on the same principles it would have left the trial by jury in criminal causes, the benefits of the writ of habeas corpus, &c. secured; they all stand on the same footing; they are the common rights of Americans, and have been recognized by the state constitutions: But the convention found it necessary to recognize or re-establish the benefits of that writ, and the jury trial in criminal cases. As to *expost facto* laws, the convention has done the same in one case, and gone further in another, It is a part of the com- [32] pact between the people of each state and their rulers, that no *expost facto* laws shall be made. But the convention, by Art. 1, Sect. 10, have put a sanction upon this part even of the state compacts. In fact, the 9th and 10th Sections in Art. 1, in the proposed constitution, are no more nor less, than a partial bill of rights; they establish certain principles as part of the compact upon which the federal legislators and officers can never infringe. It is here wisely stipulated, that the federal legislature shall never pass a bill of attainder, or *expost facto* law; that no tax shall be laid on articles exported, &c. The establishing of one right implies the necessity of establishing another and similar one.

On the whole, the position appears to me to be undeniable, that this bill of rights ought to be carried farther, and some other principles established, as a part of this fundamental compact between the people of the United States and their federal rulers.

It is true, we are not disposed to differ much, at present, about religion; but when we are making a constitution, it is to be hoped, for ages and millions yet unborn, why not establish the free exercise of religion, as a part of the national compact. There are other essential rights, which we have justly understood to be the rights of freemen; as freedom from hasty and unreasonable search warrants, warrants not founded on oath, and not issued with due caution, for searching and seizing men's papers, property, and persons. The trials by jury in civil causes, it is said, varies so much in the several states, that no words could be found for the uniform establishment of it. If so, the federal legislation will not be able to establish it by any general laws. I confess I am of opinion it may be established, but not in that beneficial manner in which we may enjoy it, for the reasons beforementioned. When I speak of the jury trial of the vicinage, or the trial of the fact in the neighborhood, I do not lay so much stress upon the circumstance of our being tried by our neighbours: in this enlightened country men may be probably impartially tried by those who do not live very near them: but the trial of facts in the neighbourhood is of great importance in other respects. Nothing can be more essential than the cross examining witnesses, and generally before the triers of the facts in question. The common people can establish facts with much more ease with oral than written evidence; when trials of facts are removed to a distance from the homes of the parties and witnesses, oral evidence becomes intolerably expensive, and the parties must depend on written evidence, which to the common people is expensive and almost [33] useless; it must be frequently taken ex porte, and but very seldom leads to the proper discovery of truth.

The trial by jury is very important in another point of view. It is essential in every free country, that common people should have a part and share of influence, in the judicial as well as in the legislative department. To hold open to them the offices of senators, judges, and offices to fill which an expensive education is required, cannot answer any valuable purposes for them; they are not in a situation to be brought forward and to fill those offices; these, and most other offices of any considerable importance, will be occupied by the few. The few, the well born, &c. as Mr. Adams calls them, in judicial decisions as well as in legislation, are generally disposed, and very naturally too, to favour those of their own description.

The trial by jury in the judicial department, and the collection of the people by their representatives in the legislature, are those fortunate inventions which have procured for them, in this country, their true proportion of influence, and the wisest and most fit means of protecting themselves in the community. Their situation, as jurors and representatives, enables them to acquire information end knowledge in the affairs and government of the society; and to come forward, in turn, as the centinels and guardians of each other. I am very sorry that even a few of our countrymen should consider jurors and representatives in a different point of view, as ignorant, troublesome bodies, which ought not to have any share in the concerns of government.

I confess I do not see in what cases the congress can, with any pretence of right, make a law to suppress the freedom of the press; though I am not clear, that congress is restrained from laying any duties whatever on printing, and from laying duties particularly heavy on certain pieces printed, and perhaps congress may require large bonds for the payment of these duties. Should the printer say, the freedom of the press was secured by the constitution of the state in which he lived, congress might, and perhaps, with great propriety, answer, that the federal constitution is the only compact existing between them and the people; in this compact the people have named no others, and therefore congress, in exercising the powers assigned them, and in making laws to carry them into execution, are restrained by nothing beside the federal constitution, any more than a state legislature is restrained by a compact between the magistrates and people of a county, city, or town of which the people, in forming the state constitution, have taken no notice.

It is not my object to enumerate rights of inconsiderable [34] importance; but there are others, no doubt, which ought to be established as a fundamental part of the national system.

It is worthy of observation, that all treaties are made by foreign nations with a confederacy of thirteen states—that the western country is attached to thirteen states—thirteen states have jointly and severally engaged to pay the public debts.— Should a new government be formed of nine, ten, eleven, or twelve states, those treaties could not be considered as binding on the foreign nations who made them. However, I believe the probability to be, that if nine states adopt the constitution, the others will.

It may also be worthy our examination, how far the provision for amending this plan, when it shall be adopted, is of any importance. No measures can be taken towards amendments, unless two-thirds of the congress, or two-thirds of the legislature of the several states shall agree.—While power is in the hands of the people, or democratic part of the community, more especially as at present, it is easy, according to the general course of human affairs, for the few influential men in the community, to obtain conventions, alterations in government, and to persuade the common people that they may change for the better, and to get from them a part of the power: But when power is once transferred from the many to the few, all changes become extremely difficult; the government, is this case, being beneficial to the few, they will be exceedingly artful and adroit in preventing any measures which may lead to a change; and nothing will produce it, but great exertions and severe struggles on the part of the common people. Every man of reflection must see, that the change now proposed, is a transfer of power from the many to the few, and the probability is, the artful and ever active aristocracy, will prevent all peaceful measures for changes, unless when they shall discover some favorable moment to increase their own influence. I am sensible, thousands of men in the United States, are disposed to adopt the proposed constitution, though they perceive it to be essentially defective, under an idea that amendments of it, may be obtained when necessary. This is a pernicious idea, it argues a servility of character totally unfit for the support of free government; it is very repugnant to that perpetual jealousy respecting liberty, so absolutely necessary in all free states, spoken of by Mr. Dickinson.— However, if our countrymen are so soon changed, and the language of 1774, is become odious to them, it will be in vain to use the language of freedom, or to attempt to rouse them to free enquiries: But 1 shall never believe this is the case with them, whatever present appearances may be, till I shall have very strong evidence indeed of it.

    Your's, &c.
    THE FEDERAL FARMER.

---

[35]     LETTER V.

        OCTOBER 15th, 1787.
DEAR SIR,

Thus I have examined the federal constitution as far as a few days leisure would permit. It opens to my mind a new scene; instead of seeing powers cautiously lodged in the hands of numerous legislators, and many magistrates, we see all important powers collecting in one centre, where a few men will possess them almost at discretion. And instead of checks in the formation of the government, to secure the rights of the people against the usurpations of those they appoint to govern, we are to understand the equal division of lands among our people, and the strong arm furnished them by nature and situation, are to secure them against those usurpations. If there are advantages in the equal division of our lands, and the strong and manly habits of our people, we ought to establish governments calculated to give duration to them, and not governments which never can work naturally, till that equality of property, and those free and manly habits shall be destroyed; these evidently are not the natural basis of the proposed constitution. No man of reflection, and skilled in the science of goverment, can suppose these will move on harmoniously together for ages, or even for fifty years. As to the little circumstances commented upon, by some writers, with applause—as the age of a representative, of the president, &c.—they have, in my mind, no weight in the general tendency of the system.

There are, however, in my opinion, many good things in the proposed system. It is founded on elective principles, and the deposits of powers in different hands, is essentially right. The guards against those evils we have experienced in some states in legislation are valuable indeed; but the value of every feature in this system is vastly lessened for the want of that one important feature in a free government, a representation of the people. Because we have sometimes abused democracy, I am not among those men who think a democratic branch a nuisance; which branch shall be sufficiently numerous to admit some of the best informed men of each order in the community into the administration of government.

While the radical defects in the proposed system are not so soon discovered, some temptations to each state, and to many classes of men to adopt it, are very visible. It uses the democratic language of several of the state constitutions, particularly that of Massachusetts; the eastern states will receive advantages so far as the regulation of trade, by a bare majority, is committed to it: Connecticut and New Jersey will receive their share of a [36] general impost: The middle states will receive the advantages surrounding the seat of government; The southern states will receive protection, and have their negroes represented in the legislature, and large back countries will soon have a majority in it. This system promises a large field of employment to military gentlemen, and gentlemen of the law; and in case the government shall be executed without convulsions, it will afford security to creditors, to the clergy, salary-men and others depending on money payments. So far as the system promises justice and reasonable advantages, in these respects, it ought to be supported by all honest men; but whenever it promises unequal and improper advantages to any particular states, or orders of men, it ought to be opposed.

I have, in the course of these letters observed, that there are many good things in the proposed constitution, and I have endeavored to point out many important defects in it. I have admitted that we want a federal system—that we have a system presented, which, with several alterations may be made a tolerable good one—I have admitted there is a well founded uneasiness among creditors and mercantile men. In this situation of things, you ask me what I think ought to be done? My opinion in this case is only the opinion of an individual, and so far only as it corresponds with the opinions of the honest and substantial part of the community, is it entitled to consideration. Though I am fully satisfied that the state conventions ought most seriously to direct their exertions to altering and amending the system proposed before they shall adopt it—yet I have not sufficiently examined the subject, or formed an opinion, how far it will be practicable for those conventions to carry their amendments. As to the idea, that it will be in vain for those conventions to attempt amendments, it cannot be admitted; it is impossible to say whether they can or not until the attempt shall be made; and when it shall be determined, by experience, that the conventions cannot agree in amendments, it will then be an important question before the people of the United States, whether they will adopt or not the system proposed in its present form. This subject of consolidating the states is new: and because forty or fifty men have agreed in a system, to suppose the good sense of this country, an enlightened nation, must adopt it without examination, and though in a state of profound peace, without endeavouring to amend those parts they perceive are defective, dangerous to freedom, and destructive of the valuable principles of republican government—is truly humiliating. It is true there may be danger in delay; but there is danger in adopting the system in its present form; and I see the danger in either case will arise principally from the conduct and views of [37] two very unprincipled parties in the United States—two fires, between which the honest and substantial people have long found themselves situated. One party is composed of little insurgents, men in debt, who want no law, and who want a share of the property of others; these are called levellers, Shayites, &c. The other party is composed of a few, but more dangerous men, with their servile dependents; these avariciously grasp at all power and property; you may discover in all the actions of these men, an evident dislike to free and equal government, and they will go systematically to work to change, essentially, the forms of government in this country; these are called aristocrats, m——ites, &c..&c. Between these two parties is the weight of the community; the men of middling property, men not in debt on the one hand, and men, on the other, content with republican governments, and not aiming at immense fortunes, offices, and power. In 1786, the little insurgents, the levellers, came forth, invaded the rights of others, and attempted to establish governments according to their wills. Their movements evidently gave encouragement to the other party, which, in 1787, has taken the political field, and with its fashionable dependants, and the tongue and the pen, is endeavoring to establish in a great haste, a politer kind of government. These two parties, which will probably be opposed or united as it may suit their interests and views, are really insignificant, compared with the solid, free, and independent part of the community. It is not my intention to suggest, that either of these parties, and the real friends of the proposed constitution, are the same men. The fact is, these aristocrats support and hasten the adoption of the proposed constitution, merely because they think it is a stepping stone to their favorite object. I think I am well founded in this idea; I think the general politics of these men support it, as well as the common observation among them, That the proffered plan is the best that can be got at present, it will do for a few years, and lead to something better. The sensible and judicious part of the community will carefully weigh all these circumstances; they will view the late convention as a respectable body of men—America probably never will see an assembly of men, of a like number, more respectable. But the members of the convention met without knowing the sentiments of one man in ten thousand in these states respecting the new ground taken. Their doings are but the first attempts in the most important scene ever opened. Though each individual in the state conventions will not, probably, be so respectable as each individual in the federal convention, yet as the state conventions will probably consist of fifteen hundred or two thousand men of abilities, and versed in the science of government, [38] collected from all parts of the community and from all orders of men, it must be acknowledged that the weight of respectability will be in them—In them will be collected the solid sense and the real political character of the country. Being revisers of the subject, they will possess peculiar advantages. To say that these conventions ought not to attempt, coolly and deliberately, the revision of the system, or that they cannot amend it, is very foolish or very assuming. If these conventions, after examining the system, adopt it, I shall be perfectly satisfied, and wish to see men make the administration of the government an equal blessing to all orders of men. I believe the great body of our people to be virtuous and friendly to good government, to the protection of liberty and property; and it is the duty of all good men, especially of those who are placed as sentinels to guard their rights—it is their duty to examine into the prevailing politics of parties, and to disclose them—while they avoid exciting undue suspicions, to lay facts before the people, which will enable them to form a proper judgment. Men who wish the people of this country to determine for themselves, and deliberately to fit the government to their situation, must feel some degree of indignation at those attempts to hurry the adoption of a system, and to shut the door against examination. The very attempts create suspicions, that those who make them have secret views, or see some defects in the system, which, in the hurry of affairs, they expect will escape the eye of a free people.

What can be the views of those gentlemen in Pennsylvania,

who precipitated decisions on this subject? What can be the views of those gentlemen in Boston, who countenanced the Printers in shutting up the press against a fair and free investigation of this important system in the usual way. The members of the convention have done their duty——why should some of them fly to their states—almost forget a propriety of behaviour, and precipitate measures for the adoption of a system of their own making? I confess candidly, when I consider these circumstances in connection with the unguarded parts of the system I have mentioned, I feel disposed to proceed with very great caution, and to pay more attention than usual to the conduct of particular characters. If the constitution presented be a good one, it will stand the test with a well informed people: all are agreed that there shall be state conventions to examine it; and we must believe it will be adopted, unless we suppose it is a bad one, or that those conventions will make false divisions respecting it. I admit improper measures are taken against the adoption of the system as well for it——all who object to the plan proposed ought to point out the defects [39] objected to, and to propose those amendments with which they can accept it, or to propose some other system of government, that the public mind may be known, and that we may be brought to agree in some system of government, to strengthen and execute the present, or to provide a substitute. I consider the field of enquiry just opened, and that we are to look to the state conventions for ultimate decisions on the subject before us; it is not to be presumed, that they will differ about small amendments, and lose a system when they shall have made it substantially good; but touching the essential amendments, it is to be presumed the several conventions will pursue the most rational measures to agree in and obtain them; and such defects as they shall discover and not remove, they will probably notice, keep them in view as the ground work of future amendments, and in the firm and manly language which every free people ought to use, will suggest to those who may hereafter administer the government, that it is their expectation, that the system will be so organized by legislative acts, and the government so administered, as to render those defects as little injurious as possible. Our countrymen are entitled to an honest and faithful government; to a government of laws and not of men; and also to one of their chusing—as a citizen of the country, I wish to see these objects secured, and licentious, assuming, and overbearing men restrained; if the constitution or social compact be vague and unguarded, then we depend wholly upon the prudence, wisdom and moderation of those who manage the affairs of government; or on what, probably, is equally uncertain and precarious, the success of the people oppressed by the abuse of government, in receiving it from the hands of those who abuse it, and placing it in the hands of those who will use it well.

In every point of view, therefore, in which I have been able, as yet, to contemplate this subject, I can discern but one rational mode of proceeding relative to it: and that is to examine it with freedom and candour, to have state conventions some months hence, which shall examine coolly every article, clause, and word in the system proposed, and to adopt it with such amendments as they shall think fit. How far the state conventions ought to pursue the mode prescribed by the federal convention of adopting or rejecting the plan in toto, I leave it to them to determine. Our examination of the subject hitherto has been rather of a general nature. The republican characters in the several states, who wish to make this plan more adequate to security of liberty and property, and to the duration of the principles of a free government, will, no doubt, collect their opinions to certain points, and accurately define those [40] alterations and amendments they wish; if it shall be found they essentially disagree in them, the conventions will then be able to determine whether to adopt the plan as it is, or what will be proper to be done.

Under these impressions, and keeping in view the improper and unadvisable lodgment of powers in the general government, organized as it at present is, touching internal taxes, armies and militia, the elections of its own members, causes between citizens of different states, &c. and the want of a more perfect bill of rights, &c. I drop the subject for the present, and when I shall have leisure to revise and correct my ideas respecting it, and to collect into points the opinions of those who wish to make the system more secure and safe, perhaps I may proceed to point out particularly for your consideration, the amendments which ought to be ingrafted into this system, not only in conformity to my own, but the deliberate opinions of others—you will with me perceive, that the objections to the plan proposed may, by a more leisure examination be set in a stronger point of view, especially the important one, that there is no substantial representation of the people provided for in a government in which the most essential powers, even as to the internal police of the country, is proposed to be lodged.

I think the honest and substantial part of the community will wish to see this system altered, permanency and consistency given to the constitution we shall adopt; and therefore they will be anxious to apportion the powers to the features and organizations of the government, and to see abuse in the exercise of power more effectually guarded against. It is suggested, that state officers, from interested motives will oppose the constitution presented——I see no reason for this, their places in general will not be effected, but new openings to offices and places of profit must evidently be made by the adoption of the constitution in its present form.

Your's, &c.

THE FEDERAL FARMER.

*To the* REPUBLICAN.

The Objections of the / Hon. George Mason, / to the proposed Fœderal Constitution. / Addressed to the Citizens of Virginia. / ..... / Printed by Thomas Nicholas.

<dl><dd>Folio, Broadside.</dd></dl>

---

George Mason was a member of the Federal Convention, but refused to sign the Constitution, and was a leader of the opposition to its ratification in the Virginia Convention.

"I take the liberty to enclose to you my objections to the new Constitution of government, which a little moderation and temper at the end of the convention might have removed.... You will readily observe, that my objections are not numerous (the greater part of the enclosed paper containing reasonings upon the probable effects of the exceptionable parts), though in my mind some of them are capital ones." Mason to Washington, October 7th, 1787.

Madison's letter to Washington of October 18th, 1787, contains a cursory answer to Mason's "Objections," and a more elaborate one by James Iredell is printed in this volume.

P. L. F.

THERE is no declaration of rights: and the laws of the general government being paramount to the laws and constitutions of the several states, the declarations of rights, in the separate states, are no security. Nor are the people secured even in the enjoyment of the benefit of the common law, which stands here upon no other foundation than its having been adopted by the respective acts forming the constitutions of the several states.

In the House of Representatives there is not the substance, but the shadow only of representation; which can never produce proper information in the legislature, or inspire confidence in the people.—The laws will, therefore, be generally made by men little concerned in, and unacquainted with their effects and consequences.\*

The Senate have the power of altering all money-bills, and of originating appropriations of money, and the salaries of the officers of their appointment, in conjunction with the President of the United States—Although they are not the representatives of the people, or amenable to them. These, with their other great powers, (viz. their powers in the appointment of ambassadors, and all public officers, in making treaties, and in trying all impeachments) their influence upon, and connection with, the supreme executive from these causes, their duration of office, and their being a constant existing body, almost continually sitting, joined with their being one complete branch of the legislature, will destroy any balance in the government, and enable them to accomplish what usurpations they please, upon the rights and liberties of the people.

The judiciary of the United States is so constructed and extended, as to absorb and destroy the judiciaries of the sev-

---

\* This objection has been in some degree lessened, by an amendment, often before refused, and at last made by an erasure, after the engrossment upon parchment, of the word forty, and inserting thirty, in the third clause of the second section of the first article.

eral states; thereby rendering laws as tedious, intricate, and expensive, and justice as unattainable by a great part of the community, as in England; and enabling the rich to oppress and ruin the poor.

The President of the United States has no constitutional council (a thing unknown in any safe and regular government.) he will therefore be unsupported by proper information and advice; and will generally be directed by minions and favorites—or he will become a tool to the Senate—or a council of state will grow out of the principal officers of the great departments—the worst and most dangerous of all ingredients for such a council, in a free country; for they may be induced to join in any dangerous or oppressive measures, to shelter themselves, and prevent an inquiry into their own misconduct in office. Whereas, had a constitutional council been formed (as was proposed) of six members, viz., two from the eastern, two from the middle, and two from the southern states, to be appointed by vote of the states in the House of Representatives, with the same duration and rotation of office as the Senate, the executive would always have had safe and proper information and advice; the president of such a council might have acted as Vice-President of the United States, *pro tempore*, upon any vacancy or disability of the chief magistrate; and long continued sessions of the Senate, would in a great measure have been prevented. From this fatal defect of a constitutional council, has arisen the improper power of the Senate, in the appointment of the public officers, and the alarming dependence and connexion between that branch of the legislature and the supreme executive. Hence, also, sprung that unnecessary officer, the Vice-President, who, for want of other employment, is made President of the Senate; thereby dangerously blending the executive and legislative powers; besides always giving to some one of the states an unnecessary and unjust pre-eminence over the others.

The President of the United States has the unrestrained power of granting pardon for treason; which may be sometimes exercised to screen from punishment those whom he had secretly instigated to commit the crime, and thereby prevent a discovery of his own guilt. By declaring all treaties supreme laws of the land, the executive and the Senate have, in many cases, an exclusive power of legislation, which might have been avoided, by proper distinctions with respect to treaties, and requiring the assent of the House of Representatives, where it could be done with safety.

By requiring only a majority to make all commercial and navigation laws, the five southern states (whose produce and circumstances are totally different from those of the eight northern and eastern states) will be ruined: for such rigid and premature regulations may be made, as will enable the merchants of the northern and eastern states not only to demand an exorbitant freight, but to monopolize the purchase of the commodities, at their own price, for many years, to the great injury of the landed interest, and the impoverishment of the people: and the danger is the greater, as the gain on one side will be in proportion to the loss on the other. Whereas, requiring two-thirds of the members present in both houses, would have produced mutual moderation, promoted the general interest, and removed an insuperable objection to the adoption of the government.

Under their own construction of the general clause at the end of the enumerated powers, the Congress may grant monopolies in trade and commerce, constitute new crimes, inflict unusual and severe punishments, and extend their power as far as they shall think proper; so that the state legislatures have no security for the powers now presumed to remain to them; or the people for their rights. There is no declaration of any kind for preserving the liberty of the press, the trial by jury in civil cases, nor against the danger of standing armies in time of peace.

The state legislatures are restrained from laying export duties on their own produce—the general legislature is restrained from prohibiting the further importation of slaves for twenty odd years, though such importations render the United States weaker, more vulnerable, and less capable of defence. Both the general legislature, and the state legislatures are expressly prohibited making *ex post facto* laws, though there never was, nor can be, a legislature, but must and will make such laws, when necessity and the public safety require them, which will hereafter be a breach of all the constitutions in the union, and afford precedents for other innovations.

This government will commence in a moderate aristocracy; it is at present impossible to foresee whether it will, in its operation, produce a monarchy, or a corrupt oppressive aristocracy; it will most probably vibrate some years between the two, and then terminate in the one or the other.

GEO. MASON.

[Answers to Mr. Mason's objections to the new Constitution, recommended by the late Convention. By Marcus. Newbern: Printed by Hodge and Wills. 1788.]

By James Iredell, member of the first North Carolina Convention. This argument was originally published in the *State Gazette of North Carolina*, and was republished in pamphlet form, together with pieces by Archibald Maclaine and William R. Davie. The most careful search has not enabled me to find the pamphlet, so I am forced to reprint the "answers" from McRee's *Life of James Iredell*, a work of considerable rarity; and in consequence the above title is certainly not that of the pamphlet.

"I have read with great pleasure your answer to Mr. Mason's objections; and surely every man who read them, and on whom Mr. Mason's observations, or indeed the arguments of those in opposition in general have had any effect, must be convinced that the objections to the constitution are without foundation." *Witherspoon to Iredell, April* 3, 1788.

P. L. F.

## I. Objection.

"THERE is no declaration of rights, and the laws of the general government being paramount to the laws and constitutions of the several States, the declarations of rights in the separate States are no security. Nor are the people secured even in the enjoyment of the benefit of the common law, which stands here upon no other foundation than its having been adopted by the respective acts forming the Constitutions of the several States."

### Answer.

1. As to the want of a declaration of rights. The introduction of these in England, from which the idea was originally taken, was in consequence of usurpations of the Crown, contrary, as was conceived, to the principles of their government. But there no original constitution is to be found, and the only meaning of a declaration of rights in that country is, that in certain particulars specified, the Crown had no authority to act. Could this have been necessary had there been a constitution in being by which it could have been clearly discerned whether the Crown had such authority or not? Had the people, by a solemn instrument, delegated particular powers to the Crown at the formation of their government, surely the Crown, which in that case could claim under that instrument only, could not have contended for more power than was conveyed by it. So it is in regard to the new Constitution here: the future government which may be formed under that authority certainly cannot act beyond the warrant of that authority. As well might they attempt to impose a King upon America, as go one step in any other respect beyond the terms of their institution. The question then only is, whether more power will be vested in the future government than is necessary for the general purposes of the union. This may occasion a ground of dispute—but after expressly de-

fining the powers that are to be exercised, to say that they shall exercise no other powers (either by a general or particular enumeration) would seem to me both nugatory and ridiculous. As well might a Judge when he condemns a man to be hanged, give strong injunctions to the Sheriff that he should not be beheaded.*

2. As to the common law, it is difficult to know what is meant by that part of the objection. So far as the people are now entitled to the benefit of the common law, they certainly will have a right to enjoy it under the new Constitution until altered by the general legislature, which even in this point has some cardinal limits assigned to it. What are most acts of Assembly but a deviation in some degree from the principles of the common law? The people are expressly secured (contrary to Mr. Mason's wishes) against *ex post facto* laws; so that the tenure of any property at any time held under the principles of the common law, cannot be altered by any future act of the general legislature. The principles of the common law, as they now apply, must surely always hereafter apply, except in those particulars in which express authority is given by this constitution; in no other particulars can the Congress have authority to change it, and I believe it cannot be shown that any one power of this kind given is unnecessarily given, or that the power would answer its proper purpose if the legislature was restricted from any innovations on the principles of the common law, which would not in all cases suit the vast variety of incidents that might arise out it.

## II. OBJECTION.

"In the House of Representatives there is not the substance, but the shadow only of representation; which can never produce proper information in the legislature, or inspire

---

* It appears to me a very just remark of Mr. Wilson's, in his celebrated speech, that a bill of rights would have been dangerous, as implying that without such a reservation the Congress would have had authority in the cases enumerated, so that if any had been omitted (and who would undertake to recite all the State and individual rights not relinquished by the new Constitution?) they might have been considered at the mercy of the general legislature.

confidence in the people; the laws will therefore generally be made by men little concerned in, and unacquainted with their effects and consequences."

### Answer.

This is a mere matter of calculation. It is said the weight of this objection was in a great measure removed by altering the number of 40,000 to 30,000 constituents. To show the discontented nature of man, some have objected to the number of representatives as being too large. I leave to every man's judgment whether the number is not sufficiently respectable, and whether, if that number be sufficient, it would have been right, in the very infancy of this government, to burthen the people with a great additional expense to answer no good purpose.*

### III. Objection.

"The Senate have the power of altering all money bills, and of originating appropriations of money, and the salaries of the officers of their own appointment, in conjunction with the President of the United States; although they are not the representatives of the people or amenable to them.—These, with their other great powers (viz. their powers in the appointment of Ambassadors, and all public officers, in making treaties and trying all impeachments) their influence upon and connection with the supreme Executive, from these causes, their duration of office, and their being a constant existing body almost continually sitting, joined with their being one complete branch of the legislature, will destroy any balance in the government, and enable them to accomplish what usurpations they please upon the rights and liberties of the people."

---

* I have understood it was considered at the Convention, that the proportion of one Representative to 30,000 constituents, would produce at the very first nearly the number that would be satisfactory to Mr. Mason. So that I presume this reason was wrote before the material alteration was made from 40,000 to 30,000, which is said to have taken place the very last day just before the signature.

## Answer.

This objection, respecting the dangerous power of the Senate, is one of that kind which may give rise to a great deal of gloomy prediction, without any solid foundation: An imagination indulging itself in chimerical fears, upon the disappointment of a favorite plan, may point out danger arising from any system of government whatever, even if angels were to have the administration of it; since I presume none but the Supreme Being himself is altogether perfect, and of course every other species of beings may abuse any delegated portion of power. This sort of visionary scepticism therefore will lead us to this alternative, either to have no government at all, or to form the best system we can, making allowance for human imperfection. In my opinion the fears as to the power of the Senate are altogether groundless, as to any probability of their being either able or willing to do any important mischief. My reasons are,

1. Because, though they are not immediately to represent the people, yet they are to represent the representatives of the people who are annually chosen, and it is therefore probable the most popular, or confidential, persons in each State, will be elected members of the Senate.

2. Because one-third of the Senate are to be chosen as often as the immediate representatives of the people, and as the President can act in no case from which any great danger can be apprehended without the concurrence of two-thirds, let us think ever so ill of the designs of the President, and the danger of a combination of power among a standing body generally associated with him, unless we suppose every one of them to be base and infamous (a supposition, thank God, bad as human nature is, not within the verge of the slightest probability), we have reason to believe that the one-third newly introduced every second year, will bring with them from the immediate body of the people, a sufficient portion of patriotism and independence to check any exorbitant designs of the rest.

3. Because in their legislative capacity they can do nothing

without the concurrence of the House of Representatives, and we need look no farther than England for a clear proof of the amazing consequence which representatives of the people bear in a free government. There the King (who is hereditary, and therefore not so immediately interested, according to narrow views of interest which commonly govern Kings, to consult the welfare of his people) has the appointment to almost every office in the government, many of which are of high dignity and great pecuniary value, has the creation of as many Peers as he pleases, is not restricted from bestowing places on the members of both houses of Parliament, and has a direct negative on all bills, besides the power of dissolving the Parliament at his pleasure. In theory would not any one say this power was enormous enough to destroy any balance in the constitution? Yet what does the history of that country tell us?—that so great is the natural power of the House of Commons (though a very imperfect representation of the people, and a large proportion of them actually purchasing their seats) that ever since the revolution the Crown has continually aimed to corrupt them by the disposal of places and pensions; that without their hearty concurrence it found all the wheels of government perpetually clogged; and that notwithstanding this, in great critical emergencies, the members have broke through the trammels of power and interest, and by speaking the sense of the people (though so imperfectly representing them) either forced an alteration of measures, or made it necesary for the Crown to dissolve them. If their power, under these circumstancrs, is so great, what would it be if their representation was perfect, and their members could hold no appointments, and at the same time had a security for their seats? The danger of a destruction of the balance would be perhaps on the popular side, notwithstanding the hereditary tenure and weighty prerogatives of the Crown, and the permanent station and great wealth and consequence of the Lords. Our representatives therefore being an adequate and fair representation of the people, and they being expressly excluded from the possession of any places, and not holding their existence upon any precarious tenure, must have vast influence, and considering that in every popular government the danger of faction is often very serious and alarming, if such a danger could not be checked in its instant operation by some other power more independent of the immediate passions of the people, and capable therefore of thinking with more coolness, the government might be destroyed by a momentary impulse of passion, which the very members who indulged it might for ever afterwards in vain deplore. The institution of the Senate seems well calculated to answer this salutary purpose. Excluded as they are from places themselves, they appear to be as much above the danger of personal temptation as men can be. They have no permanent interest as a body to detach them from the general welfare, since six years is the utmost period of their existence, unless their respective legislatures are sufficiently pleased with their conduct to re-elect them. This power of re-election is itself a great check upon abuse, because if they have ambition to continue members of the Senate they can only gratify this ambition by acting agreeably to the opinion of their constituents. The House of Representatives, as immediately representing the people, are to *originate* all money bills. This I think extremely right, and it is certainly a very capital acquisition to the popular representative. But what harm can arise from the Senate, who are nearly a popular representative also, proposing amendments, when those amendments must be concurred with by the original proposers? The wisdom of the Senate may sometimes point out amendments, the propriety of which the other House may be very sensible of, though they had not occurred to themselves. There is no great danger of any body of men suffering by too eager an adoption of any amendment proposed to any system of their own. The probability is stronger of their being too tenacious of their original opinion, however erroneous, than of their profiting by the wise information of any other persons whatever. Human nature is so constituted, and therefore I think we may safely confide in the free admission of an intercourse of opinion on the detail of business, as well as to taxation as to other points. Our House of Representatives surely could not have such reason to dread the power of a Senate circumstanced as ours must be, as the House of Commons in England the permanent authority of the Peers, and therefore a jealousy, which may be well grounded in the one case would be entirely ill-directed in the other. For similar reasons I dread not any power of originating appropriations of money as mentioned in the objection. While the concurrence of the other House must be had, and as that must necessarily be the most weighty in the government, I think no danger is to be apprehended. The Senate has no such authority as to awe or influence the House of Representatives, and it will be as necessary for the one as for the other that proper active measures should be pursued: And in regard to appropriations of money, occasions for such appropriations may, on account of their concurrence with the executive power, occur to the Senate, which would not to the House of Representatives, and therefore if the Senate were precluded from laying any such proposals before the House of Representatives, the government might be embarrassed; and it ought ever to be remembered, that in our views of distant and chimerical dangers we ought not to hazard our very existence as a people, by proposing such restrictions as may prevent the exertion of any necessary power. The power of the Senate in the appointment of Ambassadors, &c., is designed as a check upon the President. They must be appointed in some manner. If the appointment was by the President alone, or by the President and a *Privy* Council (Mr. Mason's favorite plan), an objection to such a system would have appeared much more plausible. It would have been said that this was approaching too much towards monarchical power, and if this new Privy Council had been like all I have ever heard of, it would have afforded little security against an abuse of power in the President. It ought to be shown by reason and probability (not bold assertion) how this concurrence of power with the President can make the Senate so dangerous. It is as good an argument to say that it will not as that it will.* The

---

*It seems by the letter which has been published of Mr. Elsworth and Mr. Sherman, as if one reason of giving a share in these appointments to the Senate was, that persons in what are called the lesser States might have an equal

power of making treaties is so important that it would have been highly dangerous to vest it in the Executive alone, and would have been the subject of much greater clamor. From the nature of the thing, it could not be vested in the popular representative. It must therefore have been provided for with the Senate's concurrence, or the concurrence of a Privy Council (a thing which I believe nobody has been mad enough to propose), or the power, the greatest monarchical power that can be exercised, must have been vested in a manner that would have excited universal indignation in the President alone.—As to the power of trying impeachments:—Let Mr. Mason show where this power could more properly have been placed. It is a necessary power in every free government, since even the Judges of the Supreme Court of Judicature themselves may require a trial, and other public officers might have too much influence before an ordinary and common court. And what probability is there that such a court, acting in so solemn a manner, should abuse its power (especially as it is wisely provided that the sentences shall extend only to removal from office and incapacitation) more than any other court? The argument as to the possible abuse of power, as I have before suggested, will reach all delegation of power, since all power may be abused when fallible beings are to execute it; but we must take as much caution as we can, being careful at the same time not to be too wise to do any thing at all.— The bold assertions at the end of this objection are mere declamation, and till some reason is assigned for them, I shall take the liberty to rely upon the reasons I have stated above, as affording a belief that the popular representative must for ever be the most weighty in this government, and of course that apprehensions of danger from such a Senate are altogether ill-founded.

### IV. OBJECTION.

" The judiciary of the United States is so constructed and extended, as to absorb and destroy the judiciaries of the sev-

chance for such appointments, in proportion to their merit, with those in the larger, an advantage that could only be expected from a body in which the States were equally represented.

eral States; thereby rendering law as tedious, intricate and expensive and justice as unattainable by a great part of the community, as in England; and enabling the rich to oppress and ruin the poor."

ANSWER.

Mr. Mason has here asserted, "That the judiciary of the United States is so constructed and extended, as to absorb and destroy the judiciaries of the several States." How is this the case? Are not the State judiciaries left uncontrolled as to the affairs of that *State* only? In this, as in all other cases, where there is a wise distribution, power is commensurate to its object. With the mere internal concerns of a State, Congress are to have nothing to do: In no case but where the Union is in some measure concerned, are the federal courts to have any jurisdiction. The State Judiciary will be a satellite waiting upon its proper planet: That of the Union, like the sun, cherishing and preserving a whole planetary system.

In regard to a possible ill construction of this authority, we must depend upon our future legislature in this case as well as others, in respect to which it is impracticable to define every thing, that it will be provided for so as to occasion as little expense and distress to individuals as can be. *In parting with the coercive authority over the States as States, there must be a coercion allowed as to individuals. The former power no man of common sense can any longer seriously contend for; the latter is the only alternative.* Suppose an objection should be made that the future legislature should not ascertain salaries, because they might divide among themselves and their officers all the revenue of the Union.* Will not every man see how

* When I wrote the above, I had not seen Governor Randolph's letter. Otherwise, I have so great a respect for that gentleman's character I should have treated with more deference an idea in some measure countenanced by him. One of his objections relates to the Congress fixing their own salaries. I am persuaded, upon a little reflection, that gentleman must think this is one of those cases where a trust must unavoidably be reposed. No salaries could certainly be fixed now so as to answer the various changes in the value of money that in the course of time must take place. And in what condition would the supreme authority be if their very existence depended on an inferior power! An abuse in this case too would be so gross that it is very unlikely to happen, but if it should it would probably prove much more fatal to the authors than injurious to the people.

irrational it is to expect that any government can exist which is to be fettered in its most necessary operations for fear of abuse?

### V. OBJECTION.

"The President of the United States has no constitutional Council (a thing unknown in any safe and regular government), he will therefore be unsupported by proper information and advice, and will generally be directed by minions and favorites—or he will become a tool to the Senate—or a Council of State will grow out of the principal officers of the great departments; the worst and most dangerous of all ingredients for such a Council in a free country, for they may be induced to join in any dangerous or oppressive measures, to shelter themselves, and prevent an inquiry into their own misconduct in office: Whereas, had a constitutional Council been formed (as was proposed) of six members, viz., two from the eastern, two from the middle, and two from the southern States, to be appointed by a vote of the States in the House of Representatives, with the same duration and rotation of office as the Senate, the Executive would always have had safe and proper information and advice: The President of such a Council might have acted as Vice-President of the United States, *pro tempore*, upon any vacancy or disability of the Chief Magistrate, and long-continued sessions of the Senate would in a great measure have been prevented. From this fatal defect of a constitutional Council has arisen the improper power of the Senate, in the appointment of public officers, and the alarming dependence and connection between that branch of the legislature and the Supreme Executive. Hence also sprung that unnecessary and dangerous officer, the Vice-President, who for want of other employment, is made President of the Senate; thereby dangerously blending the Executive and Legislative powers; besides always giving to some one of the States an unnecessary and unjust pre-eminence over the others."

### ANSWER.

Mr. Mason here reprobates the omission of a particular

Council for the President, as a thing contrary to the example of all safe and regular governments. Perhaps there are very few governments now in being deserving of that character, if under the idea of safety he means to include safety for a proper share of personal freedom, without which their safety and regularity in other respects would be of little consequence to a people so justly jealous of liberty as I hope the people in America ever will be. Since however Mr. Mason refers us to such authority, I think I cannot do better than to select for the subject of our inquiry in this particular, a government which must be universally acknowledged to be the most safe and regular of any considerable government now in being (though I hope America will soon be able to dispute that pre-eminence). Every body must know I speak of Great Britain, and in this I think I give Mr. Mason all possible advantage, since in my opinion it is most probable he had Great Britain principally in his eye when he made this remark, and in the very height of our quarrel with that country, so wedded were our ideas to the institution of a Council, that the practice was generally if not universally followed at the formation of our governments, though we instituted Councils of a quite different nature, and so far as the little experience of the writer goes, have very little benefited by it. My inquiry into this subject shall not be confined to the actual present practice of Great Britain; I shall take the liberty to state the Constitutional ideas of Councils in England, as derived from their ancient law subsisting long before the Union, not omitting however to show what the present practice really is. By the laws of England * the King is said to have four Councils,— 1, The High Court of Parliament; 2, The Peers of the realm; 3, His Judges; 4, His Privy Council. By the first, I presume is meant, in regard to the making of laws; because the usual introductory expressions in most acts of Parliament, viz., " By the King's most excellent Majesty, by and with the advice and consent of the Lords spiritual and temporal, and Commons," &c., show that in a constitutional sense, they are deemed the

* See Coke's Commentary upon Littleton, 110. 1. Blackstone's Commentary, 227 and seq.

King's laws, after a ratification in Parliament. The Peers of the realm are by their birth hereditary Counsellors of the Crown, and may be called upon for their advice, either in time of Parliament, or when no Parliament is in being: They are called in some law books *Magnum Concilium Regis* (the King's Great Council). It is also considered the privilege of every particular Peer to demand an audience of the King, and to lay before him anything he may deem of public importance. The Judges, I presume, are called "Council of the King," upon the same principle as the Parliament is, because the administration of justice is in his name, and the Judges are considered as his instruments in the distribution of it. We come now to the Privy Council, which I imagine, if Mr. Mason had any particular view towards England when he made this objection, was the one he intended as an example of a *Constitutional Council* in that kingdom. The Privy Council in that country is undoubtedly of very ancient institution, but it has one fixed property invariably annexed to it, that it is a mere creature of the Crown, dependent on its will both for number and duration, since the King may, whenever he thinks proper, discharge any member, or the whole of it, and appoint another.\* If this precedent is of moment to us, merely as a precedent, it should be followed in all its parts, and then what would there be in the regulation to prevent the President being governed by "minions and favorites?" It would only be the means of riveting them on constitutional ground. So far as the precedents in England apply, the Peers being constitutionally the *Great Council* of the King, though also a part of the legislature, we have reason to hope that there is by no means such a gross impropriety as has been suggested in giving the Senate, though a branch of the legislature, a strong control over the Executive. The only difference in the two cases is, that the Crown in England may or may not give this consequence to the Peers at its own pleasure, and accordingly we find that for a long time past this great Council has been very seldom consulted; under our constitution the President is allowed no option in respect to certain points wherein he cannot act with-

---

\* 1. Blackstone's Commentaries, 232.

out the Senate's concurrence. But we cannot infer from any example in England, that a concurrence between the Executive and a part of the legislative is contrary to the maxims of their government, since their government allows of such a concurrence whenever the Executive pleases. The rule, therefore, from the example of the freest government in Europe, that the Legislative and Executive powers must be altogether distinct, is liable to exceptions; it does not mean that the Executive shall not form a part of the Legislative (for the King, who has the whole Executive authority, is one entire branch of the legislature, and this Montesquieu, who recognizes the general principle, declares is necessary); neither can it mean (as the example above evinces) that the Crown must consult neither House as to any exercise of the Executive power. But its meaning must be, that one power shall not include *both authorities*. The King, for instance, shall not have the sole Executive and sole Legislative authority also. He may have the former, but must participate the latter with the two Houses of Parliament. The rule also would be infringed were the three branches of the legislature to share jointly the Executive power. But so long as the people's representatives are altogether distinct from the Executive authority, the liberties of the people may be deemed secure. And in this point surely, there can be no manner of comparison between the provisions by which the independence of our House of Representatives is guarded, and the condition in which the British House of Commons is left exposed to every species of corruption. But Mr. Mason says, for want of a Council, the President may become "a tool of the Senate." Why? Because he cannot act without their concurrence. Would not the same reason hold for his being "a tool to the Council," if he could not act without their concurrence, supposing a Council was to be imposed upon him without his own nomination (according to Mr. Mason's plan)? As great care is taken to make him independent of the Senate as I believe human precaution can provide. Whether the President will be a tool to any persons will depend upon the man, and the same weakness of mind which would make him pliable to one body of control, would certainly attend him with another. But Mr. Mason objects, if he is not directed by minions and favorites, nor becomes a tool of the Senate," a Council of State will grow out of the principal officers of the great departments; the worst and most dangerous of all ingredients for such a Council in a free country; for they may be induced to join in any dangerous or oppressive measures, to shelter themselves, and prevent an inquiry into their own misconduct in office." I beg leave to carry him again to my old authority, England, and ask him, what efficient Council they have there but one formed of their great officers. Notwithstanding their important *Constitutional Council*, everybody knows that the whole movements of their Government, where a Council is consulted at all, are directed by their *Cabinet Council*, composed entirely of the principal officers of the great departments; that when a Privy Council is called, it is scarcely ever for any other purpose than to give a formal sanction to the previous determinations of the other, so much so that it is notorious that not one time in a thousand one member of the Privy Council, except a known adherent of administration, is summoned to it. But though the President under our constitution may have the aid of the "principal officers of the great departments," he is to have this aid, I think, in the most unexceptionable manner possible. He is not to be assisted by a Council summoned to a jovial dinner perhaps, and giving their opinions according to the nod of the President; but the opinion is to be given with the utmost solemnity *in writing*. No after equivocation can explain it away. It must for ever afterwards speak for itself, and commit the character of the writer, in lasting colors, either of fame or infamy, or neutral insignificance, to future ages, as well as the present. From those *written reasons*, weighed with care, surely the President can form as good a judgment, as if they had been given by a dozen formal characters, carelessly met together on a slight appointment; and this further advantage would be derived from the proposed system (which would be wanting if he had constitutional advice to screen him), that the President must be *personally responsible* for everything—for though an ingenious gentleman has proposed, that a Council should be responsible for *their opinions*, and the same sentiment of justice might be applied to these opinions of the great officers, I am persuaded it will in general be thought infinitely more *safe*, as well as more *just*, that the President who *acts* should be responsible for his *conduct*, following advice at his peril, than that there should be a danger of punishing any man for an erroneous opinion which might possibly be sincere. Besides the morality of this scheme, which may well be questioned, its inexpediency is glaring, since it would be so plausible an excuse and the insincerity of it so difficult to detect, the hopes of impunity this avenue to escape would afford would nearly take away all dread of punishment. As to the temptation mentioned to the officers joining in dangerous or oppresssve measures to shelter themselves, and prevent an inquiry into their own misconduct in office, this proceeds upon a supposition that the President and the great officers may form a very wicked combination to injure their country, a combination that in the first place it is utterly improbable, in a strong respectable government should be formed for that purpose, and in the next, with such a government as this constitution would give us, could have little chance of being successful, on account of the great superior strength and natural and jealous vigilance of one at least, if not both the weighty branches of legislation. This evil, however, of the possible depravity of *all public officers*, is one that can admit of no cure, since in every institution of government the same danger in some degree or other must be risked; it can only be guarded against by strong checks, and I believe it be difficult for the objectors to our new Constitution to provide stronger ones against any abuse of the Executive authority then will exist in that. As to the Vice President, it appears to me very proper he should be chosen much in the same manner as the President, in order that the States may be secure, upon any accidental loss by death or otherwise of the President's service, of the services in the same important station of the man in whom they repose their second confidence. The complicated manner of election wisely prescribed would necessarily occasion a considerable delay in the choice of another, and in the mean time the President of the Council, though very fit for the purpose of advising, might be very ill qualified, especially in a critical period, for an active Executive department. I am concerned to see, among Mr. Mason's other reasons, so trivial a one as the little advantage one State might accidentally gain by a Vice President of their country having a seat, with merely a casting vote, in the Senate. Such a reason is utterly unworthy of that spirit of amity, and rejection of local views, which can alone save us from destruction. It was the glory of the late Convention, that by discarding such they formed a general government upon principles that did as much honor to their hearts as to their understandings. God grant, that in all our deliberations, we may consider America as *one* body, and not divert our attention from so able a prospect to small considerations of partial jealousy and distrust. It is in vain to expect upon any system to secure an exact equilibrium of power for all the States. Some will occasionally have an advantage from the superior abilities of its members; the field of emulation is however open to all. Suppose any one should now object to the superior influence of Virginia (and the writer of this is not a citizen of that State), on account of the high character of General Washington, confessedly the greatest man of the present age, and perhaps equal to any that has existed in any period of time; would this be a reason for refusing a union with her, though the other States can scarcely hope for the consolation of ever producing his equal?

### VI. OBJECTION.

" The President of the United States has the unrestrained power of granting pardons for treason; which may be sometimes exercised to screen from punishment those whom he had secretly instigated to commit the crime, and thereby prevent a discovery of his own guilt."

### ANSWER.

Nobody can contend upon any rational principles, that a power of pardoning should not exist somewhere in every government, because it will often happen in every country that men are obnoxious to a lawful conviction, who yet are entitled, from some favorable circumstances in their case, to a merciful interposition in their favor. The advocates of monarchy have accordingly boasted of this, as one of the advantages of that form of government, in preference to a republican; nevertheless this authority is vested in the Stadtholder in Holland, and I believe is vested in every Executive power in America. It seems to have been wisely the aim of the late Convention, in forming a general government for America, to combine the acknowledged advantages of the British constitution with proper republican checks to guard as much as possible against abuses, and it would have been very strange if they had omitted this, which has the sanction of such great antiquity in that country, and if I am not mistaken, a universal adoption in America.* Those gentlemen who object to other parts of the constitution as introducing innovations, contrary to long experience, with a very ill grace attempt to reject an experience so unexceptionable as this, to introduce an innovation (perhaps the first ever suggested) of their own. When a power is acknowledged to be necessary, it is a very dangerous thing to

* I have since found that in the constitutions of some of the States there are much stronger restrictions on the Executive authority in this particular than I was aware of. In others the restriction only extends to prosecutions carried on by the General Assembly, or the most numerous branch of legislature, or a contrary provision by law; Virginia is in the latter class. But when we consider how necessary it is in many cases to make use of accomplices to convict their associates, and what little regard ought in general to be paid to a guilty man swearing to save his own life, we shall probably think that the jealousies which (by prohibiting pardons before convictions) even disabled the Executive authority from procuring unexceptionable testimony of this sort, may more fairly be ascribed to the natural irritation of the public mind at the time when the constitutions were formed, than to an enlarged and full consideration of the subject. Indeed, it could scarcely be avoided, that when arms were first taken up in the cause of liberty, to save us from the immediate crush of arbitrary power, we should lean too much rather to the extreme of weakening than of strengthening the Executive power in our own government. In England, the only restriction upon this power in the King, in case of Crown prosecutions (one or two slight cases excepted) is, that his pardon is not pleadable in bar of an impeachment. But he may pardon after conviction, even on an impeachment; which is an authority not given to our President, who in case of impeachments has no power either of pardoning or reprieving.

prescribe limits to it, for men must have a greater confidence in their own wisdom than I think any men are entitled to, who imagine they can form such exact ideas of all possible contingencies as to be sure that the restriction they propose will not do more harm than good. The probability of the President of the United States committing an act of treason against his country is very slight; he is so well guarded by the other powers of government, and the natural strength of the people at large must be so weighty, that in my opinion it is the most chimerical apprehension that can be entertained. Such a thing is however possible, and accordingly he is not exempt from a trial, if he should be guilty or supposed guilty, of that or any other offence. I entirely lay out of the consideration of the probability of a man honored in such a manner by his country, risking like General Arnold, the damnation of his fame to all future ages, though it is a circumstance of some weight in considering whether for the sake of such a remote and improbable danger as this, it would be prudent to abridge this power of pardoning in a manner altogether unexampled, and which might produce mischiefs the full extent of which it is not perhaps easy at present to foresee. In estimating the value of any power it is possible to bestow we have to choose between inconveniences of some sort or other, since no institution of man can be entirely free from all. Let us now therefore consider some of the actual inconveniences which would attend an abridgment of the power of the President in this respect. One of the great advantages attending a single Executive power is the degree of secrecy and dispatch with which on critical occasions such a power can act. In war this advantage will often counterbalance the want of many others. Now suppose, in the very midst of a war of extreme consequence to our safety or prosperity, the President could prevail on a gentleman of abilities to go into the enemy's country, to serve in the useful, but dishonorable character of a spy. Such are certainly maintained by all vigilant governments, and in proportion to the ignominy of the character, and the danger sustained in the enemy's couutry, ought to be his protection and security in his own. This man renders very useful services; perhaps by timely information, prevents the destruction of his country. Nobody knows of these secret services but the President himself; his adherence however to the enemy is notorious: he is afterwards intercepted in endeavoring to return to his own country, and having been perhaps a man of distinction before, he is proportionably obnoxious to his country at large for his supposed treason. Would it not be monstrous that the President should not have it in his power to pardon this man? or that it should depend upon mere solicitation and favor, and perhaps, though the President should state the fact as it really was, some zealous partisan, with his jealousy constantly fixed upon the President, might insinuate that in fact the President and he were secret traitors together, and thus obtain a rejection of the President's application. It is a consideration also of some moment, that there is scarcely any accusation more apt to excite popular prejudice than the charge of treason. There is perhaps no country in the world where justice is in general more impartially administered than in England, yet let any man read some of the trials for treason in that country even since the revolution; he will see sometimes a fury influencing the judges, as well as the jury, that is extremely disgraceful. There may happen a case in our country where a man in reality innocent, but with strong plausible circumstances against him, would be so obnoxious to popular resentment, that he might be convicted upon very slight and insufficient proof. In such a case it would certainly be very proper for a cool temperate man of high authority, and who might be supposed uninfluenced by private motives, to interfere and prevent the popular current proving an innocent man's ruin. I know men who write with a view to flatter the people, and not to give them honest information, may misrepresent this account as an invidious imputation on the usual impartiality of juries. God knows no man more highly reverences that blessed institution than I do; I consider them the natural safeguard of the personal liberties of a free people, and I believe they would much seldomer err in the administration of justice than any other tribunal whatever. But no man of experience and candor will deny the probability of such a case as I have supposed sometimes, though rarely, happening; and whenever it did happen, surely so safe a remedy as a prerogative of mercy in the Chief Magistrate of a great country ought to be at hand. There is little danger of an abuse of such a power, when we know how apt most men are in a republican government to court popularity at too great an expense, rather than do a just and beneficent action in opposition to strong prevailing prejudices among the people. But says Mr. Mason, "The President may sometimes exercise this power to screen from punishment those whom he had secretly instigated to commit the crime, and thereby prevent a discovery of his own guilt." This is possible, but the probability of it is surely too slight to endanger the consequences of abridging a power which seems so generally to have been deemed necessary in every well regulated government. It may also be questioned, whether supposing such a participation of guilt, the President would not expose himself to greater danger by pardoning, than by suffering the law to have its course. Was it not supposed, by a great number of intelligent men, that Admiral Byng's execution was urged on to satisfy a discontented populace, when the administration, by the weakness of the force he was entrusted with, were perhaps the real cause of the miscarriage before Minorca? Had he been acquitted, or pardoned, he could have perhaps exposed the real fault: as a prisoner under so heavy a charge his recrimination would have been discredited, as merely the effort of a man in despair to save himself from an ignominious punishment. If a President should pardon an accomplice, that accomplice then would be an unexceptionable witness. Before, he would be a witness with a rope about his own neck, struggling to get clear of it at all events. Would any men of understanding, or at least ought they to credit an accusation from a person under such circumstances?*

* The evidence of a man confessing himself guilty of the same crime is undoubtedly admissable, but it is generally, and ought to be always received with great suspicion, and other circumstances should be required to corroborate it.

## VII. OBJECTION.

"By declaring all treaties the supreme law of the land, the Executive and the Senate have, in many cases an exclusive power of legislation; which might have been avoided by proper distinctions with respect to treaties, and requiring the assent of the House of Representatives, where it could be done with safety."

## ANSWER.

Did not Congress very lately unanimously resolve, in adopting the very sensible letter of Mr. Jay, that a treaty when once made pursuant to the sovereign authority, *ex vi termini* became immediately the law of the land? It seems to result unavoidably from the nature of the thing, that when the constitutional right to make treaties is exercised, the treaty so made should be binding upon those who delegated authority for that purpose. If it was not, what foreign power would trust us? And if this right was restricted by any such fine checks as Mr. Mason has in his imagination, but has not thought proper to disclose, a critical occasion might arise, when for want of a little rational confidence in our own government we might be obliged to submit to a master in an enemy. Mr. Mason wishes the House of Representatives to have some share in this business, but he is immediately sensible of the impropriety of it, and adds "where it can be done with safety." And how is it to be known whether it can be done with safety or not, but during the pendency of a negotiation? Must not the President and Senate judge whether it can be done with safety or not? If they are of opinion it is unsafe, and the House of Representatives of course not consulted, what becomes of this boasted check, since, if it amounts to no more than that the President and Senate may consult the House of Rrepresentatives if they please, they may do this as well without such a provision as with it. Nothing would be more easy than to assign plausible reasons, after the negotiation was over, to show that a communication was unsafe, and therefore surely a precaution that could be so easily eluded, if it was not impolitic to the greatest degree, must be thought trifling indeed. It is also to be observed, that this authority, so obnoxious in the new Constitution (which is unfortunate in having little power to please some persons, either as containing new things or old), is vested indefinitely and without restriction in our present Congress, who are a body constituted in the same manner as the Senate is to be, but there is this material difference in the two cases, that we shall have an additional check, under the new system of a President of high personal character chosen by the immediate body of the people.

### VIII. Objection.

"Under their own construction of the general clause at the end of the enumerated powers, the Congress may grant monopolies in trade and commerce, constitute new crimes, inflict unusual and severe punishment, and extend their power as far as they shall think proper; so that the State Legislatures have no security for the powers now presumed to remain to them: or the people for their rights. There is no declaration of any kind for preserving the liberty of the press, the trial by jury in civil causes, nor against the danger of standing armies in time of peace."

### Answer.

The general clause at the end of the enumerated power is as follows:—

"To make all laws which shall be necessary and proper for carrying into execution the *foregoing powers, and all other powers vested by this Constitution in the United States, or in any department or office thereof.*"

Those powers would be useless, except acts of legislation could be exercised upon them. It was not possible for the Convention, nor is it for any human body, to foresee and provide for all contingent cases that may arise. Such cases must therefore be left to be provided for by the general Legislature as they shall happen to come into existence. If Congress, under pretence of exercising the power delegated to them, should in fact, by the exercise of any other power, usurp upon the rights of the different Legislatures, or of any private citizens, the people will be exactly in the same situation as if there had been an express provision against such power in particular, and yet they had presumed to exercise it. It would be an act of tyranny, against which no parchment stipulations can guard; and the Convention surely can be only answerable for the propriety of the powers given, not for the future virtues of all with whom those powers may be intrusted. It does not therefore appear to me that there is any weight in this objection more than in others. But that I may give it every fair advantage, I will take notice of every particular injurious act of power which Mr. Mason points out as exercisable by the authority of Congress under this general clause.

The first mentioned is, "That the Congress may grant monopolies in trade and commerce." Upon examining the constitution I find it expressly provided, "That no preference shall be given to the ports of one State over those of another;" and that "citizens of each State shall be entitled to all privileges and immunities of citizens in the several States." These provisions appear to me to be calculated for the very purpose Mr. Mason wishes to secure. Can they be consistent with any monoply in trade and commerce?* I apprehend therefore, under this expression must be intended more than is expressed, and if I may conjecture from another publication of a gentleman of the same State and in the same party of opposition, I should suppose it arose from a jealousy of the eastern States very well known to be often expressed by some gentlemen of Virginia. They fear, that a majority of the States may establish regulations of commerce which will give great advantage to the carrying trade of America, and be a means of encouraging New England vessels rather than Old England. Be it so. No regulations can give such advantage to New England vessels, which will not be enjoyed by all

---

* One of the powers given to Congress is, "To promote the progress of science and useful arts, by securing for limited times to authors and inventors the exclusive right to their respective writings and discoveries." I am convinced Mr. Mason did not mean to refer to this clause. He is a gentleman of too much taste and knowledge himself to wish to have our government established upon such principles of barbarism as to be able to afford no encouragement to genius.

other American vessels, and many States can build as well as New England, though not at present perhaps in equal proportion.* And what could conduce more to the preservation of the Union than allowing to every kind of industry in America a peculiar preference! Each State exerting itself in its own way, but the exertions of all contributing to the common security, and increasing the rising greatness of our country! Is it not the aim of every wise country to be as much the carriers of their own produce as they can be? And would not this be the means in our own of producing a new source of activity among the people, giving to our fellow-citizens what otherwise must be given to strangers, and laying the foundation of an independent trade among ourselves, and of gradually raising a navy in America which, however distant the prospect, ought certainly not to be out of our sight. There is no great probability however that our country is likely soon to enjoy so glorious an advantage. We must have treaties of commerce, because without them we cannot trade to other countries. We already have such with some nations; we have none with Great Britain, which can be imputed to no other cause but our not having a strong respectable government to bring that haughty nation to terms. And surely no man, who feels for the honor of his country, but must view our present degrading commerce with that country with the highest indignation, and the most ardent wish to extricate ourselves from so disgraceful a situation. This only can be done by a powerful government which can dictate conditions of advantage to ourselves, as an equivalent for advantages to them; and this could undoubtedly be easily done by such a government, without diminishing the value of any articles of our own produce; or if there was any diminution it would be too slight to

* Some might apprehend, that in this case as New England would at first have the greatest share of the carrying trade, the vessels of that country might demand an unreasonable freight. But no attempt could be more injurious to them as it would immediately set the Southern States to building, which they could easily do, and thus a temporary loss would be compensated with a lasting advantage to us; the very reverse would be the case with them. Besides, that from that country alone there would probably be competition enough for freight to keep it on reasonable terms.

be felt by any patriot in competition with the honor and interest of his country.

As to the constituting of new crimes, and inflicting unusual and severe punishment, certainly the cases enumerated wherein the Congress are empowered either to define offences, or prescribe punishments, are such as are proper for the exercise of such authority in the general Legislature of the Union. They only relate to "counterfeiting the securities and current coin of the United States," to "piracies and felonies committed on the high seas, and offences against the law of nations," and to "treason against the United States." These are offences immediately affecting the security, the honor or the interest of the United States at large, and of course must come within the sphere of the Legislative authority which is intrusted with their protection. Beyond these authorities, Congress can exercise no other power of this kind, except in the enacting of penalties to enforce their acts of legislation in the cases where express authority is delegated to them, and if they could not enforce such acts by the enacting of penalties those powers would be altogether useless, since a legislative regulation without some sanction would be an absurd thing indeed. The Congress having, for these reasons, a just right to authority in the above particulars, the question is, whether it is practicable and proper to prescribe limits to its exercise, for fear that they should inflict punishments unusual and severe. It may be observed, in the first place, that a declaration against "cruel and unusual punishments" formed part of an article in the Bill of Rights at the revolution in England in 1688. The prerogative of the Crown having been grossly abused in some preceding reigns, it was thought proper to notice every grievance they had endured, and those declarations went to an abuse of power in the Crown only, but were never intended to limit the authority of Parliament. Many of these articles of the Bill of Rights in England, without a due attention to the difference of the cases, were eagerly adopted when our constitutions were formed, the minds of men then being so warmed with their exertions in the cause of liberty as to lean too much perhaps towards a jealousy of power to repose a proper confidence in their own government. From these articles in the State constitutions many things were attempted to be transplanted into our new Constitution, which would either have been nugatory or improper. This is one of them. The expressions "unusual and severe" or "cruel and unusual" surely would have been too vague to have been of any consequence, since they admit of no clear and precise signification. If to guard against punishments being too severe, the Convention had enumerated a vast variety of cruel punishments, and prohibited the use of any of them, let the number have been ever so great, an inexhaustible fund must have been unmentioned, and if our government had been disposed to be cruel their invention would only have been put to a little more trouble. If to avoid this difficulty, they had determined, not negatively what punishments should not be exercised, but positively what punishments should, this must have led them into a labyrinth of detail which in the original constitution of a government would have appeared perfectly ridiculous, and not left a room for such changes, according to circumstances, as must be in the power of every Legislature that is rationally formed. Thus when we enter into particulars, we must be convinced that the proposition of such a restriction would have led to nothing useful, or to something dangerous, and therefore that its omission is not chargeable as a fault in the new Constitution. Let us also remember, that as those who are to make those laws must themselves be subject to them, their own interest and feelings will dictate to them not to make them unnecessarily severe ; and that in the case of treason, which usually in every country exposes men most to the avarice and rapacity of government, care is taken that the innocent family of the offender shall not suffer for the treason of their relation. This is the crime with respect to which a jealousy is of the most importance, and accordingly it is defined with great plainness and accuracy, and the temptations to abusive prosecutions guarded against as much as possible. I now proceed to the three great cases: The liberty of the press, the trial by jury in civil cases, and a standing army in time of peace.

The liberty of the press is always a grand topic for declamation, but the future Congress will have no other authority over this than to secure to authors for a limited time an exclusive privilege of publishing their works.—This authority has been long exercised in England, where the press is as free as among ourselves or in any country in the world; and surely such an encouragement to genius is no restraint on the liberty of the press, since men are allowed to publish what they please of their own, and so far as this may be deemed a restraint upon others it is certainly a reasonable one, and can be attended with no danger of copies not being sufficiently multiplied, because the interest of the proprietor will always induce him to publish a quantity fully equal to the demand. Besides, that such encouragement may give birth to many excellent writings which would otherwise have never appeared.* If the Congress should exercise any other power over the press than this, they will do it without any warrant from this constitution, and must answer for it as for any other act of tyranny.

In respect to the trial by jury in civil cases, it must be observed it is a mistake to suppose that such a trial takes place in all civil cases now. Even in the common law courts, such a trial is only had where facts are disputed between the parties, and there are even some facts triable by other methods. In the Chancery and Admiralty Courts, in many of the States, I am told they have no juries at all. The States in these particulars differ very much in their practice from each other. A general declaration therefore to preserve the trial by jury in all civil cases would only have produced confusion, so that the courts afterwards in a thousand instances would not have known how to have proceeded.—If they had added, "as heretofore accustomed," that would not have answered the purpose, because there has been no uniform custom about it.—If therefore the Convention had interfered, it must have been by entering into a detail highly unsuitable to a fundamental constitution of government; if they had pleased some States they

---

* If this provision had not been made in the new constitution no author could have enjoyed such an advantage in all the United States, unless a similar law had constantly subsisted in each of the States separately.

must have displeased others by innovating upon the modes of administering justice perhaps endeared to them by habit, and agreeable to their settled conviction of propriety. As this was the case it appears to me it was infinitely better, rather than endanger everything by attempting too much, to leave this complicated business of detail to the regulation of the future Legislature, where it can be adjusted coolly and at ease, and upon full and exact information. There is no danger of the trial by jury being rejected, when so justly a favorite of the whole people. The representatives of the people surely can have no interest in making themselves odious, for the mere pleasure of being hated, and when a member of the House of Representatives is only sure of being so for two years, but must continue a citizen all his life, his interest as a citizen, if he is a man of common sense, to say nothing of his being a man of common honesty, must ever be uppermost in his mind. We know the great influence of the monarchy in the British government, and upon what a different tenure the Commons there have their seats in Parliament from that prescribed to our representatives. We know also they have a large standing army. It is in the power of the Parliament, if they dare to exercise it, to abolish the trial by jury altogether. But woe be to the man who should dare to attempt it. It would undoubtedly produce an insurrection, that would hurl every tyrant to the ground who attempted to destroy that great and just favorite of the English nation. We certainly shall be always sure of this guard at least upon any such act of folly or insanity in our representatives. They soon would be taught the consequence of sporting with the feelings of a free people. But when it is evident that such an attempt cannot be rationally apprehended, we have no reason to anticipate unpleasant emotions of that nature. There is indeed little probability that any degree of tyranny which can be figured to the most discolored imagination as likely to arise out of our government, could find an interest in attacking the trial by jury in civil cases;—and in criminal ones, where no such difficulties intervene as in the other, and where there might be supposed temptations to violate the personal security of a citizen, it is sacredly preserved.

The subject of a standing army has been exhausted in so masterly a manner in two or three numbers of the Federalist (a work which I hope will soon be in every body's hands) that but for the sake of regularity in answering Mr. Mason's objections, I should not venture upon the same topic, and shall only presume to do so, with a reference for fuller satisfaction to that able performance. It is certainly one of the most delicate and proper cases for the consideration of a free people, and so far as a jealousy of this kind leads to any degree of caution not incompatible with the public safety, it is undoubtedly to be commended. Our jealousy of this danger has descended to us from our British ancestors; in that country they have a Monarch, whose power being limited, and at the same time his prerogatives very considerable, a constant jealousy of him is both natural and proper. The two last of the Stuarts having kept up a considerable body of standing forces in time of peace for the clear and almost avowed purpose of subduing the liberties of the people, it was made an article of the bill of rights at the revolution, "That the raising or keeping a standing army within the kingdom in time of peace, unless it be with the consent of Parliament, is against law;" but no attempt was made, or I dare say even thought of, to restrain the Parliament from exercise of that right. An army has been kept on foot annually by authority of Parliament, and I believe ever since the revolution they have had some standing troops; disputes have frequently happened about the number, but I don't recollect any objection by the most zealous patriot, to the keeping up of any at all. At the same time, notwithstanding the above practice of an annual vote (arising from a very judicious caution), it is still in the power of Parliament to authorize the keeping up of any number of troops for an indefinite time, and to provide for their subsistence for any number of years. Considerations of prudence, not constitutional limits to their authority, alone restrain such an exercise of it—our Legislature however will be strongly guarded, though that of Great Britain is without any check at all. No appropriations of money for military services can continue longer than two years. Considering the extensive services the general government may have to provide for upon this vast continent, no forces with any serious prospect of success could be attempted to be raised for a shorter time. Its being done for so short a period, if there were any appearance of ill designs in the government, would afford time enough for the real friends of their country to sound an alarm, and when we know how easy it is to excite jealousy of any government, how difficult for the people to distinguish from their real friends, those factious men who in every country are ready to disturb its peace for personal gratifications of their own, and those desperate ones to whom every change is welcome, we shall have much more reason to fear that the government may be overawed by groundless discontents, than that it should be able, if contrary to every probability such a government could be supposed willing, to effect any designs for the destruction of their own liberties as well as those of their constituents; for surely we ought ever to remember, that there will not be a man in the government but who has been either mediately or immediately recently chosen by the people, and that for too limited a time to make any arbitrary designs consistent with common sense, when every two years a new body of representatives with all the energy of popular feelings will come, to carry the strong force of a severe national control into every department of government. To say nothing of the one-third to compose the Senate coming at the same time, warm with popular sentiments, from their respective assemblies. Men may be sure to suggest dangers from any thing, but it may truly be said that those who can seriously suggest the danger of a premeditated attack on the liberties of the people from such a government as this, could with ease assign reasons equally plausible for mistrusting the integrity of any government formed in any manner whatever; and really it does seem to me, that all their reasons may be fairly carried to this position, that inasmuch as any confidence in any men would be unwise, as we can give no power but what may be grossly abused, we had better give none at all, but continue as we are, or resolve into total anarchy at once, of which indeed our present condition falls very little short. What sort of a government would that be which, upon the most certain intelligence that hostilities were meditated against it, could take no method for its defence till after a formal declaration of war, or the enemy's standard was actually fixed upon the shore? The first has for some time been out of fashion, but if it had not, the restraint these gentlemen recommend, would certainly have brought it into disuse with every power who meant to make war upon America. They would be such fools as to give us the only warning we had informed them we would accept of, before we would take any steps to counteract their designs. The absurdity of our being prohibited from preparing to resist an invasion till after it had actually taken place* is so glaring, that no man can consider it for a moment without being struck with astonishment to see how rashly, and with how little consideration gentlemen, whose characters are certainly respectable, have suffered themselves to be led away by so delusive an idea. The example of other countries, so far from warranting any such limitation of power, is directly against it. That of England has already been particularly noticed. In our present articles of confederation there is no such restriction. It has been observed by the Federalist, that Pennsylvania and North Carolina appear to be the only States in the Union which have attempted any restraint of the Legislative authority in this particular, and that their restraint appears rather in the light of a caution than a prohibition; but notwithstanding that, Pennsylvania had been obliged to raise forces in the very face of that article of her bill of rights. That great writer from the remoteness of his situation, did not know that North Carolina had equally violated her bill of rights in a similar manner. The Legislature

---

* Those gentlemen who gravely tell us that the militia will be sufficient for this purpose, do not recollect that they themselves do not desire we should rely solely on a militia in case of actual war, and therefore in the case I have supposed they cannot be deemed sufficient even by themselves, for when the enemy landed it would undoubtedly be a time of war, but the misfortune would be, that they would be prepared; we not. Certainly all possible encouragement should be given to the training of our militia, but no man can really believe that they will be sufficient, without the aid of any regular troops, in time of foreign hostility. A powerful militia may make fewer regulars necessary, but will not make it safe to dispense with them altogether.

of that State in November, 1785, passed an act for raising 200 men for the protection of a county called Davidson county against hostilities from the Indians; they were to continue for *two years* from the time of their first rendezvous, unless sooner disbanded by the Assembly, and were to be subject to the same "rules with respect to their government as were established in the time of the late war by the Congress of the United States for the government of the Continental army." These are the very words of the act. Thus, from the examples of the only two countries in the world that I believe ever attempted such a restriction, it appears to be a thing incompatible with the safety of government. Whether their restriction is to be considered as a caution or a prohibition, in less than five years after peace the caution has been disregarded, or the prohibition disobeyed.* Can the most credulous or suspicious men require stronger proof of the weakness and impolicy of such restraints?

### IX. OBJECTION.

"The State Legislatures are restrained from laying export duties on their own produce."

### ANSWER.

Duties upon exports, though they may answer in some particulars a convenience to the country which imposes them, are certainly not things to be contended for, as if the very being of a State was interested in preserving them. Where there is a kind of monopoly they may sometimes be ventured upon, but even there perhaps more is lost by imposing such duties, than is compensated for by any advantage. Where there is not a species of monopoly, no policy can be more absurd. The American States, are so circumstanced that some of the States necessarily export part of the produce of neighboring

---

* I presume we are not to be deemed in a state of war whenever any Indian hostilities are committed on our frontiers. If that is the case I don't suppose we have had six years of peace since the first settlement of the country, or shall have for fifty years to come. A distinction between peace and war would be idle indeed, if it can be frittered away by such pretences as those.

ones. Every duty laid upon such exported produce operates in fact as a tax by the exporting State upon the non-exporting State. In a system expressly formed to produce concord among all, it would have been very unwise to have left such a source of discord open; and upon the same principle, and to remove as much as possible every ground of discontent, Congress itself are prohibited from laying duties on exports, because by that means those States which have a great deal of produce to export would be taxed much more heavily than those which had little or none for exportation.

## X. OBJECTION.

"The general Legislature is restrained from prohibiting the further importation of slaves for twenty odd years, though such importation renders the United States weaker, more vulnerable; and less capable of defence."

### ANSWER.

If all the States had been willing to adopt this regulation, I should as an individual most heartily have approved of it, because even if the importation of slaves in fact rendered us stronger, less vulnerable and more capable of defence, I should rejoice in the prohibition of it, as putting an end to a trade which has already continued too long for the honor and humanity of those concerned in it. But as it was well known that South Carolina and Georgia thought a further continuance of such importations useful to them, and would not perhaps otherwise have agreed to the new constitution, those States which had been importing till they were satisfied, could not with decency have insisted upon their relinquishing advantages themselves had already enjoyed. Our situation makes it necessary to bear the evil as it is. It will be left to the future legislatures to allow such importations or not. If any, in violation of their clear conviction of the injustice of this trade, persist in pursuing it, this is a matter between God and their own consciences. The interests of humanity will, however, have gained something by the prohibition of this inhuman trade, though at a distance of twenty odd years.

## XI. OBJECTION.

"Both the general Legislature and the State Legislatures, have expressly prohibited making *ex post facto* laws, though there never was, nor can be, a legislature but must and will make such laws, when necessity and the public safety require them; which will hereafter be a breach of all the constitutions in the Union, and offer precedents for other innovations."

## ANSWER.

My ideas of liberty are so different from those of Mr. Mason, that in my opinion this very prohibition is one of the most valuable parts of the new constitution. *Ex post facto* laws may sometimes be convenient, but that they are ever absolutely necessary I shall take the liberty to doubt, till that necessity can be made apparent. Sure I am, they have been the instrument of some of the grossest acts of tyranny that were ever exercised, and have this never failing consequence, to put the minority in the power of a passionate and unprincipled majority, as to the most sacred things, and the plea of necessity is never wanting where it can be of any avail. This very clause, I think, is worth ten thousand declarations of rights, if this, the most essential right of all, was omitted in them. A man may feel some pride in his security, when he knows that what he does innocently and safely to-day in accordance with the laws of his country, cannot be tortured into guilt and danger to-morrow. But if it should happen, that a great and overruling necessity, acknowledged and felt by all, should make a deviation from this prohibition excusable, shall we not be more safe in leaving the excuse for an extraordinary exercise of power to rest upon the apparent equity of it alone, than to leave the door open to a tyranny it would be intolerable to bear? In the one case, every one must be sensible of its justice, and therefore excuse it; in the other, whether its exercise was just or unjust, its being lawful would be sufficient to command obedience. Nor would a case like that, resting entirely on its own bottom, from a conviction of invincible necessity, warrant an avowed abuse of another authority, where no such necessity existed or could be pretended.

## ANSWER TO MASON'S OBJECTIONS BY IREDELL.

I have now gone through Mr. Mason's objections; one thing still remains to be taken notice of, his prediction, which he is pleased to express in these words: "This government will commence in a moderate aristocracy; it is at present impossble to foresee, whether it will in its operation produce a monarchy, or a corrupt, oppressive aristocracy; it will most probably vibrate some years between the two, and then terminate in the one or the other." From the uncertainty of this prediction, we may hope that Mr. Mason was not divinely inspired when he made it, and of course that it may as fairly be questioned as any of his particular objections. If my answers to his objections are, in general, solid, a very different government will arise from the new constitution, if the several States should adopt it, as I hope they will. It will not probably be too much to flatter ourselves with, that it may present a spectacle of combined strength in government, and genuine liberty in the people, the world has never yet beheld. In the mean time, our situation is critical to the greatest degree. Those gentlemen who think we may at our ease go on from one convention to another, to try if all objections cannot be conquered by perseverance, have much more sanguine expectations than I can presume to form. There are critical periods in the fate of nations, as well as in the life of man, which are not to be neglected with impunity. I am much mistaken if this is not such a one with us. When we were at the very brink of despair, the late excellent Convention with a unanimity that none could have hoped for, generously discarding all little considerations formed a system of government which I am convinced can stand the nicest examination, if reason and not prejudice is employed in viewing it. With a happiness of thought, which in our present awful situation ought to silence much more powerful objections than any I have heard, they have provided in the very frame of government a safe, easy and unexceptionable method of correcting any errors it may be thought to contain. Those errors may be corrected at leisure; in the mean time the acknowledged advantages likely to flow from this constitution may be enjoyed. We may venture to hold up our head among the other powers of the world. We may talk to them with the confidence of an independent people, having strength to resent insults; and avail ourselves of our natural advantages. We may be assured of once more beholding justice, order and dignity taking place of the present anarchical confusion prevailing almost every where, and drawing upon us universal disgrace. We may hope, by proper exertions of industry, to recover thoroughly from the shock of the late war, and truly to become an independent, great and prosperous people. But if we continue as we now are, wrangling about every trifle, listening to the opinion of a small minority, in preference to a large and most respectable majority of the first men in our country, and among them some of the first in the world, if our minds in short are bent rather on indulging a captious discontent, than bestowing a generous and well-placed confidence in those who we have every reason to believe are entirely worthy of it, we shall too probably present a spectacle for malicious exultation to our enemies, and melancholy dejection to our friends; and the honor, glory and prosperity which were just within our reach, will perhaps be snatched from us for ever.

MARCUS.

*January*, 1788.

An / Address / to the / Freemen / of / South Carolina, / on the subject of the / Federal Constitution, / Proposed by the Convention, which met in / Philadelphia, May, 1787. / Charleston, / Printed by Bowen and Co., No. 31, Bay.

16 mo., pp. 12.

---

Written by Dr. David Ramsay, member of the Continental Congress and of the South Carolina State Convention which ratified the Constitution.

*Friends, Countrymen, and Fellow Citizens:*

YOU have, at this time a new federal constitution proposed for your consideration. The great importance of the subject demands your most serious attention. To assist you in forming a right judgment on this matter, it will be proper to consider,

1st. It is the manifest interest of these states to be united. Internal wars among ourselves, would most probably be the consequence of disunion. Our local weakness particularly proves it to be for the advantage of South Carolina to strengthen the federal government; for we are inadequate to secure ourselves from more powerful neighbours. [4]

2d. If the thirteen states are to be united in reality, as well as in name, the obvious principle of the union will be, that the congress, or general government, should have power to regulate all general concerns. In a state of nature, each man is free, and may do what he pleases: but in society, every individual must sacrifice a part of his natural rights; the minority must yield to the majority, and the collective interest must controul particular interests. When thirteen persons constitute a family, each should forego everything that is injurious to the other twelve. When several families constitute a parish, or county, each may adopt what regulations it pleases with regard to its domestic affairs, but must be abridged of that liberty in other cases, where the good of the whole is concerned.

When several parishes, counties, or districts, form a state, the separate interests of each must yield to the collective interest of the whole. When several states combine in one government, the same principles must be observed. These relinquishments of natural rights, are not real sacrifices: each person, county, or state, gains more than it loses, for it only gives up a right of injuring others, and obtains in return aid and strength to secure itself in the peaceable enjoyment of all remaining rights. If then we are to be an united people, and the obvious ground of union must be, that all continental concerns should be managed by Congress—let us by those principles examine the new constitution. Look over the 8th section, which enumerates the powers of Congress, and point out one that is not essential on the before recited principles of union. The first is a power to lay and collect taxes, duties, imposts, and excises, to pay the debts, and provide for the [5] common defence and general welfare of the United States.

When you authorised Congress to borrow money, and to contract debts, for carrying on the late war, you could not intend to abridge them of the means of paying their engagements, made on your account. You may observe that their future power is confined to provide *common defence* and *general welfare* of the United States. If they apply money to any other purposes, they exceed their powers. The people of the United States who pay, are to be judges how far their money is properly applied. It would be tedious to go over all the powers of Congress, but it would be easy to show that they all may be referred to this single principle, "that the general "concerns of the union ought to be managed by the general "government." The opposers of the constitution cannot show a single power delegated to Congress, that could be spared consistently with the welfare of the whole, nor a single one taken from the states, but such as can be more advantageously lodged in the general government, than in that of the separate states.

For instance, the states cannot emit money: This is not intended to prevent the emission of paper money, but only of state paper money. Is not this an advantage? To have thirteen paper currencies in thirteen states is embarrassing to commerce, and eminently so to travellers. It is *therefore*, obviously our interest, either to have no paper, or such as will circulate from Georgia to New Hampshire. Take another instance—the Congress are authorized to provide and maintain a navy.—Our sea-coast, in its whole extent needs the protection thereof; but if this was to be done [6] by the states, they who build ships, would be more secure than they who do not. Again, if the local legislatures might build ships of war at pleasure, the Eastern would have a manifest superiority over the Southern states. Observe, how much better this business is referred to the regulations of Congress. A common navy, paid out of the common treasury, and to be disposed of by the united voice of a majority for the common defence of the weaker as well as of the stronger states, is promised, and will result from the federal constitution. Suffer not yourselves to be imposed on by declamation. Ask the man who objects to the powers of Congress two questions, *is* it not necessary that the supposed dangerous power should be lodged somewhere? And secondly, where can it be lodged, consistently with the general good, so well as in the general government? Decide for yourselves on these obvious principles of union.

It has been objected, that the eastern states have an advantage in their representation in Congress. Let us examine this objection—the four eastern states send seventeen members to the house of representatives, but Georgia, South-Carolina, North-Carolina and Virginia, send twenty-three. The six northern states send twenty-seven, the six southern thirty. In both cases, we have a superiority;—but, say the objectors, add Pennsylvania to the northern states, and there is a majority against us. It is obvious to reply, add Pennsylvania to the southern states, and they have a majority. The objection amounts to no more than that seven are more than six. It must be known to many of you, that the Southern states, from their vast extent of uncultivated country, are daily receiving new settlers; but in New England their country is [7] so small, and their land so poor, that their inhabitants are constantly emigrating. As the rule of representation in Congress is to vary with the number of inhabitants, our influence in the general government will be constantly increasing. In fifty years, it is probable that the Southern states will have a great ascendency over the Eastern. It has been said that thirty-five men, not elected by yourselves, may make laws to bind you. This objection, if it has any force, tends to the destruction of your state government. By our constitution, sixty-nine make a quorum; of course, thirty-five members may make a law to bind all the people of South-Carolina.—Charleston, and any one of the neighboring parishes send collectively thirty-six members; it is therefore possible, in the absence of all others, that three of the lower parishes might legislate for the whole country. Would this be a valid objection against your own constitution? It certainly would not—neither is it against the proposed federal plan. Learn from it this useful lesson—insist on the constant attendance of your members, both in the state assembly, and Continental Congress; your representation in the latter, is as numerous in a relative proportion with the other states as it ought to be. You have a thirteenth part in both houses; and you are not, on principles of equality, entitled to more.

It has been objected, that the president, and two-thirds of the senate, though not of your election, may make treaties binding on the state. Ask these objectors—do you wish to have any treaties? They will say yes. Ask then who can be more properly trusted with the power of making them, than they to whom the convention have referred it? Can the state legislature? They would con- [8] sult their local interests.— Can the Continental House of Representatives? When sixty-five men can keep a secret, they may.—Observe the cautious guards which are placed round your interests. Neither the senate nor president can make treaties by their separate authority.—They must both concur.—This is more in your favour than the footing on which you now stand. The delegates in Congress of nine states, without your consent, can now bind you; by the new constitution there must be two-thirds af the members present, and also the president, in whose election you have a vote. Two-thirds are to the whole, nearly as nine to thirteen. If you are not wanting to yourselves by neglecting to keep up the state's compliment of senators, your situation with regard to preventing the controul of your local interests by the Northern states, will be better under the proposed constitution than it is now under the existing confederation.

It has been said, we will have a navigation act, and be restricted to American bottoms, and that high freight will be the consequence. We certainly ought to have a navigation act, and we assuredly ought to give a preference, though not a monopoly, to our own shipping.

If this state is invaded by a maritime force, to whom can we apply for immediate aid?—To Virginia and North-Carolina? Before they can march by land to our assistance, the country may be overrun. The Eastern states, abounding in men and in ships, can sooner relieve us, than our next door neighbours. It is therefore not only our duty, but our interest to encourage their shipping. They have sufficient resources on a few months notice, to furnish tonnage enough to carry off all your exports; and they can afford, and doubtless will undertake [9] to be your carriers on as easy terms as you now pay for freight in foreign bottoms.

On this subject, let us consider what we have gained, also what they have lost, by the revolution. We have gained a free trade with all the world, and consequently a higher price for our commodities; it may be said, and so have they. But they who reply in this manner, ought to know, that there is an amazing difference in our favour; their country affords no valuable exports, and of course the privilege of a free trade is to them of little value, while our staple commodity commands a higher price than was usual before the war. We have also gained an exemption from quit-rents, to which the eastern states were not subjected. Connecticut and Rhode Island were nearly as free before the revolution as since. They had no royal governor or councils to controul them, or to legislate for them. Massachusetts and New Hampshire were much nearer independence in their late constitution than we were. The eastern states, by the revolution, have been deprived of a market for their fish, of their carrying trade, their ship-building, and almost of every thing but their liberties.

As the war has turned out so much in our favour, and so much against them, ought we to grudge them the carrying of our produce, especially when it is considered, that by encouraging their shipping, we increase the means of our own defence? Let us examine also the federal constitution, by the principles of reciprocal concession. We have laid a foundation for a navigation act. This will be a general good; but particularly so to our northern brethren. On the other hand, they have agreed to change the federal rule of paying the continental debt, according to the value of land, as laid down in the confede- [10] ration, for a new principle of apportionment, to be founded on the numbers of inhabitants in the several states respectively. This is an immense concession in our favour. Their land is poor; our's rich; their numbers great; our's small; labour with them is done by white men, for whom they pay an equal share; while five of our negroes only count as equal to three of their whites. This will make a difference of many thousands of pounds in settling our continental accounts. It is farther objected, that they have stipulated for a right to prohibit the importation of negroes after 21 years. On this subject observe, as they are bound to protect us from domestic violence, they think we ought not to increase our exposure to that evil, by an unlimited importation of slaves. Though Congress may forbid the importation of negroes after 21 years, it does not follow that they will. On the other hand, it is probable that they will not. The more rice we make, the more business will be for their shipping; their interest will therefore coincide with our's. Besides, we have other sources of supply—the importation of the ensuing 20 years, added to the natural increase of those we already have, and the influx from our northern neighbours, who are desirous of getting rid of their slaves, will afford a sufficient number for cultivating all the lands in this state.

Let us suppose the union to be dissolved by the rejection of the new constitution, what would be our case? The united states owe several millions of dollars to France, Spain, and Holland. If an efficient government is not adopted, which will provide for the payment of our debt, especially of that which is due to foreigners—who will be the losers? Most certainly the southern states. Our ex- [11] ports, as being the most valuable, would be the first objects of capture on the high seas, or descents would be made on our defenceless coasts, till the creditors of the United States had paid themselves at the expense of this weaker part of the union. Let us also compare the present confederation with the proposed constitution. The former can neither protect us at home, nor gain us respect abroad; it cannot secure the payment of our debts, nor command the resources of our country, in case of danger. Without money, without a navy, or the means of even supporting an army of our own citizens in the field, we lie at the mercy of every invader; our sea-port towns may be laid under contribution, and our country ravaged.

By the new constitution, you will be protected with the force of the union, against domestic violence and foreign invasion. You will have a navy to defend your coast.—The respectable figure you will make among the nations, will so far command the attention of foreign powers, that it is probable you will soon obtain such commercial treaties, as will open to your vessels the West-India islands, and give life to your expiring commerce.

In a country like our's, abounding with free men all of one rank, where property is equally diffused, where estates are held in fee simple, the press free, and the means of information common, tyranny cannot reasonably find admission under any form of government; but its admission is next to impossible under one where the people are the source of all power, and elect either mediately by their representatives, or immediately by themselves the whole of their rulers.

Examine the new constitution with candor and liberality. Indulge no narrow prejudices to the disadvantage of your brethren of the [12] other states; consider the people of all the thirteen states, as a band of brethren, speaking the same language, professing the same religion, inhabiting one undivided country, and designed by heaven to be one people. Content that what regards all the states should be managed by that body which represents all of them; be on your guard against the misrepresentations of men who are involved in debt; such may wish to see the constitution rejected, because of the following clause, "no state shall emit bills of credit, make any thing but gold and silver coin, a tender in payment of debts, pass any *expost facto* law, or law impairing the obligation of contracts." This will doubtless bear hard on debtors who wish to defraud their creditors, but it will be real service to the honest part of the community. Examine well the characters and circumstances of men who are averse to the new constitution. Perhaps you will find that the above recited clause is the real ground of the opposition of some of them, though they may artfully cover it with a splendid profession of zeal for state privileges and general liberty.

On the whole, if the proposed constitution be not calculated to better your country, and to secure to you the blessings for which you have so successfully contended, reject it: but if it be an improvement on the present confederation, and contains within itself the principles of farther improvement suited to future circumstances, join the mighty current of federalism, and give it your hearty support. You were among the first states that formed an independent constitution; be not among the last in accepting and ratifying the proposed plan of federal government; it is your sheet anchor; and without it independence may prove a curse.

CIVIS.

# BIBLIOGRAPHY

### AND

# REFERENCE LIST

### OF THE

# HISTORY AND LITERATURE

### OF THE

# UNITED STATES CONSTITUTION

### 1787–1788.

# NOTE.

The titles in the following list are arranged alphabetically, by the authors or editors names if known, or by the first word of the title, omitting participles, with the exception of the editions of the Constitution, which are brought together under that head, and the debates and journals of the State Conventions, which are placed under each State.

The initials which precede the numbers at the end of the description, indicate certain public libraries in which the work may be consulted.

| | | |
|---|---|---|
| A. | signifies | Astor Library. |
| A. A. S. | " | Am. Antiquarian Society Library. |
| B. | " | Boston Public Library. |
| B. A. | " | Boston Athenæum Library. |
| B. M. | " | British Museum Library. |
| C. | " | Library of Congress. |
| H. | " | Library of Harvard University. |
| M. | " | Mass. Historical Society Library. |
| N. | " | N. Y. Historical Society Library. |
| P. | " | Library Company of Philadelphia. |
| P. H. S. | " | Penn. Historical Society Library. |
| S. | " | New York State Library. |
| S. D. | " | Department of State Library. |
| ... | " | A line omitted in the title. |
| ..... | " | Two or more lines omitted in the title. |
| + | " | That what is omitted is already sufficiently given in title of previous edition. |

The numbers attached to certain titles in the reference list are cross refererences to the same title in the bibliography.

I am under obligation to Mr. C. A. Cutter, Mr. W Eames, Mr. William Kelby, Mr. E. M. Barton and Mr. Bumford Samuels, for aid in compiling this list.

# BIBLIOGRAPHY.

*Account of the Grand Federal Procession.* *See Nos.* 77–8.

*Additional number of Letters.* *See No.* 90.

The / Address and Reasons of Dissent / of the / Minority of the Convention, / Of the State of Pennsylvania, to their Constituents. [Colophon] Philadelphia: Printed by E. Oswald, at the Coffee House.

Folio. pp. (3)      A. A. S.   1

Reprinted in Carey's *American Museum*, ii, 536, and answered by Noah Webster's "To the Dissenting members of the late Convention of Pennsylvania," in his " *Collection of Essays*. . . . *Boston:* 1790," page 142.

Address and Reasons of Dissent of the Minority of the Convention of the State of Pennsylvania, to their Constituents. [Philadelphia: 1787.]

8vo. pp. 22.      B. A.   2

Title from Sabin's *Dictionary of Books relating to America.* See No. 108.

Address / to the / Citizens of Pennsylvania. / Calculated to shew the Safety,—Advantages—and Necessity of adopting the proposed Constitution of the / United States. / In which are included answers to the objections that have been made to it. / [Colophon] Philadelphia: Printed by Hall and Sellers.

Folio. pp. (4)      N.   3

A Federalist compilation, containing

    Reply to the Address of the seceding members of the Pennsylvania Legislature.

    To the Freemen of Pennsylvania [in reply to the Address of the seceding members], by Federal Constitution.

    Speech of James Wilson, October 6th, 1787.

    Examination of the Federal Constitution, by An American [Tench Coxe.]

    Circular Letter from the Federal Convention.

*Address to the Freemen of S. C.* *See Nos.* 114–15.

*Address to the People of N. Y.* *See Nos.* 83–4 *and* 120–21.

*American Citizen.* *See Nos.* 3, 21–2.

*Aristides.* *See Nos.* 74–5.

*Articles. See No.* 6.

*Baldwin (Simeon).*

An / Oration / pronounced before the / Citizens of New Haven, / July 4th, 1788 ; / in commemoration of the / Declaration / of / Independence / and establishment of the Constitution / of the / United States of America. / By Simeon Baldwin, Esquire, / New Haven. / Printed by J. Meigs, / M,DCC,-LXXXVIII.

8vo. pp. 16.     4

*Bancroft (George).*

History / of the / Formation of the Constitution / of the / United States of America. / By George Bancroft. / In two volumes, / Vol. I. / New York : / D. Appleton and Company, / 1, 3, and 5 Bond Street, / 1882.

2 Vols., 8vo. pp. xxiv, 520—xiv, 501 (2).     5

Each volume contains not only Mr. Bancroft's History, but a series of hitherto unpublished "Letters and Papers," adding greatly to the value of the work. In 1885 a one volume edition was published, from the same plates, but omitting these documents—pp. xxii., 495.

Reviewed by B. F. De Costa, in the *Mag. of Am. Hist.*, viii, 669; and in *The Nation*, xxxiv, 524 and xxxvi, 127.

*Bryan, Samuel. See No.* 108.

*Centinel. See No.* 108.

*Childs, Francis. See No.* 103.

*Citizen of America. See Nos.* 130–31.

*Citizen of New York. See No.* 83.

*Citizen of Philadelphia. See Nos.* 132–4.

*Civis. See Nos.* 82, 114–15.

*Columbian Patriot. See Nos.* 69–71.

*Constitution.*

In the following list of editions, I have only attempted to include such as were published during the discussion of the Constitution, prior to its ratification, and so conscious am I of its imperfections, that I should omit it altogether, were it not that no such list has ever been attempted, and this may make the task an easier one to some future bibliographer. It is almost certain that the Federal Convention, the Continental Congress, and each of the states printed public official editions, (of which, excepting Massachusetts, New York, and possibly Pennsylvania, I have been unable to trace copies) while the editions printed for the use of the people were undoubtedly numerous. The list includes every edition that I could find, in any bibliographies or library catalogues that I have examined, except the "Portsmouth, N. H. 1787" given in the Library of Congress catalogue, which cannot now be found. I have also included the two drafts (Nos. 19 and 20) used by the Convention, which, though not properly editions of the Constitution, nevertheless seemed best classed among them. The arrangement is alphabetical, by the first word of the title or caption participles excepted.

See also—View of the Proposed Constitution. No. 125.

*Constitution. New York.* 1787.

Articles agreed upon by the Federal Convention of the United States of / America, his Excellency, General Washington, Esq., President, / .... / New York: Printed by J. M'Lean, No. 41, Hanover Square [1787].

Folio. pp. 4.      N. 6

*Constitution. Albany.* 1788.

De / Constitutie, / eenpariglyk gea ecordeerd by de / Algemeene Conventie,/ gehonden in de / Stad von Philadelphia, / in 't Jaar 1787: / en gesubmitteer aan hit / Volk de Vereenigde Staaten / van Noord—Amerika: / Zynde van ses derzelvir Staaten alreede / geadopteerd, namentlyk, / Massachusetts, Connecticut, Nieuw-Jersey, Pennsylvania, Delaware en Georgia / Vertaald door Lambertus de Ronde, V. D. M. / Gedrukt by Ordervan de Federal Committee, in de Stad van Albany, / Door Charles R. Webster, in zyne Vrye Boek- / Druking, No. 36, Staat-Straat, na by de / Engelsche Kirke in dezelvde Stad, 1788.

Sq. 12mo. pp. 32.      B. 7

*Constitution. Boston.* 1787.

The / Constitution / or Frame of / Government, / For the United States of / America,/ as reported by the Convention of Delegates, from the / United States, begun and held at Philadelphia on the / first Monday of May, 1787, and continued by Adjournments to / the seventeenth Day of September following—[Colophon at p. 16] Printed by Thomas and John Fleet, in Boston.

8vo. pp. 20      M. 8

Includes the resolves of the Continental Congress and the Massachusetts General Court. Sabin gives a copy "12mo. pp. 16," but it is this edition, lacking the last four leaves, or the "resolves."

*Constitution. Boston.* 1787.

The / Constitution / or Frame of / Government, / for the /

United States / of / America. / As reported by the Convention of Delegates, from / the United States, begun and held at Philadel- / phia, on the first Monday of May, 1787, and continued / by adjournments to the seventeenth Day of September fol- / lowing.—Which they resolved should be laid before the / United States in Congress assembled ; and afterwards be / submittted to a Convention of Delegates, chosen in each State, / by the People thereof, under the recommendation of its Le- / gislature, for their Assent and Ratification / Together with the Resolutions of the General Court of the / Commonwealth of Massachusetts, for calling said Convention, agreea- / ble to the recommendation of Congress. / Published by order of Government. / Printed at Boston, Massachusetts, By Adams & Nourse, / Printers to the Honourable the General Court. / M,DCC,LXXXVII.

8vo.  pp. 32.          C. M., A. A. S.  9

*Constitution. Philadelphia.* 1787.

The / Constitution / proposed for / The Government of the United States of / America, by the Fœderal Conven- / tion, held at Philadelphia, in the / Year One Thousand Seven Hundred / and Eighty-seven. / To which is Annexed, / The Ratifications thereof by the Dele- / gates of Pennsylvania in the / State Convention. / Philadelphia: Printed by Hall & Sellers. / M,DCC.LXXXVII.

8vo.  pp. 24.                  C.  10

*Constitution. Philadelphia.* 1787.

The / Constitution / as formed for the / United States / by the / Fœderal Convention, / Held at Philadelphia, / In the year 1787, / With the Resolves of / Congress,/ and of the / Assembly of Pennsylvania / thereon. / Philadelphia : / Printed by T. Bradford, / in Front-Street, four doors below the Coffee House / M,DCC,LXXXVII.

12mo.  pp. 16.            C. H. S.  11

*Constitution. Richmond.* 1787 or 8.

The / Federal Constitution / for the United States of America, &c. [Colophon] Richmond: Printed by Augustin Davis.

4to.  pp. 11.                    12

*Constitution. London.* 1787.

Plan / of the / New Constitution / for the / United States of America, / Agreed upon in a / Convention of the States / with / a Preface by the Editor. / London : / Printed for J. Debrett, Piccadilly. / M.DCCLXXXVII.

8vo. pp. (2) 30,8.     13

*Constitution. Boston.* 1787.

(1) Proceedings / of the / Federal Convention. / [Colophon at p. 16] Printed by Thomas and John Fleet, in Boston.

8vo. pp. 20.     P. 14

The Constitution, with the resolutions, etc., of the Massachusetts General Court. See No. 8.

*Constitution. Philadelphia.* 1787.

Proceedings / of the / Federal Convention. / Held at / Philadelphia / in the Year 1787. / And the Twelfth Year / of / American Independence. / Philadelphia : / Printed by T. Bradford, / in Front-street, four doors below the Coffee-House / M,DCC,LXXXVII

8vo. pp. 15.     C. 15

*Constitution. Philadelphia.* 1787.

Results / of the Deliberations / of the / Federal Convention. / In Convention, Sept. 17, 1787 [Philadelphia : ? 1787].

8vo. pp. 16.     P. H. S. 16

*Constitution. New York.* 1787.

Supplement to the Independent Journal, / Saturday, September 22, 1787. / Copy of the Result of the Deliberations of the / Federal Convention / In Convention, September 17, 1787, / [New York : J. M'Lean. 1787].

Folio. pp. 4.     S. L. 16*

*Constitution. Hartford.* 1787.

We the People / of the United / States, / . . . . . / . . . do ordain and esta- / blish this Constitution for the United States of / America. / Hartford : / Printed and sold by Nathaniel Patten. / M,DCC,LXXXVII.

Sq. 16mo. pp. 16.     P. H. S. 17

*Constitution. Poughkeepsie.* 1788.

We the People of the United States, in order to form a / more perfect Union, establish Justice, insure domestic

Tran- / quillity, provide for the common Defense, promote the ge- / neral Welfare, and secure the Blessings of Liberty to ourselves / and our Posterity, do ordain and establish this Constitu- / tion for the United States of America. [Poughkeepsie: Nicholas Power, 1788.]

4to. pp. 20.      S. 18

The official edition printed for the use of the New York Convention. The text is only printed on one side of page, to page 17—after that on both sides.

*Constitution. Philadelphia.* 1787.

We, the People of the United States in order to form / a more perfect union, to establish justice, insure domestic tranquility, provide / for the common defense, promote the general welfare, and secure the blessings / of liberty to ourselves and our posterity, do ordain and establish this Constitution for the / United States of America. . . .

Folio, 4 ll.      S. D., C., M. 19

The "Report" of the "Committee on style and arrangement" of the Federal Convention, brought in September 13th, 1787. It was printed for the use of the members only and with the utmost secrecy.

*Constitution. Philadelphia.* 1787.

We the People of the States / of New-Hampshire, Massachusetts, / Rhode Island and Providence Plan- / tations, Connecticut, New York, New Jersey, Penn- / sylvania, Delaware, Maryland, Virginia, North-Caro- / lina, South-Carolina, and Georgia, do ordain, declare / and establish the following Constitution for the Government of Ourselves and our Posterity.

Folio, 7 ll.      S. D., C., M. 20

The "Report" of the "Committee of five," of the Federal Convention, brought in August 6th, 1787. Printed only for the use of the members, as a basis for a continuation of the discussion. Both these last two editions, it is needless to say, are of the greatest rarity, the number printed being probably not over sixty copies, and as confidential documents, were saved by few of the members. The Department of State possesses Washington's copy of No. 19, and David Brearly's and James Madison's copies of both drafts. The Library of Congress possesses William Samuel Johnson's copies, and the Massachusetts Historical Society has those of Elbridge Gerry. All of these contain Mss. alterations by their respective owners, and George Mason's copy of No. 19 in the possession of Miss Kate Mason Rowland of Virginia, contains not only alterations, but the objections of Mason to the Constitution, in his own handwriting. What are apparently the original Mss. compilations from which these drafts were printed are in the Wilson Papers, now in the Pennsylvania Historical Society.

[*Coxe* (*Tench*)].

An / Examination / of the / Constitution / for the / United States / of / America, / Submitted to the People / by the / General Convention, / at Philadelphia, the 17th Day of September, 1787, / and since adopted and ratified / by the / Conventions of Eleven States, / chosen for the purpose of considering it, being all / that have yet decided on the subject. / By an American Citizen. / To which is added, / a Speech / of the / Hon. James Wilson, Esquire./ on the same subject. / Philadelphia: / Printed by Zachariah Poulson, Junr. in Fourth / Street, between Market and Arch-Streets. / M.DCC.LXXXVIII.

8vo. pp. 33. P. 21

Reprinted in Ford's *Pamphlets on the Constitution* and in No. 3, and the Letters by "An American Citizen" are printed in No. 99, and in Carey's *American Museum*, ii, pp. 301 and 387.

*Coxe* (*Tench*).

[An Examination of the Constitution. Reprinted, Brooklyn, N. Y.: 1887.]

8vo. pp. 22. 22

A few copies separately printed from No. 68.

*Curtis* (*George Ticknor*).

History / of the / Origin, Formation, and Adoption / of the / Constitution of the United States ; / with / notices of its principal framers. / By / George Ticknor Curtis. / In two volumes. / Volume I. / New York: / Harper and Brothers,/ Franklin Square. / 1854 [–8].

2 vols., 8vo. pp. xxxvi, 518—xvi, 663. 23

This work, which is by far the best history of our Constitution, has been for several years out of print, and is difficult to procure in second hand condition. There are issues with different dates. It was reviewed, by C. C. Smith, in *The Christian Examiner*, lviii, 75, lxv, 67 ; in *The Methodist Review*, xv, 187 ; in *The American Quarterly Church Review*, xv, 541 ; and in *The North American Review*, lxxx, 259, by A. P. Peabody.

[*Davie* (*William Richardson and others*)].

[An Address to the People of North Carolina, by Publicola. Answer to George Mason's Objections to the new Constitution recommended by the late Convention, by Marcus, etc. Newbern: Printed by Hodge and Wills. 1788.]

pp. 24

A hypothetical title of a tract frequently alluded to in McRee's *Life of James Iredell*, but which I have been able to find no other trace. William R. Davie wrote Publicola, James Iredell wrote Marcus, and Archibald Maclaine apparently contributed as well. See No. 81.

*Debates of the State Conventions (Elliot). See Nos. 27–30.*

*Decius's Letters. See Nos.* 100 *and* 105.

[*Dickinson (John)* ].

The / Letters / of / Fabius, / in 1788, / on the Federal Constitution, / and / in 1797, / on the present situation / of / public affairs. / Copy-Right Secured. / From the office of the Delaware / Gazette, Wilmington, / by W. C. Smyth. / 1797.

8vo. pp. iv, 202 (1).      H.   25

Reprinted in *Political Writings of John Dickinson*, and the first series is in Ford's *Pamphlets on the Constitution*.

See Washington's *Writings*, xi, 354.

The first series of *Fabius* were also printed in *The New Hampshire Gazette*, from which Mr. Dawson reprinted a single number in the *The Historical Magazine*, xviii, 359; apparently under the impression that it was an original New Hampshire essay.

*Dickinson ( John).*

[The Letters of Fabius, Brooklyn, N. Y.; 1888].

8vo. pp. 54.      26

A few copies separately printed from No. 68.

*Examination into the leading principles. See Nos.* 130–1.

*Examination of the Constitution. See Nos.* 21–2.

*Fabius. See Nos.* 25–6.

*Federal Constitution. See No.* 12.

*Federal Farmer. See Nos.* 86–90.

*Elliot (Jonathan). First edition.*

The / Debates, / Resolutions, and other Proceedings, / in / Convention, / on the adoption of the / Federal Constitution, / as recommended by the / General Convention at Philadelphia, / on the 17th of September, 1787 : / With the yeas and nays on the decision of the / main question. / Collected and revised, from contemporary publications, / by Jonathan Elliot. / .... / .... / Washington, / Printed by and for the Editor, / on the Pennsylvania Avenue. / 1827 [–30].

3 vols., 8vo.      27

"Volume   I. / Containing the Debates in Massachusetts and New York."
pp. viii, 358, *8.
"Volume  II. / Containing the Debates in the Commonwealth of Virginia."
pp. viii, 33–487.
"Volume III. / Containing the Debates in the States of North Carolina and
Pennsylvania."   pp. (8), 17–322.

The star leaves in Volume I. were originally issued in Volume III., and are sometimes found bound in that volume. They are a fragment of the debates in the New York Convention.

An additional volume was issued in 1830, with the following title:

Journal / and / Debates of the Federal Convention, / Held at Philadelphia, from May 14, to September 17, 1787 / with the / Constitution / of the / United States, / illustrated by the opinions of twenty / successive Congresses, / and a / Digest of Decisions in the Courts of the Union, / involving constitutional principles: / thus shewing / the rise, progress, present condition, and practice / of the Constitution, / in the / National Legislature and Legal Tribunals of the Republic. / With / full indexes on all subjects embraced in the Work. / By Jonathan Elliot. / Volume IV. / (Supplementary to the State Constitutions, in 3 Vols. on adopting the Federal Constitution) / Washington, / Printed and sold by the Editor, / on the Pennsylvania Avenue. / 1830. /

8vo. pp. (8), 272, 404, (4).   28

Reviewed by Jared Sparks in the *North American Review*, xxv. 249.

*Elliot (Jonathan). Second Edition.*

The / Debates / in the several / State Conventions, / on the adoption of the / Federal Constitution, / as recommended by the / General Convention at Philadelphia, / in / 1787. / Together with / the Journal of the Federal Convention, Luther / Martin's Letter, Yates' Minutes, Congressional / Opinions, Virgina & Kentucky Resolutions of '96–'99, / and other illustrations of the Constitution. / In four volumes— Volume I. / Second Edition, / with considerable additions, / collected and revised from contemporary publications, / by Jonathan Elliot. / Published under the Sanction of Congress. Washington : / Printed by and for the Editor. / on the Pennsylvania Avenue. / 1836.

4 vols. 8vo.   29

I.   pp. vii, (3), xix–xxxii, 33–*79, 73–551.
II.  pp.
III. pp.
IV.  pp. (4), vii–xvi, 33–662, xvi.

*Elliot (Jonathan).  [Third] Edition.*

The / Debates / in the several / State Conventions, / on

the adoption of the / Federal Constitution, / as recommended by the / General Convention at Philadelphia, in 1787. / together with the / Journal of the Federal Convention, / Luther Martin's Letter, / Yates' Minutes, / Congressional Opinions, / Virginia and Kentucky Resolutions of '98–'99, / and / other illustrations of the Constitution. / In Four Volumes. / Vol. I. / Second Edition, with considerable additions. / Collected and Revised from contemporary publications, / by Jonathan Elliot. / Published under the sanction of Congress. / Washington: Printed for the Editor. / 1836.

4 vols. 8vo.

30

I. pp. xvi, 508 Ante-Constitutional History, Journal of Convention, Martin's Genuine Information, Yates' Minutes, Ratifications and Amendments, Official letters of Delegates, Partizan arguments, and private letters.
II. pp. xi, 556. Debates in the Conventions of Massachusetts, Connecticut, (fragmentary), New Hampshire, (fragmentary), New York, and Pennsylvania (fragmentary.) Account of Maryland and Harrisburg Conventions.
III. pp. xi, 663. Debates in the Virginia Convention.
IV. pp. xii, 639. Debates in the (first) North Carolina Convention and in the Legislature and and Convention (fragment) of South Carolina, Opinions on Constitutional questions, 1789-1836.

In 1845 a supplementary volume was added, with the following title :

Debates / on the / adoption of the Federal Constitution, / in the Convention held at Philadelphia, / in / 1787; / with a diary of the debates of / the Congress of the Confederation; / as reported / By James Madison, / a member, and deputy from Virginia. / Revised and newly arranged / By Johnathan Elliot. / Complete in one volume. Vol. V. / Supplementary to Elliot's Debates. / Published under the sanction of Congress. / Washington: / Printed for the Editor. / 1845.

8vo. pp. xxii, 641.

31

Elliot's Debates (especially this edition), in spite of its imperfections, is the great store house of American constitutional history. It is almost impossible to exaggerate its importance, and though Nos. 92 and 99 have rendered the portion relating to Massachusetts and Pennsylvania of little value, the remaining contents are only to be found in contemporary publications of greater or lesser rarity.

In 1858 the plates passed into the hands of J. B. Lippincott & Co., who have printed several issues, with change of date only.

The Fœderalist. No. I. To the People of the State of New York....[signed] Publius.

32

This is the heading to the first of the series of eighty-five essays, now known as the *The Federalist*, and was first published October 27, 1787. With occasional breaks in its regularity, it continued to be published by at least two New York newspapers until August 16, 1788.

Nos. 1-7, 11, 13, 15, 17, 19, 21, 26, 31, 33, 35, 37-8, 55, 65, 71, and 76 first appeared in *The Independent Journal*. Nos. 8, 12, 16, 18, 20, 22, 27, 29, 30, 32, 56, 64, 70, 72 and 75 first appeared in *The New York Packet*. Nos. 10 and 36 first appeared in *The Daily Advertiser*. Nos. 9, 14, 23-5, and 34 appeared simultaneously in two or more papers. Nos. 77-85 first appeared in the first edition in book form. The first publication of the remaining essays I have not been able to find.

Jay wrote Nos. 2, 3, 4, 5 and 64; Madison, Nos. 10, 14, 37 to 48 inclusive; Nos. 18, 19 and 20 are the joint work of Madison and Hamilton; Nos. 49 to 58, 62 and 63 are claimed by both Madison and Hamilton; the rest of the numbers are by Hamilton. The authorship of the 12 numbers clamed by both Madison and Hamilton are fully discussed by Mr. Lodge in *The Proceedings of the American Antiquarian Society for* 1882, and Volume ix of *The Works of Hamilton;* by Mr. Dawson and Mr. J. C. Hamilton in the introductions to their respective editions of *The Federalist;* by Mr. Rives in his *History of the Life and Times of James Madison;* by Mr. Bancroft, in the *History of the Formation of the Constitution*, ii, 236; and in *The Historical Magazine*, viii, 305.

"He is certainly a judicious and ingenious writer, though not well calculated for the common people.—*Maclaine to Iredell, March* 4, 1788.

"In a series of essays in the New York Gazettes, under title of *Fedaralist*, it [the Constitution] has been advocated with great ability. *Washington to Luzerne*, Feb. 7, 1788.

"The Federalist, as he terms himself, or Publius, puts me in mind of some of the gentlemen of the long robe when hard pressed, in a bad cause, with a rich client. They frequently say a good deal, which does not apply; but yet if it will not convince the judge and jury, may perhaps, help to make them forget some part of the evidence—embarass their opponents, and make the audience stare." *N. Y. Journal*, Feb. 14, 1788.

"It would be difficult to find a treatise, which, in so small a compass, contains so much valuable political information, or in which the true principles of republican government are unfolded with such precision." *American Magazine* for March, 1788.

See also,

A / List of Editions / of / "The Federalist." / By / Paul Leicester Ford, / Brooklyn, N. Y., / 1886. 8vo, pp. 25.

*The Federalist. New York.* 1788.

The / Federalist : / A Collection / of / Essays, / written in Favour of the / New Constitution, / as agreed upon by the Federal Convention, / Sepfember 17, 1787. / In Two Volumes. / Vol. I. / New York : / Printed and Sold by J. and A. M'Lean, / No. 41, Hanover-Square. / M,DCC,LXXXVIII.

2 vols. 12mo, pp. vi, 227—vi, 384. C., P., N., B.A.

The first edition in book form. It is difficult to find in uncut condition, or on thick paper. Ordinary copies were priced by Leon at $30, and Hawkins' copy sold for $48.

Reviewed in *The American Magazine*, 1788. 260, 327, 423, 503.

*The Federalist. Paris.* 1792.

Le Fédéraliste, / ou / Collection de quelques Écrits en faveur de / la Constitution proposée aux États-Unis / de / l'Amérique, par la Convention convoquée / en 1787 ; / Publiés dans les États-Unis de l'Amérique par / MM. Hamilton, Madisson et Gay, / Citoyens de l'État de New York. / Tome Premier. / A Paris, / Chez Buisson, Libraire, rue Hautefeuille, / No. 20. / 1792.

        2 vols., 8vo. pp. lii, 366—(4), 511.        34

        2 vols., 8vo. pp. (5), xxii–lii, 366—(4), 511.        S.

The two variations noted above are identical as to matter and composition, with the exception of the introduction, which is omitted in the second.

Translated by Trudaine de la Sablière, who added an Introduction, and Notes, most of which are merely explanatory of such parts of the text as would be unintelligible to the French reader.

"Both issues of this first French edition are of the utmost rarity. I have heard of but one example of the first issue, the imperfect copy in the library of Harvard College, referred to by Mr. Dawson. The second is almost equally rare. There is one copy in the New York State Library (mentioned by Mr. Dawson), another in the library of Yale College, and a third was sold at auction not long since, in Boston for twenty-five dollars a volume." *Mr. Lodge's Introduction to The Federalist.*

*The Federalist. Paris.* 1795.

Le Fédéraliste, / ou / Collection de quelques Écrits en faveur / de la Constitution proposée aux États-Unis / de / l'Amérique, par la Convention convoquée / en 1788 ; / Publiés dans les États-Unis de l'Amérique par / MM. Hamilton, Madisson et Jay. / Citoyens de l'Etat de New York. / Seconde Edition. / Tome Premier, / A Paris, / Chez Buisson, Librarie, rue Hautseuille, No. 20. / An 3e. de la Republique.

        2 vols., 8vo. pp. (5), xxii–lii, 366—(4), 511.        35

A reissue with new titles of the second issue of No. 34.

*The Federalist. New York.* 1799.

The / Federalist: / A Collection of / Essays, / written in favour of the / new Constitution, / as agreed upon by the / Federal Convention, / September 17, 1787. / In Two Volumes.

/ Vol. I. / New-York: / Printed and sold by John Tiebout, / No. 358 Pearl-Street. / 1799.

2 vols., 12mo. pp. vi, 227—vi, 384.   36

Of the first edition of *The Federalist* a few copies remain unsold, which passed into the hands of John Tiebout, who reissued it with new titles only.

"It is said that in the year 1799, a new edition of *The Federalist*, the fifth in book-form, was published by John Tiebout... The most diligent search has been made for a copy of that edition, but without finding it or obtaining any other information concerning it. It is not in any of the principal public libraries, nor, so far as can be learned, is a copy of it in any private library in this part of the country. The newspapers of that period—both Fœderal and Republican—have been carefully examined, with the hope of finding the Proposals for its publication; personal enquiries have been made of Mr. Tiebout's sons, and of several of the older inhabitants of the city; and those whose intimate knowledge of books entitles them to the respect of every student have been applied to on the suject; yet no trace whatever, beyond the single allusion above referred to, has been obtained from any quarter concerning this or any other edition of *The Federalist* from the press of John Tiebout." *Mr. Dawson's Introduction to The Federalist*, lxvii

"Mr. Dawson, after the most exhaustive research, failed to find a copy, and only heard of one, or what appeared to be one, in the collection of Mr. Force, while his own volume was passing through the press, and he was therefore compelled to leave the existence of such an edition largely a matter of conjecture. This gap is now filled. There is a copy of this edition, probably unique, for the Force copy has disappeared, in the Long Island Historical Society." *Mr. Lodge's Introduction to The Federalist.*

This copy mentioned by Mr. Lodge is however, imperfect, there being but one volume.

*The Federalist. New York.* 1802.

The / Federalist, / on the New Constitution. / By Publius. / Written in 1788. / To which is added, / Pacificus, / on the Proclamation of Neutrality. / Written in 1793. / Likewise, / The Federal Constitution, / with all the Amendments. / Revised and Corrected. / In Two Volumes. / Vol. I. / Copy-right secured. / New-York: / Printed and sold by George F. Hopkins, / At Washington's Head. / 1802.

2 vols., 8vo pp. viii, 317, (1)—v, 351.   C., H., N.   37

Mr. Dawson hazards the guess that this edition was edited by William Coleman, but by Mr. Hopkins statement, he appears in error.

"Mr. Hopkins informed me to-day that this edition was in the first instance corrected by John Wells, who compared it with the original edition, published by McLean [sic] in 1788, and that it was subsequently revised by my father, at whose casual suggestion Pacificus was printed with it." *Memoranda by J. C. Hamilton, Feb.* 6, 1847.

From the "prefatory remarks" prefixed to the Washington edition, it would appear that Mr. Jay also revised in this edition the numbers contributed by him. See No. 41.

"In the year 1802, Mr. Hopkins, printer, of this city, intending to publish a new edition of The Federalist, took this opportunity to apply to Gen. Hamilton, and solicit him to correct and revise the numbers, and, so far succeeded, as to obtain his consent to assist in the revisal, provided a gentleman of competent literary talents would undertake to make the first verbal corrections, for the original idea was to be strictly adhered to :—He then examined the whole with his own eye, previous to its being committed to the press, and saw that it was free from literary blemishes." William A. Coleman in the *N. Y. Evening Post*, March 25, 1817.

*The Federalist. New York.* 1810.

The / Federalist, / on the New Constitution; / written in 1788, / by Mr. Hamilton, Mr. Jay, and Mr. Madison. / To which is added, / Pacificus, / on the Proclamation of Neutrality; / written in 1793, / by Mr. Hamilton. / A new edition, with the Names and Portraits of the several Writers. / In Two Volumes. / Vol. I. / New-York: / Published by Williams & Whiting, / at their Theological and Classical Bookstore, / No. 118, Pearl-Street. / Printed by J. Seymour. / 1810.

2 vols., 8vo. pp. iv, 368, 2 portraits—iv, 368, portrait. 38

A separate edition of volumes ii. and iii. of the "*Works of Hamilton*," as edited by John Wells, in 1810. It is identical in matter with No. 37, with the addition of the names of the authors from "a private memorandum in his (Hamilton's) own handwriting."

*The Federalist. Philadelphia,* 1817.

The / Federalist, / on the New Constitution ; / written in 1788, / by Mr. Hamilton, Mr. Jay, and Mr. Madison, / A New Edition, / with the Names and Portraits of the several Writers. / Philadelphia : / Published by Benjamin Warner, No. 147, Market Street. / William Greer., Printer. Harrisburg. / 1817.

8vo. pp. 477, 3 portraits.

The first single volume edition. It follows the 1810 edition in text. 39

*The Federalist. Philadelphia.* 1818.

The / Federalist, / on the New Constitution ; / written in 1788, / by Mr. Hamilton, Mr. Jay, and Mr. Madison. / A New Edition, / with the Names and Portraits of the several Writers. / Philadelphia : / Published by Benjamin Warner,

No. 147, Market Street, / and sold at his stores, Richmond, Virginia, / and Charleston, South Carolina. / 1818.

8vo, pp, 504, 3 portraits.     B. 40

Printed from the same forms as No. 39, with the addition of an appendix containing the Articles of Confederation and the Constitution.

*The Federalist. Washington.* 1818.

The / Federalist, / on / the New Constitution, / written in / the Year 1788, / by / Mr. Hamilton, Mr. Madison, and Mr. Jay, / with / an Appendix, / Containing / the Letters of Pacificus and Helvidius, / on the / Proclamation of Neutrality of 1793 ; / Also, the / Original Articles of Confederation, / and / the Constitution of the United States, / with the / Amendments made thereto. / A New Edition. / The Numbers written by Mr. Madison corrected by Himself. / City of Washington: / Printed and published by Jacob Gideon, Jun. / 1818.

8vo, pp. 671.     41

"The present edition of the Federalist contains all the numbers of that work, as revised by their authors, and is the only one to which the remark will apply. Former editions, indeed, it is understood, had the advantage of a revisal from Mr. Hamilton, and Mr. Jay, but the numbers written by Mr. Madison still remain in the state in which they originally issued from the press, and contain many inaccuracies. The publisher of this volume has been so fortunate as to procure from Mr. Madison the copy of the work which that gentleman had preserved for himself, with corrections of the papers of which he was the author, in his own hand." Prefatory remarks by Jacob Gideon, Jr.

Mr. Madison claims the authorship, in this edition, of Nos. 18, 19 and 20, which Hamilton had given as their joint work; and 49 to 58, 62 and 63, which Mr. Hamilton had claimed for himself. In spite of the research and study devoted to the dispute, it is to-day impossible to give the authorship to either with any certainty.

*The Federalist. Washington.* 1821.

The / Federalist, / on / the New Constitution, / Written in / the Year 1788, / by/Mr. Hamilton, Mr. Madison, and Mr. Jay, / with / an Appendix, / Containing / the Letters of Pacificus and Helvidius, / on the / Proclamation of Neutrality of 1793 ; / Also, the / Original Articles of Confederation, / and / the Constitution of the United States, / with the / Amendments made thereto. / A New Edition. / The Numbers written by

Mr. Madison corrected by Himself. / City of Washington : / Printed and published by Jacob Gideon, Jun. / 1821.

8vo. pp. 671.      42

A reissue of No. 41 with new titles only. It is not in Mr. Dawson's list of editions.

*The Federalist. Hallowell.* 1826.

The / Federalist, / on the New Constitution, / Written in / the Year 1788, / by/ Mr. Hamilton, Mr. Madison, and Mr. Jay :/ With / an Appendix, / Containing / the Letters of Pacificus and Helvidius, / on the / Proclamation of Neutrality of 1793 ; / Also, the / Original Articles of Confederation, / and the / Constitution of the United States, / with the / Amendments made thereto. / A New Edition. / The Numbers written by Mr. Madison corrected by Himself. / Hallowell, (Me.): / Printed and published by Glazier & Co. / 1826.

8vo. pp. 582.      H. 43

A reprint of Gideon's edition of 1818.

*The Federalist. Philadelphia.* 1826.

The / Federalist, / on the New Constitution, / written in the year / 1788, / by / Mr. Hamilton, Mr. Madison and Mr. Jay : / With / an Appendix, / containing / The Letters of Pacificius and Helvidius / on the Proclamation of Neutrality of 1793 ; / Also the / Articles of Confederation, / and the / Constitution of the United States, / with the amendments made thereto. / A New Edition. / The numbers written by Mr. Madison corrected by himself. / Philadelphia : / Published by McCarty and Davis, / 171 Market-street. / 1826.

8vo. pp. 582.      44

Identical with No. 43, excepting title page. It is not in Sabin's or Dawson's lists, or in Ford's *List of editions of "The Federalist."*

*The Federalist. Hallowell.* 1831.

The / Federalist / on / the New Constitution,/ written in the Year 1788, / by / Mr. Hamilton, Mr. Madison, and Mr. Jay : / With / an Appendix, / Containing / the Letters of Pacificus and Helvidius, / on the / Proclamation of Neutrality of 1793 ; / also, the / Original Articles of Confederation, and the Con- / stitution of the United States, / with the Amendments made thereto. / A New Edition. / The Numbers written by Mr. Madison corrected by Himself. / Hallowell : / Printed and published by Glazier, Masters & Co. / 1831.

8vo. pp. 542.                                    45

Not in Mr. Sabin's *Dictionary of Books relating to America*, and Mr. Dawson, who had heard of such an edition, was unable to find a copy.

*The Federalist. Washington.* 1831.

The / Federalist, / on / The New Constitution, / written in / the Year 1788, / by / Alexander Hamilton, James Madison and John Jay, / With an Appendix, / Containing the Original Articles of Confederation ; the / Letter of General Washington, as President of the / Convention, to the President of Congress ; the Consti- / tution of the United States, and the Amendments to / the Constitution. / A New Edition, / with a Table of Contents, / and / a copious Alphabetical Index. / The Numbers written by Mr. Madison corrected by Himself. / Washington : / Published by Thompson & Homans. / Way & Gideon, Printers. / 1831.

12mo. pp. vii, 3–420.                         C. 46

The first edition with an index, prepared by Phillip R. Fendall.

*The Federalist. Hallowell.* 1837.

The / Federalist, / on / the New Constitution, / written in the year 1788, / by / Mr. Hamilton, Mr. Madison, and Mr. Jay : / with / an Appendix, / Containing / the Letters of Pacificus and Helvidius / on the / Proclamation of Neutrality of 1793 ; / also, / the Original Articles of Confederation, and the / Constitution of the United States, / with the Amendments made thereto. / A New Edition. / The Numbers written by Mr. Madison corrected by Himself. / Hallowell : / Glazier, Masters & Smith. / 1837.

8vo. pp. 500.                             A., C. 47

*The Federalist. Rio de Janiero.* 1840.

O Federalista, publicado em inglez por Hamilton, Madisson e Jay, cidadãos de Nova-York, e tradizido em portuguez por . . . Rio de Janeiro : Typ. Imperial e Const. de J. Villeneuve & Ca. 1840.

3 vols. 8vo. pp. 244—285—246.                 48

Title from Mr. Sabin's *Dictionary of Books relating to America.* It is unknown to Mr. Dawson, and I have been unable to find a copy. From the misspelling of Madison's name, it is apparently a translation of the Paris edition, No. 34.

*The Federalist. Hallowell.* 1842.

The / Federalist, / on / the New Constitution, / Written in 1788, / by / Mr. Hamilton, Mr. Madison, and Mr. Jay: / With / an Appendix, / Containing / the Letters of Pacificus and Helvidius / on the / Proclamation of Neutrality of 1793 ; / also, / the Original Articles of Confederation, / and the / Constitution of the United States. / A New Edition. / The Numbers written by Mr. Madison corrected by Himself. / Hallowell : / Glazier, Masters & Smith. / 1842.

8vo. pp. 484.

49

Reviewed by J. Parker, in the *North American Review*, xciv, 435.

*The Federalist. Washington.* 1845.

The / Federalist, / on / the New Constitution, / Written in / the Year 1788, / by / Alexander Hamilton, James Madison, and John Jay, / With an Appendix, / Containing / the Original Articles of Confederation ; the Letter of General Wash- / ington, as President of the Convention, to the President of Con- / gress ; the Constitution of the United States ; the Amend- / ments to the Constitution ; and the Act of Congress in / Relation to the election of President, passed / January 23, 1845. / Sixth Edition, / with / a Copious Alphabetical Index. / The numbers written by Mr. Madison corrected by Himself. / Washington: / Printed by J. & G. S. Gideon. / 1845.

8vo. pp. (2), v, (1), 391.

50

Neither in Mr. Dawson's nor Mr. Sabin's lists of editions.

*The Federalist. Philadelphia.* 1847.

The / Federalist, / on / the New Constitution, / Written in / the Year 1788, / by / Alexander Hamilton, James Madison, and John Jay. / With an Appendix, / Containing / the Letters of Pacificus and Helvidius on the Proclamation of Neu- / trality of 1793 ; the Original Articles of Confederation ; the Let- / ter of General Washington, as President of the Convention, to the President of Congress; the Constitution of the / United States ; the Amendments to the Constitution ; / and the Acts of Congress in Relation to the Elec- / tion of President, passed January 23, 1845. / Sixth edition, / with / a

Copious Alphabetical Index. / The Numbers written by Mr. Madison corrected by Himself. / Philadelphia : / R. Wilson Desilver, 18 South Fourth Street, / 1847.

8vo. pp. (2), v, 392, 102.    B. M., 51

The "Letters of Pacificus and Helvidius," has a separate title-page and pagination, and is often found as a separate work.

*The Federalist. Washington.* 1847.

The Federalist, on the New Constitution..... Washington: J. & G. S. Gideon  1847.

8vo. pp.    52

Title quoted by Sabin from " Mr. Bartlett's List."

*The Federalist. Hallowell.* 1852.

The / Federalist, / on / the New Constitution, / Written in 1788. / by / Mr. Hamilton, Mr. Madison, and Mr. Jay: / With / an Appendix, / Containing the / Letters of Pacificus and Helvidius / on the / Proclamation of Neutrality of 1793 ; / Also, / the Original Articles of Confederation, / and the / Constitution of the United States. / New Edition : / The Numbers written by Mr. Madison corrected by Himself. / Hallowell : / Masters, Smith, & Company. / 1852.

8vo. pp. 496.    53

*The Federalist. Hallowell.* 1857.

The / Federalist, / on the / New Constitution, / Written in 1788, / by / Mr. Hamilton, Mr. Madison, and Mr. Jay : / With / an Appendix, / Containing Letters of / Pacificus and Helvidius / on the / Proclamation of Neutrality of 1793 ; / Also, / the Original Articles of Confederation, / and the Constitution of the United States. / New Edition : / The Numbers written by Mr. Madison corrected by Himself. / Hallowell : / Masters, Smith, & Co. / 1857.

8vo. pp. 496.    B. 54

*The Federalist. New York.* 1863.

The Fœderalist : / A / Collection of Essays, Written in Favor / of the New Constitution, as / agreed upon by / the Fœderal Convention, / September 17, 1787. / Reprinted from the Original Text. / with an / Historical Introduction and Notes, / By Henry B. Dawson. / In Two Volumes. /

Vol. I. / New York: / Charles Scribner, 124 Grand Street, / London: Sampson Low, Son & Co. / 1863.

8vo. pp. cxlii, (2), 615. portrait.     55

All ever printed. This volume contains the text of *The Federalist*, entire, and an Introduction, containing a history of the origin, original publication, the controversy over the disputed numbers, and a bibliographical list of editions, all being treated with great thoroughness. It was Mr. Dawson's intention to give, in the second volume, the alterations which had been made in the text of the various editions, and MSS. notes from copies of the work which had belonged to the authors and other statesmen. The Introduction gave offense to the Hamilton and Jay families, and occasioned the following pamphlets:

Correspondence / between / John Jay and Henry B. Dawson, / and between / James A. Hamilton and Henry B. Dawson, / concerning / The Federalist. / New York: / Printed by J. M. Bradstreet & Son. / 1864.

8vo. and 4to. pp. 48, covers.     56

Of the 4to. edition only 25 copies were printed. The title on the cover reads *Current Fictions tested by Uncurrent Facts*. Mr. Dawson advertised *Current Fictions No. II.*, but it was never printed.

New Plottings in Aid of the Rebel Doctrine of / State Sovereignty. / Mr. Jay's Second Letter / on / Dawson's Introduction to the Federalist, / Exposing its Falsification of the History of the Constitution; its / Libels on Duane, Livingston, Jay and Hamilton; and / its relation to recent efforts by Traitors at home, and / Foes abroad, to maintain the Rebel Doctrine of State / Sovereignty, for the subversion of the Unity of / the Republic and the Supreme Sovereignty of / the American People / . . . . . / New York: / A. D. F. Randolph. / 1864. / 8vo. pp. 54, viii, covers.     57

[Same.] New York: / American News Company, 121 Nassau street. / London: / Trubner & Company, 60 Paternoster Row. / 1864. / 8vo. pp. 54. vii, covers.     58

[Same.] London: Samson Low . . . 1864. 8vo. pp. 50.     59

All three editions were suppressed by Mr. Jay, and the bulk of the copies burnt. See *Current Fictions*, p. 26.

This edition is reviewed by H. W. Torrey in *The North American Review*, cxcviii, 586; and by Historicus in *The New York Times*, Feb. 17, 1864.

*The Federalist. New York.* 1864.

The Fœderalist: / A / Collection of Essays, Written in Favor / of the New Constitution, as / agreed upon by / the Fœderal Convention, / September 17, 1787. / Reprinted from the Original Text. / With an / Historical Introduction and Notes, / By Henry B. Dawson. / In Two Volumes. / Vol. I. / New York: / Charles Scribner & Co. . . . / . . . 1864.

8vo. pp. cxlii, (2), 615, portrait.     60

*The Federalist. Morrisania.* 1864.

The Fœderalist: / A Collection of Essays, written in

Favor / of the New Constitution, as agreed / upon by the Fœderal Conven- / tion, September 17, 1787. / Reprinted from the Original Text, / with an / Historical Introduction and Notes / By Henry B. Dawson. / In Two Volumes. / Vol. I. / Morrisania, N. Y.: / 1864.

Royal 8vo. pp. cxlii, (2), 615, portrait.     61

Printed from the same plates as the New York editions of 1863 and 1864. 250 copies printed.

*The Federalist. Philadelphia.* 1865.

The / Federalist: / A Commentary / on the / Constitution of the United States. / A Collection of Essays, / By Alexander Hamilton, / Jay, and Madison. / Also, / The Continentalist, and other Papers, / By Hamilton. / Edited by / John C. Hamilton, / Author of " The History of the Republic of the United States." / Philadelphia: / J. B. Lippincott & Co. / 1864.

8vo. pp. clxv, (1), 659, vi, portrait.     B. A.   62

Many reissues, with a change of date only.

Contains an " Historical Notice," which is an endeavor to prove Hamilton the author of the doubtful numbers ; in fact, the whole tendency is to magnify Hamilton's part of the work, even the names of the other authors being printed in much smaller type on the title page.

The alterations in the text made by the different editions is added, as also the papers signed " Philo-Publius " by William Duer.

Reviewed by Mr. Horace Binney in the following:

A Review of Hamilton's Edition of the Federalist. Philadelphia : 1864.<br>8vo. pp. 8.     63

*The Federalist. Philadelphia.* 1865.

The / Federalist: / A Commentary / on the / Constitution of the United States. / A Collection of Essays / By Alexander Hamilton, / Jay, and Madison. / Also, / The Continentalist, and other Papers, / By Hamilton. / Edited by John C. Hamilton, / Author of " The History of the Republic of the United States." / Vol. I. / Philadelphia : / J. B. Lippincott & Co. / 1865.

2 vols. Rl. 8vo. pp. clxv, (1), 242.—(2), 243–659, vi, portrait.     64

From the same plates as No 62, but divided into two volumes, and printed on larger and finer paper. 100 copies only printed.

*The Federalist. New York.* 1876.

University Edition, / The Federalist: / A / Collection of

Essays, written in Favor / of the New Constitution, as / agreed upon by / Federal Convention, / September 17, 1787 / Reprinted from the Original Text / under the Editorial Supervision of / Henry B. Dawson. / New York: / Scribner, Armstrong and Co. / 1876.

8vo. pp. lvi, 615.          65

Also issues with no date. A cheap edition from the plates of No. 55, with the omission of the Introduction, a short Preface taking its place.

*The Federalist. New York.* 1886.

The Works / of / Alexander Hamilton / Edited by / Henry Cabot Lodge / . . . . . / Vol. IX. / New York & London / G. P. Putnam's Sons / The Knickerbocker Press / 1886.

8vo. pp. xlv, 598.          66

*Federal Republican.* See No. 119.

Ford (*Paul Leicester*).

A List of the Members of the Federal Convention of 1787. By Paul Leicester Ford. Brooklyn, N. Y.: 1888.

67

100 copies privately printed.

"In 1819, when John Quincy Adams, by direction of Congress, edited and published the Journal of the Federal Convention, he drew up ... a list of the members... This list was accepted and republished by Elllot, ... by Curtis ... and more recently in the Official Programme of the Constitutional Centenial, and no additions are promised in the forthcoming memorial of that celebration—Thus this list prepared in 1819, has become a fixture ... There are, however, several omissions and by reference to original documents, acts, etc., I have increased the list to seventy-four. To this I have added, in such cases as I have been able, the reasons of members for declining the appointment, and non-attendance of such as failed to be present in the Convention ; the day of arrival of attending members; the absence of attending members; the date of leaving of those who failed to sign the Constitution, with their reasons, and the part the non-attending and non-signing members took in their own States in support or opposition to the ratification." *Extract from preface.*

Ford (*Paul Leicester*).

Pamphlets / on the / Constitution of the United States / Published during / its discussion by the People / 1787-1788. / Edited / with notes and a bibliography / by / Paul Leicester Ford. / Brooklyn, N. Y.: / 1888.

8vo, pp.          68

Includes reprints of the following pamphlets, and a bibliography and reference list to the literature relating to the formation and adoption of the Constitution.

[GERRY (ELBRIDGE)]. Observations on the New Constitution, and on the Federal and State Conventions. By a Columbian Patriot.

[WEBSTER (NOAH)]. An Examination into the leading principles of the Federal Constitution. By a Citizen of America.

[JAY (JOHN)]. An Address to the People of the State of New York. By a Citizen of New York.

[SMITH (MELANCTHON)]. Address to the People of the State of New York. By a Plebeian.

[WEBSTER (PELATIAH)]. The Weakness of Brutus exposed: or some remarks in vindication of the Constitution. By a Citizen of Philadelphia.

[COXE (TENCH)]. An Examination of the Constitution of the United States of America. By an American Citizen.

WILSON (JAMES). Speech on the Federal Constitution, delivered in Philadelphia.

[DICKINSON (JOHN)]. Letters of Fabius on the Federal Constitution.

[HANSON (ALEXANDER CONTEE)]. Remarks on the Proposed Plan of a Federal Government. By Aristides.

RANDOLPH (EDMUND). Letter on the Federal Constitution.

[LEE (RICHARD HENRY)]. Observations on the System of Government proposed by the late Convention. By a Federal Farmer.

MASON (GEORGE). Objections to the Federal Constitution.

[IREDELL (JAMES)]. Observations on George Mason's Objections to the Federal Constitution. By Marcus.

[RAMSAY (DAVID)]. An Address to the Freemen of South Carolina on the Federal Constitution. By Civis.

[*Gerry (Elbridge)*].
Observations / On the new Constitution, and on the Federal / and State Conventions. / By a Columbian Patriot. / . . . . . [Boston : 1788.]
        12mo. pp. 19.   C., M., B. A. 69

The above title is merely a caption on the first page. It is not advertised in any Massachusetts paper that I have been able to find, and was probably printed for Gerry for limited circulation only. It is reprinted in Ford's *Pamphlets on the Constitution*, and as below.

[*Gerry (Elbridge.)*]
Observations / on the / New Constitution, / and on the / Fœderal and State Conventions. / By a Columbian Patriot / . ., Boston Printed / New York Re-printed, / M,DCC.LXXXVIII.
        8vo. pp. 22.   N., C., S. 70

Printed by Thomas Greenleaf, in the N. Y. Journal, and reprinted, from the same forms, for the "New York [Anti] Federal Committee," who distributed 1630 copies among the county committees in the State.

*Gerry (Elbridge).*

[Observations on the New Constitution. Brooklyn, N. Y.: 1887].

8vo. pp. 23.     71

A few copies separately printed from No. 68.

*Hall, Aaron.*

An / Oration, / delivered at the Request / of the / Inhabitants of Keene, June 30, 1788; / To Celebrate the Ratification / of the / Federal Constitution / by the / State of New-Hampshire. / By Aaron Hall, M. A. / Member of the late State Convention. / Keene: State of New-Hampshire: / Printed by James D. Griffith. / M,DCC,LXXXVIII.

8vo. pp. 15.     B. A. 72

*Hamilton (Alexander). See also Nos. 32-66.*

Propositions / of Col. Hamilton, of New York, / In Convention for Establishing a Consti- / tutional Government for the / United States. / Also / a Summary of the Political Opinions of / John Adams, / . . . . . / Pittsfield : Printed by Phineas Allen. 1802.

8vo. pp. 32.     N. 73

[*Hanson (Alexander Contee)*].

Remarks / on the / Proposed Plan / of a / Federal Government, / Addressed to the Citizens of the / United States of America, / and Particularly to the People of / Maryland, / By Aristides. / . . . / . . . / . . . / . . . / . . . / Annapolis ; / Printed by Frederick Green, / Printer to the State.

8vo. pp. 42.     N., P. H. S., M. 74

Reprinted in Ford's *Pamphlets on the Constitution.*

*Hanson (Alexander Contee).*

[Remarks on the Proposed Plan of a Federal Government. Brooklyn, N. Y.: 1888].

8vo. pp. 39.     75

A few copies separately printed from No. 68.

*Hitchcock (Enos).*

An / Oration : / delivered July 4, 1788, / at the request of the Inhabitants / of the / Town of Providence, / in / celebration / of the / Anniversary / of / American Independence, / and of / the accession of nine States / to the / Federal Con-

stitution. / By Enos Hitchcock, A. M. / Providence : / Printed by Bennett Wheeler.
8vo. pp. 24. 76

[*Hopkinson* (*Francis*)].
Account / of the / Grand Federal / Procession, / Philadelphia, July 4, 1788. / To which is added, / a / Letter / on the / same Subject. / . . . / [Philadelphia :] M. Carey, Printer. [1788.]
8vo. pp. (2), 22. 77

Appeared originally in Carey's *American Museum*, iv, 57, and the same forms were used to print this edition. Only the "Account" and Wilson's speech are reprinted in Hopkinson's *Miscellaneous Essays*, ii, 349, showing that the " Letter " is not by him.

[*Hopkinson* (*Francis*)].
Account / of the / Grand Federal / Procession, / Philadelphia, July 4, 1788. / . . . / To which is added, / Mr. Wlson's [Sic] Oration, / and a / Letter / on the / Subject of the Procession. / [Philadelphia: M. Carey. 1788.]
8vo. pp. (2), 22. 78

An / Impartial / Address, / to the / Citizens / of the / City and County of Albany : / or, the / 35 Anti-Federal Objections / refuted. / By the Federal Committee / of the City of Albany. / Printed by Charles R. Webster, at / his Free Press, No. 36, State-street, near / the English Church, Albany.
12mo. pp. 28 S. 79

Interesting Documents, / Containing : / An Account of the Federal Procession, &c. July 23, 1788. / Sketch of the Proceedings of the Convention of the State of New York, which adopted the Constitution 2 days after the Procession. / The Articles of Confederation and perpetual Union between Thirteen United States, as proposed by the Congress of the United States, 17th Nov. 1777, and approved by this State; Feb. 6, 1778. / The Constitution of the U. S. with all its Amendments. / The Constitution of the State of New-York, with its Amendments. / The Declaration of Independence, New York. / Published by John S. Murphy, Southwick & Pelsue, Print. 9 Wall St. 1819.
12mo. pp. 128 N. 80

*Introduction. See No* 105.

*Iredell (James.) See also No.* 24.
Answers to Mr. Mason's Objections to the New Constitution, recommended by the late Convention at Philadelphia. By Marcus. [Brooklyn, N. Y.: 1888.]

8vo. pp. 38. 81

Printed in Ford's *Pamphlets on the Constitution*, from which a few copies were separately printed as above. The original tract is described in No. 24.

*[Jackson (Jonathan)]*.
Thoughts / upon the / Political Situation / of the / United States of America, / in which that of / Massachusetts / Is more particularly considered. / With some / Observations on the Constitution / for a / Federal Government. / Addressed to the People of the Union. / By a Native of Boston. / . . . / . . . / . . . / Printed at Worcester, Massachusetts, / by Isaiah Thomas. MDCCLXXXVIII.

8vo. pp. 209. M., B. A., S. 82

Signed at end "Civis." The authorship of this pamphlet is also frequently given to G. R. Minot, but both Sabin and Cushing give it as above. Reviewed in *The American Magazine*, 744 and 804.

*[Jay (John)]. See also Nos.* 32-66.
An / Address / to the / People / of the / State of New-York / On the Subject of the Constitution, / Agreed upon at Philadelphia, / the 17th of September, 1787. / New-York: / Printed by Samuel London, Printer to the State.

4to. pp. 19. N., B. A., C. S. 83

Reprinted in Ford's *Pamphlets on the Constitution*.

*Jay (John).*
An Address to the People of the State of New York, on the Subject of the Constitution. [Brooklyn, N. Y.: 1887.]

8vo. pp. 20. 84

A few copies separately printed from No. 68.

Journal, / Acts and Proceedings, / of the Convention, / assembled at Philadelphia, Monday, May 14, and dis- / solved Monday, September 17, 1787, / which formed / The Constitution of the United States, / Published under the direction of the President of the United States, conformably to a / Resolution of Congress of March 27, 1818. / Boston : / Printed and Published by Thomas B. Wait. / 1819.

8vo. pp. 510.      N., P., B., H.   85

Edited by John Quincy Adams. Reviewed in the *Southern Review*, ii, 432, and in Taylor's *New Views of the Constitution. Washington:* 1823. See also No. 28.

[*Lee (Richard Henry)*].

Observations / leading to a fair examination / of the / System of Government, / proposed by the late / Convention; / and to several essential and necessary / alterations in it. / In a number of / Letters / from the / Federal Farmer to the Republican. / Printed in the Year M,DCC,LXXVII.

8vo. pp. 40.      A. A. S.   86

The *Letters of a Federal Farmer*, was, to the Anti-Federalists, what *The Federalist* was to the supporters of the Constitution. Reprinted in Ford's *Pamphlets on the Constitution*.

[*Lee (Richard Henry)*].

Observations / leading to a fair examination / of the / System of Government, / proposed by the late / Convention ; / and to several essential and neces- / sary alterations in it. / In a number of / Letters / from the / Federal Farmer to the Republican. / Printed [in New York, by Thomas Greenleaf] in the Year M,DCC,LXXXVII.

8vo. pp. 40.    B. A., H., A. A. S., N., C.   87

[*Lee (Richard Henry)*].

Observations / leading to a fair examination / of the / System of Government ; / proposed by the late / Convention ; / and to several essential and necessary / alterations in it. / In a number of / Letters / from the / Federal Farmer to the Republiean. / Reprinted [in New York by Thomas Greenleaf] by order of a Society of Gentlemen. / M.DCC.LXXXVII.

8vo. pp. 40.      A. A. S.   88

Lee (*Richard Henry*).

Observations leading to a fair examination of the System of Government, Proposed by the late Convention. [Brooklyn, N. Y.: 1888.]

8vo. pp. (2), 47.      89

A few copies separately printed from No. 68.

[*Lee (Richard Henry)*].

An / Additional number / of / Letters / from the / Federal Farmer / to the / Republican ; / leading to fair examination / of the / System of Government, / proposed by the late / Convention ; / to several essential and neces- / sary alterations in it ; / And calculated to Illustrate and Support the / Principles and Positions / Laid down in the preceding / Letters. / Printed [in New York by Thomas Greenleaf] in the year M,DCC,LXXXVIII.

8vo. pp. [41]–181.     B. A., H., C.   90

*Letters of Fabius. See Nos.* 25–6.

*Lloyd, Thomas. See Nos.* 91–110.

*Maclaine, Archibald. See No.* 24.

*M'Kean (Thomas), and Wilson (James).*

Commentaries / on the / Constitution / of the / United States of America, / with that Constitution prefixed, / In which are unfolded, / the / Principles of Free Government, / and the Superior / Advantages of Republicanism Demonstrated. / By James Wilson, L.L.D. / . . . . . / and Thomas M'Kean, L.L.D. / . . . / The whole extracted from Debates published in Philadelphia by / T. Lloyd. / London : / Printed for J. Debrett, opposite Burtington-House, Piccadilly ; / J. Johnson's, St. Paul's Church Yard ; and J. S. Jordan, / No. 166 Fleet Street. / 1792.

8vo. pp. (2), 5—23. 25—147, (1).     91

This is a reissue of the remainder of the edition of Lloyd's *Debates in the Convention of Pennsylvania* (No. 110) with a new title and pp. 20-23, which were printed in England.

*McMaster (John Bach), and Stone (Frederick D).*

Pennsylvania / and the / Federal Constitution / 1787–1788 / Edited by / John Bach McMaster / and / Frederick D. Stone / Published for the Subscribers by / The Historical Society of Pennsylvania / 1888

8vo. pp. viii, 803, 15 portraits.     92

A most valuable volume, including a history of the struggle over the ratification, the debates in the convention, now for the first time collected, sketches of the Pennsylvania members of the Federal Convention, and of the Pennsylvania Convention, and the letters of Centinel.

*Madison (James). See Nos.* 31–66.

The / Papers / of / James Madison, / purchased by order of Congress; / being / his Correspondence and Reports of Debates during / the Congress of the Confederation / and / his Reports of Debates / in the / Federal Convention; / now published from the original manuscripts, depos- / ited in the Department of State, by direction of / the joint library committee of Congress, / under the superintendence / of / Henry D. Gilpin. / Volume I. / Washinton : / Lantree & O'Sullivan. / 1840.

3 vols. 8vo. pp. (2) lx, 580, xxii, (2), xxii, (2), (581)–1242, (2), xiv, (2), (1243)–1624, ccxlvi, 16 ll.                 93

Also issues with change of date in New York and Mobile and Boston. The whole of these three volumes were also embodied in the fifth volume of *Elliot* (No. 31), but this edition is much preferable from the larger type.

Reviewed in *The Democratic Review*, v, 243 ; vi, 140, 337: in *The American Church Review* xv, 541, and by C. F. Adams in *The North American Review*, liii, 41.

*Marcus. See Nos.* 24 *and* 81.

*Martin (Luther).*

The / Genuine Information, / delivered to the / Legislature of the State of / Maryland, / Relative to the Proceedings / of the / General Convention, / Lately held at Philadelphia ; / By / Luther Martin, Esquire, / Attorney-General of Maryland, / and / One of the Delegates in the said Convention. / Together with / A Letter to the Hon. Thomas C. Deye / Speaker of the House of Delegates, / An Address to the Citizens of the United / States, / And some Remarks relative to a Standing / Army, and a Bill of Rights. / . . . / Philadelphia ; / Printed by Eleazer Oswald, at the Coffee-House. / M,DCC,LXXXVIII.

8vo. pp. viii, 93.                 94

By direction of the Legislature of Maryland, Mr. Martin reported the proceedings of the Federal Convention to them. It is a work of the greatest value from the inside light that this member, and opposer of the Constitution, sheds on this secret history of the Convention, but must be taken as a partizan statement. It is reprinted in *Elliot* and in Nos. 138–42.

*Mason (George).*

The Objections of the / Hon. George Mason, / to the proposed Fœderal Constitution. / Addressed to the Citizens of Virginia. / ..... / Printed by Thomas Nicolas [in Richmond : 1787 or 8].

Folio. Broadside.     S. 95

Reprinted in Ford's *Pamphlets on the Constitution* and "extracts" are given in *Elliot*, i.

*Mason (George).*

[The objections of the Hon. George Mason, to the proposed Fœderal Constitution. Brooklyn, N. Y. : 1888].

8vo. pp. 6.     96

A few copies separately printed from No. 68.

*Massachusetts Debates. Boston:* 1788.

Debates, / Resolutions and other Proceedings, / of the / Convention / of the / Commonwealth of Massachusetts, / Convened at Boston, on the 9th of January, 1788, / and continued until the 7th of February follow- / ing, for the purpose of assenting to and ratify- / ing the Constitution recommended by the / Grand Federal Convention. / Together with / The Yeas and Nays on the / Decision of the Grand Question. / To which / The Federal Constitution / is prefixed. / Boston : / Printed and sold by Adams and Nourse, in Court-Street; and / Benjamin Russell, and Edmund Freeman, in State-Street. / M,DCC,LXXXVIII.

8vo. pp. 219.     C., M., B. A. 97

Reported by Benjamin Russell, printer of *The Massachusetts Centinel.* His own account is given in Buckingham's *Specimens of Newspaper Literature,* ii, 49.

*Massachusetts Debates. Boston:* 1808.

Debates, / Resolutions and other proceedings / of the / Convention / of the / Commonwealth of Massachusetts. / Convened at Boston, on the 9th of January, / 1788, and continued until the 7th of Februa- / ry following, for the purpose of assenting / to and ratifying the Constitution recom- / mended by the grand Federal Convention. / Together with the / Yeas and Nays / on / the decision of the grand question. / To which / The Federal Constitution is prefixed ; / and to which are added, / the Amendments / which have been made therein. / Boston: / Printed and sold by Oliver & Monroe, / and Joshua Cushing, State-Street, / 1808.

12mo. pp. 236.        H. 98

*Massachusetts Debates. Boston:* 1856.

Debates and Proceedings / in the / Convention / of the / Commonwealth of Massachusetts, / held in the year / 1788, / and which finally ratified the / Constitution of the United States. / Printed by authority of Resolves of the Legislature, 1856. / Boston: / William White, / Printer to the Commonwealth. / 1856.

8vo. pp. (16), 442.        99

Edited by Bradford K. Pierce and Charles Hale. It contains not only the debates as printed in the two former editions, but the ante and post proceedings of the General Court; Gerry's official letter; the Journal of the Convention; Judge Parsons "Minutes" of the debates; an account of the reception of the news of the ratification, and of the procession which followed; the "Letters of an American;" Speeches of Franklin in the Federal Convention, and Wilson in the Pa. Convention; 4 "Letters of Brutus," and a series of personal letters relating to the proceedings in Massachusetts, mostly taken from Spark's *Writings of Washington.*

It is a most valuable volume for the history of the struggle over ratification in Massachusetts, but it is a little strange that the editors should pass over the essays on the Constitution from Massachusetts pens and select the letters of "An American" and of "Brutus"—the first a Pennsylvania series, by Tench Coxe, and the second by a New York writer.

*Minot, George R. See No.* 82.

*Minutes of the Convention. See Nos.* 101–2 *and* 111.

[*Montgomery, James*].

Decius's / Letters / on the / Opposition / to the / New Constitution / in / Virginia, / 1789. / Richmond: / Printed by Aug. Davis.

8vo. pp. 134.        C. 100

"Written by Dr. Montgomery, except the dedication, which was by John Nicholas, of Albemarle. MS. notes by John Nicholas." MS. note by Jefferson, in his own copy now in the Congressional Library.

This volume includes, not only the Letters signed Decius, contributed to the *Virginia Independent Chronicle,* between December, 1788 and July, 1789, but also many answers to the same, signed "Juvenal," "Philo Pat. Pat. Patria," "Anti Decius," "Honestus," and others.

It is a most scathing attack on the Anti-Federalists in Virginia, and especially on their leader, Patrick Henry. Perhaps nothing illustrates better the rarity and difficulty of finding the pamphlets of this period than the fact that Mr. Tyler, so well read in American literature, has in his *Life of Patrick Henry*, entirely overlooked this most plain spoken laying bare of the motives and actions of Henry, of which I have been able to discover only a single (imperfect) copy.

I have been able to find nothing concerning Dr. Montgomery, except that he was a member of the Virginia Convention. The so called third edition is under John Nicholas—No. 105.

*Native of Boston. See No. 82.*

*New Jersey Journal.*

Minutes / of the / Convention / of the / State of New Jersey, / Holden at Trenton the 11th Day of December 1787. / Trenton : / Printed by Isaac Collins, Printer to the State. / M,DCCC,LXXXVIII.

4to. pp. 31. P. H. S. 101

750 copies printed.

*New Jersey Journal.*

Minutes / of the / Convention / of the / State of New Jersey, / Holden at Trenton the 11th Day of December 1787. / Trenton : / Printed by Isaac Collins, Printer to the State. / M,DCC,LXXXVIII. / Trenton — Reprinted by Clayton L. Traver, MDCCCLXXXVIII.

4to. pp. 31. 102

*New York Debates.*

The / Debates / and / Proceedings / of the / Convention / of the / State of New-York, / Assembled at Poughkeepsie, / on the 17th June, 1788. / To deliberate and decide on the Form of Federal Govern- / ment recommended by the General Convention at / Philadelphia, on the 17th September, 1787. / Taken in shorthand. / New-York : / Printed and sold by Francis Childs. / M,DCC,LXXXVIII.

8vo. pp. (2), 144. N. S. 103

From a letter in the Lamb papers (N. Y. Historical Soc.) it appears probable that at least Hamilton, Jay and Lansing revised their speeches, though Francis Childs, the reporter, virtually, in his preface, says that no such revision took place. It is reprinted in *Elliot*, ii.

*New York Journal.*

Journal / of the / Convention / of the / State of New-York, / Held at Pougheeepsie, in Dutchess County, the 17th of June, 1788. / Poughkeepsie : / Printed by Nicholas Power, a few rods East from the Court-house. [1788.]

4to. pp. 86. S. 104

[*Nicholas (John)*].

[½ title] Introduction / and Concise View of / Decius's Letters, / With the Title-page, and the Substance and contents of the whole work, / Hereafter to be published at full length in a volume / . . .

Decius's Letters, / on the / opposition to the / Federal Convention, / in Virginia: / Written in 1788 and 1789. / The Third Edition. / With / a new Introduction, / and additional pieces and notes, / on the / Principles and Operation of Party Spirit since. / With an Appendix. / consisting of / Various Interesting Letters, &c. / from Washington, Jefferson, Madison, / and other High Characters, / in support of the last Letters; / Written in 1818. / Richmond: / Published by the Author. / Printed at the office of the Virginia Patriot. / 1818

8vo. pp. 48. B. A. 105

"Written by John Nicholas, Esqr. formerly a member of Congress from Virginia now resident in the State of New York. Boston 25 Sept 1818 W. S. Shaw Sec. Bost. Athen."

Mr. Shaw probably derived his note given above, from John Adams, whose copy this was.

The first edition (No. 100) is referred by Jefferson, apparently on Nicholas' own authority to Dr. Montgomery, so that we seemingly have Jefferson giving the authorship to Montgomery, and Adams giving it to Nicholas. They may both be right, however, for the above pamphlet is merely the prospectus of a new edition, and therefore might be written by an entirely different man than the author.

The prospectus was issued immediately after the appearance of Wirt's *Life of Patrick Henry*, with the avowed purpose of neutralizing that rose-colored narrative. It was never however, carried further than the prospectus.

*North Carolina Amendments.*
State of North Carolina: / In Convention, August 1, 1788.

Folio. 1 l. S. 106

The Declaration of Rights, and Amendments, of the first Convention of North Carolina.

*North Carolina Debates.*

Proceedings / and / Debates / of the / Convention / of / North-Carolina, / Convened at Hillsborough on Monday the 21st Day / of July, 1788, for the Purpose of deliberating / and determining on the Constitution recom- / mended by the General Convention at Philadel- / phia the 17th Day of September 1787. / To which is prefixed / The Federal Constitution. / Edentown : / Printed by Hodge & Wills, Printers to the State. / M,DCC,LXXXIX.

8vo.   pp. 280.         N., C., S., A. A. S.   107

Reported by David Robertson. 1000 copies printed at the expense of a few Federalists for distribution among the people. Reprinted in *Elliot*, iv. 1. The debates of the second Convention are only to be found, in fragmentary condition, in the North Carolina papers of that date.

*Observations leading to.   See Nos.* 86–9.

*Observations on the New Constitution.   See Nos.* 69–71.

Observations / on the / Proposed / Constitution / for the / United States of America. / clearly shewing it to be a complete System / of / Aristocracy and Tyranny, and / Destructive / of the / Rights and Liberties / of the / People. / Printed in the State of New-York, / M,DCC,LXXXVIII.

8vo.   pp. 126.              S., B., B. A.   108

An Anti-Federal compilation, containing :
  Address and Reasons of Dissent of the Minority of the Convention of Pennsylvania.  (No. 2 infra.)
  Letter of Edmund Randolph (No. 116 infra.)
  Letters of Centinel.
  The Constitution.

Two hundred and twenty-five copies were distributed by the New York Anti-Federal committee to the local county committees of the State.

The " Letters of Centinel," were by Samuel Bryan, of Philadelphia, and appeared originally in *The Independent Gazetteer* of that city. The letters were exceedingly personal, and especially severe on Washington and Franklin, so it is rather amusing to find Bryan writing to George Clinton in 1790 and requesting that he use his influence with Washington to obtain for his father a judgeship in the new government, and using his authorship of the letters as the reason for Clinton's furthering his request.

Order of Procession, / In Honor of the Establishment of the Constitution of the United States. / To parade . . . Friday the 4th of July, 1788. / . . . . . Philadelphia : / Printed by Hall and Sellers.

Folio.   1 l.                                 109

*Pennsylvania Debates.*

Debates / of the / Convention, / of the / State of Pennsylvania, / on the / Constitution, / proposed / for the / Government / of the / United States. / In Two Volumes. / Vol. I / Taken accurately in Short-Hand, by / Thomas Lloyd, / . . .

BIBLIOGRAPHY. 419

/ . . . / Printed by Joseph James, / in Philadelphia, A. D. M.DCC.LXXXVIII.
8vo. pp. 147. (2 ll.) 110

All ever published, being only the speeches of M'Kean and Wilson, on the Federal side of the argument. It is reviewed in *The American Magazine*, 262. See Nos. 1-2, and 92.

*Pennsylvania Journal.*

Minutes / of the / Convention / of the / Commonwealth / of / Pennsylvania, / which commenced at Philadelphia, on Tuesday, the / Twentieth Day of November, One Thousand / Seven Hundred and Eighty-Seven, / for the purpose of / Taking into Consideration the Constitution framed by / the late Fœderal Convention for the United States of America. / Philadelphia : / Printed by Hall and Sellers, in Market-street. / M,DCC,LXXXVII.
Folio. pp. 28. P. H S., H. 111

*Pennsylvania Resolution.*

[Resolution of the Pennsylvania General Assembly, September 29, 1787.]
112

The resolve for holding a Convention to discuss the Constitution. 3000 copies ordered to be printed, 1000 of which were to be in German.

*Pinckney (Charles).*

Observations / on the / Plan of Government / submitted to / Federal Convention, / In Philadelphia, on the 28th of May, 1787. / By the Hon. Charles Pinckney, Esq. L.L.D. / Delegate from the State of South-Carolina / Delivered at different Times in the course of their Discussions. / New York:— Printed by Francis Childs [1787]
4to. pp. 27. B. A., N., M., A., 113

This is really the speech of Pinckney, introducing his draft of a constitution in the Convention, May 29, 1787, which for some reason was omitted by both Yates and Madison in their minutes. Though it does not include the proposed draft, it nevertheless enables one to form a clear idea of what it was, and proves that the draft furnished by Pinckney at the request of J. Q. Adams, for publication in the Journal, and from that generally copied into other places, to be fictitious in both form and substance.

*Plan of the New Constitution. See No.* 13.

*Plebeian (A). ·See Nos.* 120-1.

*Proceedings of the Federal Convention. See Nos.* 14-5.

[*Ramsay (David)*].
An / Address / to the / Freemen / of / South Carolina, / on the Subject of the / Federal Constitution, / Proposed by the Convention, which met in / Philadelphia, May, 1787. / Charleston, / Printed by Bowen and Co., No. 31, Bay.

16mo. pp. 12. C. 114

Signed Civis. Reprinted in Ford's *Pamphlets on the Constitution*.

*Ramsay (David)*.
[An Address to the Freemen of South Carolina, on the Subject of the Federal Constitution. Brooklyn, N. Y.: 1888].

8vo. pp. 10. 115

A few copies separately printed from No. 68.

*Randolph (Edmund)*.
Letter on the Federal Constitution, October 16, 1787. By Edmund Randolph. [Richmond: Printed by Augustin Davis. 1787.]

16mo. pp. 16. 116

Reprinted in Ford's *Pamphlets on the Constitution* and in No. 108.

*Randolph (Edmund)*.
[Letter on the Federal Constitution, October 16, 1787. By Edmund Randolph. Brooklyn, N. Y.; 1888.]

8vo. pp. 18. 117

A few copies separately reprinted from No. 68.

The / Ratifications / of the / New Fœderal Constitution, / together with the Amendments, / proposed by the / Several States. / . . . / Richmond ; / Printed by Aug. Davis / M,DCC,-LXXXVIII.

12mo. pp. (4), 32. A. A. S. 118

*Remarks on the Address.* See No. 132

*Remarks on the proposed* See Nos. 74-5.

*Result of the Debates.* See No. 16.

A Review of the Constitution Proposed by the late Convention, Held at Philadelphia, 1787. By a Federal Republican. . . . . . Philadelphia: Printed by Robert Smith and James Prang. 1787.

8vo. pp. 39. 119

A copy was sold in the O'Callaghan sale, (lot 668), and a copy is mentioned in the Bowdoin College Library Catalogue, which cannot now be found. Other

BIBLIOGRAPHY.                                       421

wise I have seen no mention of this pamphlet except in the original advertments, from which the above title is taken.

*Robertson, David.* See Nos. 107 and 127-8.

*Russell, Benjamin.* See Nos. 97-8.

*Secret Proceedings.* See Nos. 138-42.

[*Smith (Melancthon)*].

An / Address / to the / People / of the / State of New-York : / Showing the Necessity of Making / Amendments / to the / Constitution, proposed for the United States, / previous to its / Adoption. / By a Plebeian, / Printed [by Robert Hodge, in New York] in the State of New York, / M,DCC,LXXXVIII.

8vo.   pp. 26.              B. A., A. A. S.   120

Reprinted in Ford's *Pamphlets on the Constitution.*

*Smith (Melancthon).*

[An Address to the People of the State of New York: Shewing the Necessity of making Amendments to the Constitution. Brooklyn, N. Y., 1888].

8vo.   pp. 27.                              121

A few copies separately printed from No. 68.

*South Carolina*

Debates / which arose in the / House of Representatives / of South Carolina, / on the Constitution framed for the / United States, / by a Convention of Delegates, / Assembled at Philadelphia. / Charleston : / Collected by R. Haswell, and published at the City Gazette / Printing Office, No. 47, Bay. / M,DCC,XXXVIII.

4to.   pp. 55.                         B. A.   122

*South Carolina.*

Debates / which arose in the / House of Representatives / of / South-Carolina, / on the Constitution framed for the United States, / by a / Convention of Delegates assembled at Philadelphia. / Together with such / notices of the Convention / as could be procured. / . . . / . . . / . . . / . . . / Charleston : / Printed by A. E. Miller, / No. 4 Broad Street. / 1831.

8vo.   pp. (4), 95.                       M.   123

The first edition of Elliot's *Debates* contained nothing relating to South Carolina, and this volume was prepared by some citizen of the State to piece out the omission. In the later editions of Elliot, he reprinted this volume entire.

*State of North Carolina. See No.* 106.
*Stone, Frederick D. See No.* 92
*Supplement to the Independent Journal. See No.* 16.
*Thoughts upon the Political. See No.* 83
*Tucker (John Randolph).*
The History / of the / Federal Convention of 1787 and its Work. / An Address / delivered before the graduating classes / at the / Sixty-third Anniversary / of the / Yale Law School, / on / June 28th, 1887 / by / Hon. John Randolph Tucker, LL.D. / New Haven: / Published by the Law Department of Yale College. 1887.

8vo. pp. 54.     H. 124

A / View / of the / Proposed Constitution / of the / United States, / as agreed to by the / Convention / of Delegates from several States at Philadelphia, the 17th Day of September, / 1787—Compared with the present Confederation. / With sundry Notes and Observations. / Philadelphia : / Printed by R. Aitken & Son, at Popes Head / in Market Street. / M.DCC.-LXXXVII.

8vo. pp. 37.     B. A., N., B. 125

A comparison in parallel columns between the Articles of Confederation, and the proposed Constitution, with anti-federal notes.

*Virginia. Act calling Convention.*

Virginia, to wit: / General Assembly begun and held at the Capitol in the city of / Richmond on Monday the fifth day of October, in the year / of our Lord, one thousand seven hundred and eighty seven / An Act / concerning the convention to be held / in June next. / Passed December 12th, 1787.

Folio. Broadside.     S. 126

*Virginia. Debates.* 1788-9.

Debates / and other / Proceedings / of the / Convention / of / Virginia, / Convened at Richmond, on Monday the 2d day of / June, 1788, for the purpose of deliberating on the / Constitution recommended by the Grand Federal / Convention. / To which is prefixed, / the / Federal Constitution. / Petersburg : / Printed by / Hunter and Prentis. / M,DCC,LXXXVIII.

3 vols. 8 vo. pp. 194; 195; 228.     N., C., B. A., 127

The imprints of volumes II. and III. vary slightly from the above, being +

/ Federal Constitution. / Volume II. [III]. Petersburg: / Printed by William Prentis, / M,DCC,LXXXIX. /

Printed without being proof read. In 1805 it was already described as a rare book, and at present is only equalled in rarity in the state debates, by those of North Carolina. Volumes two and three are of much greater rarity than the first.

*Virginia. Debates. Richmond.* 1805.

Debates / and other / Proceedings / of the / Convention of Uirginia, [sic] convened at Richmond, on Monday the second day of June, / 1787, for the purpose of deliberating on the Con- / stitution recommended by the grand / Federal Convention. / To which is prefixed / the Federal Constitution. / Taken in short hand, / by David Robertson—of Petersburg. / Second Edition. / Richmond : / Printed at the Enquirer-Press / for Ritchie & Worsley and Augustine Davis. / 1805.

8vo. pp. viii, 477. N., C., A. A. S. 128

This edition was corrected and compared with a portion of the original stenographic notes, by the reporter.

*Virginia Journal.*

Journal / of the / Convention / of / Virginia ; / held in the / City of Richmond, / on the / First Monday in June, / in the Year of our Lord One thousand seven hundred and / eighty-eight. / Richmond : / Printed by Thomas W. White, / Main-st. opposite the Bell Tavern. / 1827.

8vo. pp. 39. B. A., P. 129

*Weakness of Brutus. See No.* 133-4.

[*Webster (Noah)*].

An / Examination / into the / leading principles / of the / Federal Constitution / proposed by the late / Convention / held at Philadelphia. / With / Answers to the principal objections / that have been raised against the system. / By a Citizen of America. / . . . / . . . / Philiadelphia : / Printed and sold by Prichard & Hall, in Market Street, / the second door above Lætitia Court. / M.DCC.LXXXVII.

8vo. pp. 55. C., B. A., P., H. 130

Reprinted, from the Author's annotated copy, in Ford's *Pamphlets on the Constitution.*

*Webster, Noah.*

[An Examination into the leading principles of the Federal Constitution.  Brooklyn, N. Y.:  1887.]

8vo.  pp. 41.    131

A few copies separately printed from No. 68.

[*Webster* (*Pelatiah*)].

Remarks / on the / Address of Sixteen Members / of the / Assembly of Pennsylvania, / to their / Constituents, / Dated September 29, 1787. / With some Strictures on the Objections to the / Constitution, / Recommended by the late Federal Convention, / Humbly offered to the Public / By a Citizen of Philadelphia. /. Philadelphia: / Printed by Eleazer Oswald, at the Coffee-House. / M,DCC,LXXXVII.

8vo.  pp. 28.    B. A., M.  132.

Also (abridged) in Webster's *Political Essays*, and (entire) in No. 92.

[*Webster* (*Pelatiah*)].

The Weaknesses of Brutus exposed : / or some / Remarks / in / Vindication of the Constitution / proposed by the late / / Federal Convention, / against the / Objections and gloomy Fears of that Writer. / Humbly offered to the Public. / By / A Citizen of Philadelphia. / Philadelphia: Printed for and to be had of John Sparhawk, Market-street, / near the Court House / M.DCC.LXXXVII.

8vo.  pp. 23.    B. A., A. A. S., M.  133

Reprinted in Webster's *Political Essays*, and in Ford's *Pamphlets on the Constitution*. In reprinting this pamphlet I suggested, with a question mark, that Brutus was written by Thomas Tredwell, having found that he used that signature to a newspaper essay published in 1789. I have since concluded that they were from the pen of Robert Yates, member of the Federal Convention from New York.

*Webster* (*Pelatiah*).

[The Weakness of Brutus exposed: or some Remarks in Vindication of the Constitution proposed by the late Federal Convention.  Brooklyn, [N. Y.: 1888.]

8vo.  pp. 15.    134

A few copies separately printed from No. 68.

*We the People.  See Nos.* 17-20.

*Williamson* (*Hugh*).

Address to the Freemen of Edentown and the County of Chowan, etc. on the New Plan of Government.

8vo.    135

Title from the *N. Y. Historical Society Catalogue*, but an examination shows it to be merely a newspaper clipping mounted on sheets of writing paper.

*Wilson (James).* See No. 91.

Substance of an Address / to a / meeting of the Citizens of Philadelphia, / delivered, October sixth, MDCCLXXXVII, / by the honorable / James Wilson, Esquire, one of the delegates from the State of Pennsylvania to the / late Continental Convention. [Brooklyn, N. Y.: 1888.]

8vo. pp. 7. 136

A few copies separately printed from No. 68.

"Mr. Wilson's speech is read with much approbation here by *one party;* the other party see nothing but nonsense in it."

"It has varnished an iron trap."

*Wilson (James).*

The Substance / of a / Speech / delivered by / James Wilson, Esq. / Explanatory of the general Principles of the proposed / Federal Constitution; / Upon a Motion made by the / Honorable Thomas McKean, / in the Convention of the State of Pennsylvania. / On Saturday the 24th of November, 1787. / Philadelphia: / Printed and Sold by Thomas Bradford, in Front-Street, / four Doors below the Coffee-House, MDCCLXXXVII.

8vo. pp. 10. 137

Reported by Alexander J. Dallas, Editor of *The Pennsylvania Herald.* Thomas Lloyd charged Dallas in a communication to the papers, with misrepresenting what Wilson had said.

*Yates (Robert). Secret Proceedings. Albany.* 1821

Secret / Proceedings and Debates / of the / Convention / assembled at Philadelphia, in the Year 1787, for the purpose / of forming the / Constitution / of / the United States of America. / From the Notes taken by the late Robert Yates, Esq. Chief / Justice of New-York, and copied by John Lansing, Jun. / Esq. late Chancellor of that State, Members / of that Convention. / Including / "The Genuine Information," laid before the Legislature of / Maryland, by Luther Martin, Esq. then Attorney Gen- / eral of that State, and a member of the same / Convention. / Also, / other Historical Documents relative to the Federal Compact / of the North American Union. / Albany: / Printed by Webster and Skinners, / at their Bookstore, in the White House, corner of State and Pearl Streets./ 1821.

8vo. pp. 308.     138

An outline of Yate's Minutes appeared in Hall's *American Law Journal*, iv, 563. 1813.

Yates was a member of the Federal Convention and though his memoranda only is to July 5, at which time he left the Convention, it is only second to Madison's *Debates* in importance. It is noticed in Taylor's *New Views of the Constitution*.

This first edition is by no means a common volume.

*Yates (Robert).  Secret Proceedings.  Washington.  1836.*

Secret / Proceedings and Debates / + / Washington : / Printed for G. Templeman, / Bookseller and Stationer, Pennsylvania Avenue. / 1839.

8vo. pp 308.     139

*Yates (Robert).  Secret Proceedings.  Richmond.  1839*

Secret / Proceedings and Debates / + / Richmond, Va. / Published by Wilbur Curtiss. / 1839.

8vo. pp. xi, 335.

*Yates (Robert).  Secret Proceedings.  Louisville.  1844*

Secret / Proceedings and Debates / + / Louisville, Ky. / Published by Alston Mygatt. / 1844.

8vo. pp. xi, 335.     140

Also copies dated 1845.

*Yates (Robert).  Secret Proceedings.  Cincinnati.*

Secret / Proceedings and Debates, / + / Cincinnati. / Published by Alston Mygatt. / [184—?]

8vo. pp. xi, 335.     141

# REFERENCE LIST.

*General Works—Histories.*

Allen (T.) Facts . . . in the origination of the American Union (new Series). Boston: 1870.
Bancroft (G.) History of the Constitution. No. 5.
Cocke (W. A.) Constitutional History of the U. S. Phila.: 1858.
Coffin (C. C.) Building the Nation. N. Y.: 1883.
Curtis (G. T.) History of the Constitution. No. 23.
Elliot (J.) Debates in the several State Conventions. No. 30.
Frothingham (R.) Rise of the Republic of the United States. Boston: 1872.
Hildreth (R.) History of the U. S. (1st series, iii). N. Y.: 1852.
McMaster (J. B.) History of the People of the U. S. (i). N. Y.: 1883.
McMaster (J. B.) Making a Government, in *The* [Philadelphia] *Press.* Sept. 15, 1887.
Miller (S. F.) Oration at the 100 Anniversary of the Constitution. Phila.: 1887.
Patton (J. H.) Concise History of the American People. N. Y.: 1882.
Porter (L. H.) Outlines of the Constitutional History of the U. S. N. Y.: 1883.
Schouler (J.) History of the U. S. (i). N. Y.: 1881.
Sterne (S.) Constitutional History . . . of the U. S. N. Y.: 1883.
Thorpe (F. N.) Origin of the Constitution, in *Mag. of Am. Hist.* xviii, 130.

Towle (N. C.) History and Analysis of the U. S. Constitution. Boston: v. d.
Von Holst (H.) Constitutional and Political History of the U. S. (i). Chicago: 1876.
Winsor (J.) Narrative and Critical History of America. (vii). Boston: 1888.

*General Works—Printed documentary sources.*

Ames (F.) Works of . . . Boston: 1809.
Ames (F.) Works of . . . edited by S. Ames. Boston: 1854.
Belknap Papers. (Mass. Hist. Soc. Coll. 5th series, ii and iii). Boston: 1877.
Diplomatic Correspondence of the U. S. 1783–1789. Boston: 1837.
Franklin (B.) Works of . . . edited by J. Sparks. Boston: 1840,
Franklin (B.) Works of . . . edited by J. Bigelow. N. Y.: 1887.
Hamilton (A.) Works of . . . edited by J. C. Hamilton. N. Y.: 1850.
Hamilton (A.) Works of . . . edited by H. C. Lodge. N. Y.: 1885.
Jay (J.) Writings of . . . edited by H. P. Johnson. (in preparation). N. Y.: ——
Leake (J. Q.) Life and Times of John Lamb. Albany: 1857.
Letters and Papers illustrating the formation of the Constitution, in No. 5.
McRee (G. J.) Life of James Iredell, (ii). N. Y.: 1858.
Madison (J.) Papers of . . . No. 93.
Madison (J.) Letters and other writings. Phila.: 1865.
Morris (G.) Writings of. (in preparation). N. Y.: ——
Washington (G.) Writings of . . . edited by J. Sparks. Boston: 1837.
Washington (G.) Writings of . . . edited by W. C. Ford. N. Y.: 1888.

*General Works—Periodicals.*

## New Hampshire.
Freemans Oracle and N. H. Advertiser. [Exeter].
N. H. Gazette and the General Advertiser. [Exeter].
N. H. Mercury. [Portsmouth].
N. H. Recorder and Weekly Advertiser. [Keene].
N. H Spy. [Portsmouth].

## Massachusetts.
American Herald. [Worcester].
Berkshire Chronicle.
Boston Gazette.
Cumberland Gazette. [Portland, Me].
Essex Journal. [Salem].
Hampshire Chronicle. [Springfield].
Hampshire Gazette. [Northampton].
Hampshire Herald. [Springfield].
Independent Chronicle. [Boston].
Massachusetts Centinel. [Boston].
Massachusetts Gazette. [Boston].
Massachusetts Spy. [Worcester].
Salem Mercury.
Western Star. [Stockbridge].

## Rhode Island.
Newport Herald.
Providence Gazette.
United States Chronicle. [Providence].

## Connecticut.
American Mercury. [Hartford]:
Connecticut Courant. [Hartford].
Connecticut Gazette. [New London].
Connecticut Journal. [New Haven].
Middlesex Gazette. [Middletown].
New Haven Chronicle.
New Haven Gazette.
Norwich Packet.
Weekly Monitor. [Litchfield].

## New York.
Albany Gazette.
Albany Register.
American Magazine. [New York.]
Goshen Repository.
Hudson Gazette.
Independent Journal. [New York].
New York Daily Advertiser. [New York].
New York Journal. [New York].

New York Museum. [New York].
New York Packet. [New York].
Northern Centinel or Lansingburg Advertiser.
Poughkeepsie Journal.

### New Jersey.
Brunswick Gazette. [New Brunswick].
New Jersey Gazette. [Trenton].
New Jersey Journal. [Elizabethtown].

### Pennsylvania.
American Museum. [Philadelphia].
Freemen's Journal. [Philadelphia].
Independent Gazetteer. [Philadelphia].
Pennsylvania Gazette. [Philadelphia].
Pennsylvania Herald. [Philadelphia].
Pennsylvania Journal. [Philadelphia].
Pennsylvania Mercury. [Philadelphia].
Pennsylvania Packet. [Philadelphia].
Pittsburg Gazette.

### Delaware.
Wilmington Courant.
Wilmington Gazette.

### Maryland.
Maryland Chronicle. [Frederick].
Maryland Gazette. [Annapolis].
Maryland Gazette. [Baltimore].
Maryland Journal. [Baltimore].

### Virginia.
The Norfolk and Portsmouth Chronicle.
Virginia Gazette. [Winchester].
Virginia Gazette and Petersburg Advertiser.
The Virginia Gazette and Weekly Advertiser. [Richmond].
The Virginia Herald and Independent Advertiser.
Virginia Independent Chronicle. [Richmond].
The Virginia Journal and Alexandria Advertiser.

### North Carolina.
North Carolina Chronicle. [Fayettville].
State Gazette of North Carolina. [Newberne & Edentown].

### South Carolina.
The Columbian Herald or the Independent Courier. [Charleston].
City Gazette, or Daily Advertiser. [Charleston].
State Gazette of South Carolina. [Charleston].
South Carolina Weekly Chronicle.

### Georgia.
Augusta Chronicle.
Georgia Gazette. [Savannah].

### General Works—Biographies.

See under "Federal Convention—Biographies of attending members" and "Contests in the States."

### Federal Convention—Histories.

Anecdotes of the Federal Convention, in *Living Age*, xxv, 557.
Bledsoe (A. T.) North and South in the Convention of 1787, in *Southern Review*, (new series). ii, 359.
Clason (A. W.) The Fallacy of 1787, in *Mag. of Am. Hist.*, xiv, 373.
Jameson (J. A.) The Constitutional Convention. N. Y.: v. d.
McMaster (J. B.) Framers and Framing of the Constitution, in *The Century*, xxxiv, 746.
Martin (L.) Genuine Information, No. 94.
Sparks (J.) Convention of 1787, in *North Am. Rev.*, xxv, 249.
Tucker (J. R.) History of the Federal Convention. No. 124.

### Federal Convention—Proceedings.

Journal, Acts and Proceedings of the Convention, No. 85.
King (R.) Minutes of Debates. MS. in possession of family.
Madison (J.) Minutes of Debates, No. 93.
Martin (L.) Genuine Information, No. 94.
Yates (R.) Secret proceedings and Debates, No. 138.

### Federal Convention—Drafts and Plans.

Cruger (L. N.) Authorship of the U. S. Constitution, in *Southern Monthly*, x, 635.
Hamilton (A.) Proposition in Convention, June 18, 1787, No. 73.
Hamilton (A.) Plan of Government, (p. 584) of No. 31.
New Jersey Resolutions, June 15, 1787, in Nos. 30. 31, 85 and 138.
Pinckney (C.) [Spurious] plan of Government, in Nos. 30, 31, 85 and 138.
Pinckney (C.) Observations on the Plan of Government, No. 113.

Randolph (E.) Draft of a Constitution, in *Scribners* (new) *Mag.*, ii, 313.
Randolph (E.) Draft of a Constitution, in (forthcoming) Life of Randolph, by M. D. Conway.
Report of the Committee of Detail, Aug. 6, 1787, No. 20.
Report of the Committee of Revision, Sept. 12, 1787. No. 19.
Resolutions as agreed to in Committee of the whole. June 19, 1787, in Nos. 30, 31, 85 and 138.
Resolutions referred to the Committee of Detail, July 26, 1787, in Nos. 30, 31, 85 and 138.
Virginia Resolutions, May 29, 1787, in Nos. 30, 31, 85 and 138.

*Federal Convention—Biographies of attending Members.*

General Works.
>Ford (P. L.) List of the Members of. No. 69.
>Lamb (M. J.) The Framers of the Constitution, in *Mag. of Am. Hist.* xiii, 313.
>Memorial of the Constitutional Centennial Celebration. Phila.: 1889.
>Official Programme of the Constitutional Centennial Celebration. Phila.: 1887.

Baldwin, Abraham.
>Barlow (J.) and Baldwin (H.) in Herring's *Nat. Portrait Gallery*, iv.

Blair, John.
>Biographia Americana. N. Y.: 1825.
>Miller (S. F.) The Supreme Court. Phila.: 1877.
>Grigsby (H. B.) Virginia Convention of 1776, (p. 70). Richmond: 1855.

Brearly, David.
>Elmer (L. Q. C.) Constitution and Government of N. J., (p. 274). Newark: 1872.

Butler, Pierce.
>Simpson (H.) Lives of Eminent Philadelphians, (p. 157). Phila.: 1859.

Carroll, Daniel.
>Scharf (J. T.) History of Western Maryland.

Clymer, George.
>Dickinson (W.) in *Mag. of Am. Hist.*, v, 196.
>Waln (B.) in Sanderson's *Biography of the Signers*, iv, 173.
>Simpson (H.) Lives of Eminent Philadelphians, (p. 211). Phila.: 1859.
>McMaster (J. B.) and Stone (F. D.) p. 704, of No. 92.

## Davie, William Richardson.
Garden (A.) Anecdotes of the American Revolution (p.   ). Charleston: 1822.
Hubbard (F. M.) in Spark's *American Biography*, xxv.
Davie (A. H.) in Herring's *Nat. Portrait Gallery*, iii.
*Southern Literary Messenger*, xiv, 510.

## Dickinson, John.
Armor (W. C.) Lives of the Governors of Pa., (p. 234). Phila.. 1873.
Budd (T. A.) in Herring's *Nat. Portrait Gallery*, iii.
Dickinson (W.) in *Mag. of Am. Hist.*, x, 223.
Hines (C. F.) Sketch of Dickinson College, (p. 17). Harrisburg: 1879.
Simpson (H.) Lives of Eminent Philadelphians, (p. 309). Phila.: 1859.

## Ellsworth, Oliver.
*Analytical Mag.*, iii, 382.
*American Literary Mag.*, i, 195.
Duychinck (E.) *Nat. Portrait Gallery*, i, 345.
Flanders (H.) Lives of the Chief Justices, (i). Phila.: 1855.
Miller (S. F.) The Supreme Court. Phila.: 1877.
*The Portfolio*, xxxiv, 185.
Rowland (H. A.) Eulogy on . . . Hartford: 1808,
Sigourney (L. H.) in Herring's *Nat. Portrait Gallery*, iv.

## Few, William.
Autobigraphy of . . . in *Mag. of Am. Hist.*, vii, 340.
Jones (C. C.) in *Mag. of Am. Hist.*, vii, 343.
White (G.) Historical Collections of Georgia, (p. 409). N. Y.: 1855.

## Fitzsimons, Thomas.
Flanders (H.) in *Pa. Mag. of Hist. and Biography*, ii, 307.
*American Catholic Historical Researches*, Jan. 1888.
McMaster (J. B.) and Stone (F. D.) p. 706, of No. 92.
Simpson (H.) Lives of Eminent Philadelphians, (p. 372). Phila.: 1859.

## Franklin, Benjamin.
See Lindsay Swift's *Catalogue of works relating to Benjamin Franklin.* Boston: 1883.

## Gerry, Elbridge.
Austin (J. T.) Life of . . . Boston: 1828.
Gilpin (H. D.) in Sanderson's *Biography of the Signers*, viii, 7.

## Gilman, Nicholas.
Gilman (A.) The Gilman Genealogy, (p. 108). Albany: 1869.

## Gorham, Nathaniel.
Biographia Americana. N. Y.: 1825.
Welch (T.) Eulogy on . . . Boston: 1796.

## Hamilton.
See P. L. Ford's *Bibliotheca Hamiltoniana*. *N. Y.:* 1886.

## Ingersoll, Jared.
McMaster (J. B.) and Stone (F. D.) p. 707, of No. 92.
Simpson (H.) Lives of Eminent Philadelphians, (p. 594). Phila.: 1859.

## Johnson, William Samuel.
Beardsley (E. E.) Life of . . . N. Y.: 1876.
Irving (J. T.) Discourse on Classical Learning. N. Y.: 1830.

## King, Rufus.
Curtis (G. T.) History of the Constitution, (i, 448), No. 23.
Delaplaine's *Repository*, ii, 177.
Duyckinck (E.) *Nat. Portrait Gallery.*
Herring (J.) in Herring's *Nat. Portrait Gallery*, iii.
King (C.) Homes of American Statesmen (p. 355). N. Y.: 1856.
*American Annual Register* for 1826-7, p. 341.

## Langdon, John.
Brewster (C. W.) Rambles about Portsmouth, (1st series, 364). Portsmouth: 1873.

## Lansing, John.
Street (A. B.) Council of Revision of the State of N. Y., (p. 168). Albany: 1859.

## Livingston, William.
Sedgewick (T.) Memoir of . . . N. Y.: 1833.
Elmer (L. Q. C.) Constitution and Government of N. J., (p. 56). Newark: 1872.

## M'Henry, James.
Brown (F. J.) Sketch of . . . Baltimore: 1877.
*Mag. of Am. Hist.* vii, 104.

## McClulg, James.
Duyckinck (E.) Cyclopædia of Am. Literature, (i, 283). N. Y.: 1855.
Thacher (J.) American Medical Biography. Boston: 1828.

## Madison, James.
Rives (W. C.) Life and Times of . . . Boston: 1873.
Gay (S. H.) American Statesmen, James Madison. Boston: 1884.
Stoddard (W. O.) Lives of the Presidents. N. Y.: 1885.
Curtis (G. T.) History of the Constitution, (i, 420). No. 23.
Ingersoll (C. J.) in Herring's *Nat. Portrait Gallery*, iii.

## Martin, Luther.
Lanman (J. H.) in Herring's *Nat. Portrait Gallery*, iv.
*American Law Review*, i, 273.

## Mason, George.
Rowland (K. M.) Life of . . . [in preparation].
Grigsby (H. B.) Virginia Convention of 1776, (p. 154). Richmond: 1855.
*American Historical Record*, ii, 113.
Colvin (S.) in *The Portfolio*, ii, 231, [from Poole's Index].

## Mercer, John Francis.
*Potter's American Monthly*, vii, 178.

## Mifflin, Thomas.
Budd (T. A.) in Herring's *Nat. Portrait Gallery*, iv.
Armor (W. C.) Lives of the Governors of Pa., (p. 273). Phila.: 1873.
McMaster (J. B.) and Stone (F. D.) p. 701, of No. 92.
Simpson (H.) Lives of Eminent Philadelphians, (p. 693). Phila.: 1859.

## Morris, Gouverneur.
Sparks (J ) Life and Writings of . . . Boston: 1837.
Tuckerman (H. T.) Essays, Biographical and Critical. Boston: 1857.
Meredith (C. K.) in *Pa. Mag. of History and Biography*, ii, 185.
Roosevelt (T.) Life of . . . Boston: 1888.
Curtis (G. T.) History of the Constitution, (i, 440). No. 23.
Francis (J. W.) in *Hist. Mag.*, xiii.

## Morris, Robert.
Life of . . . Phila.: 1841.
Duyckinck (E.) *Nat. Portrait Gallery*, i, 240.
Waln (R.) in Sanderson's *Biography of the Segners*, v, 189.
Delaplaine's *Repository*, iii, 139.
Hart (A. N.) in *Pa. Mag.* of History and Biography, i, 333.
Herring (J.) in Herring's *Nat. Portrait Gallery*, iv.

## Paterson, William.
Clark (J.) Funeral Sermon on . . . New Brunswick: n. d.
Messler (A.) in *Pa. Mag. of History and Biography*, iii, 429.
Elmer (L. Q. C.) Constitution and Government of N. J., (p. 77). Newark: 1872.
Barber (J. W.) and Howe (H.) Historical Collections of N. J., (p. 314). N. Y.: 1845.
Miller (S. F.) The Supreme Court. Phila.: 1877.

## Pinckney, Charles.
Biographia Americana, N. Y.: 1825.

## Pinckney, Charles Cotesworth.
Gadsden (E. C.) A Sermon on . . . Charleston: 1825,
Garden (A.) Eulogy on . . . Charleston: 1825.
Lynch (J.) in Herring's *Nat. Portrait Gallery*, iv.
Duyckinck (E.) in *Nat. Portrait Gallery*.
Garden (A.) Anecdotes of the American Revolution. Charleston: 1822.
*American Annual Register for* 1825-6, p. 207.
Curtis (G. T.) History of the Constitution, (i, 454). No. 23.
Simms (W. G.) in *Hist. Mag.*, xii, 134.

## Randolph, Edmund.
[Daniels (P. V.)] Memoir of . . . Richmond: 1869.
Conway (M. D.) Life of . . . N. Y.: 1888.
Conway (M. D.) in *Lippincott's Mag.*, Sept. 1887.

Grigsby (H. B.) Virginia Convention of 1776, (p. 76). Richmond: 1855.
Curtis (G. T.) History of the Constitution, (i, 480). No. 23.
Public Characters for 1800-1, (p. 439). London: 1801.

### Read, George.
Read (W. T.) Life of . . . Phila.: 1870.
Read (———?) in Sanderson's *Biography of the Signers*, iv, 21.
[Tilton (J.)] History of Dionysius, Tyrant of Delaware. [n. p.] 1788.

### Rutledge, John.
Gayarré (C.) Life of . . .
Van Santvoord (G.) Chief Justices of the U. S., (p. 91). N. Y.: 1854.
Flanders (H.) Lives of the Chief Justices. Phila.: 1855.
Miller (S. F.) The Supreme Court. Phila.: 1877.
Ramsay (D.) in Herring's *Nat. Portrait Gallery*, iv.
Ramsay (D) History of S. C., (ii, 510). Charleston: 1809.
Sargent (W.) in *North American Rev.*, lxxxi, 346.
*American Whig Rev.*, vi, 125, 277.
*Southern Quarterly*, xxvii, 332.

### Sherman, Roger.
Everett (E.) in Sanderson's *Biography of the Signers*, iii, 199.
Duyckinck (E) *Nat. Portrait Gallery*, i, 334.
*Harper's Mag.*, iii, 145, vii, 156.
*Worcester Mag*, i, 164.
*New Englander*, iv, 1.

### Spaight, Richard Dobbs.
Wheeler (J. H.) in *Pa. Mag. of History and Biography*, iii, 426.

### Strong, Caleb.
Bradford (A.) Biography of . . . Boston: 1820.
Lyman (J.) Sermon on . . . Northampton: 1819.
Dwight (E S.) in *The Congregational Quarterly*, ii 161.
*American Quarterly*, xii, 1.
*Polyanthus* (enlarged), ii, 225.

### Washington, George.
Marshall (J.) Life of . . . Phila.: 1805.
Irving (W.) Life of . . . N. Y.: 1855.
Lossing (B. J) Life of . . . N. Y.: 1860.

### Williamson, Hugh.
Hosack (D.) Biographical Memoirs of . . . N. Y.: 1820.
  Also in *Proceedings of the N. Y. Historical Society*, iii.
Thacher (J.) American Medical Biography. Boston: 1828.
*The Portfolio*, xxiii, 102; xxvi, 388.
Everett (A. H.) in *North American Rev*, xi, 31.

### Wilson, James.
Waln (R.) in Sanderson's *Biography of the Signers*, vi, 113.
Curtis (G. T.) History of the Constitution, (i, 462), No. 23.

Simpson (H ) Lives of Eminent Philadelphians, (p. 964), Phila.: 1859.
Wythe, George.
Jefferson (T.) in Sanderson's *Biography of the Signers*, ii, 156.
Grigsby (H. B.) Virginia Convention of 1776, (p. 120). Richmond: 1855.
Yates, Robert.
Lansing (J.) Secret Proceedings, (p. 303). No. 138.
Street (A. B.) Council of Revision of the State of N. Y., (p. 168). Albany: 1859.

*Partizan Pamphlets—Pro.*

Address to Citizens of Albany, No. 79.
[Coxe (T.)] Examination of the Constitution, No. 21.
[Dickinson (J.)] Letters of Fabius, No. 25.
Duer (W.) Philo Publius, in No. 62.
[Hanson (A. C.)] Remarks on the Constitution, No 74.
[Hamilton, Madison and Jay]. The Federalist, No. 32.
[Jackson (J.)] Thoughts upon the Political Situation, No. 82.
[Jay (J.)] Address to People of N. Y., No. 83.
[Ramsay (D.)] Address on the Constitution, No. 114.
Randolph (E.) Letter on the Constitution, No. 116.
[Webster (N.)] Examination of the Constitution, No. 130.
[Webster (P.)] Remarks on the Address, No. 132.
[Webster (P.)] The Weakness of Brutus, No. 133.
Williamson (H.) Address to the Freemen, No. 135.
Wilson (J.) Speech of October 6th, 1787, No. 136.

*Partizan Pamphlets—Con.*

[Bryan (S.)] Letters of Centinel, Nos. 92 and 97.
[Gerry (E.)] Observations on the Constitution, No. 70.
[Lee (R. H.)] Letters of a Federal Farmer, No. 88.
Letters of Brutus, No. 99.
Martin (L.) Genuine Information, No. 94.
Mason (G.) Objections to the Constitution, No. 95.
Review of the Constitution, No. 119.
[Smith (M.)] Address to the People of N. Y., No. 120.
View of the proposed Constitution, No. 125.

*Contests in the States.*

See also "General Works—Periodicals" and "Federal Convention—Biographies of attending members."

New Hampshire.
    Amory (T. C.) Life of John Sullivan. Boston: 1868.
    Barstow (G.) History of N. H. Concord: 1842.
    Belknap (J.) History of N. H. Various editions.
    Biographies of the Members of the N. H. Convention in Bouton's N. H. State Records, x, 8.
    Debates (fragment) in Convention. (ii, 202). No. 30.
    Fragment of Debate in N. H. Convention, in *N. H. Gazette*, Feb. 20, 1780.
    Hall, A. Oration, June 30, 1788, No. 72.
    Journal of the N. H. Convention, in Bouton's N. H. Records, x, 1. Also in *Hist. Mag.*, xiii, 257.
    Outlines of proceeding of the first session of Convention in *N. Y. Journal*, Feb. 28, 29, March 3, 6, 1788.
    Peabody (A. P.) Life of William Plummer. Boston: 1866.
    Sanborn (E. D.) History of N. H. Manchester: 1875.

Massachusetts.
    Ames (Fisher.) Works of . . . Boston: 1809 and 1854.
    Amory (T. C.) Life of James Sullivan. Boston: 1859.
    Austin (G. L.) History of Massachusetts. Boston: 1870.
    Barry (J. S.) History of Massachusetts. Boston: 1855.
    Belknap Papers, [Mass. Hist. Soc. Coll. Vols. II & III]. Boston: 1877.
    Bradford (A.) History of Massachusetts. Boston: 1825.
    Clason (A. W.) Outlines of Debates in Mass. Convention, in *Mag. of Am. Hist.*, xiv, 529.
    [Gerry (E.)] Observations on the Constitution, by A Columbian Patriot, No. 70.
    [Jackson (J.)] Thoughts on the Political Situation, No. 82.
    Journal of the Convention, No. 99.
    Lodge (H. C.) Life of George Cabot. Boston: 1877.
    Parsons (T.) Minutes of Debates, No. 99.
    Parsons (T. Jr.) Memoir of Theophilus Parsons. Boston: 1861.
    Procession in Boston, No. 99.
    Russell's Debates in the Convention, No. 97.
    Smith (C. C.) History of the Mass. Convention, in Supplement to *Boston Post*, Sept. 15, 1887.
    Warren (E.) Life of John Warren. Boston: 1874.
    Wells (W. V.) Life of Samuel Adams. Boston: 1866.

Rhode Island.
    Arnold (S. G.) History of the State of R. I. N. Y.: 1859.
    Hitchcock (E.) An Oration, July 4, 1788, No. 76.
    Minutes of R. I. Convention, in Staple's R. I., and the Continental Congress, (p. 641). Providence: 1870.
    Peterson (E.) History of R. I. N. Y.: 1853.
    Staples (W. R.) R. I. and the Constitution, in R. I., and the Continental Congress. Providence: 1870.

Connecticut.

# REFERENCE LIST. 439

Baldwin (S.) Oration, July 4th, 1788, No. 4.
Debates in the Convention, in *New Haven Gazette*, 1788.
Debates in Convention (fragment) in No. 30.
Hollister (G. H.) History of Conn. New Haven : 1855.
Johnson (A.) American Commonwealths. Connecticut. Boston : 1887.
Official letter from Sherman and Ellsworth, in No. 30.

## New York.
Address to Citizens of Albany, No. 81.
Campbell (W. W.) Life of DeWitt Clinton. N. Y.: 1849.
Circular Letter of Convention, (ii, 413) of No. 30.
Debates in Convention, No. 104.
Dunlap (W.) History of N. Y. N. Y. : 1840.
[Hamilton, Madison and Jay]. The Federalist, No. 32.
Hammond (J. B.) Political History of N. Y. Albany : 1842.
[Jay (J.)] Address to People of N. Y. No. 83.
Jay (W.) Life of John Jay. N. Y.; 1833.
Jenkins (J. S.) History of Political Parties in the State of N. Y. Auburn: 1846·
Journal of Convention. No. 104.
Leake (I. Q.) Memoirs of John Lamb. Albany: 1857.
Letters of Brutus, No 99.
Macauley (J.) History of the State of N. Y. Albany : 1842.
Official letters from Yates and Lansing, (i, 480), No. 30.
Roberts (E. H.) American Commonwealth. New York. Boston : 1887.
Sketch of the Proceedings of the Convention, No. 80.
[Smith (M.)] Address to the People of N. Y., No. 120.
Stevens (J. A.) N. Y. and Federal Constitution, in *Mag. of Am. Hist.*, ii. 385,
[Webster (N.)] Account of the Procession, No. 80.
[Webster (P.)] The Weakness of Brutus, No. 133.
Whitlock (W.) Life of John Jay. N. Y.: 1887.

## New Jersey.
Address to the Citizens of N. J. by a Jerseyman, in Carey's *Am. Museum*, ii. 436.
Gordon (T. F.) History of N. J. Trenton: 1834.
Minutes of the Convention, No. 102.
Mulford (G. S.) History of N. J. Phila.: 1851.
Proceedings of the Convention, in *N. Y. Journal*, Dec., 1787.
Raum (J. O.) History of N. J. Phila.: 1877.

## Pennsylvania.
Address and Dissent of Minority of Pa. Convention. No. 1.
[Bryan (S.)] Letters of Centinel, Nos. 92 and 97.
[Coxe (T.)] Examination of the Constitution, No. 21.
Debates in the Convention. No. 92.
Debates in the Convention (fragment). No. 110.
  Also in No. 30, ii, 415.

Egle (W. H.) Biographical Sketches of Members of the Pa. Convention, in *Pa. Mag. of History and Biography*, x and xi.
   Also in No. 92.
Graydon (A.) Memoirs of . . . Harrisburg: 1811.
[Hopkinson (F.)] Account of the Procession, No. 77
Illustrated History of Pennsylvania. Phila.: 1880.
McMaster and Stone. Pa. and the Federal Constitution. No. 92.
Minutes of the Convention. No. 111.
Order of Procession at Philadelphia. No. 109.
Pickering (O.) and Upham (W. C.) Life of Timothy Pickering. Boston: 1868.
Reply to Address of Seceding Members Pa. Legislature, No. 3.
Reply to Seceding Members of Pa. Legis. by "Federal Constitution," No. 3.
Report of the Deputies of Northampton Co. in late Pa. Convention, in Carey's *Am. Museum*, iii, 75.
Review of the Constitution, No. 119.
View of the Proposed Constitution, No. 125.
[Webster (P.)] Remarks on the Address, 132.
[Webster (P.)] The Weakness of Brutus, No. 133.
Wilson (J.) Speech of October 6th, 1787, No. 136.
Wilson (J.) Substance of a Speech, No. 137.
Wilson (J.) and M'Kean (J.) Commentaries on the Constitution, No. 91.

Delaware.
[Dickinson (J.)] Letters of Fabius, No. 25.
Vinton (F.) History of Delaware. Phila.: 1870.

Maryland.
[Hanson (A. C.)] Remarks on the Constitution, No. 74.
McSherry (J.) History of Maryland. Baltimore: 1849.
Martin (G.) Genuine Information, No. 94.
Outline of Proceedings in Convention, (ii, 546), of No. 30.
Scharf (J. T.) History of Maryland. Baltimore: 1879.

Virginia.
Act Calling Convention, No. 126.
Clason (A. W.) Outline of Debates in Va. Convention, in *Mag. of Am. Hist.*, xv, 566.
Cooke (J. E.) American Commonwealth, Virginia. Boston: 1883.
Debates of the Convention, No. 127.
Howe (H.) Historical Coll. of Va. Charlston: 1856.
Howison (R. R.) History of Virginia. Phila.: 1846.
Journal of the Convention. No. 129.
Lee (R. H. Jr.) Life of Richard Henry Lee. Phila.: 1825.
Mason (G.) Objections to the Constitution, No 95.
[Montgomery (J.)] Letters of Decius. Nos. 100 and 105.
Randolph (E.) Letter on the Constitution, No. 116.
Tyler (M. C.) American 'Statesmen. Patrick Henry. Boston: 1887.

Wirt (W.)  Life of Patrick Henry.  Phila.: 1818.
## North Carolina.
Amendments to the Constitution, No. 106.
Clason (A. W.)  Outline of Debates in first Convention, in *Mag. of Am. Hist.*, xv, 352.
Hawks (F. L.)  History of N. C.  Fayetteville: 1857.
McRee (G. J.)  Life of James Iredell.  N. Y.: 1858.
Moore (J. W.)  History of N. C.  Raleigh: 1880.
Proceedings and Debates of First Convention, No. 107.
Williamson (H.)  Address to the Freemen, No. 135.
## South Carolina.
Clason (A. W.)  Outline of Debates in S. C. Convention, in *Mag. of Am. Hist.*, xv, 153.
Debate in the House of Representatives on Convention, No. 122.
Fragments of Debates in Convention, No. 123.
[Ramsay (D.)]  Address to the Freemen of S. C., No. 114.
Ramsay (D.)  History of S. C.  Charleston: 1809.
Simms (W. G.)  History of S. C.  Charleston: 1850.
## Georgia.
Stevens (W. B.)  History of Georgia.  Phila.: 1859.
White (G.)  Historical Collections of Georgia.  N. Y.: 1854.

*Celebrations of Ratifications.*

Baldwin (S.)  Oration, July 4th, 1788, No. 5.
Hall (A.)  Oration June 30, 1788, No. 72.
Hitchcock (E.)  An Oration, July 4, 1788, No. 76.
[Hopkinson (F.)]  Account of the Procession, No. 77.
Order of Procession at Philadelphia, No. 109.
Procession in Boston, No. 99.
[Webster (N.)]  Account of N. Y. Federal Procession, in No. 80.

# INDEX.

Adams, Charles Francis, 413.
Adams, John, cited, 316.
Adams. J. Q., 406; 411.
Address to the people of the State of New York, 67; 87; 111.
Agriculture. diminished values of products of, 73.
Albany, committee of, 1; address to the citizens of, 409.
Algerines, method of obtaining peace with the, 112.
Amendments, *see Constitution*.
American Citizen, An, pseudonym of T. Coxe, 134; 391.
Appointment, powers of, 311; 339.
Appointing power, necessity of check on President's, 341.
Aristides, pseudonym of A. C. Hanson, 217; 408.
Aristocracy, (*see also Monarchy*.) 17; 285; 332; natural, in the U. S., 295; party of, in the U. S., 321; rarity of, genuine, 256.
Army, Standing, dangers of, 10; 150; discussion of, 363; impossibility of in America, 56; lack of restrictions on, 51; 103; 365; necessity of, 157; 235; powers of congress over, 150; 303; restriction of, by North Carolina, 365; restriction of, by Pennsylvania, 365; unnecessary fear of, 234.
Arnold, Benedict, 352.
Articles of Confederation, *see Confederation*.
Attainder, Bills of, forbidden, 314.
Austin, James T., 1.

Baldwin, Abraham, biographies of, 432.
Baldwin, Simeon, Oration of, 386.
Bancroft, George, History by, 386.
Bankrupt laws, necessity of uniform, 306.
Belhaven, Lord, quotation from speech of, 195.
Bills of Rights, 73; 114; 229; 329; adoption of, 359; necessity of, 75; 315; unnecessary in constitution, 241; 335.

Blackstone, Judge, cited, 10.
Blair, John, biographies of, 432.
Brearly, David, 390; biographies of, 432.
Brutus, pseudonym to newspaper essay, 118; 424.
Bryan, Samuel, 418.
Butler, Pierce. biographies of, 432.
Byng. admiral, 354.

Cabinet, dangers of, 330.
Carolinas, the, importance of their decision on the constitution, 21.
Carroll, Daniel, biographies of, 432.
Caucus, dangers from, 300.
Centinel, cited, 248; pseudonym of Samuel Bryan, 418.
Citizen of America, pseudonym of N. Webster, 25; 423
Citizen of New York, pseudonym of John Jay, 67; 410.
Citizen of Philadelphia, pseudonym of P. Webster, 118; 424.
Civil list, 7.
Civil service, 189; want of rotation in, 11.
Civis, pseudonym of Jonathan Jackson, 410; pseudonym of David Ramsay, 380; 420.
Clinton, George, 418.
Clymer, George, biographies of, 432.
Columbian Patriot, pseudonym of E. Gerry, 1; 407.
Commerce, (*see also, Navigation. Shipping, Treaties*.) 73; 265; 357; condition of, 358; control of, by a few states, 62; impositions on, 264; improper power to enact laws relating to, 331; powers of congress over, 357; right of English parliament over colonial, 136; should not be submitted to a mere majority of congress, 275; wretched condition of, 265.
Confederation (*see also, Congress, Continental, United States government*.) compared with constitution, 148; 379; defective nature of, 136; 228; 261; dissolution of, 268; feebleness of, 272;

# 444 INDEX.

government under the, 72; history of, 262; 283; impossibility of suitably amending, 267; necessity of amending, 96; 136; positions of the states under, in reference to the new constitution, 97; 267.

Confederacies, separate, 120; 127; 204; 247; 269; southern, 270; evils of, 278.

Congress, Continental (*see also Confederation, Impost, Paper Money.*) 156; absurd measures of, 92; bad constitution of, 267; lack of power of, 78; merging of powers in, 268; misrepresentation in, 267; omitted in consideration of new government, 14; origin of, 70; powers of, 70; 72; 374: power to amend constitution, 284; proposition to vest with impost, 283; requisitions of, 263; unsuitable to lodge powers in, 267.

Congress, (*see also, Armies, Commerce, Constitution, Election, Judiciary, Jury, Impost, Paper Money, Press, Representation, Representatives, Senate, Treaties, United States government.*) 33; 107; abuse of powers of, 122; attendance in, 376; binding effects of acts of on its own members, 124; checks on, 125 ; definition of necessary powers, 45; delegates to, 40; division into two branches, 30 ; extensive powers of, 45; 122; 233; formed of the best men, 123; great expense of, 47; interference of with states, 46; length of term, 170; limited powers of, to deal with common law, 336; members of, remarks on, 123; method of passing laws, 44; necessary powers only given to, 173; 374; necessity of a line between states and, 273; objection to two branches in, 47; powers conceded by anti-federalists to, 126; powers of, limited to what the people allow, 127; powers of taxation of 49; 303 ; powers over elections, 44 ; powers over printing, 316; powers to define and punish crime, 359; powers to grant monopolies, 357; power to provide for the general interest and welfare, 121; probable misuse of their power, 123; representation in, 12; 289; right of the people to control delegates to, 6; to determine their own salaries, 11; unnecessary power over elections, 61.

Connecticut, adopted from local causes, 104; adoption of the constitution by, 98; and the constitution, 439; construction of Senate of, 41; disagreement in legislature of, 33; hostile feelings towards New York, 84; 96; imports of, from New York, 62; legislative action on act of Congress, 33; probable refusal to attend second convention, 81; reasons for her ratification, 21; representation in House of Representatives, 293.

Constitution, (*see also Army, Bills of Rights, Congress, Continental Congress, Conventions, Elections, Judiciary, Jury, Malitia, Navy, Press, Ratification, Representation, Representatives, Senate, United States government.*)

— Adoption of, danger of delay in, 93; necessity of 62; should not be precipitate in, 280.

— Advantages of, 61; 64; 319; control over states clearly defined, 121; diverse representation in, 204; increase of values if adopted, 47; mutual checks in the departments of government as, 222; no qualification in wealth or birth under, 146; plan of accomodation, 80; 285; security in, from federal servants, 189.

— Amendments to, 15; 34; 103; adoption before making, 93; agreement in, 102; dangers of, 226; difficulty of agreeing to, prior to adoption, 99; 245; methods for obtaining, 111; 317; necessity of, prior to adoption, 99; 101; 274; necessity of, 93; 106; 273; 324; power of making, 209; state conventions should make, 322; unreasonableness of, 104.

— Compared with other constitutions, compared with articles of confederation, 148; 379; compared with Roman and English, 35; compared with Great Britain, 137; difference between the state constitutions and the, 155.

— Defects of, 318; a consolidated fabric of aristocratic tyranny, 17; agreement in, 93; a heterogeneous phantom, 7; complicated nature of, 7; contains no feature of democracy or republicanism, 8; designed for the rich, 254; executive and legislative powers dangerously blended in, 9; ignorance of the people in its formation, 284; impracticable over so vast a territory, 13; impossibility of suiting all, 63; lack of declaration of rights in, 73; 329; neither federal nor national, 279; unequal advantages enjoyed by different localities, 298; want of title, 8.

## INDEX.                                                445

— Powers of, 156; amount delegated by, 313; divisions of, 75; fundamental rights of, 313; general clauses of, 233; 312; 331; general, 356; guarantee against ex post facto laws, 147; 314; 332; 368.
— Ratification of, see *ratification*.
— Tendencies of; consolidating, 14; 102; 121; 127; 129; 282; 286; 289; 294; 299; 320; dangers of corruption of, 129; construction with reference to state constitutions, 159 ; 314; founded on monarchy and aristocracy, 7; guarded against excesses, 184; liable to result in monarchy, 195; partly federal but tending towards consolidation, 286; possibility of ending in tyranny. 169; probable encroachments under, 122; will end in monarchy or aristocracy, 254; 235.
— Absurd prospects in case of adoption, 106; character of the supporters of, 5; classes interested in, 283; division of legislature into two branches, 30; documentary sources of the history of the adoption of, 428; editions of, 386; general histories of the, 427; partizan pamphlets pro and con, 437; possibility of obtaining a better, 78; sources of objections to, 166.
Conventions, ease in obtaining, 317.
Convention, Annapolis, 284.
Convention, Federal, (*see also Constitution, States.*) 271; 285; biographies of attending members of, 432; character of members, 114; composition of 74; compromises in, 76; 158; dangers of discord in, 222; debates and proceedings of, 431; diverse interests in, 166; drafts and plans of constitutions in, 431; histories of, improper secresy of, 15; 18; journal of, 410; list of members of, 406; local interest in, 75; members of, 221; non-attendance of members, 285; not limited, 224; opinion of, 74; origin of, 284; quality of the delegates of, 285; secrecy in proceedings, 101; unauthorized powers assumed by, 14; 16; 224; want of authority, 101.
Convention, Second, 21; 210; 272; evils of, 166; great delay in obtaining, 83; impossible to agree upon a better plan, 82; necessity of, 19; 274; possibility of a successful, 80; 246; probability that the states which have already ratified will refuse to attend, 81.
Conventions, State, (*see also each State and Ratification,*) 17; 274; ratifications against the wish of the people, 19; should be allowed to amend constitution, 272; 322; value of, 322.
Council, (*see also Executive,*) necessity of, 230; objections to, 341.
Courts, *see Judiciary.*
Coxe, Tench, pamphlet by, 134; 391.
Curtis, G. T., History by, 391.
Dallas, A J., 425.
Davie, W. R., biographies of, 433; pamphlet by, 333; 391.
Dawson, H. B., editor of The Federalist, 404; correspondence about The Federalist, 404.
Debt, federal, change of system for paying, 378, condition of, 95; equalization of, 147; failure to meet, 73; probable treatment of, 105; responsibility of, 317.
Decius, pseudonym of J. Montgomery, 415; 417.
Declaration of Rights (*see Bill of Rights*).
De Costa, B F., review by, 386.
Delaware and the constitution, 433; probable refusal to attend second convention, 81; representation of, 223; selfish motives in adopting the constitution, 21.
Democracy, disapproval of, 319.
Despotism, methods of, 9.
Dickinson, John, biographies of, 433; cited, 318; pamphlet by, 163; 392.
Duties, *see Export, Import, Taxation.*

Eastern States, *see States. Eastern.*
Elections, (*see also Constitution, Congress, Representatives, House of, Senate.*) biennial found by Massachusetts, 8; control of, by congress, 103; 151; 227; 295; frequency of, 8; 11; 13; great barrier to corruption, 61; probable misuse of the power granted over, 103.
Elliot, Jonathan, debates of, 392.
Ellsworth, Oliver, biographies of, 433; cited, 341.
English Constitution, *see Great Britain.*
Entail, dangerous to liberty, 60.
Executive, (*see also Appointment, Constitution, Impeachment, Pardon, Treaty, Vice President.*)
— Council, 230; 330; lack of, 333; objections to, 345; unnecessary, 346;
— National, 64; advantage of single, 352; American compared with English, 137; composition of, 225; elec-

446                     INDEX.

tion of, 35; 171; 298; entailment of, 233; exclusion of the people in the choice of, 12; nominating power of, 228; pardoning power of, 275; 338; 351; powers of, 36; 171; 225; 232; requisite age of, 36; should be ineligible after a certain time, 275; should not fill vacancies, 275; should not nominate judiciary offices, 275; small probability of treason of, 352; term of, 231; tool of the Senate, 330; veto power of, 45
— State, (*see also State,*) restrictions on, 351.
Export duties, restraint on, 331; restriction of states from, 366.
Ex post facto laws, desirability of restrictions on, 368; guarantee against, 147; 314; 336; restraint from, 332.

Fabius, pseudonym of John Dickinson, 163; 392.
Federal administration, 394.
Federal city, advantage to middle states, 319; jurisdiction of, improperly used, 18; resolution for, by the continental congress, 32
Federal convention, *see Convention, Federal.*
Federal Constitution, pseudonym, 385. *see Constitution, Federal.*
Federal Farmer; pseudonym of Richard Henry Lee, 277; 411.
Federalist, The, authorship of, 395; list of editions, 394; opinions concerning, 395; original publication of, 395.
Federal Republican, A, 420.
Federal Republic, title invented by James Wilson, 8.
Federal requisitions, 105.
Few, William, biographies of, 433.
Fitzsimons, Thomas, 25; biographies of, 433.
Ford, P. L., list of editions of The Federalist, 395; list of members of federal convention, 406.
Foreign affairs, indifference to, 72.
Foreign goods, excessive importation of, 95.
Franklin, Benjamin, 27; 64; biographies of, 433
Fur trade, loss of, 73.

Georgia, accession of, to insure protection, 20; amendment of constitution of, 34; and the constitution, 441; probable refusal to attend second convention, 81.

Gerry, Elbridge, biographies of, 433; failure to sign constitution, 271; pamphlet by, 1; 407.
Gilman, Nicholas, biographies of, 433.
Gorham, Nathaniel, biographies of, 433.
Greenleaf, T., 1.
Great Britain, House of Commons, 42; 143; 211; constitution of, compared with the American, 35; 137;. House of Peers of, 42; paper money would destroy the credit of, 243; Privy Council of, 345; right of the colonists to constitution of, 135; standing army of, 235; union of, 195; 213.
Government, (*see also under each country.*) dangers of all strong, 131; effect on character and manners, 5; elements of, 263, instituted for protection and happiness, 6; must not be lodged in a single body, 182; nature of, 92; origin of, 174; primary principles of, 373; the result of fraud or violence, 18.

Hale, Charles, 415.
Hale, Sir Mathew, cited, 10.
Hall, Aaron, 408.
Hamilton, Alexander, biographies of, 433; The Federalist, 395; proposition in convention, 408.
Hamilton, J. A., correspondence about The Federalist, 404.
Hamilton, J. C., editor of The Federalist, 405.
Hanson, Alexander Contee, pamphlet by, 217; 408.
Helvitius, cited, 5.
Henry, Patrick, attack on, 415; 417.
Hillsborough, Lord, 8.
Hitchcock, Enos, 408.
Hopkinson, Francis, 409.
Hutchinson, Gov. T., recommends triennial elections, 8; 13.

Impeachment, (*see also Constitution, Executive. Senate*), 342; improperly lodged with senate, 300.
Imports, 62; foreign, 95.
Impost, (*see also Congress, Taxation*), 104; 283. Connecticut and New Jersey share of, 319; general acceptance of the five per cent., 253; the great source of revenue in the U. S., 160.
Imprimatur, danger of, 9.
Ingersoll, Jared, biographies of, 433.
Insurgents, party of, in the U. S., 321.
Iredell, James, pamphlet by, 327; 333; 392; 410.

Jackson, Jonathan, 410.
Jay, John, pamphlet by, 67; 410; reply to his pamphlet, 111; The Federalist, 395.
Jay, John, (Jr.) correspondence about The Federalist, 404.
Johnson, W. S., 390; biographies of, 433.
Judiciary, National (*see also Appointment, Executive, Jury, Senate,*) 275; analysis of, 343; appellate jurisdiction of, 12; 236; 308; 311; coersive powers of, 343; dangers from jurisdiction as to both law and fact, 308; discussion of, 236; impossibility of trial by jury in, 310; necessity of national, 122; power to decide law and fact, 114; powers of, 53; 149; 236; 298; 306; want of limitation in, 9; 102.
Judiciary, State, (*see also Jury, State,*) 289; 307; absorption of by national, 53; 329; position under constitution, 343.
Jury, Trial by, absence in state courts, 361; discussion of, 157; impracticable in national courts, 289; necessity of, 184; 315; not altered by constitution, 148; not a universal practice, 361; not secured in civil cases, 9; 103; 114; 307; reply to insinuations concerning, 52; should be left to wisdom of congress, 362; the birthright of Americans, 241; under Pennsylvania constitution, 148.

King, Rufus, biographies of, 434; on Elbridge Gerry, 1.

Land, (*see also Western Territory*), decline in the price of, 74.
Langdon, John, biographies of, 434.
Lansing, John, 425; biographies of, 434.
Law, (*see also Congress, Constitution, Judiciary, Ex post facto, Treaties*), multiplication of, 302; necessity of supreme, 312; people entitled to common, 336.
Lee, Richard Henry, pamphlet by, 277; 411.
Legislature, *see Congress and State Legislatures.*
Livingston, William, biographies of, 434.
Lloyd, Thomas, 412; 418.
Lodge, H. C., editor of The Federalist, 406.

Mablé, Ablé, cited, 4.
M'Henry, James, biographies of, 434.
McClurg, James, biographies of, 434.
M'Kean, Thomas, speeches of, 412.
Maclaine, Archibald, pamphlet by, 333; 392; 412; opinion of The Federalist, 395.
MacMaster, John Bach, 412.
Madison, James, 327; 390; biographies of, 434; debate of, 394; 413; quotation from, 259; The Federalist, 395.
Marcus, pseudonym of James Iredell, 333; 391; 410.
Martin, Luther, biographies of, 434; cited, 18; Genuine Information of, 413; 425.
Maryland and the constitution, 440; construction of senate of, 41; declaration of rights, 229; delay in appointing convention, 250; local actions in courts of, 239; method of electing federal representatives, 225; omnipotence of legislature of, 226; position toward Europe, 251; position under new constitution, 251; probable rejection of the constitution by, 28; proposed emission of paper money, 33; representation of, 223; resistance of the people to paper money, 244.
Mason, George, 390; biographies of, 434; failure to sign constitution, 271; pamphlet by, 327; 413; reply to, 255; 333; 391.
Massachusetts, 13; adoption of the constitution by, 98; ambiguous expressions in ratification of, 6; amendments of the convention of, 15; 103; and the constitution, 438; debates in the convention, 414; hostile feeling towards New York, 96; means used to obtain ratification of, 19; ratification by, 6.
Mediteranean, exclusion of Americans from, 73.
Mercer, J. F., biographies of, 435.
Mifflin, Thomas, biographies of, 435.
Militia, congressional power over, 52; 305; necessary general powers over, 122; 306; no longer under civil control, 11; subject to president and senate, 11
Minot, G. R., 410.
Monarchy, (*see also Aristocracy*), 7; advocates for, 19; dangers of, 195; 254; 285; partizans of, in the state conventions, 17; spirit of, in America, 5.
Money, (*see also Paper Money, Representatives, Senate, Taxation*), power to raise, necessary to general government, 122; scarcity of, 73; 113.

# 448                INDEX.

Monopolies, congressional power to grant, 357.
Montesquien, cited, 59.
Montgomery, J., pamphlet by, 415; 417.
Morris, Robert, biographies of, 435.
Morris, Gouverneur, biographies of, 435.

Native of Boston, pseudonym of J. Jackson, 410.
Navigation laws, necessity of, 377.
Navy, power of congress to form, 374; will be obtained by constitution, 379.
New England, commerce of, 357.
New Hampshire and the constitution, 438.
New Jersey, adopted from local causes, 104; and the constitution, 439; hostile feelings towards New York, 84; 96, imports of, from New York, 62; journal of the convention of, 416; probable refusal to attend second convention, 81; selfish motives in adopting the constitution, 21.
New York, address to the people of, 67; 87; 111; and the constitution, 439; anti-federal committee of, 1; constitution of, 114; dangers from contiguous states, 96; debates of the convention of, 416; failure to guarantee liberty of the press in constitution of, 76; ill feeling towards, of New Jersey and Connecticut, 84; imports for other states, 62; imports, 104; journal of the convention of, 416; lack of bill of rights, 114; position, in case nine states ratify, 86; undoubted rejection of constitution by, 21.
North Carolina and the constitution, 441; debates in the convention of, 417; forbids standing army in time of peace, 51; 365.
Nicholas, J., 415; 417.

Paine, Thomas, The Rights of Man, 164.
Paper money, 33; baneful effects of, 243; conduct of the state legislatures concerning, 244; 284; congress not restricted from issuing, 374; only the states restricted in issuing, 374; renunciation of the right to issue, 243; the secret reason of opposition to the constitution, 243.
Pardon, (*see also Executive,*) power of executive to, 351.
Parker, J., review of The Federalist, 402.

Paterson, William, biographies of, 435.
Peabody, A. P., review by, 391.
Pennsylvania, 33; address to the citizens of, 385; and the constitution, 412; advantages from new constitution, 161; aristocratic delegates in Federal convention from, 285; debates in convention of, 418; dissent of minority of convention, 102; 385; forbids standing army in time of peace, 51; 365; general assembly under her constitution 152; hasty conduct due to construction of legislature, 33; hostile feeling towards New York, 96; journal of the convention of, 419; legislature of, 34; opposition to division of congress, 30; ratification by, 20; trial by jury under constitution of, 148.
People, desire for union of the, 17; equal representation necessary in free government, 168; 288; position in adoption of constitution, 311; real power with the, 6; 57; 147; true influence of, 60; 168; 316.
Pickering, Timothy, Life of, cited, 277.
Pierce, B. K., 415.
Pinckney, Charles, biographies of, 435; pamphlet by, 419.
Pinckney, Charles C., biographies of, 435.
Plebeian, pseudonym of Melancthon Smith, 67; 87; 421.
Police, internal, 292.
President, *see Executive.*
Press, Liberty of, 9; 76; congress without power over, 361; failure to guarantee liberty of, 9; 48; 76; 113; needless to guarantee, 156; powers of congress over, 316; power to tax, 114.
Printers, refusal of, to print against the constituion, 323.
Production, difficulty in disposing of surplus, 73.
Property, equal distribution of, the foundation of a republic, 61; the basis of freedom, 60; the real power, 57.
Publicola, pseudonym of W. R. Davie, 391.

Quakers, influenced by slave trade, 54.

Ramsay, David, pamphlet by, 371; 421.
Randolph, Edmund, biographies of, 435; cited, 343; failure to sign constitution, 261; 271; independence of,

INDEX. 449

20; 271; motion of, 272; pamphlet by, 259; 418; 420.
Ratification of the constitution, (*see also Conventions, and each state,*) 420; celebrations of the ratifications of, 441; improperly hurried, 18; influences that cause opposition to, 165; methods used to aid acceptance, 7; of nine states improper, 14; probability of, by each state, 20; probability of nine states agreeing to, 104; submittal to state legislatures and coventions, 272.
Read, George, biographies of, 436.
Religion, free exercise of, should be guaranteed, 315.
Religious sentiment of America, 135.
Religious test, none required, 146.
Representation (*see also Congress, Constitution,*) 8; 12; 289; and taxation inseparable, 148; advantages of eastern states in, 375; basis for, 263; by wealth or population, 39; direct taxation apportioned by, 310; equality of the states in, 206; inadequacy of, 12; 300; 303; inequality in, 223; improvement of, in constitution, 206; origin of, 30; possibilities of equal, 296; in the constitution a compromise, 206; superior in state governments, 293; too small to secure liberty, 102; treble method in, 178.
Representatives, House of (*see Congress, Constitution, Representation, Senate, Treaties,*) 293; comparison with house of commons, 42; 143; composition and powers of, 143; 170; 225; 295; difficulties in formation of, 297; election of members of federal convention to, 221; expense of, 299; money bills in, 340; no state to have less than one member in, 143; proportion of members to population, 143; qualifications of, 144; reply to Mason's opinion of, 255; representation in, 12; 337; shadow of representation in, 329; share in treaties, 355; 376; term of, 43; the seat of local interests and parties, 41; the voice of the separate states, 41.
Republics, constitution of ancient, 189.
Revenue (*see also Impost, Taxation,*) all sources of, subject to general government, 11; necessity of equalizing, 62.
Revolutionary war caused by a difference concerning rights, 136.
Rhode Island and the constitution, 438; failure to choose representatives, 151; senate of, 32.

Robertson, David, 418; 422.
Rome, colonies of, 208; constitution compared with proposed constitution, 35; senate of, 42,
Rowland, Kate M., 390.
Russell, Benjamin, report of debates, 414.
Rutledge, John, biographies of, 436.
Sabliere, T. de la, editor of The Federalist, 396;
Sarum, English borough of, 143.
Senate, (*see also Congress, Constitution, Executive, Representation, Treaties,*) a compromise between contending interests, 158; advantages of, 30; appointing power of, 341; a restraint on the House of Representatives, 141; aristocratic tendencies in, 158; compared with Roman and English senates, 371; 148; composition and powers of, 37; 140; 297; 338; conservative nature of, 340; constitution of ancient, 189; dangers from, 172; 203; dangerous powers of, 173; 297; 329; detached from local prejudices, 142; equal suffrage in, 38; 40; 207; 275; federal formation of, 297; frequency of election of, 338; House of Representatives a check on, 338; irresponsibility of, 12; length of term, 12; 170; mixture of functions in, 103; 229; 231; 299; money bills in, 340; necessity to be small, 169; power to remove officers, 142; qualifications for, 42; 141; reply to Mason's objections to, 255; representation in the, 40; 206; the representatives of state sovereignties, 169; 224; uselessness of the, 34; useless power of impeachment, 300; vacancies in, 170.
Sherman, Roger, biographies of, 436; cited, 341.
Shipping, (*see also Commerce,*) 73; cessation of, 73; decline of, 73; necessities of encouraging, 377.
Slavery, abolition of, would bring ruin, 54; legislation left to the states, 54.
Slaves, representation of, 319.
Slave trade, desire of South Carolina and Georgia for continuance of, 367; foundation for prevention of, 146; interest of the eastern states to allow, 378; lack of restriction on, 54; necessity of the evil of, 367; power to prohibit after twenty-one years, 378; weakening effect of, 331.
Smith, C. C., review by, 391.

450    INDEX.

Smith, Melancthon, pamphlet by, 67; 87; 421.
South Carolina, address to the freemen of, 371; and the constitution, 440; debates of legislature, 421; local weakness of, 373; protection of, 377.
Southern confederacy, (*see also Confederacy*,) proposition for, 270.
Southern states, *see States*.
Spraight, R. D.., biographies of, 436.
State Conventions. *see Conventions, State*,
State Legislatures, (*see also Constitution and each state*,) absorption of, 48; 252; a check on senators, 142; control of commerce, 265; division of, 30; 32; 33; misbehaviour of, 254; omitted in consideration of constitution, 14; restraints on, 243.
State Sovereignty, *see Congress, Constitution, States*.
States, (*see also Congress, Constitution, Judiciary, Jury, Representation, Senate, United States government, and each state*,) a check on the general government, 126; 152; all necessary for present exigencies, 96; Bills of Rights in constitutions, 359; boundaries of, 62; cases between citizens and, 307; civil war during the, 97; 264; 373; constitution of, 286; 289; 294; 299; 320; constitutional control of, 46; 120; 129; 145; 292; constitutions and laws of, 262; contention between, adjusted by general government, 120; 267; controversies between the, in the convention, 297; delusory promise to guarantee republican government to, 11; differences in the governments of, 291; dissolution of, 268; embarrassment of all issuing paper money, 374; excluded from all agency in national government, 267; failure to secure liberty and property, 55; interest of, to unite, 373; jurisdiction of, as opposed to national, 48; 97; 121; 267; 275; 314; necessity of coercive power against, 266; partial confederacies of, 120; 127; 204; 247; 269; 270; 278; power over their own citizens, 128; protected from each other, 128; rebellion in, 264; reservations in constitutions of, 313; separate interests of, 39; sovereignty of, 11; 14; 38; 46; 179; 207; 379.
— Eastern, 357; advantages from new constitution, 319; advantages of encouraging the shipping of, 377; future miserable condition of, 3; loss of, by revolution, 377; loss of markets by, 377; representation of, 375.
— Southern, advantages of navy to, 374; advantages to, of union, 319; 374; danger to, from commercial laws, 331; future hopeless poverty of, 3, gain of, by revolution, 377; position of, if constitution is rejected, 378; probable ascendency over eastern, 375; representation of, 375.
Stone, Frederick D., 412.
Strong, Caleb, biographies of, 436.

Taxation, absorption of production by national, 3; and representation inseparable, 148; 186; certainty of increase under proposed government, 108; direct, 160; 253; 310; internal, 48; 302; laws of, interfering with state laws, 302; method of collection, 49; 253; 310; powers of congress over, 48; 102; 301; 303; relief from, 106; 108.
Tender laws, conduct of the state legislatures concerning, 284.
Territories, *see Constitution, Western Territory*.
Trade, (*see also Commerce, Treaties*.) 73; 379; balance against the U. S., 107; congressional power over, 107; necessity of government to, 7; regulation of, approved by the eastern states, 319.
Treaties, (*see also Commerce, Congress, Executive, Representatives, Senate*,) dangers arising from, 312; dangers of making them the supreme law, 311, necessity of commercial, 358; of the confederation not binding under, 317; power of Executive and Senate in, 376; powers to make, 356; safer in new government than under the confederation, 376; should not be trusted to House of Representatives, 376; the supreme law of the land, 355; undue influence of Executive and Senate in, 331.
Tucker, J. R., History of the Convention, 422.
Tyler, M. C., 416.

Union, not possible without adequate power, 122; true friends of opposed to constitution, 7,
United States, condition of, 94; 281; credit of, 244; extension of, 203; future additions to, 248; future of, 208; is it too large for one, 13; 122; 127; 204; 247; necessity of supreme

government for, 119; neglect of laws of, 293; opulence of, 270; parties in, 321; position if constitution is rejected, 378; suitable government for, 119; 127; 286.

United States, Government of, a moderate aristocracy 332; checks on, 152; composition of, 292; control over the states, 120; 129; 145; 292; dangers of weak, 119; division of, 228; great increase in cost predicted, 108; institution of, after the separation from England, 136; lack of, during the revolution, 136; necessary concessions in order to form, 265; necessary conditions of, 289; necessary powers of, 120; 129; 287; 301; necessity of, 280; not restricted from issuing paper money, 374; powers must be equal to territory, 123; responsibility to foreign nations, 266; separate functions of, 225; tendency of, 369; unreasonable accumulation of powers in, 299; want of independence in departments of, 103; 229.

Vermont, probable combination with New Jersey and Connecticut in opposition to New York, 84.

Veto power, *see Executive*.

Vice-President, (*see also Executive*,) method of selection, 330: 349; position in Senate, 350; qualifications of, 310; necessary, 298.

Virginia, alterations wished by, in constitution, 275; and the constitution, 441; debates in convention of, 422; delay in appointing convention, 250; delegates to federal convention, 284; hesitation of, to ratify, 20; journal of convention of, 423; possibility of her obtaining a partial confederacy, 269.

Warrants, insecurity from, 12; protection from, 315.

Washington, George, 64; 67; 390; biographies of, 436; dedication to, 218; letters to, 327; opinion of, 350; opinion of The Federalist, 395.

Webb, S. B., 67.

Webster, Noah, pamphlet by, 25; 423; reply to minority of Pa. convention, 385; review by, 67; 87; 217.

Webster, Pelatiah, pamphlet by, 118; 424.

Wells, John, editor of The Federalist, 397.

Western posts, method of obtaining, 96.

Western Territory, claims of the states to, 239; question of ownership, 317.

West Indies, exclusion of American vessels from, 73; will be opened to trade by new government, 379.

Williamson, Hugh, 424; biographies of, 436.

Wilson, James, 242; 390; 412; biographies of, 436; cited, 336; invents title of "Federal Republic," 8; speech of, 134; 155; 385; 425.

Witherspoon, D., quotation from letters of, 333.

Writs of Assistance in Massachusetts, 13.

Wyoming, action of Pennsylvania legislature in reference to, 33.

Wythe, George, biographies of, 437.

Yates, Robert, 425; 424; biographies of, 437.

FINIS.